AF600359

A Political Companion to W. E. B. Du Bois

A POLITICAL COMPANION TO

W. E. B. Du Bois

EDITED BY

Nick Bromell

Scholarly publisher for the Commonwealth,
serving Bellarmine University, Berea College, Centre College of Kentucky, Eastern Kentucky University, The Filson Historical Society, Georgetown College, Kentucky Historical Society, Kentucky State University, Morehead State University, Murray State University, Northern Kentucky University, Transylvania University, University of Kentucky, University of Louisville, and Western Kentucky University.

Editorial and Sales Offices: The University Press of Kentucky
663 South Limestone Street, Lexington, Kentucky 40508-4008
www.kentuckypress.com

Cataloging-in-Publication data is available from the Library of Congress.

ISBN 978-0-8131-7490-7 (hardcover : alk. paper)
ISBN 978-0-8131-7493-8 (epub)
ISBN 978-0-8131-7492-1 (pdf)

This book is printed on acid-free paper meeting the requirements of the American National Standard for Permanence in Paper for Printed Library Materials.

Manufactured in the United States of America.

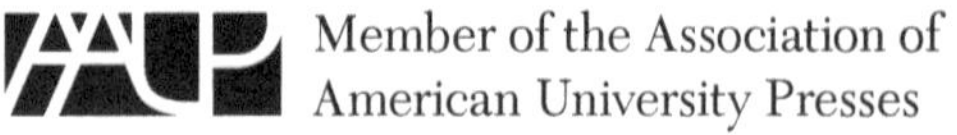

Member of the Association of
American University Presses

For Kathleen Dodd

and in memory of William H. Dodd

Contents

Series Foreword

Those who undertake a study of American political thought must attend to the great theorists, philosophers, and essayists. Such a study is incomplete, however, if it neglects American literature, one of the greatest repositories of the nation's political thought and teachings.

America's literature is distinctive because it is, above all, intended for a democratic citizenry. In contrast to eras when an author would aim to inform or influence a select aristocratic audience, in democratic times, public influence and education must resonate with a more expansive, less leisured, and diverse audience to be effective. The great works of America's literary tradition are the natural locus of democratic political teaching. Invoking the interest and attention of citizens through the pleasures afforded by the literary form, many of America's great thinkers sought to forge a democratic public philosophy with subtle and often challenging teachings that unfolded in narrative, plot, and character development. Perhaps more than any other nation's literary tradition, American literature is ineluctably political—shaped by democracy as much as it has in turn shaped democracy.

The Political Companions to Great American Authors series highlights the teachings of the great authors in America's literary and belletristic tradition. An astute political interpretation of America's literary tradition requires careful, patient, and attentive readers who approach the text with a view to understanding its underlying messages about citizenship and democracy. Essayists in this series approach the classic texts not with a "hermeneutics of suspicion" but with the curiosity of fellow citizens who believe that the great authors have something of value to teach their readers. The series brings together essays from varied approaches and viewpoints for the common purpose of elucidating the political teachings of the nation's greatest authors for those seeking a better understanding of American democracy.

Patrick J. Deneen
Series Editor

Introduction

Nick Bromell

W. E. B. Du Bois was not in any obvious sense a political theorist. He was a situated, activist intellectual who read philosophy but never saw himself as making theoretical contributions to political theory or to philosophy more broadly. Indeed, he could be sharply critical of theories and theorizing. However, as this volume and other recent work in the field amply demonstrate, his political thought can enrich, enlarge, and fundamentally transform the field. Indeed, it is precisely because his writings do not fit plainly within the canonical tradition of political thought that they have challenges and consequences for it.

As a sociologist, organizer, editor, historian, essayist, autobiographer, poet, and novelist, Du Bois changed his methods and his positions multiple times throughout his long career. Yet an obvious thread of continuity runs from its start to its close, and that is the question of race. I use the word "question" here advisedly, because Du Bois seldom (if ever) saw race as anything but a question, one that gave rise to many related questions. In his 1897 "The Conservation of Races," he shared the assumption common at the time that whatever race might be, it was certainly *something*. But this "something" was for him a starting point, the launch of an investigation: "The question, then, which we must seriously consider is this: what is the real meaning of race; what has, in the past, been the law of race development, and what lessons has the past history of race development to teach to the rising Negro people?"[1] About forty years later, he gave his 1940 book *Dusk of Dawn* the subtitle "An Essay toward an Autobiography of a Race Concept," and he titled its fifth chapter "The Concept of Race." This wording certainly signaled a shift from viewing race as something existent in the world to seeing race as an idea used to describe (or deform) the world. Yet even "concept" was perhaps too decided a term, for he went on to reflect that race "had, as I have tried to show all sorts of illogical trends and irreconcilable tendencies. Perhaps it is wrong to speak of it as 'a concept' rather than as a group of contradictory forces, facts, and tendencies."[2]

For Du Bois, the investigation of race was never an isolated inquiry. As he wrote in *Darkwater:* "There can be no permanent settlement of our problems of capital and labor, voting, women and children, which does not take into serious account the influence of color caste on these questions. And, in turn, the color line shows itself, not as a separate problem, but directly as a problem of work, rule, sex, and training."[3]As we would say in shorthand today, race cannot be disentangled from gender, sex, and class. And vice versa. Pursuing this single insight relentlessly for more than sixty years, Du Bois anticipated two major developments in more recent historical and political scholarship. One is that race is a constitutive element of Western modernity, a thesis C. L. R. James, Eric Williams, Paul Gilroy, and (subsequently) many others have elaborated. Another is that race is constitutive of US democracy's principles and its practice, as Edmund Morgan, David Roediger, Rogers Smith, and Dana D. Nelson among many others have shown. Finally, alongside these a third development is now under way. Well represented in this volume, it argues that race lies at the very heart of the Western philosophical tradition, including the branch of it we identify as political philosophy or political theory. Du Bois himself did not, as far as I know, explicitly anticipate this insight, but all of the essays in this volume argue that it is suggested in many places and in many ways throughout his immense oeuvre. Perhaps more decisively than any other single black political thinker, Du Bois challenges what Adolph Reed, in one of the first major books on Du Bois's political thought, calls "the propensity to define the history of American political thought as a narrative that marginalizes or excludes both race as an issue and nonwhites as participants."[4] This volume, therefore, seeks to work against what Lawrie Balfour, in another indispensable book on Du Bois, describes as "political theorists' reluctance to treat race and racial injustice as fundamental to the study of modern democratic life.[5]

Du Bois's insight that race is central, not peripheral, to history, culture, and politics is one reason why his work has such powerful implications for political theory. Of equal importance may be his distinctive critical practice. It is at one and the same time poetic and historical, imaginative and empirical, reserved and passionate. Take, for example, this famous passage from the last chapter of *Black Reconstruction in America,* a work of careful, empirical, historical analysis: "The most magnificent drama in the last thousand years of human history is the transportation of ten million human beings out of the dark beauty of their mother continent into the new-found Eldorado of the West. They descended into Hell; and in the third century they arose from the dead, in the finest effort to save democracy for the working millions which the world has ever seen. It was a tragedy that beggared the Greek; it was an upheaval of humanity like the Reformation and the French Revolution."[6] Today, as in his time, such intensified language does not seem to belong in a serious work of history. *Magnificent drama, dark beauty, rose from the dead:* such phrases seem to be interlopers from other discourses, genres, language games. *Why couldn't Du Bois police the borders of his prose?* we tend to ask. *What did he think he gained from these over-the-top rhetorical flourishes?* The contributors to this volume show us that these are the wrong questions to be asking. It is not Du Bois who has "lost control" of his prose, but we who shrink from seizing *all* the resources our language puts at our disposal in order to do justice to the force of the history that we are seeking to explain.

"I was extremely emotional on the race problem while I was a student at Harvard," Du Bois wrote in a letter to a friend, "and my emotion was curbed by the philosophy of William James and the historical research under Hart. They did not quench; they directed it. I was never 'primarily a historian.' If anything, I had the urge to be a creative artist but the literature which I wanted to write was not the kind which the public was willing to read."[7] It may seem so obvious as to be hardly worth mentioning that a young black scholar at Harvard would be "very emotional about the race problem." But all readers of Du Bois would do well to sit with that phrase for a moment, letting themselves feel—as most of Du Bois's black readers doubtless have felt—all the emotions Du Bois acknowledges here. Then let us consider *why* Du Bois was guided to direct, not quench, those emotions: only if those emotions burned steadily could they fuel a life's work on the problem at hand. But this channeling of emotion also means his prose is frequently saturated with pain and passion. Reading such work and striving to comprehend it fully requires us to be attuned to—and take with full seriousness—the affective register of every sentence Du Bois wrote. Consider this passage, also from the last chapter of *Black Reconstruction in America:*

> I write then in a field devastated by passion and belief. Naturally, as a Negro, I cannot do this writing without believing in the essential humanity of Negroes, in their ability to be educated, to do the work of the modern world, to take their place as equal citizens with others. I cannot for a moment subscribe to that bizarre doctrine of race that makes most men inferior to a few. But, too, as a student of science, I want to be fair, objective, and judicial; to let no searing of the memory by intolerable insult and cruelty make me fail to sympathize with human frailties and contradiction, in the eternal paradox of good and evil. But armed and warned by all this, and fortified by long study of the facts, I stand at the end of this writing, literally aghast at what American historians have done to this field.[8]

Do these words express Du Bois's "ambivalence," as one literary critic has put it?[9] Everything depends on what that term connotes. If we take it to describe a psychological state in which one's mixed feelings compel one to hesitate, or render one powerless to decide, then I think it is incorrect. If we take it to mean that the passage describes multiple strengths ("valence" derives from *valentia,* or strength, the present participle of *valere,* to be strong), then it is the perfect word. Du Bois himself says that he was "armed and warned" by the considerations he describes, not hampered by them. Thus, an incapacitating ambivalence is not what this passage is about. Rather, Du Bois suggests that he was fortified by his ambivalence as he framed his critique of white American historians. The purport of the paragraph is: If *I* who have been so wounded by insult can manage to direct my own passions through channels of objectivity, fairness, and large-minded comprehension of human frailty, what can explain the fact that white historians have allowed their own "passion" and "belief" to devastate the field? Du Bois's inability to answer this question (or even to read the conventional historiography of Reconstruction in a spirit of mere skepticism or dissent) left him "literally aghast"—terrified by a *geist,* a ghost or a spirit. What could this ghost be, if not racism that refuses to die? Here as in so many other works, Du Bois reminded his readers that the nation's racial past remains disturbingly present.

In short, there are formidable challenges to reading Du Bois adequately. One way the contributors to this volume come to terms with them is simply to read him very carefully, attending to every word and taking note of *how* he writes, not just *what* he writes. But they also go further. When they sense that our familiar lexicon will not account for his insights, they are pushed as theorists toward *poesis:* often they are compelled to remake political theory in order to render Du Bois's methods and insights legible to the field, and that is the second reason why his work is invaluable to it.

Political theory very often employs a taxonomic, or definitional method. It works in terms of large conceptual categories, asking whether a particular theorist or idea belongs in one or more of these and, if not, whether the categories themselves need reconceiving. In the case of Du Bois, this has meant asking whether he is best understood as a liberal, a Marxist, a democratic socialist, a black nationalist, an assimilationist, a democrat, or an elitist. As well, in the US context, social and political thinkers like Du Bois are usually placed under one of two headings: either they launch their critique on the basis of the "shared" values of the Founders and the Founding documents, or they propose that those values fall far short of enabling and describing a genuinely democratic order. These are all useful ways to approach Du Bois, but as we shall see, at a deep level he often evades such classification.

This is true as well when scholars of Du Bois consider what we might call his intellectual disposition. On the one hand, as all agree, he had little interest in abstract thought that did not address a particular problem or failed to point the way toward a feasible solution. For example, Aldon Morris has argued in his recent *The Scholar Denied: W. E. B. Du Bois and the Birth of Modern Sociology* that Du Bois was deeply critical of the nascent field of sociology in the United States because it was obsessed with developing grand theories of the kind being produced in the natural and physical sciences. In 1904, attending (uninvited) an early congress of sociologists in Saint Louis, Du Bois found that

> the system-building theories of Auguste Comte and Herbert Spencer loomed large in discussions regarding the future of sociology. . . . Reflecting on the debates at the conference, Du Bois claimed that such sociological reasoning was flawed by an unscientific method that gen-

> erated unsound data. He argued that for the new science of sociology to be scientific it had to be based on empirical data rather than armchair theorizing and what he called "car window sociology." . . . Du Bois, therefore, broke from the dominant theoretical stance by arguing that there were no universal laws mechanistically governing human behavior.[10]

Because (following Du Bois's own lead) so many scholars have attributed his distrust of grand theories and universal laws to the influence of William James and Thomas Bushnell Hart at Harvard, it is worth noting that he voiced such a disposition much earlier. Kenneth Barkin has shown that at the University of Berlin Du Bois was especially drawn to politically active professors with strong historical and empirical methodologies. Barker brought to light an 1894 notebook entry in which Du Bois reflected on the work of his teacher Gustav Schmoller: "Schmoller's followers do not announce an alternate theoretical aim, further than the indivisible unity of all sociological inquiry. They confine themselves in practice to careful statistical investigations of the history and development of present economic conditions and social phenomena. From this gradually increasing basis of scientific facts, they attempt to recommend remedies for certain more obvious social ills, but go no further in such recommendations and generalizations than a careful interpretation of the facts at hand. . . . They have had a significant impact. Some call Germany a great socialist state."[11] But whether he acquired it from Harvard's pragmatists or Berlin's historicists and empiricists, Du Bois's empirical bent was not the whole of his disposition. On the contrary, he frequently voiced his belief in universality and, although very critical of the black church, he repeatedly emphasized the importance of faith. In a 1922 article titled "Segregation and Race Pride," for example, he responded furiously to President Warren Harding's call for blacks to "improve themselves as a distinct race with a heredity, a set of traditions, an array of aspirations all its own. Out of such racial ambitions and pride will come a natural segregation." Du Bois wrote: "Does he not see the logical contradictions of his thought? Can he not see his failure to recognize the Universal in the Particular, the menace of all group exclusiveness and segregation in the forced segregation of American Negroes?"[12] Forty years later, in a 1963 interview, he reflected on his research for *The Philadelphia Negro* and recalled: "You could not confine yourself to Philadelphia. It is part of the U.S. Blacks are part of the working people of the world. The particular is part of the general. Without that general orientation I got in a German university, I would not have been able to do it."[13] A number of Du Bois scholars underscore that German romantic idealism was alive and well in Berlin when Du Bois studied there, and the historian Joel Williamson and political philosophers Robert Gooding-Williams and Shamoon Zamir have cogently argued that Du Bois is in important respects a deeply Hegelian thinker.[14] Stirring the pot in yet another direction, Ross Posnock has rightly pointed out that despite William James's strong opposition to the American "St. Louis school" of Hegelianism, pragmatism and Hegelianism have affinities: "William James . . . rejected Hegel's system, yet preserved what he, like Dewey, found vital in Hegel—his dialectical vision, his anti-dualist stress on concrete embodiment and on becoming."[15]

What this muddle indicates, I suggest, is that to understand fully Du Bois's equal and dialectical affiliation with both the universal and the particular, we need to consider not only the influences of his formal education but also the racial history out of which he wrote. Before he went to either Berlin or Harvard, Du Bois was strongly shaped by his experiences in a white racist society. As Leonard Harris has argued, the critical reflection produced by such experience does not resemble the detached, disembodied philosophy of the Western tradition. It is instead a "philosophy born of struggle."[16] Such philosophy, as George Yancy writes, is always working "within the concrete muck and more of *raced* embodied existence."[17] As such, it is indifferent to grand, speculative theories and focuses instead on the immediate and urgent problems experienced by persons of color in a racist order.

Yet grounded as he was in the muck and mire of his raced, embodied existence, Du Bois was also shaped by "the black natural law tradition"—as Vincent Lloyd argues in a recent book with that title. This tradition carries forward through history a deep faith in universal laws of justice, which are true at all times and in all places; it expresses as well an enduring faith in a common humanity to which all persons by nature and by right belong. But this natural law tradition is crucially different from other such traditions, Lloyd argues, most notably in its critical stance toward ideology and its commitment to act for justice: "Black natural law is suspicious of the wisdom of the world, ideology. It proclaims that we, through our own human nature, can see that the world is not as it seems. . . . Furthermore, black natural law calls us to honor the higher law that acknowledges our humanity by actively challenging the wisdom of the world. It calls us to participate in social movements that oppose, for example, slavery, segregation, and mass incarceration."[18]

What allows the black natural law tradition to embrace the universal and yet remain pluralist in spirit, respectful of particularity, is its "view that no worldly description of the human suffices. Just as God exceeds all worldly descriptions, the image of God in humanity exceeds all worldly descriptions. We offer worldly descriptions as approximations for what is ultimately unrepresentable, and those worldly descriptions succeed when they remind us how their referent exceeds them."[19] If Du Bois stood in this tradition, as Lloyd argues, then he saw the Universal as approachable only through the Particular (single consciousness), which can never grasp or comprehend it in its entirety. Conversely, he believed that when we wish to investigate and understand the nature of the Particular—be it an individual or a society—we must be ever-mindful of its relation to the Universal.

The informal education and black critical traditions he absorbed as a young black man manifest themselves in the positions Du Bois took later. In 1933, for example, he wrote: "We must have religion in the sense of striving for the infinite, the ultimate, and the best. But we must straitly curb the effort of any exclusive guild to be the single and final arbiter of individual interpretation of desired and desirable truth."[20] In his 1945 *Color and Democracy*, he sounded the same theme: "The majority of the best and earnest people of this world are organized in religious groups, and . . . without the cooperation of the richness of their emotional experience, and the unselfishness of their aims, science stands helpless before crude fact and selfish endeavor. . . . Is there not, then, a chance to find a common ground for a program of human betterment which seeks by means of known and tested knowledge the ideal ends of faith?"[21]

Du Bois's disposition to occupy the space between the general and the particular, and to remain cognizant of the truth of both, expressed itself also—and more subtly—in his way of handling many concrete issues of black politics. In an April 1934 editorial in the *Crisis*, he acknowledged the general truth that humanity itself knows no color lines: "This is the great end toward which humanity is tending, and . . . so long as there are artificially emphasized differences of nationality, race, and color, . . . there will be no real Humanity." Yet he also acknowledged the truth of the empirical facts on the ground now: "No person born will ever live to see national and racial distinctions altogether abolished and economic distinctions will last many a day." This fidelity to both long-term universal truths and shorter-term exigencies led him to advocate for tactical self-segregation when necessary: "It is perfectly certain that, not only shall we be compelled to submit to much segregation, but that sometimes it will be necessary to our survival and a step toward the ultimate breaking-down of barriers, to increase by voluntary action our separation from our fellowmen."[22]

The essays in this volume have been arranged under four headings that foreground the issues I have been discussing. Part 1 consists of essays by two distinguished philosophers, Charles W. Mills and Lewis R. Gordon. Different as their views of Du Bois are, they share the conviction that we should take him to be a major political philosopher whose work (like that of Machiavelli, Hobbes, Locke, Rousseau, and the other canonical major figures in the field) sets terms and provides a framework for theorists who are more or less content to think within established paradigms. Their arguments thus vigorously contest E. Franklin Frazier's complaint that, "We have no philosophers or thinkers who command the respect of the intellectual community at large . . . men who have reflected on the fundamental problems which have always concerned philosophers such as the nature of human knowledge and the meaning or lack of meaning of human existence."[23] Yet their interpretations of Du Bois as a philosopher differ markedly.

For Mills, Du Bois is a major political philosopher because he was the first to perceive that the entire project of Western liberal political philosophy has been infected *ab origino* by white racist assumptions flagrantly contradicting liberalism's own announced commitments and principles. Du Bois's critique thereby opens two complementary tasks for political philosophy. One is critical: to continue exposing the ways that liberalism's apparent neutral or objective political thought is actually saturated with white racist presuppositions. The other is constructive: to rebuild liberal political philosophy on its old foundations after these have been thoroughly purged of their racism. At the heart of Mills's argument, then, lies this deep paradox or irony: even as we find racism contaminating liberal thought from its historical origins to the present day, we should nonetheless regard that contamination to be contingent, not essential. Why? Because the very work of exposing liberalism's racism is itself predicated on deeply liberal commitments. That is, we have no choice but to work with what we have and are. Mills nowhere states but (in my view) everywhere implies that the longing for a total break from the past—or for a *point d'appui* outside it—expresses a well-intentioned but mistaken philosophical immaturity. The true radical goes deep to the roots of what *is* rather than dreaming of what might be.

Lewis Gordon proposes a very different reason for judging Du Bois to be a major political philosopher. For Gordon, Du Bois's greatness becomes visible when we see that he belongs not to the tradition of political philosophy with which Mills engages but to the different and independent countertradition of Africana philosophy. Making such a case confronts Gordon with a formidable rhetorical challenge, however. It is a relatively easy thing to argue to those who locate themselves within any tradition *X* that a particular figure belongs to that tradition; it is quite another and more difficult task to persuade them that that figure belongs to a tradition radically different from their own—for how can one make such a case without building it from the materials recognizable to one's audience, that is, from a conceptual vocabulary derived from their tradition, thereby encircling that figure with the tradition to which he does *not* belong? I think Mills would interject here that one *cannot* sidestep this dilemma and that (like it or not) we are stuck with the conceptual vocabulary of liberal political philosophy and that our only hope is to recast its meaning. Gordon's reply can be found in the distinctive way he sets up and unfolds his argument. His method of arguing that Du Bois is an Africana philosopher is simply to read and recognize Du Bois as such. In other words, Gordon does not move Du Bois from one place or tradition to another. He himself stands within Africana philosophy, and he proceeds to read Du Bois from that standpoint and within that tradition. What emerges, then, is less a propositional statement *that* Du Bois is an Africana philosopher than a redescription of Du Bois *as* one.

In part 2 of this volume, Anthony Reed and James Edward Ford III approach Du Bois's political thought through his poetry, reminding us of Arnold Rampersad's important insight in *The Art and Imagination of W. E. B. Du Bois* that, when we read Du Bois the thinker, we can only find him through Du Bois the writer. Anthony Reed offers a very fine-grained analysis of the ways Du Bois works within and against conventional understandings of the lyric and its relation to individual subjectivity. Du Bois's thought is to be found, he shows, as much in its poetic performativity as in its prosaic content. Focusing specifically on *The Souls of Black Folk,* he argues that its "mixed or alternating lyric mode allows [it] both to claim a centrality of authorial voice, self-consciously re-created through his revisions of its essays into a coherent text, and to undermine that voice, and with it claims to representation that, for white readers in particular, would have been a primary appeal." Simply put: at the heart of Du Bois's most famous work is "a performative engagement that announces its refusal to engage."

In a provocative reading of *Black Reconstruction,* James Edward Ford asks why Du Bois would have chosen to end each chapter of this historical work with a fragment of poetry. Using Nathaniel Mackey's suggestion that poetry sometimes provides a "paracritical hinge" that mediates among heterogeneous discourses, Ford suggests that these poetic fragments add up to an argument that is everywhere implied but nowhere stated in that book: that because white racism is in essence a political theology, "liberalism's use of the law to combat racism will inevitably fall short."

Part 3 of this volume is comprised of essays that examine Du Bois's thinking about US democracy. At the same time, they importantly underscore—as both Reed and Ford do—the ways Du Bois's thinking shuttles back and forth between what is and what might be, between the real and the imagined, between the known and the unknowable. Melvin L. Rogers's reading of Du Bois stands on two pillars. The first is that "the people" in the US democratic tradition has both descriptive meanings and an ascriptive one: it describes a given condition (that there is a polity composed of certain citizens), and it allows for almost infinite expansion as hitherto excluded persons aspire to gain citizenship and join those whom "the people" describes. The second is that Du Bois (and a number of other democratic reformers) exploit the gap between these descriptive and ascriptive meanings of the people and launch rhetorical appeals aimed at stimulating the feelings of existing citizens in ways that dispose them to expand their sense of who can and should be described as "the people." Rogers shows that the particular emotions Du Bois seeks to excite are shame (at the way whites have behaved toward black Americans) and sympathy (for the suffering black Americans experience as a consequence of white racism). Rogers's line of reasoning thus emphasizes Du Bois's attunement to the indeterminacies built into democracy, contingencies that open it toward an unknown future—for better and for worse. Rogers also helps us see that for Du Bois, both political theory and democratic citizenship involve and require not just reason and self-interest but emotion and affect. This view significantly expands our idea of what can "count" as being political theory, and it also suggests that while citizens of a democracy certainly do have rights and obligations, political philosophy must also attend to their feelings and dispositions.

My own essay moves along similar lines. Writing at a time when Progressive reformers were insisting that democracy needed more "expertise," in *Darkwater* Du Bois proposed an alternative source of democratic knowledge: what each citizen suffers is a unique and unshareable experience, one that imparts to each citizen a distinctive knowledge and perspective. A fully achieved democracy, Du Bois suggests, would be one that listened to and drew upon the totality of knowledge possessed by all its citizens. I conclude by arguing that this radical democratic epistemology distinguishes Du Bois's political theory from more conventional theories of democracy, including even those that seem most to resemble it.

Du Bois's belief that the unknowability of others can be a democratic resource is the subject of Robert W. Williams's essay also. He develops this idea by comparing Du Bois's conception of difference with that of the political theorist Iris Marion Young. Both theorists, he shows, emphasize that democratic citizens are embodied persons, not merely abstract rights-bearers or rational calculators of self-interest. And both argue that, as embodied persons, humans are ineluctably different from each other. But whereas Young sees difference itself as "unproblematically graspable," Du Bois takes it to be a radical alterity that cannot be fully known. One might conclude that such belief in the unknowable would have made Du Bois even more skeptical of science than Young was, but Williams shows that in fact the opposite is true. In a careful reading of "Sociology Hesitant," he demonstrates that although Du Bois believed that there was an ineluctable element of the "incalculable" (or "chance") operating in human affairs, the task of empirical sociology was to discover its "limit." In other words, sociologists "must assume Law and Chance [to be] working in conjunction" and to trace the line along which each met and limited the other.

Part 4, the final section of this volume, is concerned primarily with the ways Du Bois brings his critical and creative thinking to bear on concrete challenges and dilemmas of black politics. Alexander Livingston's close analysis of Du Bois's understudied book *John Brown* yields a powerful argument about Du Bois's conception of democratic sacrifice: "Against [Booker T. Washington's] path of passive integration through adjustment to white rule, *Souls* proposes a politics of assimilation through agitation and self-assertion. Du Bois's name for this program of militant striving is 'the Gospel of Sacrifice.' Here and throughout his writings Du Bois presents selfless sacrifice as paradoxically synonymous with a politics of black self-assertion."

Arash Davari takes on the contested question of Du Bois's conception of leadership in (black) social and political movements. Focusing on *The Philadelphia Negro* and *The Souls of Black Folk,* he suggests that Du Bois's work points us to a model that avoids the dangers of elite leadership on the one hand and of leaderless formations on the other. (The latter, Davari argues, are worryingly congruent with neoliberal fragmentation.) Instead, Du Bois finds a conceptual space between these alternatives, one where "positional distinctions between a leader and the led are maintained," yet "individuals from among the led may speak with the authority of leadership when and where necessary."

David H. Kim also carves out a space between by offering a new way to understand the second major phase of Du Bois's career, which is usually understood as a shift toward "Black Marxism." Kim both builds upon and complicates this now familiar picture, proposing that we should also view Du Bois as a forerunner of "decolonial" theory. Kim suggests that while Du Bois did indeed absorb and deploy a Marxist emphasis on economics and materialism, he also expanded the conventional frameworks of both Marxism and US black politics by recognizing and underscoring the importance of "coloniality"—the general historical condition produced by global Western imperialism. Du Bois, he argues, was "a distinctive type of decolonial thinker by virtue of developing an Afro-Asian conception of South-South decoloniality and . . . experimenting with a fusion of black radicalism and Gandhian notions of moksha (liberation) and satyagraha (nonviolent resistance)."

Published in 1935 and greeted by a storm of mostly critical and uncomprehending reviews, *Black Reconstruction* is now one of Du Bois's most widely read and influential books. But as Vijay Phulwani points out, it was neither the first nor the only work in which Du Bois investigated the historical and political meanings of the Reconstruction period. Indeed, Phulwani shows that when we assemble all the texts in which Du Bois wrote about Reconstruction, we find that they trace the development of his thought about "how to build durable political institutions for African Americans out of the fragmented and loosely organized forms of collective agency and organization available to them after centuries of slavery and white supremacy." Thus, while Reconstruction was the subject of Du Bois's most powerful intervention in historiography, it was also for him an ongoing resource in his political thinking about black politics.

What emerges from all these essays, then, is by no means a new vision or theory of Du Bois as a political thinker. Nor does this volume attempt to be comprehensive in scope. What we do see here, though, is a Du Bois even more deeply dialectical than his famous notion of "double-consciousness" would indicate. Taken together, Mills and Gordon show us that he can plausibly be seen to be both a radical liberal and an Africana philosopher. Rogers shows us how Du Bois worked in the space between the descriptive and the ascriptive, between what is and what might be, engaged equally with both. Bromell and Williams argue that Du Bois offers us a radical democratic epistemology and ethics based on the uniquely important knowledge each citizen gains through his or her experience, with the perspective of those who have suffered most being of particular value. Yet, as Williams shows, Du Bois also believed that the expert knowledge of the sciences could also play a critical role in governance so long as due respect was paid to both Law and Chance, the calculable and the incalculable, especially in human affairs. The essays by Reed and Ford take us further than any other work I know into the philosophical import of Du Bois's lifelong interest in poetry and its powers, arguing that Du Bois believed that the meaning of his writing was shaped as much by its form as by its content. Alexander Livingston persuasively shows that Du Bois advances a model of black "selfless sacrifice" that "is paradoxically synonymous with a politics of black self-assertion." Arash Davari reveals a Du Bois slowly working out a model of leadership that is neither the elitism of the Talented Tenth nor the total dispersal of authority advocated by many radical democratic theorists today; rather, it is an in-between path that retains a role for focused leadership but allows maximal interchange between leaders and led. David H. Kim likewise traces a productive tension between Du Bois's turn to Marxism and his long-standing commitment to what theorists would later call decoloniality. Finally, Vijay Phulwani's essay makes clear that Reconstruction was, for Du Bois, both a historical event and a philosophical resource, both a fact and a trope; in Du Bois's repeated returns to and revisions of Reconstruction's meaning, we perceive with exceptional clarity the degree to which his thinking was at once historical, theoretical, and poetic. Of course, a single volume cannot hope to represent all the kinds of political thought elaborated by and through a single figure, especially one as prolific and restless as Du Bois. However, I am particularly disappointed that I was not able to include recent—and still emergent—engagement with Du Bois by feminist political theorists and by political theorists who work with queer theory and sexuality studies.[24] Nearing the end of the second decade of the twenty-first century, we still need to keep thinking about race in all its complexity, and we have no better guide for that task than Du Bois.

Notes

1. W. E. B. Du Bois, *The Oxford W. E. B. Du Bois Reader*, ed. Eric J. Sundquist (New York: Oxford University Press, 1996), 39.

2. W. E. B. Du Bois, *Writings* (New York: Library of America, 1986), 651.

3. W. E. B. Du Bois, *Darkwater: Voices from within the Veil* (Millwood, NY: Kraus-Thomson, 1975), 9.

4. Adolph L. Reed Jr., *W. E. B. Du Bois and American Political Thought: Fabianism and the Color Line* (New York: Oxford University Press, 1997), 6.

5. Lawrie Balfour, *Democracy's Reconstruction: Thinking Politically with W. E. B. Du Bois* (New York: Oxford University Press, 2011), 5.

6. W. E. B. Du Bois, *Black Reconstruction in America 1860–1880* (New York: Free Press, 1998), 727.

7. W. E. B. Du Bois, *The Correspondence of W. E. B. Du Bois*, ed. Herbert Aptheker, vol. 2 (Amherst: University of Massachusetts Press, 1975), 204.

8. Du Bois, *Black Reconstruction*, 725.

9. Kathryne V. Lindberg, "Roots, Breaks, and the Performance of a Black Left Critique," *American Literary History* 17, no. 4 (Winter 2005): 835.

10. Aldon D. Morris, *The Scholar Denied: W. E. B. Du Bois and the Birth of Modern Sociology* (Berkeley: University of California Press, 2015), 26–27.

11. Kenneth D. Barkin, "'Berlin Days,' 1892–1894: W. E. B. Du Bois and German Political Economy," *boundary 2* 27, no. 3 (2000): 94. (From "Sketches" in Du Bois Papers at UMass.)

12. W. E. B. Du Bois, *Writings*, 1194. Du Bois goes on to declare: "For when Warren Harding or any white man comes to teach Negroes pride of race, we answer that pride is our business and not theirs, and a thing they would better fear than evoke: For the day that Black men love Black men simply because they are Black, is the day they will hate White men simply because they are White" (1194).

13. Qtd. in Barkin, "Berlin Days," 98.

14. Robert Gooding-Williams writes: "The fact remains that the argument

of *Souls* is couched in the language and spirit of an idealist philosophical tradition that James saw as the preeminent alternative to his own pragmatism" (Gooding-Williams, "Evading Narrative Myth, Evading Prophetic Pragmatism: Cornel West's *The American Evasion of Philosophy*," *Massachusetts Review* 32, no. 4 [Winter 1991–1992]: 527–28).

15. Ross Posnock, *Color and Culture: Black Writers and the Making of the Modern Intellectual* (Cambridge: Harvard University Press, 1998), 120.

16. Leonard Harris, ed., *Philosophy Born of Struggle: Anthology of Afro-American Philosophy from 1917* (Dubuque, IA: Kendall/Hunt, 1983).

17. George Yancy, "African-American Philosophy: Through the Lens of Socio-Existential Struggle," *Philosophy & Social Criticism* 37, no. 6 (2011): 552.

18. Vincent W. Lloyd, *Black Natural Law* (New York: Oxford University Press, 2016), x.

19. Ibid., xi.

20. Qtd. in Nick Bromell, *The Time Is Always Now: Black Thought and the Transformation of U.S. Democracy* (New York: Oxford University Press, 2013), 120.

21. W. E. B. Du Bois, *Color and Democracy: Colonies and Peace* (New York: Harcourt, Brace, 1945), 137

22. Du Bois, *Writings,* 1247–48.

23. Qtd. in Reed, *W. E. B. Du Bois and American Political Thought,* 8.

24. See, for example: Joy James, *Transcending the Talented Tenth: Black Leaders and American Intellectuals* (New York: Routledge, 1997); Ange-Marie Hancock, "W. E. B. Du Bois: Intellectual Forefather of Intersectionality?" *Souls* 7 (2005): 3–4, 74–84; Hazel Carby, *Race Men* (Cambridge, MA: Harvard University Press, 1998); Farah Jasmine Griffin, "Black Feminists and Du Bois: Respectability, Protection, and Beyond," *The Annals of the American Academy of Political and Social Science* 568 (March 2000): 28–40; Lawrie Balfour, "*Darkwater*'s Democratic Vision," *Political Theory* 38, no. 4 (2010): 537–63, and *Democracy's Reconstruction: Thinking Politically with W. E. B. Du Bois* (New York: Oxford University Press, 2011); Shatema Threadcraft, *Intimate Justice: The Black Female Body and the Body Politic* (New York: Oxford University Press, 2016); *Next to the Color Line: Gender, Sexuality, and W. E. B. Du Bois,* ed. Susan Gillman and Alys Eve Weinbaum (Minneapolis: University of Minnesota Press, 2007).

I

Du Bois and Political Philosophy

1

W. E. B. Du Bois

Black Radical Liberal

Charles W. Mills

The distinctive features of the black experience in modernity—the original categorization of blacks as a "slave race," Ham's grandchildren, and the continuing post-Emancipation imprint of this stigma on the black body in Africa and the African Diaspora—raise a challenge for the inherited categories and frameworks of Western political theory. Can an apparatus generally presuming free and equal citizenship and, even more fundamentally, equal recognized moral status, be adapted to the political agenda of those humans so differently related to both? Can it be adopted as is, or does it need to be fundamentally modified, or should it simply be rejected outright?[1]

Varying in its answers to these questions, what has come to be called "Afro-modern political thought" covers a wide range of political alternatives, united on the mission of overcoming racial subordination—"the regimes of white supremacy"—but divided on the diagnoses of its workings and the most effective prescriptions for its elimination. Michael Dawson's well-known taxonomy offers the following listing: radical egalitarianism, disillusioned liberalism, black Marxism, black nationalism, black feminism, black conservatism. Of course, divergences in the interpretation of these positions (even without the qualifying adjective) necessarily introduce a significant element of uncertainty and boundary fuzziness in determining their content, which is only exacerbated when the "black" is brought into the semantic equation. How does racial subordination modify the crucial terms and theoretical logics of political ideologies predicated on racial equality, or "racelessness"? Is what is produced by the synthesis still going to be recognizable by its genealogy as legitimately liberal, Marxist, nationalist, feminist, conservative? So the investigation into what a "black" political philosophy would be will necessarily have ramifications for the cartography of "white" political philosophies also, perhaps producing seismic shifts in our perception of the terrain they have been claiming to be mapping.[2]

W. E. B. Du Bois was the Afro-modern incarnate, and he is uncontroversially its greatest and most accomplished representative. "Talented Tenth" elitist, democrat, Eurocentric snob, celebrant of the folk tradition, integrationist, separatist, Marxist, black nationalist, Stalinist, radical democrat, prophetic pragmatist—the list of possible and actual descriptions of Du Bois's political identity is long and contradictory. Throughout his extended and extraordinarily productive activist and scholarly life, he engaged critically and increasingly radically with white liberalism and white Marxism, black nationalism, black conservatism, and early black feminism. In Michael Hanchard's characterization of one main purpose of black political thought, Du Bois "situate[d] racism and race-making at the core of the projects associated with Western modernity . . . [that] consequently have affected many societies and civilizations, not only black peoples. . . . [thereby exploring] the implications of racial domination for the epistemic frames, definitions, and modes of classifications for politics, polity, and society in the vocabulary and lexicon of the Western political tradition."[3]

In the process, Du Bois developed a comprehensive worldview with multidisciplinary sources and multidisciplinary implications that even now, more than a half a century after his death, the American academy, as Cornel West points out, is "just not ready" to "assimilate," "incorporate," and "render intelligible," because they so profoundly challenge scholarly orthodoxies. Ironically, Du Bois may be both "the most contemporary figure in the twenty-first century for us" and the one who for that very reason has until lately been most thoroughly ignored by mainstream scholarship.[4]

Fortunately, things are changing. Aldon Morris's recent *The Scholar Denied* makes the strongest case yet for the long-standing claim of many black sociologists that Du Bois should be seen as the real father of American sociology, not Robert Park. Historians Marilyn Lake and Henry Reynolds acknowledge his influence in their entry in Cambridge University Press's Critical Perspectives on Empire series, *Drawing the Global Colour Line: White Men's Countries and the International Challenge of Racial Equality*, as do "critical" international relations theorists Alexander Anievas, Nivi Manchanda, and Robbie Shilliam in their coedited *Race and Racism in International Relations: Confronting the Global Colour Line*. In addition, the new body of work on slavery, American capitalism, and the global economy by such writers as Walter Johnson, Edward Baptist, and Sven Beckert surely vindicates Du Bois's line of analysis, even when he is not explicitly cited.[5]

The aim of this essay and this volume—along with two recent important books by Robert Gooding-Williams and Lawrie Balfour—is to catalyze a comparable recognition of Du Bois's theoretical achievements in political philosophy. I will begin by establishing the racialized nature of Western political philosophy—certainly modern political philosophy, but possibly including the classical tradition also—and the consequent need for the black rewriting of its "epistemic frames, definitions, and modes of classifications." I will then turn to an overview of some of the key themes in Du Bois's version of this rewriting to make a case for Du Bois as being—at least for a significant stretch of his long intellectual and political career—a black radical liberal, simultaneously engaging with and critiquing the most successful ideology of modernity, and the one that has been the most consistent reference point for black political thinkers.

Racism and Western Political Philosophy

Philosophy, the oldest of the Western humanities, has—perhaps more than any other discipline—presented itself as a dialogue among "talking heads," an image literalized in the iconography of white marble busts of the classical Greek and Roman figures who are its founding fathers. Elsewhere, the body might make a difference, but not here in the world of pure thought and supposedly disincarnate thinkers. But as the pioneers of the second wave of feminist theory showed, these heads were indeed solidly attached to male bodies, and "fatherhood" was not a gender-neutral parenting but a patriarchal one. Such early texts as Susan Moller Okin's *Women in Western Political Thought* and Lorenne Clark and Lynda Lange's *The Sexism of Social and Political Theory* documented the routinely sexist assumptions in virtually all the canonical male philosophers, stretching back to antiquity, and the relegation of women to a functional reproductive role. As a result, gender bias in the putatively sexless world of philosophy is today a far less contested notion than it was thirty years ago.[6]

But if the maleness of the founding fathers has been grudgingly established as relevant, the significance of their whiteness remains more controversial, and there are far fewer texts on philosophy and race. One obvious explanation of this asymmetry is demographic: the whiteness of the profession (about 97 percent) is more pronounced than its maleness (about 80 percent). Gradually, however, a growing body of work has focused on race, attaining sufficient quantity and visibility to have earned an official designation: critical philosophy of race. This literature has explored various issues—the metaphysics of race, race and social epistemology, race and ethics, the phenomenological and existential realities of race, and others—but for our purposes its most crucial research focus has been on race and the history of philosophy, especially political philosophy. Its central question has been: Assuming that race is constructed, when does race enter the world and how does it affect Western philosophy?[7]

Two main competing answers have emerged. One, a short periodization, argues that race and racism are products of modernity or, at the earliest, of the late medieval epoch. Of course, this view does not maintain that the premodern world was free of human bigotry and prejudice of various kinds—for example, ethnocentrism, color prejudice, xenophobia, religious hostilities, etc. But these did not, it is asserted, take a "racial" form, since race as a social category did not yet exist. Thus, racism as a body of thought or a set of discriminatory institutions and practices did not exist either. Nell Painter's *The History of White People,* for example, begins: "Were there 'white' people in antiquity? . . . People with light skin certainly existed well before our own times. But did anyone think they were 'white' or that their character related to their color? No, for neither the idea of race nor the idea of 'white' people had been invented, and people's skin color did not carry useful meaning."[8]

Du Bois himself endorsed this short periodization of race. In his famous essay "The Souls of White Folk," he writes: "The discovery of personal whiteness among the world's peoples is a very modern thing,—a nineteenth and twentieth century matter, indeed. The ancient world would have laughed at such a distinction. The Middle Age regarded skin color with mild curiosity; and even up into the eighteenth century we were hammering our national manikins into one, great, universal Man, with fine frenzy which ignored color and race even more than birth."[9] Similarly, in *The Negro*, he claims:

> The world has always been familiar with black men, who represent one of the most ancient of human stocks. Of the ancient world gathered about the Mediterranean, they formed a part and were viewed with no surprise or dislike, because this world saw them come and go and play their part with other men. . . . The modern world, in contrast, knows the Negro chiefly as a bond slave in the West Indies and America. Add to this the fact that the darker races in other parts of the world have, in the last four centuries, lagged behind . . . Europe, and we face to-day a widespread assumption throughout the dominant world that color is a mark of inferiority.[10]

So according to Du Bois, racism and antiblack prejudices are modern phenomena, rooted in racial slavery and imperial European domination. Although sexism and male gender domination can be argued to have shaped and distorted Western philosophy, including Western political philosophy, from its inception, the same cannot be said of racism and white racial domination, since they did not even exist in the period.[11]

However, this short periodization has had its challengers. Even if "races" were not demarcated by skin color in antiquity, Denise McCoskey points out, this does not mean that races constructed by some other criteria did not exist. Benjamin Isaac contends in his *The Invention of Racism in Classical Antiquity* that the conventional scholarly wisdom on this subject is quite wrong (in part because of a problematic initial formulation of racism); he argues that the belief in hierarchically ordered groups with "physical, mental, and moral" "collective traits . . . which are constant and unalterable by human will" should count as racism. By this criterion, he judges Aristotle to be the progenitor of Western racism, given that his "natural slaves" are ethnically marked as non-Greeks. So even if we do not yet have a white/nonwhite racial hierarchy, we do have a Greek/non-Greek racial hierarchy, which becomes a more general civilized/barbarian racial hierarchy that influences other famous writers in Greco-Roman antiquity. Insofar as Aristotle was and is regarded as one of the towering figures in the Western political tradition, Isaac's verdict, if vindicated, would demonstrate that racism in some sense, if not the color-coded modern sense, does indeed shape Western political philosophy from the start.[12]

Nor do all historians of the subject believe that there was no specifically antiblack racism before modernity. In a later conference volume edited by Isaac and other like-minded (that is, long periodization) scholars, David Goldenberg argues that the negative associations of blackness in Greco-Roman color symbolism were the source of a differentiated antipathy—deeper and more enduring than that targeting other groups—toward "Ethiopians" (the term used at the time for Africans in general). And from the third century onward, he notes, Christianity was marked by "the identification of the devil and demons as Ethiopians." Goldenberg concludes: "Antiblack sentiment seems to be different from the hostile thinking encountered against other peoples. Against others, it is for what they do; against Blacks it is for what they are. And what they are, that is their blackness, is found to be objectionable because (a) it most visibly indicates their otherness, their somatic dissonance, and (b) its symbolic value connotes a host of negative notions. . . . The disparagement of black skin color began in classical antiquity, reached a height in Christian literature and in the literature of Christian societies."[13]

Contra Du Bois, then, medieval Christendom had a long history of negative imagery of "Ethiopians" (along with Jews, Muslims, and Mongols), who were among the "monstrous races" routinely depicted in medieval art. In her *Saracens, Demons, & Jews: Making Monsters in Medieval Art,* Debra Strickland comments on the "interchangeability of demons and Ethiopians" in the iconography of the period: "[Ethiopians] were in fact a conflation of all Blacks living in sub-Egyptian Africa, a practice that began during the Classical period. . . . In effect, the blackness of the Ethiopians obliterated their humanity, paving the way for the abstract understanding necessary for ethnic stereotyping. That is, Ethiopians were transformed from living humans into symbols, setting a dangerous precedent for the mind-set that ultimately helped justify the social discrimination and intolerance of not only dark-skinned people but also other enemy groups within medieval Christian society."[14]

These issues (whether the "monstrous races" were close enough to modern conceptions of "races" to establish at least a partial continuity) remain debated and contentious, with no scholarly consensus on the matter. But the existence of the long periodization paradigm does at least raise the possibility that Du Bois and others who locate racism and antiblack sentiment solely in modernity may have too sanguine and abbreviated a view of its longevity in the West and may be failing to appreciate how profoundly it was formed by Greco-Roman thought and the inherited iconography of Christian eschatology. Even if the European peoples we now call "white" would not formally have had that identity in the ancient world, there is still sufficient continuity over two thousand–plus years within a light-skinned Euro-descendant population identifying themselves as the heirs to ancient Greece and Rome and sharing a religion stigmatizing blackness to justify concerns about how deeply these sentiments may be rooted. Du Bois writes: "We must, then, look for the origin of modern color prejudice not to physical or cultural causes, but to historic facts. And we shall find the answer in modern Negro slavery and the slave trade." But the "material" historic factors privileged as generative in such Marxism-influenced explanations (racism as the ideology of expansionist capitalism and racial slavery) may only have been reinforcing theologico-cultural representations already deeply engrained. At any rate, with that cautionary word, let us move now to the modern period, which is, of course, the period whose ideologies are of primary and uncontested relevance for Du Bois's "Afro-modernity."[15]

The case I will briefly recapitulate here is one I have made in greater detail in a number of books and essays, starting with *The Racial Contract*. Just as feminists have shown liberalism—the dominant political philosophy of modernity—to be patriarchal, so I have suggested that we also need to see it as racial, at least in its dominant incarnations. The hedge is because Jennifer Pitts has argued that liberalism in Britain and France becomes consistently an "imperial liberalism" only after 1800 and that before that period one can find both anti-imperialist and antiracist liberals.[16]

Until recently, mainstream accounts of liberalism and the views of its leading theorists have tended to marginalize this history, either by refusing to talk about racism at all or by representing it as unfortunate "prejudice" that should not be located on the same conceptual level as the terms and apparatus of the liberal ideology itself. Racism, when acknowledged, has been depicted as an "anomaly" to a generally inclusive normative European order. But my suggestion is that we should instead see racism as so penetrating and reconstituting the rules and principles of this order that race becomes symbiotically determinant of its boundaries of inclusion and exclusion. George Mosse insisted many decades ago that "racism as it developed in Western society was no mere articulation of prejudice, nor was it simply a metaphor for suppression; it was, rather, a fully blown system of thought, an ideology like Conservatism, Liberalism, or Socialism, with its own peculiar structure and mode of discourse. . . . [Indeed it was] the most widespread ideology of the time." However, Mosse himself does not take the further step I think is warranted, which is to point out that under the circumstances, these ideologies will not remain hermetically sealed off from racism. So we will get a *racialized* conservatism, liberalism, and socialism.[17]

In her book on the Enlightenment, Dorinda Outram writes that "this contradiction between support for supposedly universal rights, and the actual exclusion of large numbers of human beings from the enjoyment of those rights, is central to, and characteristic of Enlightenment thought." But I think it would be more accurate, and more theoretically illuminating, to recognize that there is no actual "contradiction" here, since the excluded humans, even if conceded to be biologically human, were not deemed to be full persons, but *subpersons*, whether on grounds of race or gender or some other stigmatizing and morally diminishing characteristic. Acknowledging this internal historic structuring of liberalism and most other Enlightenment ideologies would both give us a more accurate picture of the recent past and sensitize us to the legacy it has left—the ways in which it is not past at all—that needs to be self-consciously corrected for.[18]

Let me illustrate this point with a quick overview of some central modern Western political philosophers, figures unquestionably canonical.

As an absolutist, Thomas Hobbes is obviously a problematic forebear for the liberal tradition. But what is commonly taken to make him an important precursor to it nonetheless is his radical individualism and (putative) egalitarianism. Unlike Aristotle and the medieval "schoolmen" he repeatedly mocks throughout *Leviathan*, he starts from the physical and mental (not moral) equality of all "men" in the state of nature. Then, on the basis of their rational self-interest in exiting the life-threatening war of all against all to which their self-seeking desires lead, he argues that they will devise rules to govern the polity that are likewise egalitarian, such as the ninth "law of Nature": "*That every man acknowledge others for his Equall by Nature.*"[19]

So it would seem that we have here an uncompromising egalitarianism, if prudentially rather than morally based. And yet Hobbes also describes Native Americans ("the savage people in many places of *America*") as real-life inhabitants of the state of nature who apparently lack the minimal threshold rationality to perceive the cooperative path out of it. How is this reconcilable with what we have just been told about the equality of all "men"? Obviously, the implication is that these are "men" of such a different and cognitively inferior sort that they belong in a different category: "savages" rather than (civilized) men in the standard sense. As Richard Ashcraft comments, "men are not recognizably different from other animals by virtue of divine creation (which may leave them, as the 'savages of America,' still in the state of other animals, i.e., the state of war); they become different only because they themselves *create* a political society." So their humanity notwithstanding, American savages are clearly not to be included as equals in the ninth of the laws of nature intended to regulate the commonwealth. They cannot be treated as persons, but rather (best-case scenario) as wards of the state or (worst-case scenario) as threats to the security of the absolutist polity who must be exterminated. The Hobbesian image of American "savages," wild subpersons, would shape not merely the British colonial project but, extrapolated to native peoples elsewhere, European expansionism in many other lands.[20]

Unlike Hobbes the proponent of absolutism, John Locke is classically its opponent, though the version he is targeting is primarily Sir Robert Filmer's biblically grounded rather than Hobbes's prudentially based kind. So Locke is indubitably central to liberalism, and, through his influence on Thomas Jefferson, he was a foundational inspiration for the property-based democracy of the young American polity. Moreover, the freedom and equality enjoyed by his "men" in the state of nature do not rest on comparative "threat advantage," as Hobbes thought, but on objective moral law, natural law in the traditional (non-Hobbesian) sense. But though all men should be self-owning, and thus possessed of equal standing in Locke's proprietarian moral universe, Native Americans seem once again to be located in a separate category, as do the Africans in whose enslavement he was earlier an investor. In the *Second Treatise*'s famous chapter 5 on property, Locke makes clear that humans are under the divine imperative to demonstrate their "industriousness" and "rationality" by appropriating the world, which in his opinion native peoples do not, so that an English day laborer lives better than an Indian king. Thus as various theorists have pointed out—including Barbara Arneil, James Tully, and Carole Pateman—Locke provides a justification for colonial appropriation of indigenous land. Nominally equal in theory, native peoples' deficient rationality makes them in practice unequal.[21]

Locke's earlier (pre–*Two Treatises*) investments in African slavery and contribution to writing the Carolina Constitution, which gave masters absolute power over their Negro slaves, also pose an obvious problem for the transracially inclusive interpretation of the *Second Treatise*'s scope. Chapter 16 does justify enslaving (or killing, if one wishes) the prosecutors of a war of aggression because they have violated natural law. But even if Locke had somehow managed to convince himself that all the captured Africans brought to the New World were in fact guilty of such crimes, he explicitly rules out hereditary enslavement of their children in that same chapter. So we have a seeming inconsistency that has generated a large body of secondary literature but that, in my opinion, can most easily be resolved by recognizing that blacks were not, for Locke, full persons in the first place. Self-ownership is legitimately denied to them because they are subpersons appropriately owned by others.

But it is in the third representative of the social contract tradition—Immanuel Kant—that the case for the philosopher seeing at least some people of color (here blacks and Native Americans) as subpersons is both most easily made and most dramatic in its theoretical repercussions. Hobbes is, as noted, not really a liberal, and his self-interest-based conception of morality locates him as the progenitor of the morally less attractive "contractarian" strain of the social contract tradition, as against the "contractual" personhood-based conception. Moreover, though Locke too (as a natural rights theorist) is part of the contractualist version, and thus with Kant central to the liberal mainstream ("deontological"/rights-based liberalism), his unqualified emphasis on the protection of property rights, while endearing him to the political Right, is rejected by ethicists concerned about society's vulnerable. Kant's prescription of respect for the "personhood" of all rational beings has seemed to them a more inspiring normative vision, arguably qualifying his own proprietarianism, and making Kant in many eyes the most important moral theorist of modernity and liberalism.[22]

Yet it turns out—shockingly, and still rejected as untrue by many mainstream philosophers—that Kant should also be considered one of the fathers of modern "scientific" racism. ("Scientific"/biological racism is usually seen as distinctively modern, as against—assuming the truth of the long periodization—the theological or cultural racism of premodernity.) His writings in anthropology and physical geography—known at the start of the twentieth century but somehow obliterated from Western consciousness after World War II—outline in detail a racial hierarchy of white Europeans/yellow Asians/black Africans/red Amerindians, a hierarchy based on the differential development of *Keime* (germs, seeds) in these different branches of the human race. So here it is not a matter of reconstructing his possibly racist views from a few scattered sentences here and there, or inferring it from his racist practice, but of an extensive body of material focused *specifically and explicitly* on the subject. Kant judged blacks and Native Americans to be natural slaves, and for most of his career countenanced African slavery and European colonialism, thereby making it difficult, at least for some of us, to see any "contradiction" here. Rather, the simple, elegant, and obvious solution is to infer that personhood as a category was racially structured for him, and that though his monogenism meant that all races were human, not all races achieved the person threshold.[23]

But Western philosophical racism is not peculiar to contract theorists; it traverses the divide between contractarian liberals and utilitarian liberals. David Hume, sometimes characterized as a proto-utilitarian, observes in a footnote to his essay "Of National Characters":

> I am apt to suspect the negroes and in general all other species of men (for there are four or five different kinds) to be naturally inferior to the whites. There never was a civilized nation of any other complexion than white, nor even any individual eminent either in action or speculation. No ingenious manufactures amongst them, no arts, no sciences. . . . Such a uniform and constant difference could not happen, in so many countries and ages if nature had not made an original distinction between these breeds of men. Not to mention our colonies, there are negro slaves dispersed all over Europe, of whom none ever discovered any symptoms of ingenuity.[24]

Or consider John Stuart Mill, leading Enlightenment theorist and nineteenth-century humanitarian utilitarian reformer, whose famous antipaternalist "harm principle" is usually taken as a cornerstone of liberalism's commitment to the individual's freedom to make his/her own life without interference. Once again, it depends on who gets to be counted as an individual. Mill, the colonial employee of the British East India Company, quickly specifies that "this doctrine is meant to apply only to human beings in the maturity of their faculties," not children, obviously, nor what could be thought of as child races, "those backward states of society in which the race itself may be considered as in its nonage": "Despotism is a legitimate mode of government in dealing with barbarians, provided the end be their improvement, and the means justified by actually effecting that end."[25] Mill's racism is not just a matter of philosophical opinion, but a position he intended to guide public policy. As Uday Singh Mehta points out, referencing Mill's text on representative government: "Representative institutions are appropriate for Europe and its predominantly white colonies and not for the rest of the world. The bracketing of India, among others, is not therefore the mark of an embarrassing theoretical inconsistency, precisely because at the theoretical level, the commitment to representative institutions is subsequent, and not prevenient, to considerations of utility. . . . [For backward nations] alternative norms are required to remain consistent with the progress associated with utility."[26]

British colonial policy must therefore maintain colonial rule, given the backward state of these nations. So what needs to be appreciated is that the person/subperson divide, the racialization of the liberal apparatus, cuts across standard demarcations between natural rights liberalism, deontological liberalism, and utilitarian liberalism, or the contrast between biological racism and cultural racism. Mill's racism is cultural, a doctrine of advanced and retarded races, as is made clear in his famous debate with Thomas Carlyle (*The Nigger Question/The Negro Question*). But while more "progressive" than the overtly reactionary Carlyle, he is still an agent of Empire, no more calling for an end to European colonialism than the biologically racist Kant did. And the same could be said for other theorists less central to the Anglo-American philosophical canon. Georg Wilhelm Hegel was not a biological racist either, but his oddly hybrid "environmental-cultural" racism, in the diagnosis of Teshale Tibebu, nonetheless provides, in the planetary itinerary of the World-Spirit, a clear demarcation between prehistorical, ahistorical, and world-historical peoples that apotheosizes Europe and the civilizing mission. Nor should we assume that the radicalized, materialistically inverted version of this story in revolutionary Marxism escapes the taint of Eurocentrism. Marx may have located primitive capitalist accumulation in "the extirpation, enslavement and entombment in mines of [Amerindians and] . . . the conversion of Africa into a preserve for the commercial hunting of blackskins." But this brief acknowledgment should not be read as grounding any distinctive vision of a *racial* exploitation different from that exemplified in white working-class wage-labor, or a sense of the specifically *racial* dimensions of global Euro-capitalist domination and its creation of a global "whiteness." As John M. Hobson concludes, Marx's theory of history rests on "paternalistic-Eurocentric foundations" that "faithfully reproduce the teleological Orientalist story" except that now "the Western proletariat [rather than the Western bourgeoisie] is global humanity's 'chosen people.'" Transformative agency, now in its revolutionary form, still inheres in whites, here the white working class of the Global North, whose mission it will be to liberate the Global South.[27]

Whether springing up only in modernity, then, or originating much further back in Aristotle's anti-Persian distinction between those who are slaves only contingently and those who are slaves by nature, Western racism deeply shapes Western political theory, becoming the demarcation in a modern world between those humans who do actually attain "person" status and those who do not. This distinction is orthogonal to, cuts across, other theoretical divisions internal to the field. If this history has now been erased, if these political ideologies are now anachronistically read as being in their time racially inclusive, we will be disadvantaged not merely in understanding their actual historical logics of development but handicapped in the necessary task of reconstructing them (to the extent that they can be) as genuinely rather than merely nominally racially inclusive. W. E. B. Du Bois, I suggest, needs to be recognized as the most important thinker in the Africana tradition undertaking this task, identifying both the liberalism and the Marxism of his day as racialized, and seeking, at different times and in different ways, to rewrite both.

W. E. B. Du Bois as Black Radical Liberal

In the pages that follow, I want to make a case for W. E. B. Du Bois as being—at least for a significant stretch of his long and self-reinventing life—a "black radical liberal." This will be an unfamiliar phrase that might seem, prima facie, to be a contradiction in terms, which is part of my reason for taking up the challenge. (That Du Bois was for many years a black Marxist—perhaps the preeminent black Marxist—is old news, certainly not something that needs to be established or refuted at this point.) *Black radical liberalism* is obviously meant to be contrasted with *black liberalism*, but what is the contrast supposed to be?[28]

Let me try to explain. Black liberalism in the mainstream unqualified sense, as I interpret it, is a liberalism that operates within a conventional liberal framework of individualist assumptions and then tries to bring race into the picture. Race and racism are not seen, as in the black radical liberalism for which I am arguing, as necessitating a fundamental rethinking of that framework. Black radicalism, usually regarded as subsuming two main variants, black nationalism and black Marxism, is taken to be categorically opposed to black liberalism. Whether individually or in attempted synthesis, the theoretical commitments of these political ideologies (either presupposing an analytic framework of white supremacy or an analytic framework of capitalist class domination) are viewed as requiring a foundational rejection of liberalism's assumptions.[29]

But what I am claiming is that this judgment is mistaken and that the most valuable elements of black nationalism and black Marxism can indeed be incorporated into a suitably revised liberalism. A liberalism whose traditional social ontology has been reconceptualized to admit the centrality of racial and class domination to the making of the modern world is not merely possible, but desirable, enabling us to mainstream into the dominant political discourse of modernity the traditionally marginalized perspectives and demands of black radicals. Black radical liberalism is a liberalism informed by the realities of *racial capitalism* and self-consciously oriented accordingly by the need to rethink white liberal theory in that light. So it is not merely a matter of arguing for a left/social-democratic/"socialist" liberalism, mindful of the failures of both free-market/neoliberal capitalism and Stalinist "socialism" (a familiar enough project by now), but of taking into account liberalism's historic complicity with white supremacy, both nationally and internationally. As such, it is, I am contending, a liberalism better equipped than mainstream liberalism, whether black or white, to carry out an emancipatory racial agenda. For in claiming above that the dominant varieties of liberalism in modernity have been racialized, I meant to refer not merely to racist representations of people of color in the theory's vocabulary but to a racialized logic in its conceptual and normative apparatus. Originally, this will have been a logic of overt racist exclusion; today, it will present itself as a nominally "color-blind" inclusion that, by failing to acknowledge the legacy of the past (and ongoing practices in the present), will guarantee its perpetuation. A black radical liberalism will therefore need to undertake a deracializing reconstruction of liberalism.[30]

Let me begin by clarifying how I understand "liberalism" as a concept. I will draw here on a characterization by the well-known British political theorist John Gray:

> Common to all variants of the liberal tradition is a definite conception, distinctively modern in character, of man and society. . . . It is *individualist,* in that it asserts the moral primacy of the person against the claims of any social collectivity; *egalitarian,* inasmuch as it confers on all men the same moral status and denies the relevance to legal or political order of differences in moral worth among human beings; *universalist,* affirming the moral unity of the human species and according a secondary importance to specific historic associations and cultural forms; and *meliorist* in its affirmation of the corrigibility and improvability of all social institutions and political arrangements. It is this conception of man and society which gives liberalism a definite identity which transcends its vast internal variety and complexity.[31]

Against collectivist political philosophies, then (as Marxism and black nationalism are often represented as being), which subordinate individual rights to a putative greater social good, liberalism affirms the moral centrality of the individual. Against racist and other discriminatory political philosophies (as black nationalism, again, is often represented as being), liberalism endorses egalitarianism and universalism. And against conservative political philosophies pessimistic about the possibilities for progressive social change, whether because of religious skepticism or biologically determinist fatalism, liberalism holds out the hope of a better world, a vision that is this-worldly rather than otherworldly.

Now as an articulation of an *ideal* liberalism, Gray's account is a very attractive picture, but it obviously bears no correspondence whatsoever to *actual,* real-world liberalism. As Domenico Losurdo summarizes things, the sordid (and therefore, understandably, usually airbrushed) history of actual liberalism reveals that it has been "illiberal" for most of humanity throughout its reign. Even the white male working class did not get the rights we associate with modernity and the Enlightenment (such as the franchise) until well into the modern period, while for white women and people of color the exclusions were even more dramatic (and arguably endure to this day). Nonwhites were not generally seen as "morally equal" "individuals" but, as I suggested above, as "subpersons" whose unqualified membership even in "the human species" was sometimes questioned, and whose "improvability" was either denied altogether or deemed to be achievable only under white tutelage. So actual liberalism was illiberalism, when class, race, or gender are taken into account. Any race-sensitive liberalism needs to acknowledge this history if it is to be accurate and effective in diagnosing and trying to eliminate social injustice.[32]

Let us appropriate some language from John Rawls to mark this distinction. In *A Theory of Justice,* Rawls distinguishes between the principles of justice appropriate for ideal, "well-ordered" (perfectly just) societies of "perfect compliance" with its rules and norms, and nonideal (imperfect) societies of only "partial compliance." The former principles come under ideal theory; the latter, under nonideal theory. I suggest the distinction is more generally useful and can in fact be applied, more globally, to liberalism itself. Most discussions of liberalism historically have presupposed ideal or near-ideal conditions and then asked what form liberal rights and freedoms should take in this context. But even under liberal modernity, which is supposed to usher in the age of individualism, oppression is the norm for all but a small minority of the population. My claim will be that a liberalism forced to face the realities of group domination in putatively liberal societies would be very different from the liberalisms familiar to us, in part because—at the meta level—a revisionist liberalism of this kind would need to critically engage with *existing* liberalism's complicity in this domination. A white-supremacist society, such as the United States has historically been (and some would say continues to be), is obviously not a well-ordered society, and the liberalism appropriate for guiding us in institutional reform and institutional reconstruction needs to reflect this radical difference in its identity. One simple way of bringing Du Bois into the realm of Rawlsian discourse, then, is to categorize him as a political philosopher centrally focused throughout his life on *nonideal theory*—that is, the world of sociopolitical oppression and the challenge, in the United States in particular, of how to overcome illiberal white supremacy in what was supposedly a liberal democratic state.[33]

Black Radical Liberalism

Against this background, then, let us turn to the details of what I am claiming can illuminatingly be seen as Du Bois's reconstruction of a nonideal-theory liberalism shaped and theoretically oriented by the experience of black racial subordination: a black radical liberalism. Unlike mainstream black liberalism, black radical liberalism views race and racism as symbiotically incorporated into the liberal body politic, not an anomaly to it, thereby requiring a deep rethinking of crucial liberal categories and framings—its social and moral ontology, its marginalization of the reality and significance of exploitation, and its consequent failure to theorize the implications of these inequitable relationships for social and political transparency. So we will look at Du Bois's reconstruction job under these four categories: the descriptive and moral metaphysics of the society, racial exploitation, and racial opacity.

The Racial Descriptive Metaphysics of the Social Order

To begin with, Du Bois has to work out the metaphysics of the social order, given that races are entities central to that order and perforce entities to be categorically recognized in theorizing about it. The crucial question is whether this metaphysics is compatible with liberalism or not. I will contend that it is indeed compatible and that in fact once we recognize how dramatic a difference the self-conscious location of liberalism in a nonideal-theory oppressive context makes, we can appreciate that many of the criticisms historically directed against liberalism as such are really targeted at ideal-theory liberalism.

Consider the Gray quote. The "individualism" he highlights is supposed to be one of the crucial demarcating features of liberalism, and indeed it is routinely critiqued by the Left for its atomistic individualist ontology. But even for mainstream liberalism, this accusation is unfair. It is most true for a contractarian liberalism based on Hobbesian individuals in self-seeking conflict with each other in the state of nature. It is less true for Lockean liberalism, which, though also contractarian, assumes a state of nature that is virtually "social," with extensive human commercial intercourse even before the formal decision to create a community. And it is not at all true for utilitarian liberalism, which grounds the basic moral imperatives on social welfare, or for the "communitarian" liberalism of the British Hegelians T. H. Green and his colleagues, which conceives of individuals as fundamentally shaped by their communities and social identities.[34]

What liberalism is really committed to is *moral* individualism, the individual as the locus of moral value (as in the Gray quote). But this is quite separate from—neither coextensive with nor implying nor implied by—*descriptive* individualism, the individual conceptualized as extracted out of her social identity and sociohistorical setting. We can affirm from a normative standpoint that the liberal bottom line should be the flourishing of individuals, with the flourishing of collectives being valuable only insofar as it is instrumental to that end. That affirmation does not at all necessarily commit us to understanding individuals in a desocialized and dehistoricized way.

Once we disambiguate terms, we should see that even mainstream liberalism has the resources to accommodate a "social" individualism. The real problem, I suggest, is that the overarching commitment to the ideal-theory framing of liberalism (across these different variants: contractarian, utilitarian, and Greenean) has precluded the exploration of the ontologies of *oppressive* liberal societies ("liberal" in that they give at least lip service to liberal principles and norms). Whether in an atomistic individualist ontology or more socially informed ontologies, liberal theory has not made it a priority to understand how group domination within liberal polities necessarily shapes the human beings enmeshed in their relations. The populations of liberal theory may be portrayed as desocialized atomic individuals or as social individuals, but in both cases they are symmetrically positioned with respect to each other as equi-powerful. Either no sociohistorical background is recognized at all, or a common sociohistorical background is presupposed that can then be factored out precisely because it is a common factor. But for nonideal-theory liberalism—the liberalism of actual liberal states—individuals cannot be theorized in this decontextualized way, since structures of domination and oppression position them so differently in the society and the polity. Here it is *asymmetry* that rules, with correspondingly profound ontological consequences for the privileged and the subordinated.[35]

So a nonideal-theory liberalism will have to register these differences in its apparatus. Assuming that such a society is radically rather than slightly deviant from ideality, its ontology will be affected also. But far from such a metaphysics being incompatible with liberalism, as is standardly assumed, it should be seen as a *prerequisite* for properly guiding it. A group ontology is not inconsistent with normative liberal individualism since it orients us to the structures that illicitly privilege and disadvantage liberal individuals and obstruct the latter's achievement of their individuality. What would be problematic would be a group ontology that elevated group flourishing *above* the individual, and/or that denied equal moral status to some individuals because of their group membership.

With these points having been made, let us turn to "The Conservation of Races" (1897), which can be argued to be Du Bois's first detailed attempt to spell out what the metaphysics of the social order are. The text is, of course, famously ambiguous, resulting in widely different interpretations of what the underlying ontology is supposed to be. On the one hand, we have reference to "families," "common blood," "physical differences of blood, color and cranial measurements," "the cleavage of physical race distinctions" that "play a great part" in dividing the "eight distinctly differentiated races" of the modern world. On the other hand, we are informed that "subtle forces," "spiritual" and "psychic," "infinitely transcend" the "physical [differences]," even if "based" on them, so that to understand them we need "the eye of the historian and sociologist." So is Du Bois offering us a biologically essentialist view of race, a socially constructivist view of race (and if so, is it culturally or politically constructivist), or a confused and inherently self-contradictory view of race?[36]

Obviously we have no time to enter and try to resolve this debate here. The point I want to make is that of all the different possible readings, none are *unequivocally* antiliberal in their implications. If a constructivist reading is ultimately vindicated—Du Bois as saying with confusing rhetorical flourishes in 1897 what he would later spell out more lucidly in 1940 in his classic epigram that "the black man is a person who must ride 'Jim Crow' in Georgia"—then clearly there is no tension here with liberalism, since most contemporary critical philosophers of race are both constructivists and liberals. It is true that Du Bois contrasts recognition of "the race idea, the race spirit, the race ideal" with "the individualistic philosophy of the Declaration of Independence." But in context, I suggest, this is just the racial equivalent of the Marxist rejection of the "Great Man Theory of History," the insistence that "groups [make] history," and that "the Pharaohs, Caesars, Toussaints and Napoleons" must be related to their sociohistorical milieu and the epochal forces at work within it. In other words, both are rejections of the idea that individuals are the prime movers of the social order. And note that the simultaneous invocation of the social and the biological, which might seem, prima facie, to be simply contradictory and incoherent, has been defended (if not in Du Bois's narrative) by such respectable contemporary figures as Robin Andreasen and Philip Kitcher.[37]

Moreover, even if the biologistic interpretation were correct, it would not necessarily be in contradiction with contemporary liberalism, since in the interwar years before World War II, the dominant liberal position on race would have been that races did indeed exist as biological entities, but that the races were morally equal. It is really only after the war, as the result of the Holocaust and the UNESCO declarations on race, that biologism was repudiated, and even today many theorists believe that such claims are decidedly premature. So if Du Bois thought that the races were natural, but of equal moral status, he would obviously be a liberal by our standards. And whatever his changes of position on other issues, he never wavered on human beings' moral equality. Thus in this essay he speaks of "the whole scientific doctrine of human brotherhood" (that is, racial differences scientifically proven to be less important than racial commonalities), and the duty of Negro Americans "to maintain their race identity until . . . the ideal of human brotherhood has become a practical possibility." Biological race would be inconsistent with (contemporary) liberal commitments only if it were taken by Du Bois to imply one or more of three alternatives. First, a moral hierarchy that lowers some races below the level of equal personhood. Second, a racial determinism of behavior that compels us to treat our fellow humans as less than equal (even if they are equal). Or third, a racial teleology that makes races themselves—rather than the individuals of which these races are composed—the bearers of moral value.[38]

Du Bois clearly did not believe the first two. What about the third? His language about each race having "its particular message, its particular ideal," and the "great races . . . giv[ing] to civilization the full spiritual message which they are capable of giving," via the "natural laws" that guide racial development may be read as valorizing a racial telos in itself. So if such a reading can be convincingly established, and the competing liberal interpretation refuted (racial advance for the sake of the well-being of the individual members *of* the race), then this 1897 Du Bois would be a nonliberal.[39]

But evidence for the correctness of the Du Bois–as-liberal interpretation can be found in "Of Our Spiritual Strivings," an essay written around the same time and reprinted as the first and most famous essay in his 1903 collection *The Souls of Black Folk.* In this essay, Du Bois explicitly declares his faith in the possibility "for a man to be both a Negro and an American," affirms "the ideal of human brotherhood," states that "there are to-day no truer exponents of the pure human spirit of the Declaration of Independence than the American Negroes," and concludes that "merely a concrete test of the underlying principles of the great republic is the Negro Problem." Since it can hardly be denied that the principles of that republic are liberal ones, this seems an unequivocal endorsement of liberalism, at least in its ideal (nondiscriminatory) form. Note also the clearly instrumental role Du Bois attributed to race and black racial organization: the "ideal of human brotherhood" is to be achieved "through the unifying ideal of Race; the ideal of fostering and developing the traits and talents of the Negro, *not in opposition to or contempt for other races* [my emphasis], but rather in large conformity to the greater ideals of the American Republic."[40] This instrumentalist conception echoes his conclusion in "Conservation" that "we must strive by race organization, by race solidarity, by race unity to the realization of that broader humanity which freely recognizes differences in men, but sternly deprecates inequality in their opportunities of development. For the accomplishment of these ends we need race organizations. . . . Not only is all this necessary for positive advance, it is absolutely imperative for negative defense."[41]

I suggest that, read in context, passages like these undercut the notion that Du Bois held an antiliberal interpretation of races as entities whose teleological destinies are self-validating, independent of their consequences for the fates of the human beings who are their constituents. On the contrary, Du Bois is endorsing neither a racially differentiated personhood, nor hatred for whites, nor an ineluctable racial determinism, nor an antiliberal ideal. Rather, he is placing liberalism in its actual racialized context and recognizing what has to be done to realize liberal ideals in a society where white liberals fail to treat their black cocitizens with "color-blind" liberal respect. Black group organization to achieve these ends is not only not *prohibited* by a liberalism sensitized to these racial realities but (more strongly) it is arguably *mandated* by any objective apprehension of the actual racial dynamics of the society, one in which real-life liberalism—from the Founders on—has been deeply racialized.

The Racial Moral Metaphysics of the Social Order

I turn now to what could be termed the "moral metaphysics" of the social order, as distinct from its "descriptive metaphysics." If this concept is unfamiliar, it is, I suggest, because neither of the two main competing modern Western political traditions, liberal and Marxist, have felt the need to theorize critically about the moral status of the "persons" whose ontologies in modernity they are supposed to be mapping. In today's sanitized versions of (originally racist) liberal individualism and Marxist class theory, these political philosophies' history of racially differentiating among people is obfuscated, and the "individuals" in both theories are conceived of as morally equal.

But a white-supremacist society is demarcated not merely by the *material* subordination of the "inferior" races but by their *moral* derogation, a derogation not limited to individual prejudicial depictions and actions but socially embedded in practices and institutions. People of color will originally have been conceptualized in this racist optic not as equal "persons" but as "subpersons." This does not, of course, literally *make* them subpersons—I endorse the morally objectivist position that moral status is socio-independent. But it does mean that, assuming the capacity of white power to bring into existence a racially hierarchical society, the failure to attain "socially recognized" personhood will have a profound effect on the psyches not merely of nonwhites but of whites also. Personhood and subpersonhood will become materially embedded in everyday transactions, in corporeality, spatiality, and institutionality, in such a way as to create a moralized topography of the social order, a relief map of dignity and indignity.[42]

It is the distinctive contribution of Du Bois and other thinkers in the black radical tradition to have recognized and pioneered the theorization of this aspect of a society's social ontology. (Along a different axis—that of gender domination—feminist thinkers have, of course, also offered an innovative perspective not found in "masculinist" theory.) The psychosocial reality and consequences of this partitioned personhood would be a central theme in Du Bois's writings for the rest of his life, applying not just to the United States but to the colonial world as a whole. In the conclusion of *The Philadelphia Negro* (1899), he writes, "We grant full citizenship in the World Commonwealth to the 'Anglo-Saxon' (whatever that may mean), the Teuton and the Latin. . . . [B]ut with the Negroes of Africa we come to a full stop, and in its heart the civilized world with one accord denies that these come within the pale of nineteenth-century Humanity." In "Strivings," he characterizes white prejudice as "that personal disrespect and mockery, the ridicule and systematic humiliation, the distortion of fact and wanton license of fancy . . . the all-pervading desire to inculcate disdain for everything black." In *Darkwater* (1920), he states: "By reason of a crime [Atlantic slavery] (perhaps the greatest crime in human history) the modern world has been systematically taught to despise colored peoples. . . . [A]ll this has unconsciously trained millions of honest, modern men into the belief that black folk are sub-human." Twenty years later, in *Dusk of Dawn* (1940), he reminisces about how he "knew from the days of my childhood . . . that in all things in general, white people were just the same as I," "and yet this fact of racial distinction based on color was the greatest thing in my life and absolutely determined it" because of the "unending inescapable sign of slavery." At the end of his life, he was still moved to describe how white civilization "taught the world that a black man was by the grace of God and law of nature so evil and inferior that slavery, insult, and exploitation were too good for him."[43]

What Du Bois is diagnosing, then, is the social ontology of a nonideal world characterized not merely by material subordination (as in a Marxist class ontology) but by institutionally denied equal moral personhood. Marx's white working class are systematically disadvantaged by the lack of material resources that constrains them (according to Marx) to sell their labor power. But their moral equality *is* recognized. Blacks, by contrast, are not just materially handicapped but in addition viewed as moral *unequals*. The social inferiority of blacks is not an intrinsic feature of their "race," but the product of historical and current oppression. But in terms of intersubjective dynamics, this imputed biological inferiority does profoundly shape society and social interactions, not merely among races but within races. In ideal-theory liberalism, everybody's Kantian personhood is respected. In nonideal-theory racial liberalism, by contrast, blacks and other people of color are seen by whites (and sometimes by themselves) as less than full persons. "Respect," which is a race-independent moral relationship in ideal (as against actual) Kantianism, becomes racialized, with racial disrespect for nonwhites being the norm. The affirmation of self-respect and dignity, then—which Rawls sees as the most important primary good—will require a race-based rejection of white racial contempt, since one is being disrespected, dissed, not as an individual but *as* a member of an inferior race.

Hence the need—in our own time no less than in Du Bois's—to insist that "Black lives matter!"

So what is a seemingly completely familiar liberal value, especially for deontological liberalism—respect—takes on unfamiliar racial dimensions when that liberalism has been racialized. And "the facing of so vast a prejudice" is likely to bring "self-questioning" and "self-disparagement," resulting in a people "that laughs at itself, and ridicules itself, and wishes to God it was anything but itself." The uncontroversial liberal value of self-respect taken for granted by white philosophers amnesiac about the past and obtuse about their racial privilege becomes the black radical liberal value of *racial* self-and-group respect in the actual racialized world. Correspondingly, the long tradition of historical "vindicationism" in texts from colonial/postcolonial Africa and the Africana Diaspora—the vindication of blacks as a race with historical achievements and important contributions to global civilization like any other race—which might seem puzzling to outsiders with a sanitized account of this past, becomes unmysterious once it is recognized how deeply respect/disrespect was tied to race. We are still solidly in the liberal normative universe but now forced to admit the coloring of concepts normally (today) represented as colorless.[44]

Moreover, the theorization of this moral ontology is going to be crucial for explaining the moral psychology and patterns of motivation of the racially privileged. Equal raceless liberal individuals for whom reciprocal respect is the "default mode" may have pathological reasons peculiar to their life histories to need and crave a differential respect, but this will not be a general phenomenon. If whites are positioned by racial membership as the superior race, however, it is obviously a completely different story. Deference is their due *as members of this race,* and their moral psychology will be deeply shaped by racial entitlement, what we would now call white privilege: "Liberty, Justice, and Right—[are] marked 'For White People Only.'"[45] And this racialized moral psychology will have implications for the analyses and prognoses of orthodox Marxist class theory also. In *Dusk of Dawn,* Du Bois would decry as fundamentally misguided the American Communist Party's (CPUSA) mechanical "importation" of "Russian Communism" into the US context, refusing to recognize the reality of the country's racialized social ontology:

> This philosophy did not envisage a situation where instead of a horizontal division of classes, there was a vertical fissure, a complete sepa-

> ration of classes by race, cutting square across the economic layers. . . . [T]he split between white and black workers was greater than that between white workers and capitalists; and this split depended not simply on economic exploitation but on a racial folk-lore grounded on centuries of instinct, habit and thought and implemented by the conditioned reflex of visible color. This flat and incontrovertible fact, imported Russian Communism ignored, would not discuss.[46]

Whether in a white liberalism or a white Marxism, then, white sociopolitical theorists were failing to admit the centrality of race to the sociopolitical order, and its implications for white consciousness and self-regard. Originally Du Bois himself had famously thought that overcoming racism just required education as to what the facts were, as in his pioneering sociological work *The Philadelphia Negro.* In *Souls,* for example, he writes: "We may decry the color-prejudice of the South, yet it remains a heavy fact. Such curious kinks of the human mind exist and must be reckoned with soberly. . . . They can be met in but one way,—by the breadth and broadening of human reason, by catholicity of taste and culture. . . . the one panacea of Education leaps to the lips of all."[47]

But what he came to realize is that white supremacy had far deeper foundations, both psychological and material. It was not at all a matter of an innocent ignorance, to be remedied by education, but a vested interest in the existing order tied up with one's identity as a white person, and including unconsciously held assumptions about what conferred worth and self-worth upon persons. As he would later conclude in *Dusk of Dawn*: "My basic theory had been that race prejudice was primarily a matter of ignorance on the part of the mass of men. . . . All human action to me in those days was conscious and rational." But now he saw that "not simply knowledge . . . will reform the world." Rather, "The present attitude and action of the white world is not based solely upon rational, deliberate intent. It is a matter of conditioned reflexes; of long followed habits, customs and folkways; of subconscious trains of reasoning and unconscious nervous reflexes. To attack and better all this calls for more than appeal and argument."[48]

White personhood becomes intricately interrelated with nonwhite subpersonhood, establishing deep psychic barriers to the achievement of racial equality.

The Racial Exploitation of the Social Order

The material foundation of the white-supremacist social order is racial exploitation. Here again, as with the idea of a racialized social metaphysic, the black radical tradition, and Du Bois in particular, has arguably played a pioneering role in developing the concept. "Exploitation" is, of course, classically associated with the Marxist tradition, and as a result of Du Bois's later encounter with and influence by Marxism, he would draw on Marxist framings from the 1920s onward. But my claim would be that the concept of racial exploitation in his work predates this influence, and even in his later more Marxist phase, he is always careful to demarcate its peculiar features. Moreover, it is not merely an exploitation local or national but *transnational*.

Marxism's critique of wage labor is that though the white working class's moral equality is recognized, seemingly fair and voluntary transactions at the level of the relations of exchange (labor power for a wage) are constrained by material compulsions at the level of the relations of production and based on the exploitative extraction of surplus value. But for blacks, not even their moral equality is recognized, and the relations whites establish with them are uncontroversially exploitative by straightforward liberal norms, without any need to invoke the now-discredited labor theory of value. So racial exploitation is not merely a form of class exploitation. Moreover, racial exploitation involves the participation of white workers as well as white capitalists and benefits the former as well as the latter. Liberalism could in theory take exploitation as a central theme, given its nominal commitment, especially in the social contract version, to a society founded on fair terms for the appropriation of the world. But the overwhelmingly ideal-theoretic orientation of contemporary liberalism—Rawls famously characterizes his ideal society as "a cooperative venture for mutual advantage" and later explicitly rules out the appropriateness to understanding such a society of any concept of exploitation—together with the sanitization of the historical record, and the guilt-by-Marxist-association of the concept, have marginalized exploitation as a topic in contemporary liberal philosophy. For nonideal-theory liberalism, on the other hand, society is *not* to be conceptualized as a cooperative venture but as a coercive and exploitative one: exploitation of the subordinated is precisely the unacknowledged (today anyway) underpinning of the social order.[49]

In *Souls,* Du Bois describes how in the postbellum period, "in well-nigh the whole rural South the black farmers are peons, bound by law and custom to an economic slavery, from which the only escape is death or the penitentiary." In the concluding chapter of *The Negro,* he says of various European "solutions" to "the Negro problem" (in Africa and the Americas) that "back of practically all these experiments stands the economic motive—the determination to use the organization, the land, and the people, not for their own benefit, but for the benefit of white Europe." So racial exploitation is not merely domestic but transcontinental. In the famous "The Souls of White Folk," this analysis is located in a more Marxist framework:

> [By the time of the Boxer Rebellion,] white supremacy was all but world-wide. . . . The using of men for the benefit of masters is no new invention of modern Europe. It is quite as old as the world. But Europe proposed to apply it on a scale and with an elaborateness of detail of which no former world ever dreamed. . . . The scheme of Europe was no sudden invention, but a way out of long-pressing difficulties. It is plain to modern white civilization that the subjection of the white working classes cannot much longer be maintained. . . . The day of the very rich is drawing to a close, so far as individual white nations are concerned. But there is a loophole. There is a chance for exploitation on an immense scale for inordinate profit, not simply to the very rich, but to the middle class and to the laborers. This chance lies in the exploitation of darker peoples.[50]

As with Lenin's *Imperialism: The Highest Stage of Capitalism,* Du Bois identifies the "inordinate profits" of colonial exploitation as a source for neutralizing the demands of the white "Northern" proletariat. But unlike the class-reductionist Lenin (who mentions "race" a grand total of two times in his book)—an analysis entirely typical of white Marxism—Du Bois recognizes that the ontology of such a world must recognize white supremacy as well as imperial capitalism, and not shy away from the collusion of white workers and their socialist representatives. Capitalism is not colorless but racial: it is *white-supremacist* capitalism. And race has its own causality, affecting the social identity of white workers and the supposed dialectic of proletarian internationalism:

> Even the broken reed on which we had rested high hopes of eternal peace,—the guild of the laborers—the front of that very important movement for human justice on which we had builded [*sic*] most, even this flew like a straw before the breath of king and Kaiser. Indeed, the flying had been foreshadowed when in Germany and America "international" Socialists had all but read yellow and black men out of the kingdom of industrial justice. Subtly had they been bribed, but effectively: were they not lordly whites and should they not share in the spoils of rape?[51]

So the revisionism of the black radical tradition demands that we acknowledge the centrality to the social order (both national and global) of a kind of exploitation much broader in scope than class exploitation, benefiting white workers as well as white capitalists and providing a motivation for whites as a group to maintain the existing architecture of systemic unfair advantage that materially privileges them.[52]

The Racial Opacity of the Social Order

And that brings us finally to what I have termed elsewhere "white ignorance," but which—respecting Du Bois's vocabulary—I am going to call here "white self-veiling." As Donald Gibson points out in his introduction to the Penguin *Souls of Black Folk*, "the central metaphor of the book" is "the veil," and blacks are, for whites, both veiled and invisible: "invisible to those who need them to be invisible, veiled to those who need them veiled." Similarly, the subtitle of *Darkwater* is *Voices from within the Veil*. The veil is a cognitive barrier to whites' veridical apprehension of the situation of blacks, a barrier erected not merely by particular white individuals but by a white society willfully ignorant in general. (James Baldwin's essays can, in significant measure, be seen as a lifelong attempt to overcome white ignorance, which he often calls "innocence." The continuing relevance of this insight is illustrated by Nicholas Kristof's 2014 five-part *New York Times* series, "When Whites Just Don't Get It.") As such, the veil will have deleterious epistemic consequences not merely for whites' perceptions of blacks but for white *self*-perception, their understanding of themselves.[53]

In a Marxist framework, of course, such distortions of social cognition on the part of the class-privileged are a familiar theme, explored through the category of "ideology" and a society's "dominant ideology." But liberalism also has the resources to theorize this issue, once we recognize that we are starting from a nonideal-theory rather than an ideal-theory liberalism. The liberal commitment to what Rawls calls "publicity," or what we would now term "transparency," is necessarily going to be affected by these nonideal circumstances. Especially in the Kantian ("deontological") tradition of liberalism that is now dominant in the West, it is taken for granted that the liberal state, the *Rechtsstaat*, should be guided by morality rather than *realpolitik* in its transactions, and as such should be unafraid of, indeed should welcome, public scrutiny. A liberal society genuinely composed of equally and equitably positioned individuals would have no need for cognitive misrepresentation, since its moral metaphysics and economic foundations are egalitarian. But a putatively liberal society that is really composed of differentially and unjustly positioned racial groups will necessarily have to avoid transparency, since its exploitative foundations must either be rationalized and justified (in the slave and Jim Crow periods) or denied altogether (in the post–civil-rights epoch). If nonracial liberal transparency is the ideal and norm for the former, racialized liberal opacity will (in practice) be the ideal and the norm for the latter. Nonideal-theory liberalism will thus be forced to overcome not just the standard obstacles to knowledge and research accuracy faced by all attempted investigations of the world, whether natural or social, but the far more daunting barriers that conceal and protect white interests in the established unjust order.

From an early stage in his life, in a passage earlier cited from "Strivings," Du Bois recognized that white disrespect for and humiliation of blacks required "the distortion of fact and wanton license of fancy." In *Darkwater*, he refers to "belief not based on science . . . [or] history . . . [but] passionate, deep-seated heritage, and as such can be moved by neither argument nor fact." In *Black Reconstruction in America* (1935), one of Du Bois's main tasks is to expose, in the concluding chapter 17, "the propaganda of history," the professional manifestations of these "distortions" and "fancies" in the work of contemporaneous white southern historians seeking to paint Reconstruction as a disaster and glorify the noble "Lost Cause": "Herein lies more than mere omission and difference of emphasis. . . . We have too often a deliberate attempt so to change the facts of history that the story will make pleasant reading for Americans. . . . It is propaganda like this that has led men in the past to insist that history is 'lies agreed upon.'" One of the most famous passages in *Dusk of Dawn* seeks to dramatize through the metaphor of a cave the cognitive plight of blacks trying to communicate with their white overlords. But in a black inversion of Plato's Cave, in which the entombed, deluded, are locked in the world of shadows while the Form of the Sun illuminates the reality above, this is a cave whose black "entombed souls" are the ones illuminated as to the realities of their situation but unable to reach the conscience and awareness of the deluded white world above, indifferent and obtuse to black oppression: "It gradually penetrates the minds of the prisoners that the people passing do not hear; that some thick sheet of invisible but horribly tangible plate glass is between them and the world. . . . [The passing white world] either do not hear at all, or hear but dimly, and even what they hear, they do not understand." In *The World and Africa* (1947), Du Bois extrapolates this insight to the global level and points out how the intercontinental domination and exploitation of the non-European world by Europe came to distort the sciences that, had they been uninfluenced by white group interest, would have indicted the existing order:

> Even the evidence of the eyes and senses was denied by the mere weight of reiteration. . . . Education was so arranged that the young learned not necessarily the truth, but that aspect and interpretation of the truth which the rulers of the world wished them to know and follow. . . . To prove the unfitness of most human beings for self-rule and self-expression, every device of science was used: evolution was made to prove that Negroes and Asiatics were less developed human beings than whites; history was so written as to make all civilization the development of white people; economics was so taught as to make all wealth due mainly to the technical accomplishments of white folks supplemented only by the brute toil of colored peoples.[54]

These systemic distortions are disastrous not merely for objective cognition of the way things actually are but for perceptions of moral obligations and moral responsibilities also. The opacity of racial liberalism provides a veil to screen off from whites their moral complicity with a social order based on racial exploitation, generating the contradictory logics of self-deception that have been analyzed in the Western philosophical tradition since the days of Socrates, but that are greatly exacerbated here through a reciprocally reinforcing *group* dynamic of white ignorance:

> Moral judgment of the industrial process is therefore difficult, and the crime [for those in Europe] is more often a matter of ignorance rather than of deliberate murder and theft; but ignorance is a colossal crime in itself. . . . How far is such a person [a young white middle-class woman in Britain] responsible for the crimes of colonialism? . . . [I]t may be true that her income is the result of starvation, theft, and murder . . . the suppression, exploitation, and slavery of the majority of mankind. Yet just because she does not know this . . . she is content to remain in ignorance of the source of her wealth and its cost in human toil and suffering. . . . The whole world emerges into the Syllogism of the Satisfied: "This cannot be true. This is not true. If it were true I would not believe it. If it is true I do not believe it. Therefore it is false!"[55]

Taking from liberalism its supposed commitment to transparency, a black radical liberalism will have to make one of its primary tasks the cognitive struggle against the opacities and mystifications, the racial veiling and self-veiling, of white racial liberalism. Du Bois's scholarship was *engagé* from the beginning of his career to the end of his life, but what he came to realize is that the obstacles to whites' understanding the social order for what it was were deeply embedded in the very nature of that order: its racial ontology and its foundation of racial exploitation both upheld and rendered invisible, veiled, by liberal political philosophy. It is an obstacle we continue to face to this very day.

Conclusion: Toward a Just Society and a New Liberalism

Du Bois worked all of his adult life for a new society that would be able to achieve social justice. But his conception of this task and the appropriate political theoretical/political philosophical means to its achievement were very different from currently dominant understandings. Since I have been urging the importance of reclaiming his work for political philosophy, it makes good sense to compare him with John Rawls, who is widely judged to be the most important twentieth-century American political philosopher.[56] Rawls was uncontroversially a liberal, one whose achievement is generally seen to be the revival of Anglo-American political philosophy and its reorientation away from the traditional question of political obligation to the question of social justice. Du Bois's liberalism is more controversial, but his self-identification as a socialist is not incompatible with liberalism in the sense of left-liberal social democracy, which at least up to the 1940s is what he seems to have been espousing.[57] Long before Rawls, his primary concern was social justice, but his orientation was radically divergent from Rawls's. From his first publications on the African slave trade and the Philadelphia Negro through his Pan-Africanism and engagement with Marxism, in both his academic writings and his activist pamphleteering, Du Bois was seeking to understand and analyze and overcome social oppression, specifically racial oppression. So in the Rawlsian lexicon, he was unequivocally located in the realm of nonideal political theory.

In Rawls and the vast secondary literature on Rawls, "social justice" is conceived of in a way very different from its lay conception. Justice is not (as it is understood on the popular level) about correcting social injustices, but, as earlier mentioned, about delineating the principles for regulating a well-ordered, perfectly just society, a society of strict compliance with its rules. What Rawls calls "compensatory justice" is mentioned only in passing and is never discussed in any of his five books. But for societies characterized by systemic oppression rather than ideality or near-ideality, such a marginalization is, I suggest, clearly indefensible, even if it is taken for granted by the overwhelmingly white community of today's American political philosophers. The normative commitments of liberalism—the moral primacy of equal individuals highlighted by Gray, demanding the "correction and improvement" of social institutions where appropriate—should under the stipulated nonideal circumstances make *corrective justice* the liberal priority. In a white-supremacist state, the achievement of racial justice should be an imperative for social justice theorists, and the fact that it is not is a sad indication of the extent to which today's liberalism continues to be racialized, albeit in a fashion different from in Du Bois's time. The "black radical liberalism" I have attributed to Du Bois, with its explicitly revisionist social and moral ontology, and demystifying diagnosis of the centrality of racial exploitation and corresponding "white ignorance" to the making of the modern world, is a liberalism that—so far from being dated—is as relevant as ever. We need to reclaim it.

Notes

I would like to thank Nick Bromell for his keen editorial eye, which has undoubtedly much improved the initial draft of this chapter.

1. David M. Goldenberg, *The Curse on Ham* (Princeton, NJ: Princeton University Press, 2003).

2. Robert Gooding-Williams, *In the Shadow of Du Bois: Afro-Modern Political Thought in America* (Cambridge: Harvard University Press, 2009), 2–3; Michael C. Dawson, *Black Visions: The Roots of Contemporary African-American Political Ideologies* (Chicago: University of Chicago Press, 2001), 14–23. I would subsume "radical egalitarianism" and "disillusioned liberalism" into a "black liberalism" that admits of different variants.

3. Michael Hanchard, "Contours of Black Political Thought: An Introduction and Perspective," *Political Theory* 38, no. 4 (2010): 512.

4. Cornel West, in Christa Buschendorf, "'A Figure of Our Times': An Interview with Cornel West on W. E. B. Du Bois," *Du Bois Review* 10, no. 1 (2013): 262, 263.

5. Gooding-Williams, *Shadow;* Lawrie Balfour, *Democracy's Reconstruction: Thinking Politically with W. E. B. Du Bois* (New York: Oxford University Press, 2011); Aldon D. Morris, *The Scholar Denied: W. E. B. Du Bois and the Birth of Modern Sociology* (Oakland: University of California Press, 2015); Marilyn Lake and Henry Reynolds, *Drawing the Global Colour Line: White Men's Countries and the International Challenge of Racial Equality* (New York: Cambridge University Press, 2008); Alexander Anievas, Nivi Manchanda, and Robbie Shilliam, eds., *Race and Racism in International Relations: Confronting the Global Colour Line* (New York: Routledge, 2015); Walter Johnson, *River of Dark Dreams: Slavery and Empire in the Cotton Kingdom* (Cambridge: Harvard University Press, 2013); Edward E. Baptist, *The Half Has Never Been Told: Slavery and the Making of American Capitalism* (New York: Basic, 2014); Sven Beckert, *Empire of Cotton: A Global History* (New York: Knopf, 2014).

6. Susan Moller Okin, *Women in Western Political Thought* (1979; Princeton, NJ: Princeton University Press, 2013); Lorenne M. G. Clark and Lynda Lange, eds., *The Sexism of Social and Political Thought: Women and Reproduction from Plato to Nietzsche* (Toronto: University of Toronto Press, 1979).

7. See Paul C. Taylor's edited four-volume collection of reprints of classic essays on the topic in Routledge's Critical Concepts in Philosophy series, *The Philosophy of Race* (New York: Routledge, 2012); and the new (2013) journal *Critical Philosophy of Race,* housed at the Penn State Philosophy Department.

8. George M. Fredrickson, *Racism: A Short History* (Princeton, NJ: Princeton University Press, 2002); Ivan Hannaford, *Race: The History of an Idea in the West* (Baltimore: Johns Hopkins University Press, 1996); Nell Irvin Painter, *The History of White People* (New York: Norton, 2010), 1.

9. W. E. B. Du Bois, "The Souls of White Folk," in *Darkwater: Voices from within the Veil* (1920; New York: Oxford University Press, 2007), 15.

10. W. E. B. Du Bois, *The Negro* (1915; New York: Oxford University Press, 2007), 2.

11. Cf. the conclusion of Frank M. Snowden Jr., *Blacks in Antiquity: Ethiopians in the Greco-Roman Experience* (Cambridge: Harvard University Press, 1970): "There is nothing in the evidence . . . to suggest that the ancient Greek or Roman established color as an obstacle to integration into society. . . . The Greeks and Romans counted black peoples in" (217–18).

12. Denise Eileen McCoskey, *Race: Antiquity and Its Legacy* (New York: Oxford University Press, 2012); Benjamin Isaac, *The Invention of Racism in Classical Antiquity* (Princeton, NJ: Princeton University Press, 2004), 23, 175–81.

13. David Goldenberg, "Racism, Color Symbolism, and Color Prejudice," in *The Origins of Racism in the West*, ed. Miriam Eliav-Feldon, Benjamin Isaac, and Joseph Ziegler (New York: Cambridge University Press, 2009), 99, 104–5.

14. Debra Higgs Strickland, *Saracens, Demons, & Jews: Making Monsters in Medieval Art* (Princeton, NJ: Princeton University Press, 2003), 81, 79, 86.

15. Similarly, in *The Negro* he seems (6, 10) to limit the influence of the Curse on Ham/Canaan story to the past few hundred years, whereas contemporary scholars like Goldenberg (*The Curse on Ham*) trace its impact back much further. Du Bois, *The Negro,* 64.

16. Charles W. Mills, *The Racial Contract* (Ithaca, NY: Cornell University Press, 1997); Charles W. Mills, "Racial Liberalism," *Publications of the Modern Language Association of America* 123, no. 5 (2008): 1380–97; Jennifer Pitts, *A Turn to Empire: The Rise of Imperial Liberalism in Britain and France* (Princeton, NJ: Princeton University Press, 2005).

17. George L. Mosse, *Toward the Final Solution: A History of European Racism* (Madison: University of Wisconsin Press, 1985), ix, 231. The well-known distinction between the "anomaly" and "symbiosis" view of racism in American political culture can be generalized, I have argued elsewhere, to describe competing understandings of the political culture of the racialized states of modernity (see David Theo Goldberg, *Racist Culture: Philosophy and the Politics of Meaning* [Cambridge, MA: Blackwell, 1993]; Rogers M. Smith, *Civic Ideals: Conflicting Visions of Citizenship in U.S. History* [New Haven, CT: Yale University Press, 1997]; and Charles W. Mills, "Modernity, Persons, and Subpersons," in *Race and the Foundations of Knowledge: Cultural Amnesia in the Academy*, ed. Joseph Young and Jana Evans Braziel (Urbana: University of Illinois Press, 2006).

18. Dorinda Outram, *The Enlightenment* (New York: Cambridge University Press, 2005), 135.

19. Thomas Hobbes, *Leviathan,* rev. student ed. (New York: Cambridge University Press, 1996), chap. 13, 107.

20. Ibid., chap. 13; Richard Ashcraft, "Leviathan Triumphant: Thomas Hobbes

and the Politics of Wild Men," in *The Wild Man Within: An Image in Western Thought from the Renaissance to Romanticism*, ed. Edward Dudley and Maximillian E. Novak (Pittsburgh: University of Pittsburgh Press, 1972), 157.

21. John Locke, *Two Treatises of Government*, ed. Peter Laslett (New York: Cambridge University Press, 1988), *Second Treatise*, chap. 2; Locke, *Second Treatise*, §41; James Tully, *An Approach to Political Philosophy: Locke in Contexts* (New York: Cambridge University Press, 1993); Barbara Arneil, *John Locke and America: The Defence of English Colonialism* (Oxford: Clarendon, 1996); Carole Pateman, "The Settler Contract," in *Contract and Domination*, Pateman and Charles W. Mills (Malden, MA: Polity, 2007).

22. Stephen Darwall, ed., *Contractarianism/Contractualism* (Malden, MA: Blackwell, 2003).

23. For an extensive bibliography of recent English-language literature on the issue, see the first endnote of my "Kant and Race, *Redux*," *Graduate Faculty Philosophy Journal* 35, nos. 1–2 (2014): 125–57. Various theorists, such as Sankar Muthu and Pauline Kleingeld, have argued that Kant later changed his mind, either in the 1780s (Muthu) or the 1790s (Kleingeld); others, such as Robert Bernasconi and Mark Larrimore, have argued that he did not. Again, see my endnote for the relevant sources.

24. David Hume, "Of National Characters" (1754 version), in *Race and the Enlightenment: A Reader*, ed. Emmanuel Chukwudui Eze (Cambridge, MA: Blackwell, 1997), 33.

25. John Stuart Mill, *On Liberty* with *The Subjection of Women* and *Chapters on Socialism*, ed. Stefan Collini (New York: Cambridge University Press, 1989), 13–14.

26. Uday Singh Mehta, *Liberalism and Empire: A Study in Nineteenth-Century British Liberal Thought* (Chicago: University of Chicago Press, 1999), 73, 90.

27. *Thomas Carlyle: The Nigger Question; John Stuart Mill: The Negro Question*, ed. Eugene R. August (New York: Crofts Classics, 1971); Teshale Tibebu, *Hegel and the Third World: The Making of Eurocentrism in World History* (Syracuse, NY: Syracuse University Press, 2011); Karl Marx, *Capital*, vol. 1, trans. Ben Fowkes (Harmondsworth, UK: Penguin, 1976), 915; John M. Hobson, *The Eurocentric Conception of World Politics: Western International Theory, 1760–2010* (New York: Cambridge University Press, 2012), 57 (italics removed from "Western").

28. Cf. Kristin Waters's "black revolutionary liberalism" as a characterization of the positions of nineteenth-century black American political activists David Walker and Maria Stewart: "Crying Out for Liberty: Maria W. Stewart and David Walker's Black Revolutionary Liberalism," *Philosophia Africana* 15, no. 1 (Winter 2013): 35–60.

29. Cedric J. Robinson, *Black Marxism: The Making of the Black Radical Tradition* (1983; Chapel Hill: University of North Carolina Press, 2000).

30. See, for example, Tommie Shelby's reconciliation of liberalism with certain strains of black nationalism in his *We Who Are Dark: The Philosophical Foundations of Black Solidarity* (Cambridge: Harvard University Press, 2005).

31. John Gray, *Liberalism* (Minneapolis: University of Minnesota Press, 1986), x.

32. Domenico Losurdo, *Liberalism: A Counter-History,* trans. Gregory Elliott (New York: Verso, 2011); Carole Pateman, *The Sexual Contract* (Stanford: Stanford University Press, 1988); Mills, *Racial Contract.*

33. John Rawls, *A Theory of Justice,* rev. ed. (Cambridge: Harvard University Press, 1999). Note that this is *not* the same as the contrast between normative theory and descriptive theory, or between moralized approaches and *realpolitik.* Both ideal and nonideal theory are normative theory, but the former presupposes ideal circumstances whereas the latter presupposes nonideal circumstances. What justice calls for in oppressive societies thus counts as nonideal theory, and (arguably) a nonideal-theory liberalism.

34. See Derrick Darby's *Rights, Race, and Recognition* (New York: Cambridge University Press, 2009) for an account of this neglected strain of the liberal tradition, and a case for bringing it back to theoretical centrality in contemporary liberal discussions.

35. Ann E. Cudd, *Analyzing Oppression* (New York: Oxford University Press, 2006).

36. W. E. B. Du Bois, "The Conservation of Races," in *The Oxford W. E. B. Du Bois Reader,* ed. Eric J. Sundquist (New York: Oxford University Press, 1996), 40–41. For the distinction, see Chike Jeffers, "The Cultural Theory of Race: Yet Another Look at Du Bois's 'The Conservation of Races,'" *Ethics* 123 (2013): 403–26.

37. W. E. B. Du Bois, *Dusk of Dawn: An Essay Toward an Autobiography of a Race Concept* (1940; New York: Oxford University Press, 2007), 77; Du Bois, "Conservation," 40; Robin O. Andreasen, "A New Perspective on the Race Debate" (1998), in *The Philosophy of Race,* ed. Paul C. Taylor, 4 vols., vol. 2: *Racial Being and Knowing* (New York: Routledge, 2012); Philip Kitcher, "Does 'Race' Have a Future?" (2007), ibid.

38. Du Bois, "Conservation," 40, 46.

39. Ibid., 42.

40. W. E. B. Du Bois, *The Souls of Black Folk* (1903; New York: Penguin, 1989), 11, 5, 11.

41. Du Bois, "Conservation," 44.

42. Mills, *The Racial Contract*; Mills, "Racial Liberalism." See my critique on this score of Darby, *Rights, Race, and Recognition:* Charles W. Mills, "Racial

Rights and Wrongs: A Critique of Derrick Darby," in "Confronting State and Theory," ed. Tommy J. Curry and Leonard Harris, special issue, *Radical Philosophy Review* 18, no. 1 (2015): 11–30.

43. W. E. B. Du Bois, *The Philadelphia Negro: A Social Study* (1899; New York: Oxford University Press, 2007), 269; Du Bois, *Souls,* 10; Du Bois, *Darkwater,* 35; Du Bois, *Dusk of Dawn,* 69; W. E. B. Du Bois, "Whites in Africa after Negro Autonomy" (1962), in *Oxford Du Bois,* ed. Sundquist, 668.

44. Du Bois, *Souls,* 10; Du Bois, "Conservation," 44.

45. Du Bois, *Souls,* 168.

46. Du Bois, *Dusk of Dawn,* 103.

47. Du Bois, *Philadelphia Negro;* Du Bois, *Souls,* 76.

48. Du Bois, *Dusk of Dawn,* 141, 111, 87.

49. Marx, *Capital,* vol. 1; Rawls, *Theory,* 4, 271–72.

50. Du Bois, *Souls,* 34; Du Bois, *The Negro,* 108; Du Bois, *Darkwater,* 21.

51. Vladimir I. Lenin, *Imperialism: The Highest Stage of Capitalism* (1916; Chicago: Pluto, 1996); Du Bois, *Darkwater,* 23.

52. Admittedly, in a famous passage from his later *Black Reconstruction in America, 1860–1880* (1935; New York: Oxford University Press, 2007), 573–74, Du Bois seems to suggest, in keeping with orthodox Marxist analysis, that the "public and psychological wage" enjoyed by white workers was largely honorary and "had small effect upon [their] economic situation." So I am placing greater significance here on those of his other writings that *do* recognize the substantial material advantaging of whites and that in the end are the ones that have been borne out by the social scientific literature on comparative black and white wealth (see, for example, Melvin L. Oliver and Thomas M. Shapiro, *Black Wealth/White Wealth: A New Perspective on Racial Inequality,* 10th anniversary ed. [New York: Routledge, 2006]).

53. Charles W. Mills, "White Ignorance," in *Race and Epistemologies of Ignorance,* ed. Shannon Sullivan and Nancy Tuana (Albany: State University of New York Press, 2007); Donald B. Gibson, introduction to *Souls,* xi, xiv; Du Bois, *Darkwater;* James Baldwin, *Collected Essays,* ed. Toni Morrison (New York: Library of America, 1998). For a valuable reconstruction of Baldwin as a political theorist, see Lawrie Balfour, *The Evidence of Things Not Said: James Baldwin and the Promise of American Democracy* (Ithaca, NY: Cornell University Press, 2000).

54. Du Bois, *Souls,* 10; Du Bois, *Darkwater,* 36; Du Bois, *Black Reconstruction,* 584–85; Du Bois, *Dusk of Dawn,* 66; W. E. B. Du Bois, *The World and Africa* and *Color and Democracy* (1947, 1945; New York: Oxford University Press, 2007), 15, 16, 23.

55. Du Bois, *World and Africa,* 26–27.

56. Samuel Freeman, *Rawls* (New York: Routledge, 2007).

57. I have phrased it in this vague way because in an already overlong essay, I decided there was no space to enter the controversy about whether some of his 1950s declarations and writings could be read as signaling a turn to Stalinist Marxism. As I said at the start, all I need for my thesis is that Du Bois can be categorized as a black radical liberal for a major part of his life.

2

An Africana Philosophical Reading of Du Bois's Political Thought

Lewis R. Gordon

As his last autobiography, *A Soliloquy on Viewing My Life from the Last Decade of Its First Century*, attests, W. E. B. Du Bois's life took a path from New England liberalism to international radicalism with an eye steadily fixed on what is today called the Global South. After nearly a century as a "race man" fighting for the humanity of African-descended peoples in the United States, he spent the last two years of his life as a member of the Communist Party and, at the invitation of President Kwame Nkrumah, as a resident of Ghana, where he became a citizen in 1963, the year of his passing. Although there were many black political thinkers more radical than Du Bois during his younger years, one would be remiss to consider his earlier liberal political location as without its own radical import.[1] His expectation of equality for the then "Negro" was in the United States of the nineteenth century nothing short of a radical idea. As this was not the view of many liberals (of any racial background), the reasons for that position must have been rooted in independent sources. A similar conclusion applies to his subsequent affiliation with communism. Marxism for Du Bois was more a matter of affinity than influence. This is because Du Bois was engaged throughout his career with a black tradition of addressing social contradictions and imagining a future of grappling with, if not overcoming, them. His efforts, like those of many major intellectuals of African descent, amounted to the recurring adage: "Why we can't wait."[2] The immediate answer? "We" cannot afford a foreclosed future, even when it promises salvation. I will explore in this chapter some of the complexity of what I shall call a Du Boisian dialectics premised on a contingent future. It is the heart, I will argue, of his philosophical anthropology, which unveils not only ways in which power is produced but also how knowledge is one of its manifestations.

Locating Du Bois in Africana Political Thought

The task at hand emerges from reflections on Du Bois in Africana thought, of which Africana political philosophy and political theory are subfields. The term "Africana" refers to the African Diaspora, of which African America is a part. Though located primarily in the African American wing of Africana thought, Du Bois's global influence, which includes his studies of African history and his work in global black politics, such as his co-organizing the first Pan-African Congress, makes him one of the main pillars of the broader project of Africana thought. His contributions are also in nearly every area across the human sciences: economics, history, philosophy, sociology, and even literature. In terms of Africana political philosophy and political theory, at least three major themes—philosophical anthropology, philosophy of freedom, and the metacritique of reason—come to the fore.[3] The Africana political theorist must assert the humanity of African-descended peoples in political life, which requires not only explaining why they are agents capable of citizenry but also offering a theory of what went wrong with hegemonic models of "the human" in the Euro-modern world.[4] That theorist must also offer a theory of freedom that addresses the shortcomings of avowed commitments to freedom in a country such as the United States. And finally, such a theorist must deal with the metatheoretical elephant in the room: What is the point of theory when so much of it has been advanced, with much success, *against* the dignity and freedom of African-descended peoples? Doesn't this create, at least for black peoples, a crisis of theory and its founding concept—reason?[5] Du Bois's oeuvre exhibits all the characteristics of Africana philosophy.

Du Bois's Phenomenological Anthropology

Although Du Bois commenced his career as a historian with most of the criteria fulfilled for his doctorate in economics, which he subsequently received from the University of Berlin, his effort to bring science to bear on the study of the so-called "Negro problem" took many innovative forms, one of the most crucial of which emerged from his time devoted to studying the Seventh Ward in Philadelphia. Out of that research grew not only his monumental study *The Philadelphia Negro* but also a series of crucial reflections with continued bearing on social science.[6] "On the Conservation of the Races," presented before the Negro Academy, which was organized and presided over by Alexander Crummell, was his early articulation of what could be formulated as problems of identity and social change.[7] The former pertained to what, ultimately, are races, and, given that, what could be hoped for in such terms. I have argued elsewhere that the context of those reflections made it reasonable to consider the possibility of impending genocide, as witnessed by a near fait accompli with regard to the First Nation peoples of North America.[8] The language of the day pretty much suggested that the United States was ultimately better off with the *absence* of black peoples. Since black people didn't control the mechanisms of state power, it was reasonable to believe, as the evidence of state-sanctioned lynching and the undermining of black political efficacy suggested, that such power would be abused for the worst. Du Bois thus argued in those early writings for the *necessity* of the so-called "Negro." I state "so-called" because such an identity was one imposed on people of African descent, which raised the question of its ontological, political, and social scientific legitimacy. In fact, the problem with which social scientists in the United States had to contend was that there were people across the globe completely unaware that they were considered "Negroes." Even though the identity was created, the Negro faced the danger of extermination not only as an idea but also as a people. Genocide, in other words, could be committed against constructed peoples.

In his early formulations of race in the late 1890s, Du Bois thus made the case for blacks' existence, or survival, in terms of their "gifts" for humanity, suggesting, within that framework, what would be lost for all in the absence of certain races. As he writes in "On the Conservation of the Races": "For the development of Negro genius, of Negro literature and art, of Negro spirit, only Negroes bound and welded together, Negroes inspired by one vast ideal, can work out in its fullness that great message we have for humanity."[9] And later: "The American Negro Academy must point out a practical path of advance to the Negro people. . . . Such questions need not so much specific answers for each part as a general expression of policy, and nobody should be better fitted to announce such a policy than a representative honest Negro Academy."[10] What should be done, in other words, was to develop policies that would not only protect a race of people from genocidal machinations but also facilitate their flourishing.

In "The Study of the Negro Problems," presented before the Academy of Social and Political Science in Philadelphia in 1897, Du Bois advanced a critique that emerges in various forms in Africana thought—namely, that a problem with social science as practiced in the day (and to some extent still today) was that, when it came to the study of the so-called Negro, much of what was called research was unscientific.[11] This is a consideration posed by the Haitian anthropologist, jurist, and philosopher Anténor Firmin earlier in Haiti in his classic *The Equality of the Human Races* (1885): Much of what was being passed off as anthropology was so full of fallacies that hegemonic scholarship could hardly be considered science.[12] I bring up Firmin because what is often overlooked in identifying Eurocentric scholarship as racist is the extent to which it also failed to adhere to scientific standards. The failure to be scientific meant that valuable knowledge was not coming to the fore and that, thus, ignorance reigned. "Students," in other words, Du Bois wrote, "must be careful to insist that science as such . . . has but one simple aim: the discovery of truth."[13] Many spoke *of* the Negro but few knew anything about such people. "The American Negro," he wrote, "deserves study for the great end of advancing the cause of science in general."[14] Du Bois began there an argument to which he would return throughout his career: The failure to see the humanity of a subject of study leads to the imposition of nonhuman categories onto human beings.

Du Bois advanced there a point he would reformulate in more poetic fashion in *The Souls of Black Folk* (1903): "How does it feel to be a problem?"[15] The reference to feeling raises the question of a point of view, a subjective life, wherein there is simultaneously the normative and the descriptive. The normative emerges from its mattering, its being of value, how one feels. Notice the intersubjective structure of the query; it is asked to another. The descriptive point collapses from feeling to being. In effect, it raises at the level of social ontology the presupposition that the Negro *is* a problem.[16] This raises a double layer of problems—namely, the problem of being a problem. In effect, wherever the Negro is, there stands a problem. To become isomorphic with a problem leaves only one recourse for the Negro, then: disappearance.[17] This places Negroes in a double bind—as problems to society and, logically, problems to themselves. The whole situation is neurotic: wherever the Negro is, he or she should not be. The situation changes, however, if the humanity of the Negro is posited: Now the Negro is not a problem but instead someone on whom a problem—the problem of being Negro—has been imposed. The task then becomes to examine the nature of such imposition and the kinds of problems accompanying the designated identity. Du Bois argued for understanding such problems in *social* and *societal* terms, which means addressing how the world in which such people live produces such problems. Du Bois was offering the Academy of Social and Political Science a message its members didn't want to hear: social and intellectual accountability for the production and treatment of Negro people.

The problem of studying Negro problems raised the question of what problems are in social terms. Though this question could be addressed pragmatically—in terms of what works and what does not across aggregates and institutions—Du Bois delved further into the question of what is involved in conducting truly rigorous social science. In "Sociology Hesitant," he formulated this question in terms of social explanation hindered by a failure to understand social reality:[18]

> Of the physical scientists on the one hand who say: The laws of men's deeds are physical laws, and physics studies them; of the mass of men, on the other hand, who say: Man is not wholly a creature of unchanging law, he is in some degree a free agent and so outside the realm of scientific law. Now whatever one's whims and predilections, no one can wholly ignore either of these criticisms: If this is a world of absolute unchanging physical laws, then the laws of physics and chemistry are the laws of all action of stones and stars, and Newtons and Nortons. On the other hand, for a thousand and a thousand years, and today as strongly as, and even more strongly than, ever, men, after experiencing the facts of life, have almost universally assumed that in among physical forces stalk self-directing Wills, which modify, restrain, and re-direct the ordinary laws of nature. The assumption is tremendous in its import. It means that, from the point of view of Science, this is a world of Chance as well as Law; that the conservation of energy and correlation of forces are not universally true, but that out from some unknown Nowhere bursts miraculously now and then controlling Energy.[19]

Another word for chance is "contingency." As Du Bois put it: "Sociology, then, is the Science that seeks the limits of Chance in human conduct."[20] In the world of social reality, though, contingency is not accidental. Much depends on the problem of social meaning, which always exceeds the language of positivist science. Sociology, he suggests, must abandon categorical concepts in favor of a more limited and relevance-oriented form of social explanation. That depends on acknowledging, in effect, that human beings exceed the scope of the disciplinary methods and categories imposed upon them. Failure to understand this would produce a new kind of problem: the production of human beings as problems because of their failure to fit neatly into the methods and research practices at hand.

We have the makings here for what could be called Du Boisian phenomenological social science. It is phenomenological because it brings to the fore the question of research competence in terms of intersubjective consciousness. Here we see a problem that will recur throughout the history of this subject matter. Sylvia Wynter posed it this way a century later: What is it like to be black?[21] For a Negrophobe, this question requires contaminating an antiblack consciousness with an intrinsically unthinkable perspective. It thus makes the researcher, *qua researcher* (who supposedly *cannot be black*), limited at basic levels of social meaning. One may object that the question could be broached without positing the other point of view as phobogenic through simply subsuming that other point of view in the form, "What would it be like *for me* if I were black?" This, however, makes the black an analogue of the presumably nonblack researcher; the result would not be a *black* perspective but, where the researcher is white, that of a *white-imagining-being-both-white-and-black-at-once.* Moreover, where white is treated as human and black is presumed below human, the problem of racist social science emerges, as Jane Anna Gordon points out: The intersubjective relationship between researcher and subject of study should be a human-to-human one.[22] The question then becomes: What is it like to be a human being who lives in the world as a black *human being?* This question places a reciprocal and reflexive questioning on the questioner, for it then raises the possibility that presuming the human being to be *white* is delusional and self-interested. The interrogation, in other words, expands the scope of critical consciousness. Rigorous research requires not only acknowledging the humanity of blacks but also recognizing the presumed whiteness of all purportedly legitimate research.

Studying Blackness

Such critical consciousness takes at least two forms when raised in terms of what I will from this point simply call *the black*. The first form is the social understanding of what it means to be black. In an antiblack society, that means embodying a negative term. Thus, to be black is to be aware of oneself as negative. It is the black as seen through the eyes of an antiblack society. That society does not, however, offer itself as antiblack but instead as simply the ordinary state of affairs or the way things are. It thus makes being antiblack, in a word, "normal."[23] This raises antiblackness to an ontological level. It means that blackness and lowliness are isomorphic. To be black, then, would mean never to be normal, except as an affirmation of abnormality (which amounts to the same). Let us call this first-stage double-consciousness. It is double because it is a way of seeing the self through the perspective of those who despise what one is. The black thus sees that he or she is seen from the normative, white standpoint of the society in negative terms as black while being aware of experiencing that from a black point of view. There is thus the experience of being seen and the perspective from which one is seen. In both, one's initial point of view is without validity. In Du Bois's words:

> After the Egyptian and Indian, the Greek and Roman, the Teuton and Mongolian, the Negro is a sort of seventh son, born with a veil, and gifted with second-sight in this American world,—a world which yields him no true self-consciousness, but only lets him see himself through the revelation of the other world. It is a peculiar sensation, this double-consciousness, this sense of always looking at one's self through the eyes of others, of measuring one's soul by the tape of a world that looks on in amused contempt and pity. One ever feels his twoness,—an American, a Negro; two souls, two thoughts, two unreconciled strivings; two warring ideals in one dark body, whose dogged strength alone keeps it from being torn asunder.[24]

Now, if we bring the arguments Du Bois offered against bad social science into play, a realization emerges for the double-conscious subject. To be seen as a problem is a condition that emerges in a society that fails to see one as a human being. In effect, then, one moves from seeing oneself as a problem into seeing oneself as part of a society with, among its many problems, a tendency of treating certain groups of people as if they were not human beings. This movement is in fact a dialectical negation of the first form of double-consciousness. (In his discussion of this subject, Paget Henry refers to this movement as *potentiated double consciousness.*)[25] For our purposes, what is crucial is that the phenomenological movement is to a metalevel of critique; a metatheory is a theory *about* theory; a metacritique is one about critique; at such a level, the first form of double-consciousness is then raised as an object of critique. It becomes conscious apprehension of a mistaken consciousness. Do black people *really* live as the negative terms depicted in the first form of double-consciousness? Placed in the logic of universals and particulars, the movement is this. The first form of double consciousness is transformed into a *stage* toward a critical form of reflection that questions the social categories of the dominant system as "universal." Thus, the white point of view becomes the universal (and thus objective) view of reality, with the black viewpoint embodying a particular malediction. Realization that the white point of view is not absolute (though presenting itself as universal) makes the white perspective a particular masked as a universal. Because the white point of view avows universality, it fails to imagine there is more to reality than itself. The black point of view never takes itself as universal, however, and thus regards the particularity of the white as part of a larger schema. In effect, then, the dialectical movement to potentiated double-consciousness calls for *universalizing* versus universal practices. It is the universalizing potential that is the clue to human relations in the dynamics of social life. Antiblack racism, then, is an attempt to force human relations out of human relations. The contradiction is evident, and the implications for political theory are many, as I hope to spell out after one more foray into a specific social science.[26]

Du Bois's Critique of Hegemonic Historiography

In his later *Black Reconstruction,* Du Bois takes on the problem of how the period of Reconstruction after the American Civil War had been explained by what is now called the "Dunning School" of historical studies.[27] Based on the work of the historian and political scientist William Dunning, this approach basically argued that Reconstruction failed because of the supposed false premise on which it was based: the equality of blacks and their capacity for citizenship.[28] Du Bois suggests that the fallacy of this historiography is not just that it got the facts wrong but that it related events without regarding black people as human beings. The story is thus told in terms of blacks' inferiority, or, if they appear at all, in terms of their irrelevance—even though countless black people played central roles in those historical events. But more, if we return to the observations about double-consciousness and presumptions of universal white normativity, a more radical consideration addresses the extent to which the Dunning approach may be not an exception but rather an example of ways the norms of presumed universal history are taken to be white. In short, even some critics of Dunning and his followers may be guilty of the deeper, racist presuppositions of supposedly rigorous history. *Historiography*, in other words, had the same problem that sociology and other areas of the human sciences had. The failure to address this problem caused both the lack of scientific rigor in historical studies and also the lack of *history* in hegemonic American historiography.

Du Bois offered a series of innovations to open up the historicity and rigor of American history (and eventually "world" history in terms of his work on Africa), and the outcomes were extraordinary in political theoretical terms. The first was to pry apart the categories of chattel slavery and the concept "Negro" and thereby reveal that the fusing of the two had led to the failure to regard enslaved peoples as *workers*. Think, for example, of how different our understanding of the history of slavery might be in the minds of those who study it if the kidnapped and enslaved populations from Africa were understood as *skilled labor*. The misguided history of white intellect and brute black labor would be transformed into an understanding of the benefits enslaved Africans brought to the Americas. Those skills were also brought to the postslavery years of Reconstruction, but US society continued its effort to reap the benefits of that labor without acknowledging its legitimacy outside of the framework of enslavement. Thus, during the supposedly postslavery period of Reconstruction, the logic of slavery continued, with workers identified exclusively with whiteness. The consequence was that, through what eventually became Jim Crow (that is, American legalized segregation), the logic of workers' emancipation was being forestalled by the exclusion of whole categories of workers rendered invisible by virtue of being black. Despite its declared commitment to freedom, the United States became instead the active producer of the rationalization of unfreedom aided not only by the devices of propaganda posing as history but also by the follies of supposedly "impartial" history. As Du Bois protests:

> It was morally wrong and economically retrogressive to build human slavery in the United States in the eighteenth century. We know that now, perfectly well; and there were many Americans North and South who knew this and said it in the eighteenth century. Today, in the face of new slavery established elsewhere in the world under other names and guises, we ought to emphasize this lesson of the past. Moreover, it is not well to be reticent in describing that past. Our history tends to discuss American slavery so impartially, that in the end nobody seems to have done wrong and everyday was right. Slavery appears to have been thrust upon unwilling helpless America, while the South was blameless in becoming its center. The difference of development, North and South, is explained as a sort of working out of cosmic social and economic law.[29]

Abstract mechanisms obscure truth. An important fact overlooked by supposedly impartial approaches is the extent to which avowed commitment to emancipation was a necessary condition for winning the war. The failure to regard enslaved peoples as human beings led, as well, to the mistaken view that freedom was "given" to blacks. Yet, had formerly enslaved blacks not fought and played a decisive role in the winning of the Civil War, their fate would have been continued bondage. In short, the formerly enslaved peoples and their freed black brothers and sisters *fought* for and *won* their freedom. Du Bois was insisting that historians understand black people as *agents* of history:

> One has but to read the debates in Congress and state papers from Abraham Lincoln down to know that the decisive action which ended the Civil War was the emancipation and arming of the black slave; that, as Lincoln said: "Without the military help of black freedmen, the war against the South could not have been won." The freedmen, far from being the inert recipients of freedom at the hands of philanthropists, furnished 200,000 soldiers in the Civil War who took part in nearly 200 battles and skirmishes, and in addition perhaps 300,000 others as effective laborers and helpers. In proportion to population, more Ne-

> groes than whites fought in the Civil War. These people, withdrawn from the support of the Confederacy, with threat of the withdrawal of millions more, made the opposition of the slaveholder useless, unless they themselves freed and armed their own slaves. This was exactly what they started to do; they were only restrained by realizing that such action removed the very cause for which they began fighting. Yet one could search current American histories almost in vain to find a clear statement or even faint recognition of these perfectly well-authenticated facts.[30]

Du Bois then pointed out other cases of historians working with a presumption of black inferiority and also with the naïve presupposition that they were providing a complete record of events when in fact important records chronicling such events as the founding of the Florida public school system were destroyed because of efforts to erase the story of its founder, who was a black superintendent. In short, much of US history is premised not only on the presumed inferiority of blacks but also on the supposed absence of white antiblack racism. This amounts to a theodicean history:

> One is astonished in the study of history at the recurrence of the idea that evil must be forgotten, distorted, skimmed over. We must not remember that Daniel Webster got drunk but only remember that he was a splendid constitutional lawyer. We must forget that George Washington was a slave owner, or that Thomas Jefferson had mulatto children, or that Alexander Hamilton had Negro blood, and simply remember the things we regard as creditable and inspiring. The difficulty, of course, with this philosophy is that history loses its value as an incentive and example; it paints perfect men and noble nations, but it does not tell the truth.[31]

The occlusion of truth, Du Bois concludes, ultimately serves the purpose of rationalizing obstructions to true democracy; it elides the self-governing capacities of dominated peoples. Its result is blindness and "being led by the blind," wherein readers of such distorted histories fail to see the connection between the *revolt* of enslaved peoples during the Civil War and their efforts in the years of Reconstruction and such events as the Reformation and the French Revolution:

> Before the dumb eyes of ten generations of ten million children, it is made mockery of and spit upon; a degradation of the eternal mother; a sneer at human effort; with aspiration and art deliberately and elaborately distorted. And why? Because in a day when the human mind aspired to a science of human action, a history and psychology of the mighty effort of the mightiest century, we fell under the leadership of those who would compromise with truth in the past in order to make peace in the present and guide policy in the future.[32]

As the story told is to erase the role of blacks in the struggle for freedom, the policy for the future, to be sure, is a moribund one of renewed forms of bondage. Du Bois thus issues a critique of the shortcomings of white historiography on two levels. On the political level, there is the problem that misrepresentations of past events distort policy and obscure a people's right to citizenship. On the disciplinary and methodological level, there is a lack of rigor, which compromises truth. This second consideration brings to the fore what could be called the grammar of double-consciousness and potentiated double-consciousness. Hegemonic history could maintain its misrepresentations of events through, in effect, white normativity. The unwitting or intentional proponent of hegemonic history simply offers it as universal and truth. The critic who admits the humanity of black people would immediately see that hegemonic history is actually white history. That there could be *white history* means that history should be interrogated at its methodological level, which requires questioning its practitioners' fidelity to evidence.

Consider the epistemic anxieties stimulated in the academy by the emergence of black studies: the underlying fact to which it points is the (hitherto invisible) existence of white studies. The latter, however, is rarely referred to as such. It's simply often called the academy with its disciplines of study. Yet, when interrogated, the practice of many disciplines was historically premised on the inherent inferiority of dark peoples and the presumed integrity of the white people who not only studied them but also claimed representation for the study of all reality. Black studies demanded the accountability of all knowledge through the inclusion of a broader conception of the human being at work. As this concern requires also self-critique, that means that even black studies could at best offer itself as a more universalizing practice than *the* universal discipline. Looked at in this way, Du Bois was arguing, through his work on sociology and history, for disciplinary practices more attuned to evidence. His critique reveals that the hegemonic exemplars have a long way to go to meet at least the test of accountability with regard to reality and truth.

A Political Anthropology of Freedom

Du Bois's political theory is often occluded in studies of his political battles and policy attempts. The famous (and perhaps infamous) debate he had with Booker T. Washington is one instance. In his final autobiography, Du Bois summarized their two positions thus:

> There was first of all the ideological controversy. I believed in the higher education of a Talented Tenth who through their knowledge of modern culture could guide the American Negro into a higher civilization. I knew that without this the Negro would have to accept white leadership, and that such leadership could not always be trusted to guide this group into self-realization and to its highest cultural possibilities. Mr. Washington, on the other hand, believed that the Negro as an efficient worker could gain wealth and that eventually through his ownership of capital he would be able to achieve a recognized place in American culture and could then educate his children as he might wish and develop their possibilities. For this reason he proposed to put the emphasis at present upon training in the skilled trades and encouragement in industry and common labor.[33]

Looking back on his life, he admits that Washington and he were naïve with regard to the larger significance of such matters; politics, after all, cannot work without an economy (or at least a material infrastructure), and the latter cannot work without the former: "These two theories of Negro progress were not absolutely contradictory. Neither I nor Booker Washington understood the nature of capitalistic exploitation of labor, and the necessity of a direct attack on the principle of exploitation as the beginning of labor uplift."[34]

Despite his insistence on the importance of truth and the possibilities of rational reflection, Du Bois in the last decade of his life began to reflect on their limits. He writes:

> It was of course crazy for me to dream that America, in the dawn of the 20th century with colonial imperialism, based on the suppression of colored folk, at its zenith, would encourage, much less adequately finance [research projects at black colleges] under Negro scholars. My faith in [such a project's] success was based on the firm belief that race prejudice was based on widespread ignorance. My long-term remedy was Truth: carefully gathered scientific proof that neither color nor race determined the limits of a man's capacity or desert. I was not at the time sufficiently Freudian to understand how little human action is based on reason; nor did I know Karl Marx well enough to appreciate the economic foundations of human history.[35]

He interestingly enough appeals to Freud here to explain his naïve faith in the force of truth and rationality. At the metacritical level, rationality ironically finds its limitations in reason, where even though rational, human actions could nevertheless be unreasonable. He also rethought his Talented Tenth argument in the light of his later internationalist position, a bit of which we've already seen in his later reflections on his conflict with Booker T. Washington. I do think that critics of his quarrel with Washington and his advancement of the idea of a Talented Tenth miss some important considerations. His debate with Washington, for instance, offers an important element that should be acknowledged in any political theory and, by extension, political action—namely, the centrality of *power* in any political equation. Two additional factors of the Talented Tenth ideology are (1) the logic of what it means to build a society and (2) the logic of minimal conditions.

Regarding the first, the argument is straightforward: one has to start somewhere, and the black masses at the end of Reconstruction were in need of a professional class. Recall Du Bois's observation that to rely on white material infrastructural development *for* blacks would be unwise. Simply put, it's not a good idea for black people, *as a group*, to trust whites, *as a group*. The empirical data, so to speak, made the point clear. Du Bois's basic argument here isn't very different from E. Franklin Frazier's and Frantz Fanon's to come.[36] Frazier and Fanon lamented the emergence of a class of what could be called "race mediators." These were (and sadly, continue to be) blacks whose main source of legitimacy and wealth emerges from their role of negotiating the relations between powerful whites (and their correlative institutions) and the majority working- and underclass black populations.

Failing to translate their skills into material, infrastructural development, their "capital," so to speak, is simply race-representational. Fanon's conclusion was brutal. Such a group was, in his view, good for nothing. His point, however, was that their failures were lamentable precisely because they were *needed for something.* Every society needs people with skills that can translate into uplift. Fanon referred to such skills as a group's "mission," whereas Du Bois preferred the language of "talent." Du Bois's earlier thought wasn't engaged with debates about infrastructural class development. His later reflections revealed disillusionment akin to Fanon's concerns, interestingly enough written in the same decade: a class could emerge with needed skills that are squandered due to, as Fanon would put it, betraying its mission. Du Bois learned the hard way, as members of that group abandoned him:

> The intelligentsia, the "Talented Tenth," the successful business and professional men, were not, for the most part, outspoken in my defense. There were many and notable exceptions, but as a group this class was either silent or actually antagonistic. . . . They proposed to make money and spend it as pleased them. They had beautiful homes, large and expensive cars and fur coats. They hated "communism" and "socialism" as much as any white American. Their reaction toward Paul Robeson was typical; they simply could not understand his surrendering a thousand dollars a night for a moral conviction.[37]

With regard to Du Bois's supposedly being elitist and exclusionary, an appeal to a talented tenth of the population doesn't mean that only a tenth would be talented.[38] As Anna Julia Cooper pointed out before Du Bois in *A Voice from the South,* the logic of worth depends on what is invested. That so many black people have given far more to the Americas in the arts, labor, science, and technology than has been invested in them is a testament to their value, that is, their talent.[39] Put differently: there were simply a lot of talented black people around, most of whom were being blocked from the opportunity to transform the world with their talent. Starting from a talented tenth, then, one could instead encounter a talented half or a talented majority of the population. One, in short, doesn't know. Du Bois's argument was ultimately about *a minimum with which to begin,* not about an elite category to maintain. His argument for black leadership was premised on white leadership's being untrustworthy for the project of increased black opportunity and prosperity.[40] To make matters more complicated, if the goal were exclusion, then the project wouldn't be for an *increase* in that supposedly talented population, even in its most racist formulation. His thought on this matter went through various stages from the noxious positions of eugenics (biological and social) in the nineteenth century and early twentieth to a radically transformed position of his attitude to the bottom rung—namely, blacks who were "pure" Africans—in his later and more politically radical years.[41]

Looking back, then, to the debate with Washington, we have a clue to what Du Bois's Africana political theory offers as he in his own practice pursued and learned its contingent features through the academy, organizations such as the National Association for the Advancement of Colored People (NAACP), and still further through to his purported radicalization with Paul Robeson and William Patterson culminating in his membership of the Communist Party USA and his departure to Ghana as an ex-patriot of the United States. His final autobiography articulates that path well, but I would like to suggest here that even in his earliest work Du Bois was no stranger to the project of social transformation, since he lived in a world in which it was radical for him simply to stand up and declare that he and his fellow blacks were human beings. Such an assertion of dignity, as history attests, carried with it the threat of being strung up and dismembered.

The peculiarly *political* question at the heart of Du Boisian social science is manifold. On one hand, it is the question of methodological rigor. On the other, it is the question of how the first requires intersubjective understanding of a shared social world. Moving further, it expresses the logic of exceptions and rules, where the infelicities of the dominant group are treated as insignificant and those of the dominated, however small, overcloud their achievements and strengths. And headed even further, it reveals what is most feared in US race politics: Black Power.

Power/Knowledge and Social Justice

We have at this point explored the methodological concern of failing to study or treat human subjects as human beings. Another is the error of treating dynamics between black and white as contraries.

Du Bois learned early in his career that segregation split the category of the ordinary. While for whites, the achievement of an ordinary life is a rule, for blacks it is an exception since the entire system of racial oppression is designed to block such a possibility for black people. This feeds into a wider logic, as Du Bois himself experienced with his extraordinary education credentials. Despite outdoing his white contemporaries in sociology, Du Bois was never offered posts readily available to mediocre white scholars in prestigious American institutions of higher learning. In his day there were many well-educated blacks working in blue-collar positions. This logic worked its way through to the study of crime, where Ida B. Wells-Barnett was probably his major source. The criminalization of black people made it (supposedly) an exception to meet a black person who was not a criminal, and likewise made it an exception to meet a white person who was one. In effect, then, blacks in the United States were guilty until (very rarely) proven innocent. This means that black people have had to perform at a much higher standard simply to receive the rewards of being ordinary. For black people, being ordinary is an extraordinary achievement.

Such exceptions and rules have many implications for social justice. One is that the search for such under racist conditions requires a dialectical unmasking of the system's double-consciousness. Here we enter the realm of political theodicy. Theodicy involves accounting for the legitimacy of a god in the presence of injustice or evil. The solutions to this problem often involve demonstrating the externality of injustice and evil. Thus, infelicity is either presumed as a function of human beings' failing to see the larger and just picture or accounted for in terms of human free will gone wrong. Secularized, the logic becomes one of showing that the society is ultimately just, which means wrongdoing *must* be a function of those accused of its perpetration. We return here to the construction of problem people. Blacks and other groups of color are, in this view, justly treated as external to the system, which is supposedly intrinsically just. For such groups, however, the problem becomes one of an unjust justice. They must struggle to establish the possibility of human relations beyond the existing order of justice. This requires revolutionary change.

However, change cannot be achieved without power. Du Bois was well aware of this as early as his 1903 Atlanta University speech "The Training of Negroes for Social Power." Although this speech was given during what he later regarded as his more naïve years, its basic insight remained with him throughout his career: without material capital (much of which in the US context was destroyed during the demise of Reconstruction), black people must seek ways of affecting the world through a wide range of alternative resources, with education being the most important of them. The connection between education and power may at first seem misguided (given the limited options available even to educated blacks during Du Bois's early years) unless we think through how knowledge and power are linked. To do that requires first defining the latter.

Power, as I'll be using it here and as I suggest Du Bois eventually understood it, means the ability to make things happen. Where there is no social system, no means of communication, there would be no distinction between power and force, since both would depend on the reach of one's physical body. Intelligence could expand force through the use of a tool. But language and its correlative social world change matters greatly. The ability to affect the world, to make things happen, expands dramatically. Institutions, laws, knowledge over time, and all the means of culture born from social reality are infused with capabilities at levels of meaning transferred, where necessary, also into force. Different phenomena emerge with such abilities, and among them is the practice of politics, which, through speech, negotiates power itself. Through politics, the ability to make things happen is energized into making more things happen.

Du Bois's political thought, then, should be reread also as a long meditation on not only the knowledge through which the power of revolution could be effected but also the knowledge itself as a form of power. In the absence of sufficient material capital, knowledge became for him a crucial form of power. And as the racist state devoted its energy to limiting the power of black people—indeed, to the point of restricting the reach of most black people to that of their bodies—blacks' knowledge, as a form of power, became one of the prime enemies of the racist state. Du Bois's radicalism, then, was already present in his dignified assertion of cultivating what the racist society in which he struggled demanded all of his kind must not be. For him, knowledge was a fruit he not only wanted but also *needed*. Reflecting on his undergraduate years at Harvard in his last autobiography, he wrote: "I was in Harvard for education and not for high marks, except as marks would insure my staying. . . . I was there to enlarge my grasp of the meaning of the universe . . .; above all I wanted to study philosophy! I wanted to get hold of the basis of knowledge, and explore foundations and beginnings."[42]

However, Du Bois wasn't duped by Harvard's inflated reputation and self-esteem. Comparing the faculty there with those who had taught him at

Fisk, the historically black institution he attended before going to Harvard, he observes: "Fortunately I did not fall into the mistake of regarding Harvard as the beginning rather than the continuing of my college training. I did not find better teachers at Harvard, but teachers better known, who had had wider facilities for gaining knowledge and had a broader atmosphere for approaching truth."[43]

Du Bois's journey as a representative of his race took him to his doctorate in history at Harvard, his studies for and eventual doctorate in economics at the University of Berlin, his work as an academic first at Wilberforce and then Atlanta University, and eventually as what Jean-Paul Sartre would call an *intellectuel engagé* (committed intellectual) in the struggle, as an intellectual, for racial justice. He recounted how his faith in knowledge had blinded him to the brutality of the historical situation during his younger years as a professor: "One could not be a calm, cool, and detached scientist while Negroes were lynched, murdered and starved. . . . I regarded it as axiomatic that the world wanted to learn the truth and if the truth were sought with even approximate accuracy and painstaking devotion, the world would gladly support the effort. This was. Of course, but a young man's idealism, not by any means false, but also never universally true."[44]

Though Du Bois was referring to errors in his thinking before *Black Reconstruction,* this last point considers the meeting of psychoanalysis and Marxism in concerns about the relation between inner self-reflection and material conditions of existence. His critical reflections in that earlier work suggest, however, a third element, which is the impact of anthropological impositions such as "race" on the mediation of those two poles. As Fanon reflected nearly a decade before Du Bois's reflections offered here, the world between ontogeny (an individual organism's activities) and phylogeny (a species' activities) is *sociogeny* (the world in which human meaning is produced).[45] That is the world in which race and racism are produced not only as identities and practices of power but also as underlying conditions of hegemonic or dominant knowledge. The human sciences, in other words, faced challenges of racial, colonial imposition of the kinds Du Bois himself examined early in his career. This third element suggests, then, that even ideas from Freud and Marx needed interrogation about the forms of human being and models of political agents they presuppose. They must each address the problem of black people appearing in the world as human beings and the implications, in social scientific terms, of such appearance.[46]

In the reflections on his life and thought that Du Bois wrote in the last decade of his life, he realized this need for coming to grips with what could be called Africana historiography and its concomitant political thought. Preceding Aimé Césaire's 1950 assertion, in *Discourse on Colonialism,* that Hitlerism was actually Europe's colonial values turned upon itself, Du Bois argued in 1946, "There was no Nazi atrocity—concentration camps, wholesale maiming and murder, defilement of women or ghastly blasphemy of childhood—which the Christian civilization of Europe had not long been practicing against colored folk in all parts of the world in the name of and for the defense of a Superior Race born to rule the world."[47] His eventual decision to leave the United States and become a citizen of Ghana was prompted not only by his arrest and acquittal for treason in 1951 and his being denied a US passport until 1958 but also by Kwame Nkrumah's inviting him to direct the Encyclopedia Africana, a project to which Du Bois had been committed since 1909.[48] Knowledge, as Du Bois saw it throughout his life, is a political act—one for which he often paid a high price.

That knowledge, however, needed to take form in the material expansion of options, an example of which was his opportunity in Ghana. Du Bois came to Marxism as a radical in the later part of his life as the direction in which his thought was already headed. Like Nkrumah, he did so out of affinity. As he never endorsed the view that black people must wait to become white in order to act, his movement into the sphere of dialectical reflection was linked organically to the strivings of the people to whose humanity he had dedicated his life's work.

Obviously, I have chosen not to examine Du Bois's political thought through the usual lenses of conservatism, liberalism, nationalism, separation, or assimilation, for these are the tropes through which black political thought is often boxed in. Instead, I've offered a redescription of his thought through political ideas emanating from Africana philosophy, which explores what it means for black persons to be human, to struggle for freedom, and to question the conditions of knowledge in the white racist social, political, and epistemological order of things. Du Bois's engagements with problematic constructions of knowledge, sloppy methodologies, the meaning of freedom, and the nature of power all suggest that Du Bois's reflections continue to speak to us well into the twenty-first century. Humanity now struggles not only with what we have been but also with what we are to become. Whether that will be the best or worst in us is in our hands as we set the foundations for subsequent generations. I close, then, with the closing meditation of the "Postlude" from his *Soliloquy:*

> Suffer us not, Eternal Dead to stew in this Evil—the Evil of South Africa, the Evil of Mississippi; the Evil of Evils which is what we hope to hold in Asia and Africa, in the southern Americas and islands of the Seven Seas. Reveal, Ancient of Days, the Present in the Past and prophesy the End in the Beginning. For this is a beautiful world; this is a wonderful America, which the founding fathers dreamed until their sons drowned it in the blood of slavery and devoured it in greed. Our children must rebuild it. Let then the Dreams of the Dead rebuke the Blind who think that what is will be forever and teach them that what was worth living for must live again and that which merited death must stay dead. Teach us, Forever Dead, there is no Dream but Deed, there is no Deed but Memory.

Notes

1. Anna Julia Cooper; Ida B. Wells-Barnett, and Marcus Garvey immediately come to mind. See Joy Ann James, *Transcending the Talented Tenth: Black Leaders and American Intellectuals* (New York: Routledge, 1997) and, from a more liberal perspective, David Levering Lewis *W. E. B. Du Bois—Biography of a Race, 1868–1919* (New York: Holt, 1993) and *W. E. B. Du Bois—The Fight for Equality and the American Century, 1919–1963* (New York: Holt, 2000).

2. I'm referring, of course, to Martin Luther King Jr.'s famous "Letter from Birmingham Jail," which crystalized in succinct form black response to cries, and at times demands, for continued patience instead of action in the interest of social change (see Martin Luther King Jr., *Why We Can't Wait* [New York: Signet Classics, 2000]). For some discussion of this theme in black political thought before and alongside King, see Lewis R. Gordon, *What Fanon Said: A Philosophical Introduction to His Life and Thought* (New York: Fordham University Press, 2015), 124.

3. I offer discussion of Du Bois's specifically philosophical contributions in Lewis R. Gordon, *An Introduction to Africana Philosophy* (Cambridge: Cambridge University Press, 2008), 73–79. For a more detailed treatment, see Nahum Dimitri Chandler, *X: The Problem of the Negro as a Problem for Thought* (New York: Fordham University Press, 2014). See also Paget Henry, "Africana Philoso-

phy: Its Philosophical Implications," in *Journeys in Caribbean Thought: The Paget Henry Reader,* ed. Henry, Jane Anna Gordon, Lewis R. Gordon, Aaron Kamugisha, and Neil Roberts, 27–58 (London: Rowman and Littlefield International, 2016).

4. See, e.g., Jane Anna Gordon, "Challenges Posed to Social-Scientific Method by the Study of Race," in *A Companion to African-American Studies,* ed. Lewis R. Gordon and Jane Anna Gordon (Malden, MA: Blackwell, 2006), 279–304; and Lewis R. Gordon, *Existentia Africana: Understanding Africana Existential Thought* (New York: Routledge, 2000), chap. 4.

5. For elaboration of this problem, see Lewis R. Gordon, "Theory in Black: Teleological Suspensions in Philosophy of Culture," *Qui Parle: Critical Humanities and Social Sciences* 18, no. 2 (Spring/Summer 2010): 193–214.

6. W. E. B. Du Bois, *The Philadelphia Negro* (Philadelphia: University of Pennsylvania Press, 1899).

7. W. E. B. Du Bois, *The Conservation of the Races* (Washington, DC: Negro Academy Press, 1897).

8. Gordon, *Existentia Africana,* chap. 4.

9. Du Bois, *The Conservation of the Races,* 4.

10. Ibid., 7.

11. W. E. B. Du Bois, "The Study of Negro Problems," *Annals of the American Academy of Political and Social Science* 11 (January 1898): 1–23; reprinted in *The Annals of the American Academy of Political and Social Science* 56 (March 2000): 13–27.

12. Anténor Firmin, *Equality of Human Races: A Nineteenth-Century Haitian Scholar's Response to European Racialism,* trans. Asselin Charles (New York: Garland, 2000).

13. Du Bois, "The Study of the Negro Problems," 23.

14. Ibid., 19.

15. W. E. B. Du Bois, *The Souls of Black Folk: Essays and Sketches* (Chicago: McClurg, 1903), 1–2.

16. For elaboration, see Chandler, *X: The Problem of the Negro as a Problem for Thought,* chap. 1.

17. Gordon, *Existentia Africana,* chap. 4; see also Lewis R. Gordon, "Race, Theodicy, and the Normative Emancipatory Challenges of Blackness," *South Atlantic Quarterly* 112, no. 4 (Fall 2013): 725–36.

18. W. E. B. Du Bois, "Sociology Hesitant," *boundary 2* 27, no. 3 (Fall 2000): 37–44.

19. Ibid., 41.

20. Ibid., 44.

21. Sylvia Wynter, "Towards the Sociogenic Principle: Fanon, Identity, the Puz-

zle of Conscious Experience, and What It Is Like to Be 'Black,'" in *National Identities and Sociopolitical Changes in Latin America,* ed. Mercedes F. Duran-Cogan and Antonio Gomez-Moriana (New York: Routledge, 2001), 30–66.

22. J. A. Gordon, "Challenges Posed to Social-Scientific Method by the Study of Race."

23. Frantz Fanon later makes such observations on normativity and normality in his book *Black Skin, White Masks* (1952) and his essay "Racism and Culture," which I elaborate in Gordon, *What Fanon Said.*

24. *The Souls of Black Folk,* 3–4.

25. Henry, "Africana Phenomenology," in *Journeys in Caribbean Thought,* 27–58.

26. For more discussion along these lines, see Jane Anna Gordon, "The Gift of Double Consciousness: Some Obstacles to Grasping the Contributions of the Colonized," in *Postcolonialism and Political Theory,* ed. Nalini Persram (Lanham, MD: Lexington, 2007), 143–61; and Lewis R. Gordon, "Problematic People and Epistemic Decolonization: Toward the Postcolonial in Africana Political Thought," in *Postcolonialism and Political Theory,* 121–41.

27. See W. E. B. Du Bois, *Black Reconstruction in America: 1860–1880* (New York: Free Press, 1935), chap. 17.

28. For a history of this academic movement and its political effects, see *The Dunning School: Historians, Race, and the Meaning of Reconstruction,* ed. John David Smith and J. Vincent Lowery (Lexington: University Press of Kentucky, 2013).

29. Du Bois, *Black Reconstruction in America,* 714.

30. Ibid., 716–17.

31. Ibid., 722.

32. Ibid., 727.

33. W. E. B. Du Bois, *The Autobiography of W. E. B. Du Bois: A Soliloquy on Viewing My Life from the Last Decade of Its First Century* (New York: International, 1968), 236.

34. Ibid.

35. Ibid., 227–28.

36. See E. Franklin Frazier, *Black Bourgeoisie: The Book That Brought the Shock of Self-Revelation to Black America* (New York: Free Press, 1997; originally published in French in 1955); and Frantz Fanon, *Les damnés de la terre* (Paris: François Maspero, 1961).

37. Du Bois, *Autobiography,* 370–71.

38. Two examples of this criticism are Joy Ann James's *Transcending the Talented Tenth* (New York: Routledge, 1997) and Robert Gooding-Williams, *In the Shadow of Du Bois: Afro-Modern Political Thought* (Cambridge: Harvard University

Press, 2011). James's concern is with the idea of the Talented Tenth functioning as leadership over the black masses. Gooding-Williams is critical of the idea of what he calls "a cultured, aristocratic leadership" (10).

39. Cooper was born a slave and was by then writing as the principal of the M Street School in Washington, DC. The scholarship she received to study at St. Augustine College at age nine, her subsequent education at Oberlin and the Sorbonne, and her place in American letters made her an exemplar of her own thesis. As she was also speaking of other prominent people of African descent who were either born in servitude or a societal situation of a racist legal system prohibiting their options, that there was achievement at all supported her thesis. Beyond the elites, however, is the fact of survival and continued growth of black communities. See Cooper's *A Voice from the South,* especially the chapter "What Are We Worth?" reprinted in *The Voice of Anna Julia Cooper, Including "A Voice from the South" and Other Important Essays, Papers and Letters,* ed. Charles Lemert and Esme Bha (Lanham, MD: Rowman and Littlefield, 1998). For elaboration of Cooper's thought, see Vivian M. May, *Anna Julia Cooper, Visionary Black Feminist: A Critical Introduction* (New York: Routledge, 2007).

40. Du Bois, *Autobiography,* 236.

41. The black elite to which Du Bois belonged was primarily a mixed-race one with the trappings of biological racial logic of the nineteenth century: white ancestry offered superiority; black ancestry, inferiority. In effect, the mixed-black population presumed, in a repetition of the white-supremacist thesis, a mixed-race-supremacist one in which those of mixed race were the natural-born leaders of the "pure," and thus purely inferior, blacks. The eugenics of the day presumed a tenth of the population was, in today's language, biracial or of mostly white "stock," and various gradations led to a bottom 10 percent who were presumed "dysgenic." As with biological Darwinism, Social Darwinism took root with similar logic. The upshot was a prevailing set of arguments for racial uplift premised on in effect weeding out or eventually eliminating "pure" blacks from the American "Negro" gene pool, a goal that Frantz Fanon in *Black Skin, White Masks* (1952) called "lactification." A detailed treatment of this unfortunate history is Shantella Y. Sherman's "In Search of Purity: Popular Eugenics and Racial Uplift among New Negroes 1915–1935" (PhD diss., University of Nebraska–Lincoln, 2014). Despite the inclusive dates given in its title, the thesis offers excellent discussion from the mid-nineteenth century onward. For discussion of Du Bois's transformed views toward the "pure" blacks and Africans, see Vernon J. Williams Jr., *Rethinking Race: Franz Boas and His Contemporaries* (Lexington: University Press of Kentucky, 1996). May offers a similar criticism of Anna Julia Cooper in *Anna Julia Cooper, Visionary Black Feminist,* 52–57.

42. Du Bois, *Soliloquy,* 132–33.

43. Ibid., 133.

44. Ibid., 222.

45. See Fanon's introduction to *Black Skin, White Masks.*

46. Jane Anna Gordon offers elaboration of this imperative in "Challenges Posed to Social-Scientific Method by the Study of Race."

47. W. E. B. Du Bois, *The World and Africa: An Inquiry into the Part Which Africa Has Played in World History* (1946; New York: International, 1965), 23. Aimé Césaire, *Discourse on Colonialism,* trans. Joan Pinkham (New York: Monthly Review Press, 2000).

48. Du Bois, *Soliloquy,* 302.

II

Du Bois, Politics, and Poetry

3

Alightings of Poetry

The Dialectics of Voice and Silence in W. E. B. Du Bois's Narrative of Double-Consciousness

Anthony Reed

Discussing his prewar and interwar activism in *Dusk of Dawn,* W. E. B. Du Bois remarks, "it had always been my intention to write" and "to seek through the written word the expression of my relation to the world and of the world to me." I take this, and its peculiar phrasing, as a point of departure. It subtly suggests that the relationship between the world and him, and between him and the world, is asymmetrical and not necessarily reciprocal. I read it as a continued elaboration of his celebrated notion of double-consciousness: the spacing between literary subject and world makes the sentence's chiasmus uneven, while in his formulation of double-consciousness, that gap makes "my own" experience always partially public. For Du Bois, the relationship of the world to the subject in large part determines the subject's sense of any possible relation to the world: the world appears as already marked by differential and differentiating power relationships. Writing is at once instrumental to discovering one's relationship to the world and, assuming his use of "expression" belongs to an idealist vernacular, a medium of that relationship. Through writing, Du Bois suggests, he can transform the discrepancy between subjective "lived experience" ("my relation to the world") and objective ("the world to me") into something more than autobiography. Following this train of thought, I will argue in this essay that Du Bois stretches the limits of the autobiographical, strategically deploying the conventions of lyric expression—a particular alignment of rhetoric and tropes—to ground his "concept of race" in figurative expression.[1]

Let us start by noting that Du Bois's phrasing in *Dusk of Dawn* resonates with the famous opening of *Souls:* "Between me and the other world there is *ever* an *unasked* question . . . How does it *feel* to be a problem?" Following such scholars as Cheryl Wall and building on my brief engagement with Du Bois in another context, I will argue that Du Bois uses writing and the staging of and on the page to create a text that "exceeds the limits of textual representation." Rather than emphasizing the ways Du Bois negotiates the expectation that his writing will be testimony about the color line, this essay will focus on his literary strategies, particularly his use of the lyric mode and the autobiographical "I," which are constitutive of *Souls*' literary politics. This is not to conflate the two but to suggest that what I am calling lyric life writing might have offered Du Bois an alternative to the prevailing modes of the slave narrative, or spiritual autobiography, to name two. In *Darkwater,* he "experiments" with "little alightings of what may be poetry," which he calls "tributes to Beauty." Along similar lines, he would later declare himself "one who tells the truth and exposes evil and seeks with Beauty and for Beauty to set the world right." Drawing out the significance of these claims—explaining how beauty would set the world right—will require rethinking the status of writing, especially the function of the modern lyric, within his larger project.[2]

I will carry out this reading by engaging the famous narrative through which Du Bois introduces his concept of double-consciousness, reading it as a literary rather than exclusively philosophical or sociological concept. First, I will offer an account of the ways race intersects with the universalist assumptions underpinning the modern lyric mode, encompassing, for present purposes, both Romantic verse and the spirituals, or "sorrow songs." Next, I will offer a reading of silence as a literary technique that both informs and interrupts the tropes of voice, dialectically suspending it between individual and collective without offering it as a point of sympathetic identification. I will conclude by considering the function of gender in this early development of his race concept, which depends on the imagined stability of the biographical self as referent even as the narrative suggests an excess of referentiality, of that which stands in excess *of* referentiality, to be a motivating factor of the Negro Problem's discursive operation. Through this excess, I will argue, Du Bois both mimes and defers the recollective posture upon which rest both autobiography (a literary mode with a privileged relationship to the truth) and lyric poetry (an expressive mode that can encompass autobiography). In the process, he produces a disruption in the even flow of time, including the smooth sense of biographical time, so that double-consciousness describes both an aesthetico-epistemological state—a "peculiar sensation"—and the ways telling of that state always partially produces it. In different terms, whereas critics often retrace the contours of his "voice" as a starting point to unpacking his politics, taking autobiography as a political problem concerning his relationship to the black masses, I argue that moments where he dramatizes a withheld voice show a literary dimension to the problem of the color line.[3]

My analysis centers on the poetics of his writing, emphasizing the degree to which the literary is central—not peripheral—to Du Bois's political thought. Through literary form, including the much-analyzed epigraphs, he collects disparate aesthetic traditions. Silence, like voice, is a literary effect that depends on certain habits of thinking about rhetoric and tropes. Du Bois uses literary technique to negotiate the relationship between race, understood as a process of creating deindividualized subjects in a society organized around individuality, and aesthetics, understood as that nexus of the sensible and the beautiful, the individual and the collective.

The unstable status of the modern lyric, which occupies a position between poetic mode and, in this case, implied song text, is central to his early project. Famously, his chapter epigraphs generally mix the two, refusing a hierarchy between Anglo-European and African American aesthetic traditions. That nonhierarchical mixture mirrors the movement within the text that is, for example, equally comfortable rewriting William Wordsworth's "Intimations Ode" and allowing room for his African American subjects' own reported voices even at the expense of his own. But if the lyric is the paradigmatic genre of experience "recollected in tranquility," the paradigmatic genre of the isolated individual attempting to make contact with and transfer what William Wordsworth called "kindred feelings" to the Other, how does it function as a medium for those subjects denied both the benefits and assumptions of individuality? Blackness is the implied antistrophe to the universal: one speaks as black or as Man, not both at the same time. If, in another register, lyric indexes a metonymic chain of the human—

speech rather than noise, the voice of the subject, the subject of rights—an implied question of Du Bois's enterprise is what it means to write then from the position of the contingently unhuman. These questions get right to the heart of two of the most vexing questions around Du Bois's writing, and black writing in his wake: the status of the voice, and of representation, in his literary project. To be clear: the lyric tradition Du Bois engages develops in conjunction with the birth of capitalism and its attendant notions and rhetorics of subjectivity. Its mixed or alternating lyric mode allows *Souls* both to claim a centrality of authorial voice, self-consciously re-created through his revisions of its essays into a coherent text, and to undermine that voice, and with it claims to representation that, for white readers in particular, would have been a primary appeal. This play with lyric destabilizes the "voice" and locates the "peculiar sensation" of blackness within aesthetic traditions, which are implied but not named. Such play of implication throughout Du Bois's writing is a preliminary moment of silence; it functions structurally as a recurrent anacrusis and rhetorically as paralipsis, a performative engagement that announces its refusal to engage.[4]

Lyric serves as a bridge between phenomenological and political subjectivities, even as the generality of Man elides any distinction between them. What happens to our notions of identity if we follow a certain line of double-consciousness to the point where the distinction between narrating and narrated subject becomes undecidable? Du Bois's paraliptic silence doubles the initial silenced or veiled question "How does it feel to be a problem?" in the famous and oft-cited opening to "Of Our Spiritual Strivings." In other words, his claim to answer the "ever unasked question" with "seldom a word," the drama of coming to racial self-knowledge as a sensory-epistemological opening, duplicates that structure through a mirror: he offers his visiting card without reporting his dialogue, and she refuses it "peremptorily, with a [paraliptic, articulate] glance" whose meaning manifests as if already known. In another register, part of what is at stake in Du Bois's narration of race consciousness is the transition from one kind of lyric subject—the individual of Euro-American poetry—to another: the singer of the sorrow songs as emblematic of a fuller sense of humanity. I read that semi-dialectical transition (as we will see, he narrates it as occurring with "a certain suddenness") alongside the tension inherent in those moments that seem to belong simultaneously to individual and collective experience. One confronts the difference between identity and identification, between one's self-perception and the ways one is perceived. As Karen E. Fields and Barbara J. Fields succinctly put it, "Race as identity breaks down on the irreducible fact that any sense of self intrinsic to persons of African descent is subject to peremptory nullification by forcible extrinsic identification." The interaction of Du Bois's literary and political ambitions—the desire to tell something of the complex histories, contemporary experiences, and "spiritual strivings" of African Americans in the first half of the twentieth century—marks a *crisis* in the etymological sense of the term. It marks, that is, both a *scission* of literary consciousness and a *decision* whereby the literary "I" formally reflects its own impossible, mythic origin, as in Du Bois's narrative immersion into double-consciousness, of having the world's relation to the self impinge on the self's relation to the world, which I will discuss at length below. The self-reflection, which puts the literary subject in play and arrests the voice as privileged consciousness, makes the text's engagement with the lyric mode fundamentally *critical.*[5]

From this perspective, we can approach what Nahum Chandler calls Du Bois's "autobiographical example" from a different perspective, hewing closely to the ways the autobiographical/lyric "I," as radical effect, is made and unmade. "Radical," of course, refers to getting to the root of the "problem," and understanding what was once called the "Negro problem" to be constitutive of the modern world, including the bedrock concepts around which we organize our institutions and subjectivities. It's that strain, resting in what remains irresolvable in the very framing of American democracy and theories of the citizen that rest on what Sylvia Wynter calls a "now globally hegemonic ethnoclass world of 'Man,'" a synecdoche whereby a particular subset of human beings self-designate as the paradigm of humanity as such. To read Du Bois through the lyric's particular version of singular-plural subjectivity as it relates to double-consciousness as a senso-ry-epistemological concept is to consider the ways race shapes and interrupts and overdetermines his "autobiographical example" insofar as race is the limit—and product—of the ethnoclass upon which the concept of "Man" in political and aesthetic domains rests. Blackness stands in excess to notions of universalism predicated on Man in this sense, whose tastes and whose experiences are imagined to reproduce themselves invisibly across human history.[6]

Modern autobiography and lyric have been shaped by the development of the notion of Man in Wynter's terms. The models of subjectivity and subjecthood through which readers encounter an "I" as another version of the self, even across transhistorical contexts that allow us to read premodern verse through the lens of the lyric, speak to the pervasiveness of this ideology. Both the autobiographical and lyric subjects have been critiqued as "reinforc[ing] dominant ideologies, official histories, and founding mythologies of the subject," helping to circulate and normalize these notions of white, male, bourgeois selfhood. Literary scholars in the wake of Paul de Man have stressed the fictionality of the mode, and although there is some disagreement over the degree to which lyric (or autobiography) "knows" it is fiction, much analysis sees lyric voice and subjectivity as effects of reading, an alignment of rhetoric and trope whose effect is speech, described since John Stuart Mill as "overheard."[7]

Mill's follow-up claim, that the "peculiarity of poetry appears to us to lie in the poet's utter unconsciousness of a listener," generally does not hold for Du Bois or other African American writers. With the exception of the authors of the slave narratives, who self-consciously and strategically engaged restrictive literary genres, his foray into lyric life writing would have been all but unexampled in his moment. Literary scholar Helen Vendler's account of lyric poetry as a genre whose "purpose" is "to represent an inner life in such a manner that it assumable by others" does not fare better, although it does lay bare the universalist assumptions of the form. Although she draws different conclusions, her argument is compatible with Theodor W. Adorno's analysis of the lyric in the context of emergent capitalism. For him, each lyric poem is partially a collective document insofar as it is the "subjective expression of a social antagonism." On his account, the voice is assumable by others owing to capital's abstract reduction of human life to labor power under a regime of formal equality. If the Other's experience is knowable because it is roughly the same as one's own, then belonging to the national *demos* or the universal family of Man is a condition of intelligible lyric speech.[8]

Race, a hygienic process of ensuring differential belonging to the universal, complicates this process insofar as it creates universality's Other, as the slave in the period of the emergence of the Romantic lyric is the Other to the citizen in whose body capital's ultimate abstraction and alienation is most spectacularly visible. Because the conditions of racial identification deny the raced subject a separate space for reflective tranquility, race—perhaps blackness especially, owing to the particular ways black bodies live abstraction and alienation—internally destabilizes an already unstable genre. This is not to say that nonwhites (or nonmales and other non-normative subjects) cannot or do not write in the lyric mode. They have, and continue to. But racial themes introduce a new set of interpretive imperatives and assumptions that defer the possibility of lyric even as a mode of reading. Race changes the terms of "assumption" in Vendler's sense insofar as part of the meaning of the racially marked text is its production of knowledge about raced experience. The genre in these circumstances bends toward testimony—from art to truth—making readers much more likely to overlook the art of the written word and see the text instead as transparent self-expression. To burnish the artifice or otherwise draw attention to the instability of the lyric voice is to introduce, if only temporarily, a snag in the flow of identification, allowing something of the underlying social texture to become legible on and as the surface of the writing.

This model of lyric poetry, a historically specific way of combining rhetoric and tropes to engender the effect of utterance and thus subjectivity, has the advantage of making lyric a social relation. Thus, it helps us to see how, in this instance, Du Bois is after something other than representation. In that way, it dovetails with Du Bois's own notion of the "sorrow songs," or spirituals, whose site (and cite) of enunciation is that of what Robert Stepto terms the "quintessential, atemporal, Afro-American 'we.'" The spirituals, expressing objective racial alienation in plural-subjective voice, are the inverse of the Vendlerian lyric: they figure a group's inner life through which an individual can understand her own experience as embedded in a particular historical time and space. In the movement between these modes of inner life, of individual and group experience, is a rethinking of the very grounds of aesthetics and politics: the individual subject. Du Bois's use of the blended lyric also reveals the discrepancy (assumed to be an isomorphism) between the subject of experience and the social or political subject, the unmarked other who appears as the same insofar as both are subjects of the *demos*. More radically, accounts like Vendler's—paradigmatic in discussions of the political value of lyric poetry—strongly suggest that subjectivity only inheres in this intermixture, or what Nahum Chandler terms the "constitutive detour through the other": the creative acts of reading through which one perceives a coherent lyric speaker requires organizing one's own subjectivity so that one can answer its call.[9] Du Bois fully avails himself of both the racially marked and unmarked valences of "lyric," deploying a mode fundamentally associated with the shared nature of discourse—through conventions or actual communities—to generate a drama of refused social relation.[10]

Of particular importance to my reading is the use of ellipsis and paralipsis (saying by declaring unwillingness to say), within which he gives substance to the veil. Through those tropes, Du Bois outlines the phenomenological and temporal dimensions of his race concept. The recursive encounter around which double-consciousness becomes an object of knowledge mixes literary and experiential understandings of time—history, memory, and other modes of looking back or forward, of locating individual experience in a larger field set of experiences—to produce a concept of race as a process of subjection whose phenomenological subjects continue to be denied the rights and entailments of liberal subjecthood. Blackness, thus, is fundamentally political and signals a more or less permanent zone of nonbelonging (and the myths that maintain that zone) within the domain of the political. In different terms, one might say that blackness is a "social construct" if by that we mean it structures the intimate and public terrains of the social. The continued relevance of the color line points to the durability of the structure, while the narrative he provides gives a sense of the conventions and laws that give it substance.[11]

This narrative, which he invokes in later writings under a cover of continued silence or refusal to speak (in both *Dusk of Dawn* and the *Autobiography* he writes only that he has written this incident previously, tacitly reproducing its performative silences), is staged as a myth. It is worth quoting in its entirety:

> It is in the early days of rollicking boyhood that the revelation first bursts upon one, all in a day, as it were. I remember well when the shadow swept across me. I was a little thing, away in the hills of New England, where the dark Housatonic winds between Hoosac and Taghkanic to the sea. In a wee wooden schoolhouse, something put it into the boys' and girls' heads to buy gorgeous visiting-cards—ten cents a package—and exchange. The exchange was merry, till one girl, a tall newcomer, refused my card,—refused it peremptorily, with a glance. Then it dawned on me with a certain suddenness that I was different from the others; or like mayhap in heart and life and longing, but shut out from their world by a vast veil.[12]

The movement between the general and the particular, like the transformation of shadow—a transient nonsubstance—to veil, is noteworthy. Equally remarkable are the silences that structure the passage, through which Du Bois marks a shift from the general to autobiographically specific: the revelation "bursts upon *one,* all in a *day,*" which is one of the many "early days of rollicking boyhood." This gap is that within which the "I" is reintroduced, having undergone a hiatus of speculative infancy and European sojourn: it bursts upon one, after which "*I* remember well when the shadow fell upon *me.*" The atemporal adverb "never" belies the "certain suddenness": one learns and relearns that one is a problem, in serial experiences through which being a problem is defined. The "subject" of the veil is neither phenomenology's intending subject nor the psychological subject of cognized experience. Rather, Du Bois's narrative figures the veil as a dissimulation of the givenness of the "organic" or "natural" nature of the social world. Insofar as it is constructed to justify exploitation and discourage broader class unity, the veil—both a metaphor for race and for what race constructs—comes to seem a permanent, unassailable structure. As an ideological component linking practical and popular consciousness and cognitive activity to more rarified forms of philosophy, it is immanent to—and intimate with—thinking itself. There is not and has never been *one* Negro Problem; rather, "the Negro" exerts pressure in several directions and across several domains from the pseudo-ontological to the political. In other words, the Negro Problem is not independent of or secondary to other concerns; the "Negro" veils—renders visible and obscures—the articulation of the greater social network in which it plays a part.

The "tall newcomer" who rejects his visiting card provides a narratizable moment of racial awareness, an emotional experience to be recollected in relative tranquility. She is, presumably, either unfamiliar with the ways in which the Negro Problem is articulated and practiced in "the hills of New England," or all too aware of the open secret with which his peers had "come to terms" by refusing to speak it. In order to read the tall newcomer's silence correctly, it follows that Du Bois was aware of his racial predicament, which he confirms in later writing. The sudden epiphanic discovery, however, is an ideal lyric scenario: an intense, singular experience rendered in the first person in such a way that makes subjective horizons thinkable. Simultaneously, it outlines the limits of those forms of reading that would have its "I" interchangeable with those across the color line. In this, it offers an internal check against simple sympathetic identification, denying the fiction of an easily assumable "I" universally available for adaptation.[13]

Desire here is paradoxically *im*personal: the only way to understand the "sudden" understanding of racial difference is through a prior "sudden" understanding of gender and the heterosexual dyad that, like race, appears to be eternal—the condition of any thought. Certain "gendered structures of intellectual and political thought and feeling" (Hazel V. Carby's phrase) seem to function as the presumptive horizon of intelligibility, the support for this narrative, and are exploited. The gender dynamics, like the curious timing, are not accidental. Where, for Adorno, literary language, as exemplified by the lyric, "substitutes a poetic event for a language that is no longer present," here the poetic event stands in for an event that cannot otherwise be—the implied encounter a visiting card promises.[14]

The phrase "I was a little thing" is similarly worth pausing over for the ways it disarticulates the recollecting subject from the subject of experience. The most immediate reading involves the older man looking at the younger, naïve boy with tenderness and nostalgia, wishing at once to protect the young boy from knowledge of the world and to recover that experience of relative merriness. The "thing" is a kind of antimetaphor. It refuses to carry over sense from one domain to another, remaining peculiarly suspended between subject and object. A past subject that acted, felt, and was an agent in the world becomes the present object of narration and knowledge used to illustrate the present predicament of present-day subjects who had historically been treated as mere fungible objects. The older voice borrows authority at the expense of the younger and thus proclaims wisdom where before there had been ignorance. However, one can also read the phrase more literally, referring intimately to an "I" then relatively "little," unworthy of having its story told or speaking itself in discourse prior to this experience. Insofar as we understand the "little thing" as continuous with the older author of *Souls*, part of the "experience" of being a problem is this repetition or doubling ("one who was never anything but"). But it is also persistence—being a "bigger thing" whose speech is only warranted if it speaks to the conditions under which it is a "thing," a problem, in the first place. There is no way to answer "How does it feel to be a problem?" without affirming oneself—or the Negro, rather than the oppressive ideological and institutional norms within which the Negro comes to understand him/herself—as a problem. Lyric technique, inviting identification with a misidentified thing, allows an ironic reversal. The new knowledge is knowledge of the impossibility of knowledge. New answers affirm the problem and reinforce its apparent permanence. All the figures of instant enlightenment—"burst," "swept," "dawn," a "certain suddenness"—become code for the reinscription of the spontaneous knowledge of ideological strictures. Enlightenment appears as a remystification, a re-presentation of the Negro Problem as the outcome of the impossibility of answering the unasked question without confirming the relation of self and world it implies.

Caught between lyric expressivity and autobiography's claims to truth, the essay's modes of recollection do not sit easily with one another, especially to the extent that Du Bois at times figures himself as addressing those on the "other side" of the veil. At stake, though, is something akin to the second part of Wordsworth's famous definition of poetry as "the spontaneous overflow of powerful feeling": "the emotion is contemplated till by a species of reaction the tranquility disappears, and an emotion, kindred to that which was before the subject of contemplation, is gradually produced, and does itself actually exist in the mind." Wordsworth, as I suggested above, is responding to the historically new modes of alienation that arise out of capitalism's new modes of subject- and community-formation. If we assume that Du Bois is also addressing a heterogeneous African American audience, one can hear in this same claim a desire to claim an aesthetic community, a group of people invited to share Du Bois's understanding of how it *feels* to be a problem. The "I" of his text, thus, is suspended between synecdoche and metonymy, between the temporal disjunction of the veil, the suspended "now" of lyric utterance, and the racial embodied time of autobiographic form. The effect of the text depends both on its historical situation and the irreducible intertextuality of writing.[15]

By way of conclusion, I want to consider the tall newcomer who, like Du Bois's narrator, performs a kind of embodied paralipsis. If the play of silence—the unasked question between "me and the other world," the "seldom a word" given in response, the mute, articulate glance with which the tall newcomer rejects his visiting card—shows the different forms of reading and listening the color line requires, I want to draw out some conclusions for the relationships among gender, sexuality, and lyric as an opening onto future considerations. Gender and sexuality come together through the implicit threat of miscegenation, which functions as one of the most enduring ideological props of segregation and racial antagonism. Unearthing and exploiting the generative potentiality at the core of the children's game, Du Bois is able to reveal the two-way function of the veil: it alienates not only black subject but whites as well. The thought of a successful coupling between Du Bois, "bone of the bone and flesh of the flesh of them that live within the Veil," and this (presumably) white girl, the thought that she might accept his promise and await his future visit, would have been taboo. The intersection of race and gender is instrumental to staging the particularity of this expressive/experiential nexus. Du Bois, in this reading, uses an unspoken rejection to outline the unspeakable: the taboo of interracial desire and sex, which he mentions without mentioning when he rehearses his family genealogy, in *Souls* and subsequent writings. Blackness from this perspective interrupts distinctions between public and private, history and memory, and shows the frayed edges of the concepts upon which the normativity of the human rests.

The other reading would emphasize her allegorical function, meaning her belonging to the gendered sign complex linking women's bodies to the nation-state, on the one hand, and to the foreign lawgiver Bonnie Honig discusses on the other. Refusing a proto-sexual relationship with him defines his relation to the world on terms other than those assumed by the conventions of lyric subjectivity for whom the world is an object to incorporate. The "tall newcomer" gives what she does not have—what I can only imprecisely term "knowledge" of (and an occasion to acknowledge) the veil—to someone who cannot keep it. Knowledge of the veil awakens the impulse to offer "the Negro's gift to the world." One might say that it awakens a lyric impulse: the discovery of a voice in order to send it out beyond the confines of the narrow now. It marks the transition between modes of lyric expression—from the false universalism of conventional lyricism to the truer lyricism with which the rest of the essay begins to relate self to world and world to self.[16]

In keeping with my reading of this passage in terms of the lyric, I would suggest that time—the articulation of the timeless moment of enunciation—is also at stake. By refusing to make time for Du Bois—the proposed visit at an unknown point in the future, entrance into a shared of futurity—she makes visible the "phantom objectivity," the self-effacing veil, that invisibly orders experiences and lives. The outcome, the veil as race concept, at least implies a fundamental interrelation between racial and gendered oppression (their location at a school also implicates class and other forms of social reproduction). With "a certain suddenness" Du Bois diagnoses that differential time, and the differential histories with which races are associated, are the fundamental conflict, which *Souls* does not resolve: the Negro still has a message to give and has produced the only "true American music." The former participates in the open temporality of the visiting card; the latter suggests that black folk are already central to the development of the American folk-spirit. For Kwame Anthony Appiah, Du Bois's discussion of this conflict in terms of the affliction of warring souls in effect "reject[s] the notion that each of us could participate in only one Volksgeist; an individual person could be, in part, the product of the souls of the various folks to which she belonged." In one sense, this means that the tall newcomer already participates in a black folk-spirit to the extent that she understands herself to be American. More radically, rejecting the Negro deprives her, too, of the capacity for speech (or expression), insofar as her American voice comes about meaningfully through engagement with blackness.[17]

In miniature, this allegorical reading inscribes the color line as a theory of history: the movement between a folk-spirit and what it refuses. Though she refuses a prospective intimacy with the young Du Bois, *Souls* reveals the unacknowledged intimacy between what he represents and the (white, American) identity she protects. If Du Bois's narrator has "never been anything but" a problem, the tall newcomer has no other position from which to speak except as an American, or in this context as America. His use of lyric conventions allows Du Bois to reverse the question, revealing that he's not the problem: then as now, the problem lies with the fictional worlds white supremacy crafts as justification and enactment of its rules. Near the end of *Souls*, Du Bois engages a familiar metaphor, using a feminine pronoun to invoke the nation: "Would America have been America without *her* Negro people?" If responding to the unasked question "How does it feel to be a problem?" is a condition of lyric or autobiographical speech for the black subject that denies him or her the individuality upon which liberal and lyric subjecthood depend, refusing the blackness constitutive of American identity leaves the tall newcomer (and, implicitly, the nation she allegorizes) with nothing to say.[18]

Notes

1. Du Bois, *Writings*, ed. Nathan Huggins (New York: Library of America, 1986), 551, emphasis added.

2. Wall, "Resounding *Souls:* Du Bois and the African American Literary Tradition," *Public Culture* 17, no. 2 (2005): 218; Du Bois, *Darkwater: Voices from within the Veil* (New York: Washington Square Press, 2004), xxiii; Du Bois, "Criteria of Negro Art." in *Writings,* ed. Huggins, 995; Reed, *Freedom Time: The Poetics and Politics of Black Experimental Writing* (Baltimore: Johns Hopkins University Press, 2014).

3. I am building, in part, on Robert Gooding-Williams's arguments in *In the Shadow of Du Bois: Afro-Modern Political Thought in America* (Cambridge: Harvard University Press, 2009), esp. 77–88.

4. Some scholars, especially Virginia Jackson and, from another perspective, Jonathan Culler, have critiqued the degree to which the lyric mode has come to be overrepresented in poetry, leading to criticism that flattens the historical contours of poetic development and flattens a complicated set of practices into one genre through the process of "lyricization," or to reading practices that treat poems as miniature novels and miss what is distinct about poetry as poetry. The period of Du Bois's intellectual development overlaps the period within which the consolidation of both, related tendencies are being developed. Gooding-Williams (*In the Shadow of Du Bois*) compellingly reads the connections between Du Bois and Wordsworth, whereas Wall ("Resounding *Souls*") notes those places where Du Bois's authorial voices gives way to others.

5. Barbara Fields and Karen Fields, *Racecraft: The Soul of Inequality in American Life* (London: Verso, 2012), 157; Du Bois, *Writings*, 364.

6. Wynter, "Unsettling the Coloniality of Being/Power/Truth/Freedom: Towards the Human, After Man, Its Overrepresentation," *CR: The New Centennial Review* 3, no. 3 (Fall 2003): 262.

7. Sidonie Smith, "Who's Talking/Who's Talking Back? The Subject of Personal Narrative," *Signs* 18 (Winter 1993): 393. Lawrie Balfour cites this same passage from Smith and persuasively reads, albeit in a different way, the ways *Dusk of Dawn,* in particular, "operates within and challenges generic expectations" (*Reconstructing Democracy: Thinking Politically with W. E. B. Du Bois* [Oxford: Oxford University Press, 2012], 78). Mill's whole statement: "Poetry and eloquence are both alike the expression or utterance of feeling: but, if we may be excused the antithesis, we should say that eloquence is *heard;* poetry is *over*heard" (*Essays on Poetry* [Columbia: University of South Carolina Press, 1976], 12). Versions of Mill's argument, which draws on William Wordsworth's famous definition of poetry as the "spontaneous overflow of powerful feeling . . . recollected in tranquility" resound in the work of Northrop Frye and T. S. Eliot.

8. Vendler, *The Given and the Made: Strategies of Poetic Redefinition* (Cambridge: Harvard University Press, 1995), xi; Adorno, *Notes to Literature,* vol. 1, trans. Shierry Weber Nicholsen (New York: Columbia University Press, 1991), 45.

9. Nahum Dimitri Chandler, *X: The Problem of the Negro as a Problem for Thought* (New York: Fordham University Press, 2014), 105.

10. Stepto, *Behind the Veil: A Study of Afro-American Narrative* (Urbana: University of Illinois Press, 1979), 64.

11. Kwame Anthony Appiah, revising his earlier arguments about Du Bois, notes that with his observation that "the black man is the person who must ride 'Jim Crow' in Georgia" Du Bois "articulates . . . , in a powerful image, the core of the idea of race as an effect of social practices, as a social construction, many decades before that term became the slogan of the new cultural studies" (Appiah, *Lines of Descent: W. E. B. Du Bois and the Emergence of Identity* [Cambridge: Harvard University Press, 2014], 113).

12. Du Bois, *Writings*, 364.

13. See esp. Du Bois, *Autobiography* 83–94, where Du Bois does describe his coming to race consciousness as a more gradual process.

14. Carby, *Race Men* (Cambridge: Harvard University Press, 1998), 12; Adorno, *Notes to Literature*, 44.

15. Wordsworth, *The Major Works*, ed. Stephen Gill (Oxford: Oxford University Press, 1984), 611.

16. See Honig, *Democracy and the Foreigner* (Princeton: Princeton University Press, 2003).

17. Appiah, *Lines of Descent*, 59.

18. Du Bois, *Writings*, 545, emphasis added.

4

The Imperial Miracle

Black Reconstruction *and the End(s) of Whiteness*

James Edward Ford III

> So, comrades, let us not pay tribute to Europe by creating states, institutions, and societies which draw their inspiration from her. . . . If we wish to live up to our people's expectations, we must seek the response elsewhere than in Europe.
>
> —Frantz Fanon, *The Wretched of the Earth*

W. E. B. Du Bois's extensive use of poetry in his books of prose remains underexplored. Considering the hundreds of articles that discuss his *The Souls of Black Folk* while ignoring poetry's role in it as a central framing device, one should not be surprised that almost no scholarship considers poetry's function in Du Bois's later works, including *Black Reconstruction in America, 1860–1880.* Along with two other essays in this volume, this essay will address that omission. I suggest that we should think hard about the poetry in *Black Reconstruction* because there, as in most of Du Bois's work, argumentation proceeds on multiple levels, through form as well as content, involving both *what* is said and *how* it is said. Du Bois ends every chapter of *Black Reconstruction* with a fragment of poetry. These serve, I propose, as what Nathaniel Mackey has called a "paracritical hinge," a "door" "permitting flow between disparate modes of articulation." For this essay's purposes, those "disparate modes" consist on the one hand of Du Bois's explicit political thinking about the nation-state's relation to the global and, on the other, of his often implicit thinking about the relationship between black radical politics and black aesthetics. I suggest that Du Bois invites us to enter each chapter through the poetry that concludes each preceding chapter. With this formal decision, Du Bois invites us both to ponder why he selected specific passages from the original poems for his chapters and to figure out how these passages augment the book's prose analysis of racist national culture and imperialism. I suggest further that the tension arising from the interplay between Du Bois's connotative poetry and his denotative prose foments what I call *an interminable analysis,* such that *Black Reconstruction* never settles but remains a restless text, inviting and provoking its readers to engage deeply with it. Indeed, by using poetry as a paracritical hinge that upsets and forestalls narrative resolution, Du Bois prompts readers to shuttle within and across the book's chapters, a movement that allows them to comprehend the links between the legal codification of Jim Crowism and twentieth-century European imperial power.

Du Bois's argument connecting racist legal codes in the United States and European colonial imperialism worldwide turns, as Allison Powers has shown, on his distinctive use of the word "transubstantiation." Originally, Marx had used this word in elaborating upon the concept of commodity fetishism, whereby capitalist exchange puts products through a spiritual transformation that supersedes their material form, so they can be exchanged on the same terms as any other products. Powers suggests that Du Bois adapted this concept to American constitutional law, such that the law is both *fetishized* and *fetishizes.* As such, it conceals the fact that it assumes a racial hierarchy among humans. And because implementing or reforming that law inevitably reinforces that presumed hierarchy, new laws in themselves, however progressive and seemingly antiracist, cannot effect an antiracist revolution.

However, if *Black Reconstruction* argues that racist assumptions precede legal concepts and make the law a puppet of the racist order, then what explanation does the book provide for the *source* of these assumptions? Where do they come from? What narrative are they part of, and what is their potential endpoint? Du Bois does not devote a single chapter to answering these questions, but if, as I hope to show, we engage seriously with the poetry in the book, we will find his answers to these questions strewn throughout the long volume. These statements can be assembled into an argument if we allow the poems to serve as its connective tissue.

The poetic account Du Bois gives of the white racial assumptions informing US constitutional law lead him—as the very word "transubstantiation" might suggest—into the matrix of concerns known as political theology. (The term itself was coined by Carl Schmidt, the Nazi jurist who argued that modern political terms are nothing but secularized theological concepts, and who used that thesis as a basis for justifying the right of a sovereign to intervene in politics the way a God intervenes in the world—through what Schmidt called "miracle.") Read through its poetic fragments, *Black Reconstruction* contextualizes "transubstantiation" in a teleology developed over several centuries, one that proclaims that humanity will ultimately and inevitably fulfill itself in white supremacy. This teleology helps justify European imperial conquests and colonization. Du Bois suspected that it also explains the racist violence of US law: the law is based on this prior commitment to a racial teleology and its narrative of fulfillment. At the same time, *Black Reconstruction* also attends to the end(s) of white supremacy and the decadence at the core of its cultural-political movement.

The Imperial Miracle and Christian Typology

Du Bois ends "The White Worker" chapter with the fourth and fifth stanzas from Percy B. Shelley's eight-stanza "Song to the Men of England," a political poem appended to *Masque of Anarchy* (1842):

> Have ye leisure, comfort, calm,
> Shelter, food, love's gentle balm?
> Or what is it ye buy so dear
> With your pain and with your fear?
>
> The seed ye sow, another reaps;
> The wealth ye find, another keeps;
> The robes ye weave, another wears;
> The arms ye forge, another bears.[1]

Read through a conventional Marxist lens, these stanzas alert the white worker to their alienation from their surplus value and their fellow workers.

When placed in the broader context of the imperial miracle, as I call it, these stanzas accumulate unexpected meanings. For Powers, transubstantiation leads to "the problem of lawless legality," which "must be addressed through the *historical registers*" serving as "foundations for the working of legal precedent."[2] One such "historical register" in *Black Reconstruction* derives from a Western, Christian concept of typological fulfillment: the imperial miracle works by a semiotic structure consisting of a prophetic sign (*figura*) that a future messianic event will fulfill. The imperial miracle contrasts with Lenin's and Du Bois's theories, which articulate how a surplus overloads and negates current governance structures based on political organizing in concrete material conditions. The medieval world's religious identities were not racialized compared to today. Nevertheless, they harbored seeds of racial strife, seeing that this Christian typology, *by definition*, could only be universalized through excluding Jews, Muslims, and other non-Christians.[3]

As Europe comes under the sign of whiteness from the early modern period to the present, European imperialism retains, rather than displaces, this form of historicity, because of the solidarity it grants.[4] Du Bois places the white worker within this teleological viewpoint derived from Christianity by mockingly restaging Europe's settling of America as an Eden undone by a racialized Fall:

> America thus stepped forward in the first blossoming of the modern age and added to the Art of Beauty, gift of the Renaissance, and to Freedom of belief, gift of Martin Luther and Leo X, a vision of democratic self-government: the domination of political life by the intelligent decision of free and self-sustaining men. What an area for its realization—endless land of richest fertility, natural resources such as earth seldom exhibited before. . . . It was the Supreme Adventure, the last Great Battle for the West, for that human freedom which would release the human spirit from lower lust for mere meat, and set it free to dream and sing.
>
> *And then some unjust God leaned, laughing, over the ramparts of heaven and dropped a black man in the midst.*
>
> It transformed the world. It turned democracy back to Roman Imperialism and Fascism; it restored caste and oligarchy; it replaced freedom with slavery and withdrew the name of humanity from the vast majority of human beings.[5]

This typology's adherents fear a black stain upon Eden's lush foliage will disrupt European Man's *dominion* over the earth. The black enters prior to and triggers the need for transubstantiation, in this fiction. This does not deny liberal constitutionalism's role in producing racial difference. But it reminds one of Cedric Robinson's concept of racial capitalism since racialization has been indispensable for categorizing and disciplining laborers.[6] But even labor organization could not hold unless law serves capitalism's purposes. Thus, this religious-turned-racial typology has remained in effect. When speaking of racial capitalism, scholars presuppose links between racial and economic exploitation in modernity. This essay suggests that racial capitalism has absorbed into its ideological supports a messianic narrative derived from Christian teleology.

Over several centuries, this new racial solidarity transformed politics and ethics for Europe. David Roediger quotes *The World and Africa* to show how whiteness alters historical and political teleology. Imperial white domination has had terrible effects "upon colored people the world over," Du Bois says. But "*in the end it was even worse when one considers what this attitude did to the European worker.* His aim and ideal was distorted. . . . He began to want not comfort for all men, but power over other men for himself." "The Christian sympathy between rich and poor, the communism of medieval charity, all were thrust into the new straitjacket of thought," that "straightjacket" being capitalism: "the iron law of wags, the population doctrines of Malthus, and the bitter fight against the early trade unions."[7] *The World and Africa's* assessment of whiteness and "The White Worker's" pseudo-genesis story show how racial capitalism twists Europe's liberatory potentialities into new forms of subjugation. The European worker dons the fiction of an ideal that compels democracy to justify injustice, legislate lawlessness, and render unethical acts into ethical norms. Immediately after the Civil War, researcher Carl Schurz finds just this situation when he concludes that white southerners were "unable to conceive of the Negro as possessing any rights at all." To them, "to kill a Negro, they do not deem murder; to debauch a Negro woman, they do not think fornication; to take the property away from a Negro, they do not consider robbery."[8]

Place Shelley's stanzas in this racialized typology and they no longer inspire worker revolution. The poem originally condemned the Peterloo massacre of peacefully protesting workers. Stanzas 1 through 3 ask why the laborer submits to "lords" who "lay ye low"; stanzas 4 and 5 describe the theft of the laborer's gains; stanza 6 inspires political action, and the final stanzas explain that the nation itself will become the grave for the politically complacent. In "The White Worker," stanzas 4 and 5 place the white working class at an impasse. The stanzas accurately describe their exploitation. But stanza 4's opening couplet no longer reads like rhetorical questioning, and stanza 5 no longer incites unrest, since this alienation is a reasonable cost for belonging to this greater racial-messianic project. The greater loss would be overthrowing capitalism to lose this privileged position and, instead, become equal with workers of color, which, in this typology, counts as another sinful fall.

A passage from Du Bois's chapter on post–Civil War Mississippi and Louisiana supports this hypothesis. An observer mentions "poor whites" in northern Mississippi, living "close to the subsistence line . . . without schools, with but few churches. . . . [T]heir ignorance or prejudice bred in them after the emancipation of the Negro, a *dread of sinking to the level of the blacks*."[9] These poor workers fear being on the social level of the blacks because they already share the same (lack of) economic standing. Yet, the impossibility of strictly distinguishing the economic from the social means poor whites can never consistently ensure their social standing against their economic peers. The poor white epitomizes the worker Shelley would rally and the worker who will not risk racial privilege by full-fledged anticapitalist revolt. Their dread comes not from their material destitution, which predates abolition, but from the theoretical *possibility*, let alone the historical fact of a black social equal. In this archival evidence, the law undercuts the Emancipation it codifies but does not assuage the white worker's dread of a fall from racial grace. I now turn to "The Transubstantiation of a Poor White" to ponder the role of "personification," as Powers calls it, in (always failing at) redeeming this fall.[10]

Transubstantiation and Messianic (Un)Fulfillment

Transubstantiation strives to redeem this racial stain through the exaltation and consumption of a messiah who draws other bodies into an economy of sacrifice. The historical typology requires the fulfillment of *figura*. Throughout *Black Reconstruction*, Du Bois explores capitalism's importance to narratives of national belonging in the United States means that, for many, their path to inclusion comes through striving to fulfill the "American Assumption" that "wealth is mainly the result of its owner's effort and that any average worker can by thrift become a capitalist."[11] Since the Civil War, this ideology is almost completely divorced from the nation's economic realities. But even abolition-democracy's liberal proponents like Charles Sumner and Thaddeus Stevens did not see how their "belief in the *self-resurrection* of democracy . . . lent unconscious power to the American Assumption." Constitutionalism is essential to this movement, but so is "self-resurrection"—the materialization of the American Assumption through average workers successfully climbing the economic and social ladders. Particularly in "The Transubstantiation of a Poor White" chapter of *Black Reconstruction,* Du Bois makes Andrew Johnson's presidency a canonical instance of this process. Yes, Johnson is a literary device for debating conflicting theories of Emancipation's legality. But he also epitomizes the poor white's economic mobility while substituting a fantasy of racial superiority for the American Assumption's failure.

The clue comes when Du Bois first mentions Johnson. "The drear destiny of the Poor White South" involved "deserting its economic class and itself," becoming "the instrument by which democracy in the nation was done to death, race provincialism *deified,* and *the world* delivered to plutocracy. The man who led the way with unconscious paradox and contradiction was Andrew Johnson." This contrasts significantly with early twentieth-century historians and biographers crowning Johnson the American working class's champion. Du Bois examines evidence these writers ignored. Johnson compromised his agenda when he realized bringing it to fruition required a strong *multiracial* working class. Johnson would be responsible for upsetting the racial typology undergirding white American identity since the Founding. This, he would not do. Johnson's missteps serve Du Bois's critique of liberal labor leadership.

Remember, when Johnson ran for election, several in a crowd called him "our Moses" when he wished a leader would "arise" to "lead" Americans "safely to their promised land of freedom and happiness." After hearing audience members call him Moses, he replied, "Humble and unworthy as I am, if no other better shall be found, I will indeed be your Moses, and lead you through the Red Sea of war and bondage to a fairer future of liberty and peace." Few figures in the Christian Bible rival Moses for *prefigura* of Jesus. And whoever those figures might be, they do not rival Moses's importance to European philosophers theorizing the political.[12] By accepting this mantle, Johnson promises to fulfill the typology through the elevation of all "Loyal" members of the working classes, such that black workers will have their fair share. Johnson failed, a failure that stems from this typology motivating—and at the same time undoing—his political strivings. Johnson not only serves as a vehicle of Du Bois's critique of mainstream political leadership and its relationship to the white masses. Johnson's political contradictions demonstrate the degradation produced in the pursuit of messianic fulfillment.

Thus, Du Bois replies to Johnson's haughty identification with Moses through a stanza from William Rose Benet's poem "Falconer of God":

> My wild soul waited on as falcons hover.
> I beat the reedy fens as I trampled past.
> I heard the mournful loon
> In the marsh beneath the moon
> And then, with feathery thunder, the bird of my desire
> Broke from the cover
> Flashing silver fire.
> High up among the stars I saw his pinions spire.
> The pale clouds gazed aghast.
> As my falcon dropped upon him, and gript and held him fast.

In contrast to Shelley's poem, which works against its original intent and illustrates how imperial solidarity arrests labor movement, Benet's poem now goes farther in its original direction. In the original four-stanza work, the speaker "fl[i]ngs" their "soul" into the sky like a falcon, which aids in hunting a "heron," "the bird of my desire." Catching that heron would equate to successfully fulfilling one's desire. This effort fails by the third stanza: "My soul dropt through the air—with heavenly plunder?—Gripping the dazzling bird my dreaming knew? Nay! . . . Despoiled of silver plumage, its voice forever stilled / All of the wonder / Gone that ever filled / Its guise with glory." The poem may read like a platitude about the dissatisfaction of capturing one's desired object. That reading assumes that the object one consciously pursues corresponds to the object one unconsciously desires, and that both correspond to the object one captures. These assumptions do not apply to Johnson's "unconscious paradox and contradiction," for thinking he was after the political and economic empowerment of the masses, when he unconsciously sought their disempowerment for a seat at the table of corporate masters.

The question is, What are the political implications of this noncoincidence between conscious objectives, unconscious object of desire, and captured object? Du Bois concludes the "Transubstantiation" chapter by arguing that Johnson did achieve the object of his unconscious desire, but that object was the polar opposite of what he identified in his early political speeches. To revise an earlier quotation, although Johnson identifies himself with Moses, his presidential agenda uncovers his true hope to become Pharaoh: "This change did not come by deliberate thought or conscious desire to hurt—it was rather the tragedy of American prejudice made flesh; so that the man born to narrow circumstances, a rebel against economic privilege, *died with the conventional ambition of a poor white to be the associate and benefactor of monopolists, planters and slave drivers*."

Transubstantiation applies to the Constitution's reinvention of racist conditions, as Powers explains. In this regard, William Seward proves crucial to Johnson's efforts, especially by thwarting the Freedmen's Bureau. Furthermore, Seward's territorial acquisitions are crucial antecedents for the nation's imperial exploits in the 1890s. But in Du Bois's reading, legalism is the object worked over by a subject shaped by the forces of racialism, capitalism, and a wish to become the charismatic leader who can fulfill the messianic role *within* a racial-religious typology, that is, to be "race provincialism *deified*." Thus, Benet's second stanza allegorizes Johnson violently seizing his unconsciously desired object. His desired object—access to oligarchy's prestige and power—was made desirable and obscured by racialization. Johnson hoped it would finally confirm he need not "dread" being on the same "social level as the blacks," and it provided an avenue for fulfilling the messianic promise, the American Assumption, that was with him at every phase of his life.

This formulation identifies the white liberal ally's true challenge, namely, to undo the structures producing their privilege. Johnson could not admit that his principled opposition to corporate elites was actually jealous identification. The price for finally gaining access to their prestige and resources? Allowing the southern oligarchs the freedom to exploit and bludgeon the Negro as they wished, while using Negro bodies as the basis for strengthening a white southern voting bloc. Johnson paid this price because he could not bring himself to actually grant the Negro such economic and political stability. But, as Du Bois famously states, the natural by-product of crushing the Negro means the average white American's economic power would never outweigh the southern oligarch's or the northern industrialist's. Thus, Johnson's "falcon" violently "gript" and killed "the bird of [his] desire" by creating the conditions for a dictatorship of racial capitalism and undoing a different miracle, namely the miracle of proletarian organization.

Johnson, cowering to racial capitalism's interests, helped to stage the United States' partnership with Europe's late-nineteenth-century imperial efforts. Powers notes that "late nineteenth-century justifications for empire" "operated together in the United States," though they seemed incompatible in theory. "A progressivist telos of constitutionalism" allowed the United States to claim that its legal framework could not be accused of perpetuating barbarity. This, the United States combined with a "Burkean attachment to the authority of the Ancient Constitution as emanating out of the temporality or time immemorial."[13] These perspectives make people of color synonymous with barbarism, which means that their full participation in modern democracy would mean barbarians ruling the civilized. The immutability of the Constitution means that this racial metaphysics cannot be altered without destroying legality altogether. Across South Asia, the Caribbean, and Africa, European empires applied this legal framework to counter colonial subjects seeking greater power in colonial governments. Imperialism could declare their civilizing role but malign the colonial subject's self-governance as social retrogression. But that version of legal metaphysics hearkens back to the historical typology discussed so far, in which a narrative of religious redemption becomes an allegory for a single race's unending global supremacy. In what follows, I dig deeper into "the price of disaster" that has been paid as a result of this imperial project's success.

Degradation; or, Nemesis in Flight . . .

Nemesis I call upon you, . . .
Your all-seeing eye looks upon
The lives of man's many races . . .
All who bear the yoke
Of mortality fear you,
You care about the thoughts of all;
The arrogant soul, the reckless one, finds no escape.

—Orpheus, "Hymn to Nemesis"

Transubstantiation perpetuates racism through law and uses a leader to draw others into an economy of sacrifice.[14] Thus, "degradation" becomes much more complicated. To the racial typology's adherents, degradation solely occurs when the black threatens to achieve equal footing with the white. But *Black Reconstruction* asserts that fulfilling this racial typology ensures degradation to the majority of human beings, such that the majority of the "chosen" white few are also imperiled. Du Bois quotes Charles Sumner on this matter. With "the population of the earth" being "about thirteen hundred millions, of whom only three hundred and seventy-five millions are 'white men,'" to "claim exclusive rights for 'white men,'" would "*degrade* nearly three quarters of the Human Family." "Oligarchy" would control and contradict "Republican Government," and "Monopoly" would have "the whole world as its footstool."[15] Poet and educator Leslie Pinckney Hill shares these concerns, which is why Du Bois uses his poem "Armageddon" to conclude *Black Reconstruction's* first chapter. With the title "Armageddon" and a prefatory note extolling "the trammeled millions of colored people the world over . . . of that *spirit of the times* which well nigh destroyed civilization," Hill agrees that the Great War and Great Depression are logical outcomes of a US–European imperial project forged after Reconstruction's collapse.[16]

Hill's romanticism aids Du Bois's effort. Hill places mundane figures in the heroic, universal role, so the Negro and other colonial subjects "look out upon the world" at national and global conflicts and "look in" at their "stricken peers" to assess their political agency. They witness and participate in "the whirlwind and the thundershock, / *The agony of nations* . . . / These *tottering bastions* of mighty states, / This *guillotine of culture*." "Armageddon's" opening lines hearken back to the French Revolution and the Terror, when a potentially progressive movement devolves into a cycle so destructive, figured by "the guillotine," that resolution is impossible except through the movement annulling its own conditions.[17] In the seventh stanza, "Armageddon's" speaker sees this occurring during the Great War: "For looking *out* upon the world, I saw / no hope for future man in those who stand / Upon the heights of power, *save in the tales / Transmitted of their slow decline and fall*." Then, in the penultimate paragraph of *Black Reconstruction's* actual final chapter, the metacritical essay called "The Propaganda of History," Du Bois links national racism to imperial violence in the 1930s: "Immediately in Africa, a black back runs red with the blood of the lash; in

India, a brown girl is raped; in China, a coolie starves; in Alabama, seven darkies are more than lynched. . . . Flames of jealous murder sweep the earth, while brains of little children smear the hills." Had abolition-democracy prevailed, this violence, essential to subjecting populations, would have been drastically curbed, or rendered unnecessary. This destructive tendency means Western imperialism, however impactful it may be now, amounts to a "transient lordship."[18]

Looking inward leads the speaker of "Armageddon" to feel "*unconvinced* that we [colonial subjects] are born the dupes of Providence, / To be a nation's burden and her taunt, / Or Ishmaels of an unchosen land." The poem's title does not mean the end of humanity or, more specifically, the end of blackness. It means "the end of the end." The chaos of war and economic destitution does not confirm the typology but reveals its shortcomings. It creates an aporia it cannot escape through its own terms, subjectivities, or concept of power. The speaker turns away from imperial might to manifest the power of "the weak thing, and the foolish, and the base." Now, to the stanza concluding the "Black Worker" chapter:

> Dark, shackled knights of labor, clinging still
> Amidst a universal wreck of faith
> To cheerfulness, and foreigners to hate.
> These know ye not, these have ye not received,
> But these shall speak to you Beatitudes.
> Around them surge the tides of all your strife,
> Above them rise the august monuments
> Of all your outward splendor, but they stand
> Unenvious in thought, and bide their time.[19]

The poem seeks an exit from this economy sacrificing the majority of humanity and acknowledges the difficulty of the task. For Hill, the answer comes by switching sacrificial economies. The weak receive just reward for their "calm endurance" of racism "without revolt." Hill associates the poem with a "tragic cadence" "express[ing] the passing and the coming life of man," since, as previously stated, current circumstances offer "no hope for future man" except for the "slow decline and fall" of the powerful. But what kind of fall? In "Armageddon," that fall gets redeemed through "calm endurance" "without revolt."[20] Nothing could be further from *Black Recon-*

struction's theoretical, historical, and political account of agency. The fall takes a quite different shape when one no longer depends upon Christian teleology to absorb tragedy.

When Du Bois calls the black "Nemesis" in *Black Reconstruction,* he is not merely exposing a misrecognition among antiblack racists, contra Powers's view of the matter: "The black man is not in fact the 'Nemesis' of American politics. . . . [T]he myth of racial difference only made it seem as though this were so."[21] Nemesis (and, to a lesser extent, Actaeon) plays the more sophisticated role of dislodging historical forces from a Christian teleological framework, pulling Hill's poem and *Black Reconstruction* at large into an overdetermined, nonteleological outlook. As Johan Ludvig Heiberg notes, Nemesis "is the rational . . . in what is contingent" and "expresses unconscious reason, . . . the justice which can rule over what is still regarded contingent."[22] While Heiberg shies away from associating Nemesis with morality, scholarly consensus suggests that Nemesis aims to "restore the moral order whenever it has been violated. In *Some Aspects of the Greek Genius,* Samuel Butcher says Nemesis "punishes" "Insolence or [hubris]," which he characterizes by "pride that is untempered by the sense of human frailty," "a self-centered will recognizing no power outside itself, *and knowing no law but its own impulses.*" Butcher calls this "the deepest source of moral evil" for Greek thought.[23]

No other classical figure could be more relevant to the US situation described in *Black Reconstruction*'s final chapter of historical narrative, "Back Towards Slavery": "*A spirit of lawlessness became widespread.* . . . White men became a law unto themselves. . . . Practically all men went armed and the South reached the extraordinary distinction of being the only modern civilized country where human beings were publicly burned alive."[24] Also, Du Bois associates Seward with Actaeon, the famed hunter who insults Artemis, gets turned into a deer, and then gets devoured by his own hunting hounds. The immediate point, for Du Bois, is that Seward's advice did little to protect Johnson but swayed him into the clutches of southern oligarchs. From the "Proclamation of Amnesty and Reconstruction" onward, Seward minimized the freedperson's much-needed effort to save the Union; to many, Seward appeared increasingly like the mad colleague guiding Johnson to betray his political commitments. Western imperialism infuses whiteness with an always-recuperable messianic destiny. The-black-as-Nemesis and the imperial subject-as-Actaeon are not dei ex machina besmirching an Edenic origin or a messianic destiny. Quite the contrary, the Nemesis indicates that the empire cannot last forever, that contradictions *within* the form, even among its most privileged subjects, will scrape away at the form's coherence.

No wonder, then, that Du Bois selects that particular passage from Hill's poem. The speaker constantly addresses "they" (referring to the colonized) and "ye" (referring to the imperial subject) to acknowledge the incompatibility of the two positions. In practice, as in the poem, they cannot achieve a higher unity.[25] The second-person character in the poem represents the worker privileged (to suffer) under the terms of imperial white domination; this character in the poem disavows any connection with the workers of color, represented by the third-person-plural "they." "They" do not commit to the "American Assumption" or envy its splendorous "monuments." Whereas the white worker fears a fall from racial grace and disavows the fellow worker in this stanza, there are workers of color uninterested in replacing the white worker in the same typology; instead, these workers speak "beatitudes," meaning the meek will inherit the earth on terms incommensurable with imperialism. And that incommensurability, combined with the imperial subject's insolence, means that, too often, the white worker will not "receive" these beatitudes but will continue along the same path, convinced of their success no matter the misstep.

This worldview emerged regionally, nationally, and globally through the counter-revolution of 1876, to the point that "a solid bloc of reaction in the South can always be depended upon to unite with Northern conservatism" and form a national coalition influencing legislation, economics, elections, and more. After "winning the victory which the Fourteenth Amendment tried to deny," the South "uses the Negro population as a basis for his political representation."[26] The "paradox" of this counter-revolution is that it never completely disenfranchised black folk as it hoped to, so the only sure "result of disfranchisement is *to bind the white South hand and foot and deliver it to its own worst self*."[27] Du Bois persuasively links this to late nineteenth- and early twentieth-century imperialism: "Whatever the South gained through its victory in the revolution of 1876 has been paid for at a price which literally staggers humanity. Imperialism, the exploitation of colored labor throughout the world, thrives upon the approval of the United States, and the United States gives that approval because of the South. World war waits on and supports imperial aggression and international jealousy. This was too great a price to pay for anything which the South gained."[28]

From these passages one can arrive at several conclusions. They confirm Powers's observation that US legality allows for equal representation without equal empowerment for its nonwhite citizens. The law and its implementation frequently disrupt the connection between racial representation and effective enfranchisement. The fact that the imperial subject uses racial recognition to defuse political empowerment complicates matters. It makes it unlikely that *Black Reconstruction* inaugurates a "politics of man."[29] To achieve true inclusion, that politics would require second sight to look through the obscurities race produces in oneself and others.[30] The imperial white subject lacks *and* opposes this phenomenological mode, since it would remind this figure of its subjective, epistemological, and historical limits. Without this second sight, one cannot even consider humbling oneself to avoid Nemesis's retribution. This leads to the frustrating conclusion that this imperial attitude will not stop pursuing global domination. A national or global progressive turn will involve Western imperialism devouring itself. Correcting the hyperinflated image of whiteness as an ideal will feel like degradation, which makes it no less of a requirement for radical change.

Yet, there is more to knowing the full vent of Nemesis's righteous indignation. Attempting to rescue Eurocentrism from itself will only increase the number of its victims. The contemporary move to salvage any political ideology simply by diversifying its members appears more problematic in this light. The racialized Christian typology and economy of sacrifice it operates has always required the consumption of populations all over the world. Du Bois would not have today's readers deny the incommensurability of imperial and black perspectives, as he addressed it in 1935 in *Black Reconstruction*'s final chapter: "This, the American black man knows: his fight here is a fight to the finish. Either he dies or wins. If he wins it will be by no subterfuge or evasion of amalgamation. . . . There can be no compromise. This is the last great battle of the West."[31] To be clear, Du Bois is not condemning mixed-race identity. He complains of what one would now call tokenized forms of diversity that mistakenly equate increased representation with increased empowerment, when the very need for diversity indicates that this convenient equation is insufficient. That tokenization always requires the person of color's affective labor to process the complexities of the imperial subject's institutional positions. At its best, such work leads from recognition of the minority subject to the conversion of the imperial subject. But this revives the very narrative of redemption and fulfillment that produces racial violence. While there is much work all can do to tear down imperialism, when people of color strive to redeem the privileged subjects of imperial white domination, the former gives up the position of Nemesis and instead becomes Actaeon, vulnerable to being devoured by their own effort. It is up to those who have gained from imperial white domination to relinquish this position and the resources it offers, not to draw others back into its cycles of violence.

To clarify, a faithful reading of *Black Reconstruction* separates the Nemesis of righteous indignation from the Nemesis of divine jealousy, since the latter minimizes the goddess's epistemological and moral role. The passages from *Black Reconstruction* evoke the former, not the latter. To borrow a word from Hill, the "unenvious" position promotes justice and is uninterested in taking the imperial subject's place.[32] The racializing of redemption as a destiny for white supremacy must collapse. The logic of Nemesis would first restore the sense of human frailty to *all* humans, leaving no exception, which means no group is chosen for sacrifice any more than another is chosen to reap sacrifice's rewards. When Du Bois says that the black's battle is the "*last* Great Battle of the West," he mirrors his mock description of colonial settlers imagining America. In "The White Worker" chapter, the last battle of the West aimed to fulfill the racial typology; in "Back Towards Slavery," the last battle seeks a way out of that typology altogether.

This is a far cry from a Hegelian-style battle "*to* the death" and instead calls forth a "struggle *with* and *from* death, a struggle that seeks to go beyond the death in life."[33] The imperial subject assumes they are fully alive, that they possess the only effective standard for judging viable life, and that, at bottom, other racialized populations are striving to enter this form of life to achieve freedom, justice, truth, and so on. Although Du Bois admits that Western Europe offers several "gifts" to the world, from its medieval moment up through modernity, his use of Hill's "Armageddon" suggests that black people have given gifts to modernity as well. One would be right to assume that among several gifts Hill mentions the gift of song, which would agree with Du Bois's claim in *The Souls of Black Folk*. But for this essay's purposes, I am most interested in Hill saying that black people possess "the gift of feeling for all forms of life," and the gift of "wide / Adaptive power" for confronting contingency. Blackness's aporetic relationship to Western terms of living and belonging grant it an intellectual, affective, and performative capacity for engaging humanity's heterogeneity as an end in itself, endowed with dignity, rather than as a threat to suppress or a deviation to fix. Most of all, this means that the terms of life are not (and cannot be) finally fixed, and that *Black Reconstruction* recruits the tragic in order to make contingency and frailty central to understanding life, once again.

Black Reconstruction's problematic remains completely relevant today. Powers reminds readers of *Black Reconstruction* that racist happenings in the US South cannot be minimized to regional peculiarities. They also inform national and transnational political, legislative, and economic decisions. Powers persuasively argues that liberal responses to these problems are limited insofar as they uncritically turn to the legal codes that produce racism even as they promise to ensure long-term protections against injustice.[34] To Powers's contributions, this essay adds that the imperial miracle is an oblique but significant path by which Du Bois critiques empire. To perceive this aspect of the book, one must work through the poems closing several of *Black Reconstruction*'s chapters to move across disparate intellectual, aesthetic, and political fields. This account contends that the imperial miracle provides the broader background as to why Du Bois required a concept of transubstantiation that went beyond conventional Marxist thought, as Powers argues. The violence of law reinstates a prior commitment to a racial typology and its narrative of fulfillment. But a charismatic leader must intervene, posing himself as the embodiment of the American Assumption, and, from there, spearhead the legislative effort that substitutes a racial superiority complex for the economic degradation suffered by the masses. This leader's power is measured partly by how it wins the masses over to sacrifice their well-being on behalf of this untenable arrangement, which never fulfills its racial or economic goals for the majority of its imperial subjects, let alone for the majority of humanity. This thesis also explains why the turn away from this typology is so difficult, seeing that it promises to turn virtually any setback into another progressive step toward fulfilling the messianic dream. This morbid perseverance counts as faithfulness to the signs (*prefigura*) anticipating the messiah's arrival, when all this loss will be redeemed.

This narrative is still at work today. The transnational political and economic structures organizing the US-European imperial relationship are eroding and have yet to react effectively to the Crash of 2008—if "effective" means addressing the economic destitution of the masses, not just restoring the balance sheets of financial elites whose deregulations, manipulations of the finance economy, and outright theft caused the chaos. Beyond this, these and related financial elites have demonstrated their power to limit the mechanisms for democratic decision-making in their respective nations or transnational structures. Far Right forces have rallied effectively across the North Atlantic's imperial hubs by interpreting the global economic emergency as another instance when a laughing god has dropped into their Western Eden the refugee from the Middle East, from North Africa, or from Russia's neighboring states. Liberal and even leftist intellectuals have condemned the actions, but they have done so in ways meant to save the European intellectual legacy, though they are unable to detach this legacy from a typology that, as Sumner gets quoted saying, excludes the majority of humanity, past and present, from political agency. Meanwhile, in the United States, racist backlash to the Obama administration has reached mammoth proportions despite the irony that President Obama has outperformed all expectations in salvaging and perpetuating America's imperial might. The fact that a short-circuit in racial symbolism (with a black president, First Family, etc.), coupled with new demographics, could trigger such brutality and defenses for it, indicates that violence is the conjoined twin of racism. Violence maintains political advantages. Violence recovers political advantages. And violence expresses frustration at not being able to recover said advantages. No matter the specific circumstance, violence is constant. But it is a violence assumed to be working toward a globe-encompassing goal that will redeem all the losses of white supremacy in due time.

Black Reconstruction suggests that Europe's and America's others must allow that "guillotine of culture" to annul itself and devote their energies to the miracle of proletarian organization, once again. Critical awareness of today's circumstances suggests that carrying out the miracle of proletarian organization will not occur peacefully, for it requires a break from an epoch-shaping typology of chosenness and fulfillment. That break will be painful, even traumatic to that typology's privileged subjects. Whereas the poetry helps to link the prose episodes in this tangle of issues, tragedy reorients the reader to see the persistent attachment to this messianic narrative as hubris that triggers righteous indignation. Nemesis, as Du

Bois utilizes the figure, raises the stakes for all involved, though. The imperial miracle's privileged subjects experiencing this break will help restore a respect for contingency, natural law, and, most of all, humanity's frailty. To interfere with this experience will obscure the progressive goals in mind by reducing Nemesis's righteous indignation to mere jealous identifications and revitalize the West's economy of sacrifice. Therefore, to the *New York Times* reviewer who called *Black Reconstruction* "a solid history of the period, an economic treatise, a philosophical discussion, a poem, a work of art all rolled into one," one can reply affirmatively. *Black Reconstruction* takes this odd, inventive shape to reveal the truth about Civil War and Reconstruction, and, this essay suggests, to call upon alternative forms of justice, yet to come.

Notes

1. W. E. B. Du Bois, *Black Reconstruction in America, 1860–1880* (New York: Free Press, 1995), 31.
2. Allison Powers, "Tragedy Made Flesh: Constitutional Lawlessness in Du Bois' *Black Reconstruction*," *Comparative Studies of South Asia, Africa, and the Middle East* 34, no. 1 (2014): 121.
3. Kathleen Biddick, "Dead Neighbor Archives: Jews, Muslims, and the Enemy's Two Bodies," in *Political Theology and Early Modernity*, ed. Graham Hammill and Julia Reinhard Lupton (Chicago: University of Chicago Press, 2012).
4. Lindon Barrett, *Racial Blackness and Discontinuity of Western Modernity*, ed. Justin A. Joyce, Dwight A. McBride, and John Carlos Rowe (Urbana: University of Illinois Press, 2013).
5. Du Bois, *Black Reconstruction*, 29–30.
6. Cedric Robinson, *Black Marxism: The Making of the Black Radical Tradition* (Chapel Hill: University of North Carolina Press, 2000).
7. W. E. B. Du Bois, *The World and Africa* (Oxford: Oxford University Press, 2007), 14.
8. Du Bois, *Black Reconstruction*, 136.
9. Ibid., 471.
10. Powers, "Tragedy Made Flesh," 117.
11. Du Bois, *Black Reconstruction*, 201.
12. For more on this topic, see Graham Hammill, *The Mosaic Constitution: Political Theology and Imagination from Machiavelli to Milton* (Chicago: University of Chicago Press, 2012).
13. Powers, "Tragedy Made Flesh," 119.

14. *Epigraph:* Orpheus, *The Orphic Hymns,* trans. Apostolos N. Athanassakis and Benjamin M. Wolkow (Baltimore: Johns Hopkins University Press, 2013), 50.

15. Du Bois, *Black Reconstruction,* 197.

16. Leslie Pinckney Hill, "Armageddon," in *Wings of Oppression* (Boston: Stratford, 1921), 5.

17. On the "guillotine" as condition and hindrance of French Revolution, see Rebecca Comay, *Mourning Sickness: Hegel and the French Revolution* (Stanford, CA: Stanford University Press, 2010).

18. Hill, "Armageddon," 8.

19. Du Bois, *Black Reconstruction,* 16.

20. Hill, "Armageddon," 10.

21. Powers, "Tragedy Made Flesh," 122.

22. Heiberg qtd. in Laura Liva, "Nemesis: From the Ancient Goddess to a Modern Concept," in *Kierkegaard's Literary Figures and Motifs*, tome 2: *Gulliver to Zerlina*, ed. Katalin Nun and Jon Stewart (Surrey, UK: Ashgate, 2015), 157.

23. Samuel Butcher, "Some Aspects of the Greek Genius," (London: Macmillan, 1916), 109–10.

24. Du Bois, *Black Reconstruction,* 700.

25. Ibid., 16.

26. Ibid., 706.

27. Ibid., 705.

28. Ibid., 706.

29. Powers, "Tragedy Made Flesh," 123.

30. W. E. B. Du Bois, *The Souls of Black Folk*, in *Du Bois: Writings*, ed. Nathan Huggins (New York: Library of America, 1986), 364.

31. Du Bois, *Black Reconstruction,* 703.

32. Ibid., 16.

33. David Marriott, "Judging Fanon," *Rhizomes* 29 (2016), http://rhizomes.net/issue29/marriott.html.

34. For proof, one need only reference Kentucky's "Blues Lives Matter" law, which responds to protesters calling out racial profiling and assaults carried out by police by making assaults on police a hate crime, while the victims of police attacks are just as vulnerable, if not more.

III

Du Bois in the Space between the Known and the Imagined

5

The People, Rhetoric, and Affect

On the Political Force of Du Bois's The Souls of Black Folk

Melvin L. Rogers

> O, Let America be America again—The land that never has been yet—
> And yet must be.
>
> —Langston Hughes

In recent years, the concept of "the people" has received sustained attention from political theorists.[1] At issue is the proper understanding of the category, who comprises it, how it expands, and its boundaries in the context of globalization. Unfortunately, political theorists, especially in the American context, have said very little about its explicit or implied deployment in thinking about the expansion of the American polity along racial and gender lines.[2] How, for instance, were women and African Americans able to invoke the language of "the people" even as they were consistently identified as standing outside the boundaries of the political and affective concerns of the nation?

I do not seek to settle this question here, although I shall come back to it at the end. The more immediate purpose of this essay is twofold. First, to provide a substantive account of the meaning of the term—what I call its *descriptive* and *aspirational* dimensions. And second, to use that account as the framework for understanding the rhetorical character of W. E. B. Du Bois's classic work *The Souls of Black Folk* (1903),[3] and its relationship to what we might call the cognitive-affective dimension of judgment that has received recent attention in moral and political philosophy.[4] On the one hand, the people symbolize those individuals whose rights and privileges of citizenship are enshrined in a constitutional structure. On the other hand, the idea of the people reflexively serves as a space for refounding the polity along more inclusive lines.[5] Placed against this backdrop, Du Bois's approach illustrates the kind of normative work the category of "the people" makes possible in democracy. And the gap between the descriptive and aspirational dimensions of "the people" prompts me to attend more carefully to the various mechanisms employed to bridge this divide.

The attempt to move from description to aspiration highlights the space of contestation and uncertainty that the politically dispossessed have occupied. In this context, reformers have articulated transcendent ethical visions of what kind of community America ought to be and the virtues needed to realize and sustain that way of life, but without any certainty that those descriptions would be realized. This dual aspect of the people, I suggest, encouraged Du Bois in his effort to stimulate and direct America's political and ethical imagination. The distinction, then, between the two dimensions of the people allowed Du Bois to appeal to the polity amid exclusion—to call his fellows, in Hughes's language from the epigraph, to "the land that never has been yet"—even as the certainty of success was denied to him.

To make good on this argument, my essay unfolds in three parts. In the next section, I lay out more carefully the two dimensions of the people and the normative presupposition it implies. I focus on the transformative possibility the idea of the people makes possible in a democratic society. This prompts us to ask after ways of bridging the divide between the descriptive and aspirational views of the people.

In the second and third sections and related to this last point, I specifically take up this bridging mechanism through a reading of *Souls*. Here I argue that as a work of political theory, *Souls* draws a specific connection between rhetoric (i.e., a mode of speaking and writing to persuade one's audience), on the one hand, and emotional states such as sympathy and shame, on the other, as a way to close the gap between the descriptive people and its aspirational counterpart. By emphasizing rhetoric, I mean to suggest that *Souls* attempts to craft a common horizon for author and reader from which common emotional judgments regarding racial inequality might be reached. For Du Bois, this common horizon is not merely the result of a fortuitous union but emanates from a shared political identity that can, in turn, be used to guide the responses of the community and its inhabitants as to the justice or injustice of the judgments they make and the actions they undertake.

The theme of rhetoric, its political character, and its relationship to emotional states has oddly received little to no attention in the literature on *Souls*.[6] To be sure, I agree with, and in some instances reiterate, the importance Arnold Rampersad attaches to Du Bois's training in rhetoric, especially while a student in residence at Harvard University between 1888 and 1892. Nonetheless, my argument extends his insight by underscoring the politically transformative possibilities Du Bois accords rhetoric in potentially influencing the character of white Americans. But if the political character of rhetoric has not been attended to by Rampersad, the theme of rhetoric has equally gone unnoticed by those otherwise interested in the political vision of the text.[7]

My aim is to correct this oversight, and in doing so to elucidate how Du Bois enacts the relationship between rhetoric and emotional states, revealing the democratic character of his approach. On my view, we come to appreciate the ways in which the art of rhetoric and the political aspiration of the text are constitutively tied together as part of a single desire to enrich the judgment of the reader regarding the plight of African Americans. To appreciate this, I follow Du Bois back from his 1926 essay "Criteria of Negro Art" to his 1903 work *Souls*, where we find the key to understanding the rhetorical character of the latter: "all art is propaganda and ever must be," a mode of persuading the community in the direction of some cause that neither panders nor manipulates but enlists the judgment of the reader, what I will often refer to as Du Bois affirming the reflective agency of his audience.[8] This understanding of propaganda, I argue, formalizes his earlier training in rhetoric. Through the art of rhetoric, *Souls* attempts to project and vivify a form of citizenship, and it seeks to evoke in the reader those desires and actions commensurate with realizing that life. Du Bois's stance toward America is exemplified by his intense desire to direct the sentiments of the reader so as to address the racist division that separated blacks and whites—what he famously calls "the Veil"—and that produced political and ethical inequality. He therefore seeks to make the reader receptive to the alternative vision of America he presents. The motivating force for this specific kind of engagement is the importance to democratic life of the aspirational vision of the people. In the conclusion, I will tentatively suggest that the reading of Du Bois I offer begins to answer the much larger question with which we began.

Description and Aspiration: On the Political Force of the People

Since its modern incarnation in the eighteenth century, the idea of the people has worked to dissolve the line of demarcation between rulers and ruled that previously defined monarchical and aristocratic regimes. For if the rulers and the ruled shared a political identity—that is, were members of one and the same citizenry, equal before the law—the power held by the former was merely fiduciary in quality and so meant the latter was never alienated once and for all from the source of authority. The idea of the people served as the solution to the problem modern representative government posed to the status of the minority, who might otherwise be at the mercy of a tyrannical majority. The people, understood as the ultimate source for conferring legitimacy, rendered the position of power holders changeable. But the changeable character of power holders rested on a deeper descriptive designation—it referred to those with rights and privileges of citizenship, enshrined in a constitutional structure and often on visible display during electoral cycles. Both the Levellers of the seventeenth century and American Founders of the eighteenth century agreed on this point, despite the degrees of radicalism that separated them.

The idea of the people was also an aspirational category that formed the morally appealing core of democracy and extended beyond electoral politics. This idea called to mind an "imagined community," "dream country," or "democratic wish" to which political reformers appealed, and in which they redescribed the boundaries of the polity.[9] In the nineteenth and twentieth centuries especially, women and African Americans exploited this category. Both groups articulated their grievances to the public in the form of public addresses, treatises, and literary texts in the face of severely compromised legal standing or no legal standing whatsoever even as they sought to give the content of the public a new meaning.[10] The divergence between the people as they *were* and as reformers longed for them *to be* created a space for potentially mending fractures at the core of the polity, a space in which one's political and ethical standing might subsequently be affirmed.

To be sure, the language of the people was not consistently invoked by reformers. But both the subtle presupposition of the people that informed political action and explicit invocation in texts entailed a specific view of democratic legitimacy and, as a result, the possibility of transforming the polity. Here we might think of Elizabeth Cady Stanton's plea before the New York State Legislature in the 1850s to recognize and honor the equal standing of women.[11] We might consider, for instance, Du Bois's specific use of the term, when he remarks in *Souls* that African Americans "have pleaded with a headstrong, careless *people* to despise not Justice, Mercy, and Truth, lest the nation be smitten with a curse."[12] Still further, we might recall Martin Luther King Jr.'s classic 1963 "I Have a Dream" speech, whose central metaphor calls America to a vision of itself not yet actualized.

Stanton, Du Bois, and King are connected by their shared belief that democracy's logic of legitimacy dissolved the connection between political power, on the one hand, and those specific people, on the other, who claimed exclusive deployment of that power. Since the people could never be represented at any given time in their totality via the binding acts of the polity, legitimacy rested on a critical reflexivity—what made dreaming possible—if the risk of domination was going to be avoided. In Margaret Canovan's words, the gap between description and aspiration "left room for appeals to the people against the people's government," and this appeal process necessarily extended beyond voting itself.[13] The appeal process, as Jason Frank underscores, thus reveals a "people that are productively never at one with themselves."[14] As such, pleading with members of the American polity and eliciting their judgment, as Du Bois and others often did, implied at least one firm belief that connected those with and without political and ethical standing—namely, that who the people are at one time need not exhaust who they may yet become. Their actions suggest that the political force of the people followed from the iterative process of contestation it made possible, but which it could never finally settle. The power and magnetism of the category thus derived from its persistent indeterminacy, from the paradox that the idea of the people is both a presupposition of democratic life and a not yet realized ideal.

The space of contestation brings into view an important fact about the politically dispossessed and signals the importance of Du Bois's view of democratic development. First, the need to occupy this space points to the asymmetries in power—that is, the legal deficiencies of a society that claims to be well ordered. And this is, in the first instance, primarily about one's *political standing* as a rights-bearing member of the polity. Second, and crucially, these deficiencies cannot exclusively refer to a system of abstract rights that attach to persons by virtue of their political standing, since the problem runs deeper but must also denote the larger societal framework of valuation in which persons are located. "He simply wishes," writes Du Bois, "to make it possible for a man to be both a Negro and an American, without being cursed and spit upon by his fellows, without having the doors of Opportunity closed roughly in his face."[15] This, in the second instance, is about the *ethical life* of the community to which one belongs and is not reducible to the rights that citizens possess. Indeed, the passage quoted is located in the first chapter of *Souls*, "Of Our Spiritual Strivings," where Du Bois signals by virtue of the title his concern with the interior life of African Americans and how it is adversely affected by those who look on them "in amused contempt and pity."[16] I refer to the political-ethical character of this space to mark the basic point about *Souls:* Du Bois attempts to address and make the reader sensitive to the experiential quality of exclusion in its multiple dimensions—from African Americans' interactions with public agents and agencies to their mundane and private transactions with their fellows, and finally, to their self-understanding.[17] Du Bois's democratic vision aspires to effect a transformation at the deepest levels of the self, so that democracy becomes, in John Dewey's language, "as a way of life."[18]

Two features of the descriptive and aspirational dimensions of the people need to be underscored, since they prepare the way for what we might call the perfectionist bent of *Souls*. The first dimension relates to how we should understand the transcendent ethical vision mentioned above. Does the content of the ethical vision, in Jürgen Habermas's language, refer to an "untapped normative substance of the system of rights laid down in the original document of the constitution?"[19] Or does it entail a deeper transformation, whose aim is to reshape the normative character of the polity itself? The second issue relates to the space between description and aspiration that the politically dispossessed occupy. This space, following Claude

Lefort, denotes "the [acknowledged] dissolution of the markers of certainty" in political life, and the ever-present markers of contingency.[20]

Habermas's language above emerges in the context of addressing the paradox of founding at the heart of democratic theory, the belief that a constitutional assembly, for instance, "cannot itself vouch for the legitimacy of the rules according to which it was constituted."[21] This paradox leads, in Habermas's understanding, to an "infinite regress" in trying to ascertain legitimate foundations. I am less interested in the paradox itself and more concerned with the solution Habermas offers and what this proposal means for understanding Du Bois. It is worth citing Habermas at length, to put on full display the philosophical slippage at the core of his thinking:

> I prefer not to meet this objection [that is, the paradox of founding] by recourse to the transparent objectivity of ultimate moral insights that are supposed to bring the regress to a halt. Rather than appeal to moral realism that would be hard to defend, I propose that we understand the regress itself as the understandable expression of the future-oriented character, or openness, of the democratic constitution: in my view, a constitution that is democratic—not just in its content but also according to its source of legitimation—is a tradition-building project with a clearly marked beginning in time. All the later generations have the task of actualizing the still-untapped normative substance of the system of rights laid down in the original document of the constitution. . . . To be sure, this fallible continuation of the founding event can break out of the circle of a polity's groundless discursive self-constitution only if this process . . . can be understood in the long run as a self-correcting learning process.[22]

Observe that Habermas opens the passage by rejecting moral realism but then concludes by interpreting the transcendent ethical vision of later generations as actualizing a latent, but untapped normative substance. The ethical visions on offer do not put in place something absent; rather, they simply bring what is there, at a morally primitive level, to fruition. As such, the learning process to which Habermas refers at the end of the passage is meant to denote the acquisition of an ethical vision that is implicit but does not itself touch the substance of that vision. This most certainly sounds like the position of a moral realist. We can allay any doubts regarding my reading by attending to the line of consistency that Habermas draws through history, uniting both constitutional founders and reformers: "All participants must be able to recognize the project as *the same* throughout history and to judge it from *the same perspective*."[23]

But this does not seem right. Notice that this account muddles the descriptive and aspirational dimensions of the people, and, in Du Bois's case, Habermas's account is unable to confront the ethical disparity at the core of the American polity. What, for instance, would it mean for Du Bois to "start with the same standards as the founders" or to judge the American project from "the same perspective"? After all, it was precisely the normative basis of social life that Du Bois hoped to redescribe. The aim was to make the polity more inclusive both with respect to the juridical standing of African Americans and with respect to their social but nonpolitical position in the eyes of their white counterparts. Here we should recall the brief but important aim of the first chapter of *Souls* in which democracy is viewed not only as a system of cooperation among rights holders but also as a way of life in which those rights are sustained and ennobled. As a result, we cannot draw a line of historical consistency that ties the descriptive and aspirational views of the people together, without denying that the political-ethical world Du Bois envisioned was radically different from the one on offer by the Founders.[24] It thus seems more accurate to say that Du Bois begins with a normative horizon that is developmentally open to the cognitive-affective capacities human beings possess. In fact, these capacities—among which is included the capacity for sympathy and shame—and their cultivation are precisely what Du Bois believes is fundamental in the fight against the political and ethical inequities in the United States. This is why, as I discuss in the next section, Du Bois openly describes *Souls* as a work concerned with democratic development.

The moment we acknowledge the political-ethical disparity at the core of the American polity, we must simultaneously confront the fact that the space between description and aspiration was animated by contingency and uncertainty. For it was never certain that those who were legally recognized would respond appropriately to claims of inclusion. The uncertainty of political success made faith in the convincing character of one's appeal necessary; political action was at once encouraged, even as belief in expected outcomes was circumscribed. And this uncertainty raised the all-important issue of how to effectively bridge the divide between the people as fact and the people as ideal—that is, to think more deliberately about the art of persuasion and what it may yet make possible. It is to this issue, and the details of *Souls*, to which we must now turn.

Between Description and Aspiration: The Turn to Rhetoric

Published in 1903, *The Souls of Black Folk* is a collection of fourteen essays, some of which were based on pieces previously published. Despite the distinct methodological approaches informing the essays, which give the book an uneven character of never wholly being philosophy, history, sociology, or literature, Du Bois is clear that there is "a unity to the book, not simply the general unity of the larger topic, but a unity of purpose in the distinctively subjective note that runs in each essay."[25] The unity consists in a critical and courageous engagement to dramatize the problem of racial inequality, the institutional and psychological motivations for sustaining the second-class status of African Americans, and its impact on those who live behind the veil, including Du Bois himself. As David Levering Lewis convincingly shows, the book did not simply pass quietly into the night but was received with an intensity to match the passion with which Du Bois composed his text:

> *The Souls of Black Folk* went into its third printing in June of its first year. By October 1903, [A. C.] McClurg [and Company] was selling about two hundred copies weekly of a second edition. . . . Five years after publication, 9,595 books had been sold. For a controversial work about African-Americans by an African-American, such sales were exceptional, and, by any measure, the book enjoyed an impressive run. The London first of Constable published a British edition in the spring of 1905 and Max Weber's expectation that there would soon be a German translation was still very much alive.[26]

If the idea of "the people" so central to democratic life opened up space for evocative appeals for reimagining and reconstituting the polity, then *Souls* sought to give that reconstitution direction. In short, it sought to answer the following question: How do you move the people, and here we mean those white Americans enjoying the rights and privileges of American democracy, such that they will embrace an expanded view of themselves? In reading *Souls* as a response to this question, I argue we should see the text as working in the domain of rhetoric. In working in the domain of rhetoric, *Souls* honors the judgment of the reader, leaving their reflective agency intact.

The turn to rhetoric has received renewed attention by political theorists concerned to explore the subtleties of deliberation.[27] As Bryan Garsten notes: "When speakers or writers try to persuade us of something, they are confronting us with a particular situation in speech. . . . [T]hey are . . . drawing upon and reorganizing our existing patterns of thought and emotion—they are appealing to our capacity for judgment."[28] This formulation might easily be read as describing Du Bois's orientation as well, encouraging his readers from the outset of *Souls* to study his words with him so that they may arrive at shared judgments regarding the plight of African Americans. Attesting to the role of rhetoric in *Souls,* Arnold Rampersad explains: "For the first fifty years and more of his life [Du Bois] showed the mark of classical principles of rhetoric. . . . *The Souls of Black Folk* is overwhelming evidence" of this fact.[29]

This should not be surprising given Du Bois's training as a graduate student at Harvard University under the instruction of the English professor Barrett Wendell.[30] The central text for the course Du Bois took with Wendell was *The Principles of Rhetoric* (1878), written by Adams Sherman Hill, the Boylston Professor of Rhetoric and Oratory at Harvard (1876–1904). Located wholly in the Aristotelian and Ciceronian school of thinking, Hill underscores the purpose of rhetoric from the outset of his work: Rhetoric "uses knowledge, not as knowledge, but as power."[31] One of the important aims rhetoric serves, in good classical fashion, is political and ethical development.[32] This point was not lost on Du Bois.

But if Rampersad notes Du Bois's training in this regard, he seems unconcerned with rhetoric as power, as containing the possibility for political and ethical transformation, and with the particular formalized expression of it in *Souls.* Unfortunately, this has not been attended to by those interested in the political character of the work. Yet the power of *Souls* is bound up with its aspiration to persuade through an appeal to affirmative and negative emotional states, namely, sympathy and shame. Indeed, it is precisely Du Bois's quest to evoke in the reader sympathy for the suffering of black people and shame in being complicit in their suffering that was the key to involving and directing the judgments of his white counterparts. Sympathy and shame potentially enrich the perceptual capacity of Americans, helping them see, feel, and respond to the world and their place therein in the appropriate way. *Souls* depends on the ability of readers to use their independent judgment, and to this extent it respects their equal capacity for critical appraisal.

I begin with defending the rhetorical character of *Souls* through Du Bois's 1926 claim that all "art is propaganda, and ever must be"—that is, Du Bois's rearticulated pronouncement of Hill's earlier description of rhetoric. As Du Bois explained in *Dusk of Dawn* of 1940, reflecting on the period in which *Souls* was composed: "My attention from the first was focused on democracy and *democratic development* and upon the problem of the admission of my people into the freedom of democracy."[33] I then will turn in the next section to address the emotional states to which the rhetoric of the text is directed.

In "Criteria of Negro Art" of 1926, an essay ostensibly directed to embolden black artists against the humiliating and exclusionary standards imposed on them by white America, Du Bois offers one of his most striking statements that helps us understand what he intended much earlier in *Souls:* "Thus all art is propaganda and ever must be. . . . I stand in utter shamelessness and say that whatever art I have for writing has been used always for propaganda for gaining the right of black folk to love and enjoy."[34] In isolation the first of these sentences might well strike the reader as odd, especially for those of us who see in propaganda the opportunity to manipulate and deceive the public. And yet, the passage is prefaced by Du Bois's explicit explanation that artists are conveyers of moral and political truth, in possession of tools for bringing truth into view for their fellows: "First of all, he has used the truth—not for the sake of truth . . . but . . . as the one great vehicle of universal understanding. Again artists have used goodness—goodness in all its aspects of justice, honor, and right—not for sake of an ethical sanction but as the one true method of gaining sympathy and human interest."[35]

When Du Bois weds truth and goodness to the work of the artist and art to propaganda, he means for the reader to understand art as a vehicle for expanding the horizon of the recipient. The recipient is brought to a wider view of the world and their place within it than is currently on offer. This is why Du Bois encourages black artists to resist the need to satisfy their white audiences' desire for "literary and pictorial racial prejudgment[s] which deliberately distort truth and justice, as far as colored races are concerned."[36]

This description of art as a vehicle for persuasion is motivated by the wider context in which artists are located. But Du Bois is not simply providing direction to would-be artists; rather, he means to signal something about his own method as a writer. Importantly, Du Bois treats art as a much wider category to include his own literary engagements with the public and not simply those expressed by his works of fiction such as *The Quest of the Silver Fleece* (1911) or *Dark Princess* (1928), thus drawing *Souls* into the orbit of propaganda. This move is consistent with Hill's description of rhetoric as "*the* art" containing "principles [to] which, consciously or unconsciously, a good writer or speaker must conform."[37] *Souls* is thus the product of an artist of letters and as such exemplifies the aims stipulated decades later in "Criteria."

As an artist of letters—that is, a rhetorician—Du Bois employs propaganda in an effort to provide access for African Americans to "love and enjoy," and this consciously informs his work. Or, to put it differently, *Souls* is an attempt to persuade his white counterparts to embrace an alternative view of America. In his view, the aim is to articulate a vision not simply of what the "world could be if it were really a beautiful world" but of a world to be enjoyed by "all of America."[38] For this reason, William Ferris writes of *Souls:* "Du Bois is a literary artist who can clothe his thought in such forms of poetic beauty that we are captivated by the opulent splendor and richness of his diction, *while our souls are being stirred by his burning eloquence.*"[39] One should read the use of "souls" in this passage by Ferris as denoting the moral and emotional nature of human beings that Du Bois is seeking to transform, which is consistent with the rhetorical tradition. For the aim of rhetoric, Cicero explains, "is to rouse the people when languishing and to restrain them when impetuous." "Who," he asks, "can exhort people to virtue more passionately than the orator, and who can call them back from vice more vigorously?"[40] Hence *Souls* pleads with a "headstrong, careless people to despise not Justice, Mercy, and Truth, lest the nation be smitten with a curse."[41] Du Bois thus attends to the "souls" of black folk—both the work they may yet contribute and the deprivation they experience—in order to tell the reader something about and to redirect the "souls" of white folk.

But the artist "becomes the apostle of truth and right not by choice but by inner and outer compulsion."[42] By inner compulsion Du Bois seems to have in mind a desire to proffer grander visions of life—that is, to give content to the image of what the people may yet become. And the artist is also moved by outer compulsion because those visions of life stand in tension with and seek to address the world currently on display. Inner and outer compulsion is thus a dynamic and creative relationship that brings into view the experiential quality of black life that is in need of a response. Du Bois uses such experiences as a way to guide the moral and emotional nature of his fellows.

In fact, the aim of rhetoric is to take the reader to the experiential source from which appropriate emotions and judgments spring. The dynamic relationship between inner and outer compulsion that Du Bois describes in "Criteria" exemplifies and enacts Hill's claim: "We are made to feel by being taken to the sources of feeling."[43] This approach fuels the "storied" or "narrativized" structure of *Souls*, the way many of its chapters turn on the detailed depictions of dreams unrealized (chapters 2, 4, 12, and 13), communities destroyed (chapters 4 and 5), and lives lost (chapters 11 and 13). "Let me on the coming pages," Du Bois says at the conclusion of chapter 1 of *Souls*, "tell again in many ways, with loving emphasis and deeper detail, that men may listen to the striving in the souls of black folk."[44] To listen, for Du Bois, entails that the audience will actively seek to comprehend, interpret, and evaluate what is being heard. The aim is to evoke an emotional response in the reader that might generate a reasoned desire to alleviate the condition of African Americans specifically and to expand the political-ethical imagination of the broader citizenry. For Du Bois, then, it is the repulsive conditions African Americans endure under the weight of Jim Crow that serve as the backdrop for his reflections—a motivating force that infuses and transfigures his efforts to move his readers to a position of moral rectitude. This much he suggests in "Criteria": "I am one who tells the truth and exposes evil and seeks with Beauty and for Beauty to set the world right."[45] Of course Du Bois is sensitive to a view of the artist whose vision of beauty stands above and is unconditioned by the truth of public atrocities—a vision of the artist that, in Richard Rorty's language, pursues her craft in the service of "private perfection."[46] But Du Bois is committed to the proposition that "here and now and in the world in which I work they [beauty and the truth of life] are for me unseparated and inseparable."[47]

In describing art as propaganda, Du Bois is not merely politicizing aesthetics but, more importantly, aestheticizing politics. As to the first, he clearly sees a transformative role for art, broadly understood. He opens "Criteria" by saying "the thing [i.e., art] that we are talking about tonight is part of the great fight we are carrying on."[48] And he delivered the statement, like the wider essay, at the Chicago conference of the National Association for the Advancement of Colored People. Du Bois most certainly sees himself as engaging in this fight. Although it may seem odd that Du Bois emphasizes art rather than political action properly speaking, this mistakenly understates the fact that he sees art as a form of political action in a world of asymmetrical power relations that must stand alongside traditional modes of protest. Recounting his transition from relying exclusively on scientific rationality in addressing racial inequality, Du Bois explains: "The black world must fight for freedom. It must fight with the weapons of Truth, with the sword of the intrepid, uncompromising Spirit, with organization in *boycott, propaganda and mob frenzy*."[49]

In attributing the aestheticization of politics to Du Bois one should observe that he does not believe he is importing into the political and ethical domain something that ought to be kept out. Rather, he sees the aestheticization of politics not only as a method for African Americans to expand their self-description and the judgment of their white counterparts but also, as he indicates in the conclusion of the essay, as a vehicle for building themselves "up into that wide judgment, that catholicity of temper" that is the key to freedom.[50] For the role of the black artist generally, and the black rhetorician in letters particularly, is not simply to ask the question, "What is a Negro anyhow?" but to provide a more capacious answer to the question.[51] This is what Du Bois refers to as African Americans compelling "recognition."[52]

Notice that these two claims—politicizing aesthetics and aestheticizing politics—serve as bookends for the essay. The first keeps in view the problem of racial injustice that orients Du Bois as literary artist, whereas the second indicates that the content of his rhetoric must be aimed at expanding his white counterparts' capacity for judgment. Building blacks up into that judgment requires, as Du Bois attempted decades earlier in *Souls*, a dramatization of their struggles—a jarring presentation of those who live behind the veil, to generate sympathy for their plight and to shame those who were complicit in and unresponsive to their struggles.

Recall Du Bois's explicit call to widen the judgment of the audience in "Criteria" and my earlier gloss on his use of the word "listen" in the conclusion of the first chapter of *Souls*. The first of these helps us understand what he intends by the second. He does not intend for the readers to alienate their judgment to his authority—that is, to be dominated; rather, he asks the readers to put the capacity for judgment to work, including its ability to be expanded. Rhetoricians seek to stir the souls of those whom they engage so that they may arrive (and see themselves as participating in that arrival) at a truth hitherto unavailable. Properly conceived, Du Bois allows readers to retain their reflective agency and contribute to the participatory and binding quality essential to democratic life.

It isn't completely clear, one might think, how the rhetoric of *Souls* can hope to generate the kind of deep transformation Du Bois imagines that affirms rather than stifles reflective agency. Or to put it in the form of a question: What does it mean for Du Bois's audience to see themselves as participating in the arrival of a truth hitherto unavailable? After all, Hill describes rhetoric as the imposition of power, and Du Bois describes it as propaganda. All of this seems to point to manipulation; and certainly that would not involve us in affirming the reflective agency of the recipient, and it most certainly does not support a democratic reading of Du Bois's use of rhetoric. Why not, one might ask, interpret propaganda more straightforwardly and subsequently read *Souls* as a book simply engaged in manipulation, even if for good ends?

One way of approaching this issue is to compare persuasion and manipulation. When we manipulate someone we typically move them to a belief or action that is inconsistent with the reason for which they hold that belief or engage in that action. As a result, there is a disconnect between the belief they hold and the reason for holding that belief, making one feel that the belief in question, properly speaking, is not the person's own. To manipulate a person in this respect is to dominate them clandestinely—we substitute the manipulator's judgment and will for the person's own and elicit his or her cooperation in securing the manipulator's advantage. Indeed, this was Plato's classic concern in the *Gorgias*.[53] "The rhetorician's mastery of language," says Peter Euben of Gorgias's view, "enables his student to master anyone, anytime, anyplace, and for any ends."[54] Manipulation thus violates what we might call an *identifiability condition:* persons who are manipulated cannot recognize themselves in the belief they have now come to hold. And it is this violation that undermines one's reflective agency.

But there is another view of rhetoric that does not necessarily fall prey to this conflation and that Aristotle defends in his book *On Rhetoric*, and that was reiterated in Hill's *Principles of Rhetoric*. The Aristotelian view of rhetoric has recently been reclaimed by Garsten and Danielle Allen for thinking about contemporary reflections on deliberative democracy.[55] Properly understood, rhetoric reflects the cooperative aspirations of democratic life rather than the more tyrannical imposition of the rhetorician's views. This is because the rhetorician hopes that the audience—those to whom he or she writes and speaks—will assent to the particular views in question as being their own, so that they comport their political and ethical lives in light of those views. Du Bois is no different. I follow Garsten, then, on this distinction between rhetoric as manipulation and rhetoric as persuasion largely (*a*) because it is a division to which Du Bois was attentive given his education and what he lays out in "Criteria" and (*b*) because it helps us better understand how *Souls* can aspire to contribute to the political and ethical development of America. The latter, as he argues in "Criteria," relates to cultivating the "wide judgment" he defines as the aim of the black rhetorician.

In contrast to manipulation, when we persuade someone to hold this or that belief or engage in this or that action, there is a sense of ownership on the part of the one who is on the receiving end of persuasion. This is why Du Bois specifically uses "listen" to describe how the audience should orient themselves to his words. Having listened and read carefully, the person is able to say at the end, "I'm persuaded." This matters profoundly if what one intends is for the person or community to be able to affirm, *on their own,* the new belief they now hold. This is what we might refer to as the content of the wider judgment. As Hill explains of the role of persuasion: "Persuasion may go on long after the feelings have been reached; for it is necessary, not only that the feelings should take the right direction, but that they should take it with a will."[56] On this point Du Bois agrees. For although he rightly emphasizes the coercive force of the law in protecting African Americans, he is also convinced that the law alone does not entail the kind of deep transformation at the level of character necessary for achieving racial equality.[57] As he says elsewhere, the cure to racial injustice, if one were ever to be found, is not possible by "simply telling people the truth"; rather it comes about by "inducing them to act on the truth."[58] To induce them to act on the truth is simply to have it reflectively emanate from their will.

As such, the statement "I'm persuaded" references the process of internal transformation by the auditor that aligns his or her belief with the rhetorician. This alignment indicates the active involvement of the auditor and affirms a view of the persuader (in this case Du Bois) as a partner in bringing about the internal transformation. This is the point made in the preceding section, that Du Bois submits his views regarding both black life and the aspirational content of the people to the consideration of his readers. In contrast to Robert Stepto's claim that the "rhetorical posture" of *Souls* expresses a "strategy for greater authorial control," it appears to do the opposite.[59] This much Du Bois affirms in his own assessment of *Souls* in 1904, explicitly invoking the judgment of the reader, which must stand alongside his own: "In thus giving up the usual impersonal and judicial attitude of the traditional author I have lost in authority but gained in vividness. The reader will, I am sure, feel in reading my words peculiar warrant for *setting his judgment against mine,* but at the same time some revelation of how the world looks to me cannot easily escape him."[60]

The diminishment of his authorial voice makes sense in the context of inviting his readers to be coparticipants in arriving at shared judgments regarding the plight of African Americans. The statement, "I'm persuaded" thus expresses something that individuals who are persuaded have reflectively done for themselves, which connects the belief they now hold with reasons for holding that belief. Hence Du Bois says in the first sentence of "The Forethought," gesturing to the lack of control he exercises over his readers' judgment: "Herein lie buried many things which if read with patience *may* show the strange meaning of being black here in the dawning of the Twentieth Century."[61] As Aristotle explains of the rhetorician's lack of control, it is the one on the receiving end of persuasion that "determines the speech's end and object."[62] Listeners are, in essence, responding to a situation in light of reasons to which they take *themselves* to be committed, even as the rhetorician is a coparticipant in helping them see those reasons. This is why it makes sense to say Du Bois seeks to affirm the reflective agency of his reader.

Now, we will have missed the point of involving the judgment of the reader if we did not attend to the relational and binding character of what Du Bois is attempting. Recall that Du Bois says to his audience, study my words "with me." Arriving early on in "The Forethought" of *Souls,* this is an invitation that frames the book. But an invitation to what? What he has in mind is that speaker and listener, author and reader may arrive at *shared* judgments regarding the subject matter and the claim it makes on them. In suggesting that they (speaker and listener) will arrive at shared judgments regarding the plight of blacks and the deficiencies of the polity, they will have also tied themselves together in a community based on shared emotional dispositions regarding the subject matter.[63] This shared horizon is made possible by the space of contestation the idea of the people makes possible even as the space becomes the locus for persuading white Americans to embrace an expanded view of themselves and the political community. The relational and binding quality that *Souls* seeks to forge follows from making the reader a coparticipant in the arrival of a truth hitherto unavailable. Herein lies the force of Du Bois's claim that *Souls* is a text concerned with democratic development. For this community based on shared emotional dispositions embodies conceptions of what one's community is about and how one is related to those being dishonored. For Du Bois, crafting a political-ethical vision of the community gives direction to sympathy, but it also sets a standard meant to induce in the reader a sense of shame for having failed to honor it in practice.[64]

Cultivating Sympathy and Eliciting Shame: On the Transformative Possibility of *Souls*

Thus far I have argued that the idea of the people central to democracy opens up space for evocative appeals—that is, it makes room for moving the people such that they will embrace an expanded view of themselves. I have argued that Du Bois, as he calls for in "Criteria" and enacts in *Souls*, was engaged in just this project through his deployment of rhetoric, with its specific aim of involving the judgment of the reader. Enlisting the judgment of readers thus honors their reflective capacity and exemplifies the democratic character of this approach. *Souls* illustrates the normative work that goes on in the space between the descriptive and aspirational views of the people. In this section, I argue that the object of Du Bois's rhetoric—the keys, for him, to widening the judgment of the white reader that he calls for in "Criteria"—is the emotional states of sympathy and shame.

Why should one believe that it is the cultivation of sympathy to which the rhetoric of *Souls* is directed? The simple answer is that Du Bois often argues for the importance of sympathy throughout *Souls* for improving race relations. In chapter 6, "Of the Training of Black Men," he writes: "It was not money these seething millions want, but love and sympathy, the pulse of hearts beating with red blood."[65] In chapter 9, "Of the Sons of Master and Man," remarking on the ironic form of affection that emerged from the institution of slavery in comparison to what followed in its wake, he explains: "This is a vast change from the situation in the past, when, through the close contact of master and house-servant in the patriarchal big house, one found the best of both races in close contact and sympathy."[66] In yet another chapter, "Of Alexander Crummell," Du Bois remarks, in a passage worth citing at length: "He did his work,—he did it nobly and well; and yet I sorrow that here he worked alone, with so little human sympathy. His name today, in this broad land, means little, and comes to fifty million ears laden with no incense of memory or emulation. And herein lies the tragedy of the age: not that men are poor,—all men know something of poverty; not that men are wicked,—who is good? Not that men are ignorant,—what is Truth? Nay, but that men know so little of men."[67]

Whenever Du Bois employs the language of sympathy, it conveys a sentiment that brings the life of another into view. So little human sympathy, referenced in the first line of the passage, is dialectically tied to knowing so little of men. For Du Bois, then, sympathy means that one understands a person from their point of view (knowledge of the person) in a way that generates concern for them. This would correct the fact that Crummell works alone because of so little human sympathy. As I read Du Bois, sympathy is meant to both *register* and *consider* the specificity of situations, so that one can respond appropriately to the condition of persons. But because sympathy involves understanding from the position of those with whom one sympathizes, the capacity for sympathy is constitutively connected to our ability to *re-present*—that is, imagine—in one's mind what may potentially be neither directly seen nor felt, but which is essential to enlarging one's perspectives for decision-making.

The example of Crummell is especially telling in this regard. It is worth recounting some of the details of his life to contextualize the point Du Bois makes. After the destruction, in 1835, of the Noyes Academy interracial college where Crummell attended, he enrolled and graduated from the Oneida Institute in Whitesboro, New York. As Du Bois writes of the destruction of the Academy: "But the godly farmers hitched ninety yoke of oxen to the abolition schoolhouse and dragged it into the middle of the swamp."[68] At the Oneida Institute, Crummell came to realize his calling, one that involved the spiritual uplift of African Americans:

> A vision of life came to the growing boy,—mystic, wonderful. He raised his head, stretched himself, breathed deep of the fresh new air. Yonder, behind the forests, he heard strange sounds; then glinting through the trees he saw, far, far away, the bronzed hosts of a nation calling,—calling faintly, calling loudly. He heard the hateful clank of their chains, he felt them cringe and grovel, and there rose within him a protest and a prophecy. And he girded himself to walk down the world.
>
> A voice and vision called him to be a priest,—a seer to lead the uncalled out of the house of bondage. He saw the headless host turn toward him like the whirling of mad waters,—he stretched forth his hands eagerly, and then, even as he stretched them, suddenly there swept across the vision the temptation of Despair.[69]

The "temptation of Despair" pertains to the refusal of the General Theological Seminary to admit Crummell because of his race.

Du Bois uses Crummell's life and his unrealized calling as a result of racial exclusion as a synecdoche for African American experience. "So he grew," Du Bois explains, "and brought within his wide influence all that was best of those who walk within the Veil."[70] Crummell exemplifies what Du Bois states earlier in chapter 1: "Throughout history, the powers of single black men flash here and there like falling stars, and die sometimes before the world has rightly gauged their brightness."[71] Crummell serves as a proxy for what goes unappreciated and unnoticed about blacks in America—their striving for success, the work of their lives, the character that is exemplified by both, and the frustrated attempt at self-realization.

In narrating Crummell's life and using him as a proxy, Du Bois intends to undermine the dividing force of the veil so that the reader can come to appreciate and sympathize with those who stand behind it.[72] The veil not only divides the political-ethical status of blacks and whites—the "world within and without the Veil")[73]—but also signals an emotional geography that follows from this division (which leads to so little human sympathy). Notice, then, that the veil represents (among other things) the division between the "outer" or experiential condition of blacks in America, and the "inner" disposition that experience should properly influence among white Americans. Notice further that this division between "outer" and "inner" is precisely what, from the perspective of "Criteria," Du Bois believes the rhetorician must overcome in an effort to expand the judgment of the reader.

Overcoming the divide between "outer" and "inner" relates directly to Du Bois's ironic use of sympathy between master and house-slave, which he takes up in chapter 9. Now it is important to observe that this analysis comes in the sociological portion of the book—chapters 8–10—where he remarks, "We seldom study the condition of the Negro To-day honestly and carefully."[74] The ironic use of sympathy shows what happens when the divide is not appropriately bridged. As Du Bois explains:

> This is a vast change from the situation in the past, when, through the close contact of master and house-servant in the patriarchal big house, one found the best of both races in close contact and sympathy, while at the same time the squalor and dull round of toil among the field-hands was removed from the sight and hearing of the family. One can easily see how a person who saw slavery thus from his father's parlors, and sees freedom on the streets of a great city, fails to grasp or comprehend the world of the new picture.[75]

In this context, Du Bois emphasizes a form of sympathy born of contact, but its meaning is distorted because the truth of black life is "removed from the sight and hearing of the family." Removing the problems from sight and hearing signals the superficiality of contact. He commends proximity, but it needs to be genuine. He thus juxtaposes close contact as determined by the norms of the "big house," and the close contact that puts in view the daily "squalor" and "toil" of black life as imposed by the norms of the veil. The former gives to white Americans a distorted view of what freedom means and leaves blacks in a position where they suffer as a result.

In focusing on the details of Crummell's life and the character it represents, Du Bois means to counteract this distortion and its effects. Crummell's life allows him to stage the experiential separation between whites and blacks (revealing the substantive difference between freedom and unfreedom), even as he alerts the reader to a deeper connection between the races. It is no wonder that the chapter on Crummell comes several chapters after Du Bois takes up the distorted view of sympathy. The division between the races becomes palpable as Du Bois recounts the tragic details of Crummell's life that result from his second-class status. It is this condition that is in need of a response and accentuates the absence of freedom. But the motivating force for addressing this situation, Du Bois believes, comes about because of a fundamental human quest for self-realization that unites blacks and whites. It is this shared quest that is obscured by the veil and that he aims to uncover. Indeed, Du Bois says as much in the first line that opens the chapter: "This is the history of a *human heart,*—the tale of a *black boy* who many long years ago began to struggle with life that he might know the world and know himself."[76] In describing the chapter as a history of "a human heart," Du Bois humanizes for the reader the subject of the narrative. He is, in other words, building blacks up into that wide judgment, so that the white reader may be "touched."[77] And the result of being "touched" is that the reader will come to hear appropriately—that is, understand—the nature of Crummell's plight and those like him.

Following Du Bois on this journey reconceptualizes freedom for the reader. The meaning of freedom no longer consists in using the norms of the "big house," for that merely obscures the horrors of black life and leads to a disingenuous sense of close contact. Rather, freedom consists in removing the obstacles to self-realization. Freedom is now conceptually tied to making Crummell's goals and the goals of those like him genuine possibilities in the American world, while simultaneously helping his white audience "grasp or comprehend the whole of the new picture" this freedom entails. Only by making the goals of African Americans genuine possibilities and helping white Americans seize the transformed picture of the political and ethical life these possibilities require does America become both "great" and "new."

But Du Bois does not mean for this to be a narrow sentimentalism. This humanization aspires to bring about a perceptual shift that relocates the "black boy" from outside the affective orbit of the white reader to its inner domain. The white reader is at once, or so Du Bois hopes, moved by the *shared* quest for self-development and chastened by its specific frustration in the lives of those darker individuals with whom they share the polity:

> You will not wonder at his weird pilgrimage,—you who in the swift whirl of living, amid its cold paradox and marvelous vision, have fronted life and asked its riddle face to face. And if you find that riddle hard to read, remember that yonder black boy finds it just a little harder; if it is difficult for you to find and face your duty, it is a shade more difficult for him; if your heart sickens in the blood and dust of battle, remember that to him the dust is thicker and the battle fiercer. No wonder the

> wanders fall! . . . The Valley of the Shadow of Death gives few of its pilgrims back to the world.[78]

The specific and unjustified suffering of the "black boy" becomes the object of reflection about which one should properly feel sympathy. Here the reader comes face to face with the destructive influence of racism, but it serves to underscore the fundamental gap at the core of the polity that stifles affirmative gestures by fellow human beings.

The success of Du Bois's narrative depends not on a view of impartial judgment but rather on the partiality of the reader. When he seeks to persuade his readers he meets them where they stand; he addresses their existing bundle of commitments, values, and norms with the hope of expanding their content. As he explains in chapter 9—a chapter where sympathy is invoked by name: "Such an essentially honest-hearted and generous people cannot cite the caste-leveling precepts of Christianity, or believe in equality of opportunity for all men, without coming to feel more and more with each generation that the present drawing of the color-line is a flat contradiction to their beliefs."[79] But care is needed in reading this line. After all, Du Bois is clear that *Souls* is about democratic development. In other words, he is well aware that the content of those beliefs as currently structured do not, in fact, have African Americans in view as proper subjects of their application. (Recall, it was "godly" farmers that pulled Crummell's schoolhouse into the swamp.) This is precisely why the perceptual shift above is necessary. Thus, when Du Bois appeals to conventional wisdom (e.g., the percepts of Christianity or equality of opportunity), he does so in an effort to extend its content and move the reader to a position that they might not have otherwise adopted. It is this new, expanded view that Du Bois subsequently uses as a way to defend the proposition of contradiction or inconsistency. So in saying that Du Bois seeks to get his readers to see and feel that the suffering of African Americans is out of step with what America claims to be about, one must keep in mind that the content of this description of America is not a reality, but a vision toward which Du Bois is trying to move the nation.

In showing the inconsistency between the expanded principles—principles of equality or the dignity of persons that now includes African Americans—and the failure to apply them equally to black Americans, Du Bois seeks to generate in the reader a sense of shame for having contributed to their suffering.[80] If sympathy looks outward to others, shame looks inward to the self that has either contributed to the suffering of those on the outside or played witness to that suffering. As Bernard Williams rightly notes, "Shame looks to what I am."[81] Shame entails falling below a standard I otherwise embrace, but this falling below can only come into view because of the negative results that follow and that sympathy puts on display.

Although Du Bois does not use the language of shame, there is little doubt this is what he intends. As he says in the "The Afterthought" of *Souls*, "Let the ears of a guilty people tingle with truth."[82] There are two terms here—"guilty" and "truth"—that require elucidation. What is Du Bois after in this sentence? To be guilty, as Du Bois employs it, is to be justly chargeable with harming another (in this instance African Americans). One might think, however, that there is imprecision in this sentence, especially given that Du Bois hopes that *Souls* will touch or move the reader. The imprecision emerges because we can readily think of cases in which people are found guilty of an offense for which they do not take responsibility. But the fact that Du Bois wants the guilt to resonate with the offenders (to tingle their ears) means that he takes himself to be laying out their failure to live up to a standard with which they identify.[83]

The sympathetic identification with African Americans that contributes to an expansion of the political-ethical horizon is now employed by Du Bois to shame the reader. That sympathy is paired with shame is important, especially given that Williams and Christina Tarnopolsky typically deploy shame in isolation from other emotions.[84] The problem in doing this is that it will invariably be the case that the reaction to shame will be one of evading the situation that requires attention—one will recoil from rather than engage with shame and the source from which it springs. This is precisely why the structure of *Souls* moves from attempting to cultivate sympathetic identification in several of the early chapters to eliciting shame in the reader by the end of the book. It is the work of sympathy—creating a shared normative and affective horizon—that increases the chances that a sense of shame will emerge in the reader. (Of course, there are no guarantees where democratic transformation, with its reliance on affect, is concerned.) In doing so, Du Bois intends for his readers to feel diminished by the end of the book—a sense that something about who they are as displayed in their treatment of blacks is wrong. The psychological and characterological effect of this is to lower "the agent's self respect and diminish him in his own eyes."[85] This helps explain Du Bois's reference to truth. For the truth that will tingle the ears of white Americans is a truth about normative dissonance that is on display in their mistreatment of African Americans. To let the ears of guilty people tingle with truth, then, is meant to arouse in them a sensation of aversion to a picture of themselves and the society to which they belong as harming blacks. This is the realization that shame makes possible for the reader. Du Bois's aim here is not, properly speaking, for the readers to feel bad because they have been shamed but to feel bad because they have failed to realize the good.

Failing to realize the good crystallizes an important undercurrent to Du Bois's evocations of sympathy and shame. First, sympathizing with the plight of African Americans in their frustrated attempts to achieve self-realization (*a*) reveals to the persuaded reader something that they find central to the flourishing of life and (*b*) awakens in them a sense of disappointment over the failure of the polity and all who belong to it (including themselves) for not providing the space in which that flourishing can be actualized. Second, precisely because the reader sees self-realization as central to the flourishing of life, but nonetheless frustrated in African Americans because of racism, the reader is forced to ask and confront the following questions: Who am I? What kind of community do I belong to that obstructs the living of life? These are the questions that must be generated within and by citizens if they are going to be genuinely answered. But they are questions that allow readers to probe the justice and injustice of their community.

As these questions suggest, if shame diminishes the standing of persons in their own eyes, it is equally meant to be generative of a new way of living by alerting the reader to the demand of a just regime. Shame honors the judgment of the reader by encouraging a self-critical stance toward one's treatment of African Americans that reflexively reveals the moral deficit within oneself and one's community. As Williams explains, "shame may be expressed in attempts to reconstruct or improve oneself."[86] Shame thus provides an opportunity for self-development because it entails a view of one's political-ethical identity in relation to which transformation is made possible and rendered intelligible. This is precisely why the hope of *Souls* is that it will not fall "*still-born into the world-wilderness*"; but, rather, may "*spring . . . from out its leaves vigor of thought and thoughtful deed to reap the harvest wonderful. . . . Thus in Thy good time may infinite reason turn the tangle straight, and these crooked marks on a fragile leaf be not in-*

deed."[87] But this is simply to say, that in Du Bois's hands, shame emanates from a sense that who we are as a democratic people, need not determine who we may yet become.

I have argued that the idea of the people, with its descriptive and aspirational dimensions, creates a space in which the rhetoric of *Souls* and its explicit appeal to sympathy and shame operate. Rhetoric and its affective targets are used by Du Bois to potentially move his white audience to embrace a view that, if realized, would redefine the contours of democratic citizenship and the political-ethical standing of blacks therein. As the word *potentially* suggests, Du Bois was well aware of the uncertainty that haunted his appeals. Significantly, then, *Souls* seeks not only to fashion a vision of what the people may yet become but also necessarily reflects the uncertainty that is bound up with democratic development. And the rhetorical invitation to the judgment of readers, over whom one can never exercise complete control, reflects this uncertainty. This is the normative work that the idea of the people makes possible and the danger it courts.

And yet, *Souls* may well be an exemplar of the kinds of practices that African Americans and women historically employed in their quest to redefine the contours of the political community—to persuade their audiences to embrace that unrealized America. How might *Souls*, we should ask in this final moment, serve as a guide to understanding a much larger tradition in which it participated? Might Du Bois's mode of engagement serve as a tentative answer to the question with which we began this essay: *How were women and African Americans able to invoke the language of the people even as they were consistently identified as standing outside the boundaries of the political and affective concerns of the nation?*

I pointed earlier to Elizabeth Cady Stanton and Martin Luther King Jr. as examples of individuals who also sought to transform the American polity. Standing historically on either side of Du Bois, they mark a much wider tradition of engagement. For these thinkers, too, this gap between description and aspiration opens a space to refashion a vision of the democratic self. Consistent with Du Bois's approach, what emerges in their writings and speeches is the role and status of rhetoric as a form of political education, the transcendent vision inherent in rhetorical appeals, and the central place of the sentiments in awakening the citizenry to the demands of the moral life. Taken together, these aspects of rhetoric both clarify the challenges of democratic life and illuminate a philosophical outlook common to Stanton, Du Bois, and King.

Stanton and King are analogously related to Du Bois because they also found in rhetoric and the sentiments a vehicle for engaging their fellows. Indeed, this is the form in which they partly waged the battle for America's soul. Speaking before the New York State Legislature in 1860, Stanton graphically recounts the horror women experienced at the hands of their male counterparts without any opportunity for redress. "Call that sacred," she exclaims, "where innocent children, trembling with fear, fly to the . . . dark places of the house, to hide themselves from the wrath of drunken, brutal fathers, but, forgetting their past sufferings, rush out again at their mother's frantic screams, 'Help, oh help'?"[88] Stanton's graphic portrayals, although not uncommon in the quest for gender and racial inclusion, are directly focused on stimulating sympathy in her male audience and prefigure Du Bois's approach. "What father," she asks, "could rest at his home by night, knowing that his lovely daughter was at the mercy of a strong man drunk with wine and passion, and that, do what he might, he was backed up by law and public sentiment?"[89]

But if sympathy is central to Stanton's appeal, King is no less keen on having his audience feel that they have fallen below standards with which they otherwise identify. In his classic "I Have a Dream" speech, King argues that "they [referring to the American Founders] were signing a promissory note to which every American was to fall heir . . . a promise that all men, yes, black men as well as white men."[90] But King's rhetoric is not dissimilar to Du Bois's in *Souls;* like him, King attempts to call into existence the thing he assumes—that the Founders, did, in fact, see blacks as equal. But the appeal to the Founders is a trope of American rhetoric, even among the marginalized, and is not meant to express a belief in a preexistent consensus in a Habermasian register. King attempts to work within familiar symbols, if only to expand their conceptual content. He creates a foundation within the sacred text of the American Founding upon which he locates black equality and then moves to critically engage the nation for failing to honor this in practice—a failure, he hopes, that all will look on in disappointment, and above all else, shame.

These thinkers are similar because they share experiences of domination in a society that claimed to be well-ordered, and which prompts them to defend a constellation of ideas that rely on rhetoric and the sentiments in moving the people to embrace an expanded view of themselves. Significantly, however, what fuels their political orientation is a view of democracy that severs the connection between the people and those who might claim exclusive deployment of power in the people's name. This is the beauty of democracy that ennobles human existence through the iterative process of contestation it makes possible, and its darker undercurrent in which the outcome of contestation is never known in advance. The lack of knowledge—the existential uncertainty of action—makes democratic action for these thinkers a leap of faith. As William James remarked in 1882, perhaps unknowingly articulating the ethos of democratic action: "Faith is the readiness to act in a cause the prosperous issue of which is not certified to us in advance," and yet transformation could not come about without acting.[91] In Jamesian fashion these political actors acknowledge the danger of political engagement, but they nonetheless defend, in an Emersonian idiom, a species of perfectionism: they constantly push and prod the Nation, by virtue of the projections of life they offer, to reimagine its self-understanding.[92] Perhaps, then, to engage *Souls* is not merely to discover the approach of one thinker on behalf of a marginalized group, but it may well serve as an example of a larger tradition of thinking that gives life to the democratic world we continually aspire to realize.

Notes

Originally published as "The People, Rhetoric, and Affect: On the Political Force of Du Bois's 'The Souls of Black Folk,'" *American Political Science Review* 106, no. 1 (2012): 188–203. Reprinted with the permission of American Political Science Association.

1. A number of scholars have done interesting work on the concept of "the people" from which I have learned a great deal, even if they have not specifically or consistently had in view the issue of racial exclusion that I take up here or how the concept has been mobilized to address this problem (e.g., Sheldon Wolin, "The People's Two Bodies," *Democracy* 1, no. 1 [1981]: 9–24; Edmund Morgan, *Inventing the People* [New York: Norton, 1988]; Bernard Yack, "The Myth of the Civic Nation," *Critical Review* 10 [1996]: 193–211; Rogers Smith, *The Stories of Peoplehood* [New York: Cambridge University Press, 2003]; Danielle S. Allen, *Talking to Strangers: Anxieties of Citizenship since "Brown v. Board of Education"* [Chicago: University of Chicago Press, 2004]; Margret Canovan, *The People* [Cambridge, UK: Polity, 2005]; and Sofia Nasstrom, "The Legitimacy of the People," *Political*

Theory 35.5 [2007]: 624–58). The exceptions to this argument, in different ways, include: James Morone, *Democratic Wish: Popular Participation and the Limits of American Government,* rev. ed. (New Haven: Yale University Press, 1998); and Jason Frank's brilliant text *Constituent Moments: Enacting the People in Postrevolutionary America* (Durham, NC: Duke University Press, 2010).

2. Exceptions here include Frank, *Constituent Moments,* chap. 7; and Morone, *Democratic Wish,* chap. 6.

3. W. E. B. Du Bois, *The Souls of Black Folk* (1903), in *Du Bois: Writings,* ed. Nathan Huggins (New York: Library of America, 1986). Subsequent references to Du Bois's work will be to this volume unless otherwise noted.

4. Some of these works include Ronald de Sousa, *The Rationality of Emotion* (Cambridge: MIT Press, 1990); Robert Solomon, *True to Our Feelings* (New York: Oxford University Press, 2001); *Not Passion's Slave: Emotions and Choice* (New York: Oxford University Press, 2007); Martha Nussbaum, *Upheavals of Thought: The Intelligence of Emotions* (New York: Cambridge University Press, 2003); Benedetto Fontana, Cary J. Nederman, and Gary Remer, eds., *Talking Democracy: Historical Perspective on Rhetoric and Democracy* (State College: Pennsylvania State University Press, 2004); Cheryl Hall, *The Trouble with Passion: Political Theory beyond the Reign of Reason* (New York: Routledge, 2005); Allen, *Talking to Strangers;* Bryan Garsten, *Saving Persuasion: A Defense of Rhetoric and Judgment* (Cambridge: Harvard University Press, 2006); Sharon Krause, *Civil Passions: Moral Sentiment and Democratic Deliberation* (Princeton: Princeton University Press, 2008); Rebecca Kingston and Leonard Ferry, eds., *Bringing the Passions Back In: The Emotions in Political Philosophy* (Vancouver, BC: UBC Press, 2008); and Elizabeth Markovits, *The Politics of Sincerity: Plato, Frank Speech, and Democratic Judgment* (State College: Pennsylvania State University Press, 2008).

5. I do not deny that there were other—narrower—ways of configuring the people that were backward-looking. John C. Calhoun, for example, also invoked "the people" but only as a way to limit the orbit of affective and political concern. The aim, as far as my argument is concerned in this context, is to focus on the more expansive conception of "the people."

6. Arnold Rampersad, *The Art and Imagination of W. E. B. Du Bois* (New York: Schocken, 1976), chap. 2. To my knowledge, Rampersad's text is the only one that explicitly takes up the importance of rhetoric to Du Bois.

7. The texts I have in mind include Manning Marable, *W. E. B. Du Bois: Black Radical Democrat* (Boston: Twayne, 1986); Shamoon Zamir, *Dark Voices: W. E. B. Du Bois and American Thought,* 1888–1903 (Chicago: University of Chicago Press, 1995); Ross Posnock, *Color and Culture: Black Writers and the Making of the Modern Intellectual* (Cambridge: Harvard University Press, 1996); Adolph L.

Reed Jr., *W. E. B. Du Bois and American Political Thought: Fabianism and the Color Line* (New York: Oxford University Press, 1997); Eugene Victor Wolfenstein, *A Gift of the Spirit: Reading "The Souls of Black Folk"* (Ithaca, NY: Cornell University Press, 2007); and Robert Gooding-Williams, *In the Shadow of Du Bois: Afro-Modern Political Thought in America* (Cambridge: Harvard University Press, 2009).

8. Du Bois, "Criteria of Negro Art" (1926), 1000.

9. See Benedict Anderson, *Imagined Communities: Reflections on the Origins and Spread of Nationalism*, rev. ed. (London: Verso, 2006); Richard Rorty, *Achieving Our Country: Leftist Thought in Twentieth-Century America* (Cambridge: Harvard University Press, 1998), chaps. 3–4; and Morone, *Democratic Wish;* cf. Christopher Looby, *Voicing America: Language, Literary Form, and the Origins of the United States* (Chicago: University of Chicago Press, 1996).

10. See, for instance, Kimberly Smith, *Dominion of Voice: Riot, Reason and Romance in Antebellum Politics* (Lawrence: University of Kansas Press, 1999); Maurice S. Lee, *Slavery, Philosophy, and American Literature, 1830–1860* (New York: Cambridge University Press, 2005); and Michael Bennett, *Democratic Discourses: The Radical Abolition Movements in Antebellum American Literature* (New Brunswick, NJ: Rutgers University Press, 2005).

11. For representative examples, see Elizabeth Cady Stanton, *Elizabeth Cady Stanton Feminist as Thinker,* ed. Ellen Carol DuBois and Richard Candida Smith (New York: New York University Press, 2007), 155–79, 219–35.

12. Du Bois, *Souls,* 545 (emphasis added).

13. Canovan, *The People,* 29.

14. Frank, *Constituent Moments,* 8; cf. 18, 210.

15. Du Bois, *Souls,* 365.

16. Ibid., 364.

17. Note the multiple levels on which Du Bois articulates what is required for African Americans to enjoy equality: "The training of schools we need to-day more than ever,—the training of deft hands, quick eyes and ears, and above all the broader, deeper, higher culture of gifted minds and pure hearts. The power of the ballot we need in sheer self-defense,—else what shall save us from a second slavery? Freedom, too, the long-sought, we still seek,—the freedom of life and limb, the freedom to work and think, the freedom to love and aspire" (Du Bois, *Souls,* 370).

18. John Dewey, "Creative Democracy—The Task before Us," in *The Later Works of John Dewey, 1925–1953*, vol. 14, ed. Jo Ann Boydston (1939; Carbondale: University of Southern Illinois, 1985), 226.

19. Jürgen Habermas, "Constitutional Democracy: A Paradoxical Union of Contradictory Principles?" *Political Theory* 29 (2001): 774.

20. Claude Lefort, *Democracy and Political Theory* (Minneapolis: University

of Minnesota Press, 1989), 19; *The Political Forms of Modern Society,* ed. J. B. Thompson (Cambridge: Polity, 1986); cf. Alan Keenan, *Democracy in Question: Democratic Openness in a Time of Political Closure* (Stanford: Stanford University Press, 2003): Frank, *Constituent Moments.*

21. Habermas, "Constitutional Democracy," 774.

22. Ibid.

23. Ibid., 775 (emphasis added).

24. In his much earlier "Popular Sovereignty as Procedure" of 1988, an essay which also appeared as part of the appendix to his 1996 translated book *Between Facts and Norms,* Habermas appears to be sensitive to the position with which I am concerned (Habermas, "Popular Sovereignty as Procedures," in *Between Facts and Norms: Contributions to a Discourse Theory of Law and Democracy,* trans. William Rehg [Cambridge, UK: Polity, 1996], 463–91). There he writes of the French and American Revolutions: "The revolutionary consciousness was expressed in the conviction that a new beginning could be made. This reflected a change in historical consciousness. Drawn together into a single process, world history became the abstract system of reference for a future-oriented action *considered capable of uncoupling the present from the past.* In the background lay the experience of a break with tradition: the threshold to dealing reflexively with cultural transmissions and social institutions was crossed" (Habermas, "Popular Sovereignty," 467 [emphasis added]). Several pages later he continues in his explanation of the normative thrust of the revolution: "the revolutionary project overshoots the revolution itself: it eludes the revolution's own concepts. . . . It is only as a historical project that constitutional democracy points beyond its legal character to a normative meaning—a force at once explosive and formative" (Habermas, "Popular Sovereignty," 471). But if there is a break with the past such that its concepts do not overdetermine the present, it isn't clear to me what Habermas means to say in the 2001 essay. He cannot retreat to the procedural rules of rights and the vision of recognition that informs that account, since it is precisely this description that is the problem. He must, instead, appeal to an account of the people that is itself discontinuous with the past and never fully exhausted by the present in which contestation over the polity emerges. For it is here that we find the connection between the political and ethical standing of persons. At any rate, either he has changed his mind or his language betrays him. The first is a mistaken move for reasons which I have already discussed, and the second is terribly unfortunate.

25. Du Bois, "The Souls of Black Folk," in *The Oxford W. E. B. Du Bois Reader,* ed. Eric J. Sundquist (New York: Oxford University Press, 1996), 97–240. On the revisions of the earlier essays and compositional coherence of *Souls,* see Robert Stepto, *From Behind the Veil: A Study of Afro-American Narrative,* 2nd ed. (1979; Urbana: University of Illinois Press, 1991), chap. 3.

26. David Levering Lewis, *W. E. B. Du Bois: Biography of a Race* (New York: Holt, 1993), 226. The translation proposed by Weber unfortunately did not happen.

27. See note 3.

28. Garsten, *Saving Persuasion,* 9.

29. Rampersad, *Art and Imagination,* 36.

30. Du Bois, *Dusk of Dawn,* 581–82; cf. Rampersad, *Art and Imagination,* 35–38. For an outline of some of Du Bois's course work, see W. E. B. Du Bois, *Against Racism: Unpublished Essays, Papers, Addresses, 1887–1961,* ed. Herbert Aptheker (Amherst: University of Massachusetts Press, 1985), 35–38.

31. Adams Sherman Hill, *The Principles of Rhetoric and their Application* (New York: Harper and Brothers, 1878), iii; cf. to Hill's longer chapter titled "Persuasion," chap. 5.

32. Aristotle, *On Rhetoric: A Theory of Civic Discourse,* trans. George A. Kennedy, 2nd ed. (New York: Oxford University Press, 2007), 1.2, 1356a; Cicero, *On the Ideal Orator,* trans. James M. May and Jakob Wisse (New York: Oxford University Press, 2001), 2.35, 133. My understanding of Aristotle and Cicero's rhetoric is owed to Eugene Garver, *Aristotle's Rhetoric: An Art of Character* (Chicago: University of Chicago Press, 1994); Garsten, *Saving Persuasion,* chaps. 4 and 5; Allen, *Talking to Strangers,* chap. 10; Wendy Olmsted, *Rhetoric: An Historical Introduction* (Malden, MA: Blackwell, 2006), chap. 1.

33. Du Bois, *Dusk of Dawn,* 574 (emphasis added).

34. Du Bois, "Criteria," 1000.

35. Ibid.

36. Ibid., 1001.

37. Hill, *Principles of Rhetoric,* iii.

38. Du Bois, "Criteria," 994.

39. William H. Ferris, *The African Abroad,* vol. 1 (New Haven: Tuttle, Morehouse and Taylor, 1913), 18 (emphasis added).

40. Cicero, *On the Ideal Orator,* trans. James M. May and Jakob Wisse (New York: Oxford University Press, 2001), 2.35, 133.

41. Du Bois, *Souls,* 545.

42. Du Bois, "Criteria," 1000.

43. Hill, *Principles of Rhetoric,* 239.

44. Du Bois, *Souls,* 371.

45. Du Bois, "Criteria," 995.

46. Rorty, *Contingency, Irony, and Solidarity* (New York: Cambridge University Press, 1989).

47. Du Bois, "Criteria," 995.

48. Ibid., 993.

49. Du Bois, *Dusk of Dawn,* 557 (emphasis added).

50. Du Bois, "Criteria," 1001.

51. Ibid. This forms the core, as Robert Gooding-Williams rightly notes, of Du Bois's "politics of expressive self-realization" (Gooding-Williams, *In the Shadow of Du Bois,* chap. 1).

52. Du Bois, "Criteria," 1002.

53. Plato, *Gorgias,* trans. Donald J. Zeyl (Indianapolis: Hackett, 1987).

54. Peter Euben, "Reading Democracy: 'Socratic' Dialogues and the Political Education of Democratic Citizens," in *Demokratia,* 337, 327–59; cf. David Cohen, "The Politics of Deliberation: Oratory and Democracy in Classical Athens," in *A Companion to Rhetoric and Rhetorical Criticism,* ed. Walter Jost and Wendy Olmsted (Malden, MA: Blackwell, 2004), 22–37; Simone Chambers, "Rhetoric and the Public Sphere: Has Deliberative Democracy Abandoned Mass Democracy?" *Political Theory* 37, no. 3 (2009): 323–50.

55. Garsten, *Saving Persuasion,* 7, and chap. 4; Allen, *Talking to Strangers.*

56. Hill, *Principles of Rhetoric,* 240.

57. As he says of the Freedmen's Bureau: "This Bureau set going a system of free labor, established a beginning of peasant proprietorship, secured the recognition of black freedmen before the *courts of law,* and founded the free common school in the South. On the other hand, it failed to begin the establishment of *good-will* between ex-masters and freedmen" (Du Bois, *Souls,* 387 [emphasis added]). In *Souls,* Du Bois attaches weight to both the law (see, for instance, his criticism of Booker T. Washington's willingness to abandon the franchise and civil equality in chapter 3, "Of Mr. Booker T. Washington and Others") and a deeper exchange and engagement among whites and blacks for improving the standing of each in the eyes of the other (see, for example, chapter 9, "Of the Sons of Master and Man," where he emphasizes the importance of social contact).

58. Cited in Lewis, *W. E. B. Du Bois,* 226. It should not go unnoticed that Du Bois's concern with arriving at the truth and acting from the truth stands in sharp contrast to Plato's belief that rhetoric only produces mere belief, rather than knowledge about the world. For this argument in Plato see, *Gorgias,* 459a, 17–18.

59. Stepto, *From behind the Veil,* 53. For a similar point, see Wolfenstein, *Gift of the Spirit,* chap. 1.

60. Du Bois, "The Souls of Black Folk," 305 (emphasis added).

61. Du Bois, *Souls,* 359 (emphasis added). Although I cannot pursue the matter here, involving the judgment of the reader is not exclusively meant to refer to the white reader. Du Bois is terribly concerned to affirm the dignity of African Americans, even amid the horrors life. Here we might think of the story of Alexander Crummell (chapter 12), the fictive story of John Jones (chapter 13), and Du Bois's understanding of the sorrow songs (chapter 14). Despite the impact of white supremacy, the first two chapters underscore the excellence that African Americans

should aspire toward, while the last of the three explicates the spiritual excellence African Americans qua African Americans have already displayed and contributed to the polity in the form of the sorrow songs. As such, these chapters can be read as attempting to counteract the negative influence of measuring oneself by a world that looks on in amused contempt and pity that frames the book in chapter 1. Just as he invites the judgment of his white readers to be coparticipants in the arrival of a truth hitherto unavailable, he does the same for those who live behind the veil. In proceeding this way, and in contrast to Gooding-Williams's reading of Du Bois's politics, *Souls* aspires to render compatible two accounts of politics that are central to American political thought broadly, a vision of politics that focuses on ruling in the form of *giving direction* or *pointing the way* and one that affirms the capacity of citizens to reflect, amend, and affirm the directions that have been presented to them. Hence Du Bois says in chapter 3, where he deals with the question of leadership, yoking the two views of politics together as part of one understanding of democracy: "Honest and earnest criticism from those whose interests are most nearly touched,—criticism of writers by readers, of government by those governed, of leaders by those led,—this is the soul of democracy and the safeguard of modern society" (Du Bois, *Souls*, 395). *Souls* might be read as Du Bois standing before the judgment of the African American community who will decide if he is worthy of serving as their new representative. For Gooding-Williams's arguments on the politics of *Souls*, see *In the Shadow of Du Bois*, chap. 1. I do not mean to suggest that Du Bois was successful in consistently holding these two together, but he did not unambiguously affirm rule as the model for understanding democracy.

62. Aristotle, *Rhetoric*, 1358b.

63. To refer to a "community based on shared emotional dispositions" in no way implies that Du Bois means to refer to noncognitive states. Involving the judgment of the reader in an effort to arrive at an accurate picture of the plight of African Americans, as Du Bois does, means that the emotional states that follow have an irreducible cognitive component. That is, they are in themselves judgments of value or lack of value regarding the social world and the persons that inhabit it. In Robert Solomon's words: "Emotion is not merely a feeling, as, say, pain is a feeling. It is also an outlook, an attitude, a reaching out to the world. . . . Thus, the conceptual geography of emotion suggests that the realm of emotion is neither the mind nor the world but both together: the world as experienced" (Solomon, "The Politics of Emotion," in *Bringing the Passions Back In*, 195, 198).

64. In advancing this claim about sympathy and shame, I part ways from Virgil Aldrich, John Kekes, and Anthony O'Hear and the emphasis they place on the nonsocial character of such emotions like these, especially shame. Precisely because sympathy and shame emerge from *shared standards*, we need not worry, as they do, that the necessity of these emotional states result wholly because of what

others think about us rather than being the result of our reflective stance toward the persons for whom we should feel sympathy or actions about which we should be ashamed (see Virgil C. Aldrich, "An Ethics of Shame," *Ethics* 50 [1939]: 57–77; Anthony O'Hear, "Guilt and Shame as Moral Concepts," *Proceeding of the Aristotelian Society* 77 [1976–197]; John Kekes, "Shame and Moral Progress," *Ethical Theory: Character and Virtue,* Midwestern Studies in Philosophy, vol. 13, ed. Peter A. French, Theodore E. Uehling Jr., and Howard K. Wettstein [Notre Dame, IN: University of Notre Dame Press, 1988]).

65. Du Bois, *Souls*, 432.

66. Ibid., 477.

67. Ibid., 520.

68. Ibid., 513–14.

69. Ibid., 514.

70. Ibid., 519.

71. Ibid., *Souls,* 365. Du Bois's constant reference to "black men" and to male leadership is not without its obvious patriarchal problems, especially in the context of arguing against political-ethical inequality (see Hazel V. Carby, *Race Men* [Cambridge: Harvard University Press, 1998]). But there is ambiguity both in *Souls* and elsewhere in Du Bois's writings around the status of women that seemingly affirms and subverts their second-class status (for analysis of some of this, see Lawrie Balfour, "Representative Women: Slavery, Citizenship, and Feminist Theory in Du Bois's 'Damnation of Women,'" *Hypatia* 20, no. 3 [2005]: 127–48).

72. For a similar account of Crummell, see Gooding-Williams, *In the Shadow,* 98–111.

73. Du Bois, *Souls,* 359.

74. Ibid., 457.

75. Ibid., 477.

76. Ibid., 512 (emphasis added).

77. Ibid., 514.

78. Ibid., 519.

79. Ibid., 490.

80. I do not mean to suggest that this description of shame exhausts how the term can be understood. I fully acknowledge that, as indicated by an anonymous reviewer, persons can feel ashamed of hypocrisy even if this produces no harm to others. But feeling ashamed of oneself in this sense will be wholly a private affair and will have no material bearing on the life chances of persons. Du Bois, as indicated here, is concerned with shame that emerges precisely because the actions which one has engaged in or been a witness to impact the life chances of persons. I should further note that although I do not preclude this other, wholly interior sense of shame, at some point consistent hypocrisy will generate a material impact.

81. Bernard Williams, *Shame and Necessity* (Berkeley: University California Press, 1994), 93; cf. Andrew Morrison, *The Culture of Shame* (New York: Ballantine, 1996); and Christina Tarnopolsky, *Prudes, Perverts, and Tyrants: Plato's "Gorgias" and the Politics of Shame* (Princeton: Princeton University Press, 2010).

82. Du Bois, *Souls*, 547.

83. It is important to note that Williams distinguishes between shame and guilt by focusing on their directionality (Williams, *Shame and Necessity*, 90–95). Shame looks inward to the self, and guilt looks outward to the one who has been harmed. In Du Bois's case, these two are collapsed. Hence guilt is not simply about the one who is harmed, but in properly identifying with one's guilt, white Americans see themselves as having fallen below a standard to which they take themselves to be committed and for which they should be ashamed. For Du Bois, then, it isn't enough to simply find white Americans guilty; they must also find themselves guilty if the feeling of shame is to emerge.

84. Williams, *Shame and Necessity;* Tarnopolsky, *Prudes, Perverts, and Tyrants.*

85. Williams, *Shame and Necessity*, 90.

86. Ibid.

87. Du Bois, *Souls*, 547 (original emphasis).

88. Stanton, Address to Convention, May 11, 1860, in *Elizabeth Cady Stanton: Feminist as Thinker*, 182.

89. Ibid., 183.

90. Martin Luther King Jr. "I Have a Dream," in *A Testament of Hope: The Essential Writings and Speeches of Martin Luther King Jr.*, ed. James M. Washington (1963; New York: HarperOne, 1982), 217.

91. William James, "The Sentiment of Rationality," in *The Will to Believe and Other Essays in Popular Philosophy* (1897; New York: Dover, 1956), 90; cf. John Dewey, *A Common Faith*, in *The Later Works: 1925–1953*, ed. Jo Ann Boydston, vol. 9 (Carbondale: Southern Illinois University Press, 1986), 17.

92. See, generally, Stanley Cavell, *Conditions Handsome and Unhandsome: The Constitution of Emersonian Perfections* (Chicago: University of Chicago Press, 1990); and Jeffrey Stout, *Democracy and Tradition* (Princeton: Princeton University Press, 2004), chap. 1.

6

"Honest and Earnest Criticism" as the "Soul of Democracy"

Du Bois's Style of Democratic Reasoning

Nick Bromell

As African American political thought analyzes the consequences of racism on politics and the political, it frequently undertakes a systemic analysis of the failures of the dominant political and social structures per se. As Charles Mills has argued, black political thought and philosophy often offer "a (partially) internalist [immanent] critique of the dominant culture by those who accept many of the culture's principles but are excluded from them. In large measure, this critique has involved telling white people things that they do not know and do not want to know, the main one being that . . . the local reality in which whites are at home is only a non-representative part of the larger whole."[1] Such black political thought often addresses itself, as Mills points out, to an imagined democratic polity consisting of both whites and blacks—that is, to that "larger whole" that has been elided and even denied by the white practice (and theory) of democracy. This imagined whole is who James Baldwin often refers to when he uses the first-person-plural pronoun "we."[2]

W. E. B. Du Bois frequently addressed this larger polity by using a rhetorical structure—or style of thought—that embodies what I take to be core principles of his theory of democracy. In the pages that follow, I give an account of this style and of its implications for political theory. I begin by showing that Du Bois was extraordinarily alert to the claim of *any* part that it is the whole of the matter under consideration. I then show that he responds to such claims with a three-step argument: first, he acknowledges some truth or validity in the position he is contesting; he then moves on to expose that position's partiality or incompleteness; and he concludes by folding both his own and the other view in a more expansive, open-ended whole. I suggest further that Du Bois presents such arguments as a model of democratic reasoning, or of what he calls the "honest and earnest criticism" that is "the soul of democracy."

As we shall see, Du Bois also makes three other important points about democratic reasoning: first, he thinks of it as being situated and embodied, frequently using the verb "touch" to describe its workings; second, he privileges the knowledge gained by those who are least empowered and who suffer most in the polity, suggesting that their perspective is the one by which the polity most needs to be guided; third, he suggests that no individual's democratic reasoning is by itself truly able to comprehend the whole of any matter, and so as democratic citizens we must all be prepared to use our imagination at the point where our knowledge reaches its limit. In other words, the democratic reasoning he models tries to be aware of its own fallibility and regards the imagination as its crucial supplement or ally.

In the second section of this essay, I show how Du Bois brought this style of democratic reasoning to bear on a specific political problem—the disproportionate power of the South in national politics. And in the essay's final section, I bring the principles that animate Du Bois's rhetorical style into conversation with the democratic theorizing of George Kateb and Iris Marion Young, showing both what he shares with these two very different theorists and how his thinking might enlarge theirs and ours.

For his 1890 Harvard commencement address, delivered when he was just twenty-two years old, Du Bois chose a very surprising subject: Jefferson Davis. Even more surprising is that Du Bois begins by acknowledging that Davis was "a typical Teutonic Hero" and by seeming to applaud "the history of civilization during the last millennium," a history that has "been the development of the idea of the Strong Man of which he [Davis] was the embodiment." Davis was a "soldier and a lover," Du Bois declares, "a statesman and a ruler; passionate, ambitious and indomitable; bold reckless guardian of the peoples' All—judged by the whole standard of Teutonic civilization, there is something noble in the figure of Jefferson Davis."[3]

Many in Du Bois's mainly white audience were probably pleased by his praise of Davis; indeed, his words echo and seem to confirm the view (increasingly popular among whites at the turn of the twentieth century) that the Anglo-Saxon, or Teutonic, race had achieved its superiority through a Darwinian struggle in which the fittest and strongest were destined to prevail. But at just this point, Du Bois's argument takes a turn. He recoils from Davis by rhetorically constructing himself as a dispassionate observer wholly removed from the subject he is discussing, and then he takes his third step, enfolding the partiality of the Teutonic standard of civilization in a larger whole: "Judged by every canon of human justice," he begins, "there is something fundamentally incomplete about that standard" (243). Considered as a type, Davis is not so much wrong as partial, and so is "the type of civilization which his life represented." Such a civilization is based on "Individualism coupled with the rule of might"; its ideals are power and conquest. "Under whatever guise, . . . a Jefferson Davis may appear as man, as race, or as nation, his life can only logically mean this: the advance of a part of the world at the expense of whole; the overweening sense of the I, and the consequent forgetting of the Thou" (243). Davis's "striking contradictions of character," Du Bois observes, with what is surely a sidelong glance at his audience, "always arise when a people seemingly become convinced that the object of the world is not civilization, but Teutonic civilization" (244). However, when one steps back and takes a broader view, as Du Bois himself is modeling for his audience, what springs to view is the incompleteness of Teutonic civilization and its blindness to its own limitedness. The "world has needed and will need its Jefferson Davises," he acknowledges; "but such a type is incomplete and never can serve its best purpose until checked by its complementary ideas. Whence shall these come?" (244).

They shall come, he suggests, from "the South" and in particular from "the Negro," who can offer the world a different ideal, "an idea of submission apart from cowardice, laziness, or stupidity, such as the world never saw before." The "change made in the conception of civilization" would be profound, he argues: "The submission of the strength of the Strong to the advance of all—not in mere aimless sacrifice, but recognizing the fact that, 'To no one type of mind is it given to discern the totality of Truth,' that civilization cannot afford to lose the contribution of the very least of nations for its full development: that not only the assertion of the I, but also the submission to the Thou is the highest individualism" (244).

In this last sentence, Du Bois succinctly summarizes the core principle of his democratic reasoning: Even as his recoil has allowed him to see *more* of the truth than many in his audience, it has impressed upon him the impossibility of seeing *all* of the truth. His speech is not just about the virtues of Davis, or about his incompleteness, or about how that incompleteness can be remedied in a larger whole that includes the Negro's "complementary ideas." Most deeply, it warns his audience that representation (cultural, aesthetic, political) tends to slide into synecdoche, and it demonstrates that the best way to resist this tendency is to develop a habit of mind that moves as Du Bois's does: one must always seek for the "but also" that supplements and complements a partial representation and an incomplete understanding. The rhetorical structure that conveyed this mode of reasoning was effective. One person in the audience wrote later: "His paper was on 'Jefferson Davis,' and you would have been surprised to hear a colored man deal with him so generously. Such phrases as a 'great man,' a 'keen thinker,' a 'strong leader' and others occurred in the address."[4] A contributor to the New York *Nation* observed: "Du Bois handled his difficult and hazardous subject with absolute good taste, great moderation, and almost contemptuous fairness."[5] *Almost contemptuous fairness:* the phrase nicely captures the dynamic of recoil and recuperation that animates Du Bois's address.

Written eleven years later, Du Bois's critical essay on Booker T. Washington (1901) displays a similar structure of argument and style of thought. Du Bois begins by acknowledging Washington's achievement: "We may not agree with the man at all points, but we admire him and cooperate with him so far as we conscientiously can." Du Bois goes on to suggest that Washington's success is also a sign of weakness since it, like the age he lives in, is characterized by a "singleness of vision" that is "narrow" even as it gives him "force." Du Bois aligns himself instead with "the large and important group" of African Americans "represented by Dunbar, Tanner, Chesnutt, Miller, and the Grimkes" and tells us that these seek a broader vision of "self-development and self-realization in all lines of human endeavor." Again, Du Bois's mind moves from "not only" to "but also" with a worldly reasonableness that does not so much dispute his opponent as reframe him: "While these men respect the Hampton-Tuskegee idea to a degree, they believe it falls short of a complete program." As an alternative to Washington's narrow incompleteness, then, Du Bois offers the example of a mind with a broader and more inclusive vision, one that strives to enlarge the whole rather than defining and constraining it.[6]

A final example of Du Bois's style of democratic reasoning, his essay on Abraham Lincoln (1907) is similarly shaped by this three-step movement of thought. He begins by asserting that Lincoln's first gift was "his clear sightedness—the way that he could brush aside the cobwebs of convention and of difficulty and see with perfect clearness the right and justice and logic of life."[7] But since this quality is dangerously close to the "singleness of vision" Du Bois has criticized Washington for possessing, he goes on to point out that Lincoln "did not always see the right at first, and in that very fact lies his second claim to greatness and that is his capacity for growth" (249). Thus, the power of singleness of vision is supplemented (not displaced) by the wisdom of adaptability. Du Bois goes on to suggest that Lincoln is a model for his readers to emulate, especially in a time when "we have growing up in this country, slowly, surely, the idea that the world is not for everybody"—that it belongs instead to a "restricted class to which all human beings are not permitted" (255). Like Frederick Douglass before him, Du Bois contrasts what is "narrow" and "mean" and "strict" with "broad" and "full" and "free," warning that "there is growing up in America the idea that we must be careful how we train children," that "their heritage is to be narrow and not the full, free, broad heritage toward which Abraham Lincoln looked" (255).[8]

In all three of these essays, then, we see that Du Bois's critical reasoning first acknowledges some worth in its subject, then recoils from and criticizes it, and concludes by reconfiguring it in a wider frame. This was his most persistent style of argument throughout his career. Although its three-part structure bears a superficial resemblance to Hegelian dialectics of thesis, antithesis, and synthesis, it is crucially different insofar as it leads not to synthesis (or fusion) but to complementarity (or balanced tension). When Du Bois has taken a partiality claiming to be a totality and shown it to be what it is—limited not complete, local not universal—we are left with new and highly dynamic conception of "the whole" in which the parts retain their singularity and yet derive their meaning from their relations with each other. Perhaps the most concise articulation of this principle, which runs very deep in African American thought, was Anna Julia Cooper's: "Progressive peace in a nation," she wrote in *A Voice from the South* (1892), "is the result of conflict; and conflict, such as is healthy, stimulating, and progressive, is produced through the co-existence of radically opposing or racially different elements." She called this "the stable equilibrium of opposition." Ralph Ellison's phrase describing jazz as "antagonistic cooperation" would be equally apt.[9]

Du Bois seems to have become increasingly aware that this particular style of thought and argument was an indispensable quality of what some political theorists would now call democratic "deliberation." In *The Souls of Black Folk,* after reprising his earlier critique of Washington's narrowness, Du Bois asserts that Washington was usually disposed to try to silence such criticism. This, says Du Bois, "is a dangerous thing": "Honest and earnest criticism from those whose interests are most nearly touched,—criticism of writers by readers, of government by those governed, of leaders by those led,—this is the soul of democracy and the safeguard of modern democracy."[10]

To understand fully what Du Bois takes such criticism to be, we must begin by taking note of how much is packed into his phrase "nearly touched." *Touch* is a key word in his vocabulary of democracy—as when he writes, for example, that "Politics have not *touched* the matters of daily life which are nearest the interests of the people" or that "When voting *touches* the vital, everyday interests of all, nominations and elections will call for more intelligent activity."[11] In his *Autobiography,* Du Bois writes that teaching summer school in Tennessee (between semesters at Fisk) was an "invaluable" experience because "I *touched* the very shadow of slavery. I lived and taught school in log cabins built before the Civil War. . . . I *touched* intimately the lives of the commonest of mankind—people who ranged from barefooted dwellers on dirt floors, with patched rags for clothes, to rough, hard-working farmers, with plain, clean plenty."[12] And in another passage from his *Autobiography,* Du Bois writes: "This my training *touched* but obliquely," and "I could bring criticism from what I knew and saw *touching* the Negro" (72, 98; my emphases throughout). *Touch,* I would suggest, registers Du Bois's commitment to a mode of thought that does not stop at *theoria* (at looking upon from a disembodied distance) but actually touches its object and includes it in a more complete whole. "Criticism" is honest and earnest when it touches and is touched by something, when it engages with something rather than simply distancing itself in order to gain a critical perspective on it.

This became the basis of Du Bois's more explicit critique of white political culture's misrepresentation of itself as the whole, rather than just a part, of US democracy. His theory of democracy conceives of it as an endless process of such criticism in which the multiple perspectives of those whose interests are "touched" become aggregated or pooled in what Cooper called "stable equilibrium of opposition." "Democracy alone," he writes, "is the method of showing the whole experience of the race for the benefit of the future."[13] Democracy rests, finally, on recognition of "the worth of" a person's "feelings and experiences to all" (555). "To disenfranchise" any group "is deliberately to turn from knowledge and grope in ignorance" (556). "No state can be strong which excludes from its expressed wisdom the knowledge possessed by mothers, wives, daughters" and by other "excluded groups" (556).

The feelings and experiences that citizens contribute to the wisdom of the polity are best described as *touching* the matters being deliberated and as *touching* each other—Du Bois's verb carefully evades the tradition of Cartesian, spectatorial "knowing"—because the heart of such experience is suffering. Pain. That is, the epistemological authority of each person's perspective rests, finally, on the utter privacy of his or her suffering. "In the last analysis," Du Bois writes, "only the man himself, however humble, knows his own condition." That is, "in the last analysis only the sufferer knows his sufferings," and "all this goes to prove that human beings are, and must be, woefully ignorant of each other."[14] Democracy can transform this private pain into a political good, however, when that pain is understood to be the source of each individual's distinctive knowledge, of what he or she can contribute to the group's deliberations.

Crucially, then, Du Bois's "whole" resists representation. It can never be enclosed in definite limits and must always remain open to further expansion; it is composed of infinite splinters of human difference, all equal in their shared difference: "Human equality is not lack of difference, nor do infinite human differences argue relative superiority and inferiority." For this reason, genuine democratic inclusion cannot mean a universal sameness, the conformity of all difference to a single standard. "Of all worlds," he writes, "may the good Lord deliver us from a world where everybody looks like his neighbor and thinks like his neighbor and is like his neighbor" (561). There is a place in Du Bois's *demos* for a Booker T. Washington—and even for a Jefferson Davis if he is willing to complement his assertive self with a self that submits to the Thou of the community.[15]

In sum, Du Bois's "criticism" as the "soul of democracy" is a mode of thought that continually tries to make room for the differences it encounters by habitually seeking an enlargement of the whole. Within that whole, differences persist and coexist in Ellison's "cooperative antagonism." Democratic reasoning understood as such criticism would consist not of exchanging reasons, nor of reasoning per se, but of bringing to bear knowledge gained by suffering that can never be abstracted and then represented because it is essentially private and incommensurable with anything else. This criticism touches rather than perceives things because it is informed by individual knowledge derived from the authority of personal suffering. That touching is at once near and intimate (not distanced) and yet also cognizant that it must be, in the best sense of the word, superficial. When my knowledge *touches* upon something or someone, it does not presume to penetrate to an essence. Nor does it proceed by abstracting out what is purportedly held "in common" by all the differences that surround it. Suspicious of representation and alarmed by synecdoche, it locates knowledge precisely in what is separate and unique rather than in what is universal and shared (and shareable).

Following this trail of key words in Du Bois's vocabulary of democratic theory—*criticism, whole, touch, difference, suffering*—we should not be surprised to find ourselves coming to *infinity, imagination, dream.* For if the democratic *whole* is always open to further revision and wider inclusion, it is by definition infinite. And the infinite cannot be grasped by reason, only by imagination. Hence Du Bois's unyielding commitment to the belief that the imagination plays an indispensable role in the creation of a democratic political culture. "And first and before all, we cannot forget that this world is beautiful," he wrote in 1920.[16] Twenty years later, even as his appreciation of Karl Marx's dialectical materialism deepened, Du Bois continued to celebrate and affirm the politically transformative powers of the imagination. In his 1941 essay on Phillis Wheatley (to choose just one of many examples), Du Bois presents her as a visionary whose prophetic dreams were later realized in the work of seven major African American writers, including David Walker, William Wells Brown, Charles Chesnutt, and Paul Laurence Dunbar: "It is these imagined visions of Phillis . . . that made her Phillis the Blessed." Almost certainly implying a reference to himself in particular and to African American experience in general, Du Bois writes: "Always a certain sense of mystery lurked in the furtherest [*sic*] reaches of Phillis' consciousness—the miracle of her sudden transport to this far land; the hoarse voice of the Visions, the deep dire Visions, thus floated and drifted, loomed and died in her thoughts and dreams. In the only home she knew—and the only friends she had, she was always partly a stranger. Only her phantasy was real, only her dreams were true. She could not help but have visions—prophetic visions—she who in a single childhood had encompassed the ends of the earth."[17]

"The real argument for democracy," he had written in *Darkwater*, "is . . . that in the wisdom of the people we have that source of endless life and unbounded wisdom which the rulers of men must have" (555). Here again, in his tropes of the "endless" and "unbounded," Du Bois strives to articulate his understanding of a horizonless whole that cannot be precisely delimited because it is by nature infinite. This conception of the whole helps explain why Du Bois himself was and remained an imaginative writer throughout the entire span of his career. A secularist to the core and a rationalist master of empirical argument and icy logic, he nonetheless crowded his oeuvre with what a commitment to reasoned discourse would seem to exclude—specters of the unknown and the unknowable. Du Bois's poems, novels, and books of creative essays demand that his readers continually lift their eyes from the data of the here-and-now to contemplate a world that can be approached only through the imagination. His work may thus be said to return us to the original meaning of *theoria* as contemplation of the divine, when "the divine" is understood to be beyond knowing or naming.

This recognition of the infinite and the unknown appears even in his late and most matter-of-fact works. In *Color and Democracy*, written at the end of the Second World War in a desperate effort to influence the behavior of the great powers toward the former colonies, Du Bois begins by affirming his belief in reason. It is the lingua franca of the world, he writes, the common medium in which people may meet and resolve their differences. This is why revelation cannot be allowed to trump it: "My attitude toward organized religion is distinctly critical," he writes, explicitly rejecting the possibility "that any chosen body of people or special organization of mankind has received a direct revelation of ultimate truth which is denied by earnest scientific effort." But he goes on to make plain that his critique is directed at *claims* to *exclusive* possession of (and representation of) "ultimate truth," not to the notion of such truth per se. And so he invites into his text what a narrower conception of reason would have excluded when he supplements this critique with an acknowledgment that "the majority of the best and earnest people of this world are organized in religious groups, and that without the cooperation of the richness of their emotional experience, and the unselfishness of their aims, science stands helpless before crude fact and selfish endeavor. . . . Is there not, then, a chance to find a common ground for a program of human betterment which seeks by means of known and tested knowledge the ideal ends of faith?"[18]

The development of this "common ground" would require reciprocal sacrifices, he admits. On the one hand, organized religion would have to "surrender" its "dogma to the extent of being willing to work for human salvation this side of eternity." Likewise, the scientific community (including political secularists like himself) would have to make its own sacrifice by admitting "that what we know is vastly exceeded by what we do not know, and that there may be realms in time and space of infinitely more importance than the problems of this small world" (138).

With these words Du Bois once again expresses his vision of a whole that is boundless and thus beyond the grasp of any attempt to represent it. This is why quest for the whole, or for completeness, can never come to an end: the universe is infinite, and "What we do not know" vastly exceeds what we do know. For Du Bois, then, wholeness is a figure not of completion but of potentiality. This is also why, for Du Bois, the imagination is as essential as reason to democratic deliberation or communication. Whether that unknown faces us as a vast immensity or as the utterly private suffering of each individual with us in the democratic *polis*, we cannot claim to know it. The faculty that allows us to apprehend it, to know that it is there without knowing exactly what it is, is the imagination—which Du Bois often figures as *dreaming* or having *visions*.[19] This imaginative act is also what informs every act of empathy with others. It is what enabled Du Bois to see Jefferson Davis as a white southerner might have, and it is the faculty to which he appeals when he writes that even though "in the last analysis only the sufferer knows his suffering," democracy rests on the democratic community's recognition of "the worth of" each individual's "feelings and experiences to all." The social recognition of each individual's suffering has to be an act of imagination, not of knowing—the difference being precisely that the imagination remains cognizant at all times that "what we know is vastly exceeded by what we do not know," whereas knowing, running in a much narrower track, tends to believe that it can get to the bottom of something and really and finally know it completely, with no remainder left to haunt us.

Du Bois's mode of democratic reasoning—his earnest and honest criticism of the polity—turns to a concrete problem of US democracy in a two-part series he published in the *Crisis*. "The Possibility of Democracy in America" analyzes and critiques the power of the explicitly racist South to control US politics as the power of a part to misrepresent and control the meaning of the whole. Du Bois begins by asking why voter turnout has been so low: "The proportion of actual voters among the voting population of the United States is between twenty-five and thirty-three per cent." The cause, he argues, is not merely widespread voter apathy but the fact that such indifference has been manufactured and institutionalized by the systematic disenfranchisement of both blacks and whites, especially in the South. "This is a serious thing," he writes: "The theory of democracy does not call for equality of gift, universal college education or absolute individual integrity; but it does depend upon the widest possible consultation with the mass of citizens on the theory that only in this way can you consult ultimate authority and ultimate sovereignty."[20]

Du Bois then presents his readers with a table showing the number of votes cast in each state for the election of one representative in Congress. These figures range from 9,449 votes in South Carolina to 105,131 in New Mexico, and they plainly suggest that the southern states had deliberately restricted the franchise so that only a small number of citizens could actually participate in the election of their congressmen (521). Consequently, each one of these southerners who was permitted to vote exercised inordinate power relative to other Americans living in states where the franchise was more broadly available. Du Bois writes: "The stranger from Mars looking at this table would immediately ask, 'Why is it that citizens from South Carolina should have eleven times as much political power as the citizens of New Mexico?' . . . Surely the time has come for a careful, dispassionate consideration—not so much of the political condition of the South as of the effect which the political legislation of the South from 1890 to 1909 has had upon the politics of the nation" (523).

What such dispassionate consideration reveals, says Du Bois, is that the nation has allowed the southern states to have their cake and eat it too. They have been permitted to disenfranchise millions of black voters, but at the same time they have been allowed to count those blacks in the census rolls that determine how many representatives each state will be allowed in Congress. As a result, the power of the Solid South had actually *increased* by two-fifths (40 percent) since the abolition of slavery because each disenfranchised black southerner now counted as a whole person, instead of as three-fifths of a person, as slaves had been reckoned in the census. But this is not the worst of it, for the curtailment of democracy in the southern states has given those states disproportionate power at the federal level, which in turn has allowed them to curtail democracy nationally. In short, Du Bois argues that southern racism is not just an attitude that in some vague way poisons American politics; instead, it should be seen as an entrenched institution that has enabled a part (the South) to stand for and control the actual mechanism of American democracy (the whole).

Perhaps stunned by his own findings, Du Bois in the second article voices a suddenly deepened pessimism about the possibilities of democracy in the United States. A tone of bitterness creeps in where formerly he had expressed only anger. He now writes, he says, "to apologize and change my thesis. I was wrong in what I was predicting. I see today without any doubt . . . that . . . the problem that faces us in America and faces the world is the question as to whether we can keep the territory we thought democracy had already conquered." In a characteristic "not only, but also" move, Du Bois takes pains to show that poor whites also have been victimized and disenfranchised by the racist legacy of slavery, for "this disenfranchisement of the negro has had an astonishing effect on the voting of other persons in the states concerned and in the whole nation so far as the mass of voters is concerned."[21] The reason is that the policy of disenfranchisement, once legitimized and operative, concentrates power in fewer and fewer hands. Du Bois quotes the opinion of Henry W. Anderson, "a rich white Virginian politician," that "The machinery of discrimination, devised primarily for this purpose [of disenfranchising blacks], was then employed by the dominant party organization to effect a disqualification of a large proportion of the white population opposed to that organization" (527). To substantiate this claim, Du Bois presents two tables showing that although the population of the southern states has increased "over 200 per cent since 1870, . . . the voting population has increased only 131% over 1872, *despite woman suffrage*." The figures are even worse for Alabama, Georgia, Louisiana, Mississippi, and South Carolina: "In these five states out of a total of

5,145,282 persons 21 years of age and over, there were 635,512 votes cast in 1920. There were in this election, therefore, disenfranchised voluntarily or involuntarily, 4,489,770 persons. Subtracting 19,000 Negroes as actually voting from the total number of Negroes 21 years of age and over, we have 2,215,991 Negroes disenfranchised. But we also have 2,259,799 whites disenfranchised, which is a fair indication of the cost of Negro disenfranchisement in these five states" (528).

On the basis of this analysis, Du Bois would argue in a subsequent essay that the fatal mistake made by every third-party movement except the Socialists has been to court the Solid South instead of attacking it. The results of the 1928 election in no way mitigate this analysis, he claims. The Smith-Hoover election drew many more voters to the polls in the South, and the Republican Hoover did manage to wrest five states, with sixty electoral votes, away from the Democratic Party machine. "But was this a real triumph, and a breaking of the Solid South?" Du Bois asks. "Nothing of the sort. While they voted against the machine, these voters did so for no modern reasons. They voted because of religious prejudice [against the Catholic Smith], hatred of the party domination of New York, fear of the negro, and prohibition. . . . They had no intelligence of or intelligent answers to the problems of protecting labor, curbing monopoly and privilege, preserving natural resources, equitable taxation of incomes, and preventing crimes. *The million new voters who came into the field were densely ignorant and prejudiced*" (my emphasis).[22]

These last words indicate a very significant shift in Du Bois's thinking. Nine years earlier, he had affirmed this most radical principle of democracy: "A given people today may not be intelligent, but through a democratic government that recognizes, not only the worth of the individual to himself, but the worth of his feelings and experiences to all, they can educate, not only the individual unit, but generation after generation, until they accumulate vast stores of wisdom. Democracy alone is the method of showing the whole experience of the race for the benefit of the future." By 1929, that "future" appeared so distant as to cast doubt upon his bedrock faith in the wisdom of the people: the "densely ignorant and prejudiced" white voters of the South might *never* become sufficiently educated to participate wisely in democracy, and in the meantime their "feelings and experiences" were emphatically *not* of any worth to the democratic polity. Grappling with these facts, Du Bois became increasingly convinced that meaningful social justice would never be achieved through suffrage alone. Instead, our understanding of democracy and democratic practice would have to be enlarged so as to include economic as well as political power: He summed up his evolving position in 1933:

> A generation ago, we assumed that democratic methods of social reform in the United States were . . . working toward their goal, and that the major problem of the American Negro was to share effectively in the machinery of government, and to be counted according to his numbers as one of the objects of uplift. . . . Since then, and particularly in these post-war days, we have with some difficulty and searching of soul, come to the conclusion that the program of reform through universal suffrage is not moving as it should and might. That on the contrary, the economic and industrial organization of the world is such that democracy, even among the more advanced white nations, is singularly ineffective. And that if the masses are going to achieve incomes adequate to a decent livelihood, and the economic justice which is the only basis of a broad human culture, a revolution in the control and method of our present political activities must come.[23]

As late as the very last page of his *Autobiography* (begun in 1958), Du Bois continued to deploy his three-step style of democratic reasoning. "This is a wonderful America, which the founding fathers dreamed," begins a sentence; "until their sons drowned it in the blood of slavery," he continues. And he concludes: "Our children must rebuild it."[24] I surmise that Du Bois's "our" is deliberately ambiguous. On the one hand, it specifically addresses the African American community and affirms the indispensable role black Americans will, or must, play if US democracy is ever to become what the dream of it promises. At the same time, the pronoun points toward the broader polity who must imagine themselves as a whole and jointly undertake the reconstruction of their democracy on an enlarged foundation.

Despite his deepening pessimism about democracy, Du Bois never abandoned his conviction that a democracy must educate its people to become effective democratic citizens. Although in person and in his correspondence he could be caustic, domineering, and unshakably convinced of his own sagacity, the persona we so frequently encounter in his published works models a very different disposition. It is one that at least feigns to presuppose the limitedness and contingency of its own view, no matter how clear-sighted it might be, and therefore seeks to supplement this inevitable narrowness with the perspectives of others. In disputation and deliberation, such a mind does not seek to prove others wrong so much as it hopes to demonstrate their partialness and incompleteness, and to compensate for these shortcomings by seeking a broader view that includes them both. Such a mind eventually realizes that all human wisdom begins in individual experiences of pain and suffering; precisely because these cannot be shared with others, they constitute the source of the distinctive knowledge that any person can contribute to public deliberation. Such a mind is predisposed to understand, therefore, that the persons and groups who have suffered most because of their exclusion from democratic citizenship are precisely those who may have the most to offer democratic life—and theory.

In the spirit of Du Bois's own style of thought, I propose that in trying to relate his thinking about democracy to the theories and terminologies that are more familiar to us, we view it as *enlarging* rather than "fitting into" these. (This is why I have refrained from explicating his thought in terms of Jacques Rancière's familiar thesis about "the part that is no part." In my view, Du Bois has no need of such explication; he actually advanced this thesis well before Rancière.) To give some indication of what such an enlargement would look like, I want to bring Du Bois's thought into conversation with two current theories of democracy: the first is the idea of democratic individuality as developed by George Kateb; the second is Iris Marion Young's critical analysis of deliberative democracy and the way such theory conceives of reasoning and inclusion. Different as these two theories are, Du Bois would have welcomed—yet also criticized and enlarged—both of them.

In his now classic article "Democratic Individuality and the Claims of Politics," Kateb develops a theory drawn from the work of Ralph Waldo Emerson, Walt Whitman, and Henry David Thoreau.[25] By "democratic individuality" Kateb means a way of living that begins with an awakening to the possibilities and responsibilities of one's self-development or self-perfecting. This is an open-ended project that cannot be defined in advance but takes shape in the process of its own unfolding. It is "not an ideal that one can ever be certain has been reached. It is not meant to be so unequivocally defined as to be unambiguously reachable. It is not a permanent state of being, but an indefinite project" (338). As characterized by Emerson, Whitman, and Thoreau, writes Kateb, democratic individuality is alert to the contingency of all social conventions. It is self-reliance. It is a disposition to disobey and resist laws and conventions that one believes to be unjust. It is at the same time a feeling that one's "*dignity* resides in being, to some important degree, a person of one's own creating, making choosing, rather than in being merely a creature or a socially manufactured, conditioned, manipulated thing: half-animal and half-mechanical and therefore wholly socialized" (343). As Whitman puts it: "To become an enfranchised man, and now, impediments removed, to stand and start without humiliation, and equal to the rest; to commence, or have the road clear'd to commence, the grand experiment of development, whose end (perhaps requiring several generations,) may be the forming of full-grown man or woman—that is something" (339). Finally, the democratic individual's "rupture with external regulation" is "a necessary preparation" for something "beyond individuality or personality or character or even individuation. What is it? The soul." Acknowledging that he cannot know what "soul" is, or what it was for these writers, Kateb writes that "there is some sense that there is divinity in each human being—some kinship with either the creator or all creation—something indestructible or inexhaustible that may, at least metaphorically, be called immortal" (344).

The chief problem with this conception of democratic individuality—and Kateb bravely addresses it—is that the individual as imagined by these writers need not commit himself to sustaining the political structure that has made his flourishing possible. Kateb wrestles with his writers' seeming hostility or at least indifference to democratic political activity, and he concludes: "It may be that if one is sympathetic to their idealism, one would advocate a somewhat sharper feeling of indebtedness toward the system that allows and encourages the aspirations that then disdain it, or at least outgrow it. What would follow from a sharper feeling? Could an appeal be made to the sense of duty? Is there a duty to do one's share in actively perpetuating the indispensable resource of democratic individuality? . . . I do not think that one could plausibly answer, Yes. As long as there are countless people willing to take part, there can be no duty to do so, no matter how sharply indebted one felt" (358).

Du Bois would have been in deep accord with an aspect of Kateb's argument, for he agrees with him about the importance of recognizing the distinctiveness of each person in a democracy; and like Kateb's, his thinking about democracy doesn't hesitate to turn its face toward the metaphysical and to employ words like "soul" and "infinite." But Du Bois would also enlarge Kateb's theory and at the same time solve its chief difficulty by showing that participation in the politics of democracy is something other than a duty. A "duty," as Kateb uses the word, implies an obligation; and obligation implies a compromise of the self whose self-realization consists of a complete flowering of its own autonomy. By contrast, a sharper feeling of the fragility and contingency of "the system that allows and encourages the aspirations" of democratic individuality would incline one to regard political activism as a *necessity*, not a duty. To put the case somewhat differently: Kateb's version of Emersonian democratic thought virtually erases *conflict* from democratic politics and culture. It erases the conflict that arises because certain groups and individuals will always have a stake in destroying or subverting the democracy. And it overlooks the conflict through which democratic citizenship is gained by those who have been excluded from the system—by the disenfranchised insisting on enfranchisement. Writing as Du Bois does from a position of intense awareness of both kinds of conflict, the question of "duty" toward democratic politics is almost moot. The question is one of survival, not obligation.[26]

Before turning to the relation between Du Bois's political thought and that of Iris Marion Young, I would briefly point to what all theorists of democracy might learn from him. Instead of figuring interest-based democracy and deliberative democracy as mutually exclusive alternatives, they might reframe the former in the broader context of the latter; that is, instead of trying to replace the interest-based model, they might seek to enlarge it. Such enlargement would begin with a fresh consideration of what is meant by "interest" in the first place. Du Bois's thought helps us see that this term, like so many others in our philosophical tradition, invisibly presupposes an ontology in which individual identity has been abstracted or removed from the realm of necessity. Thus, we have on the one hand an autonomous "self" that is subject and pursuer, while on the other we have "interests" that are the objects being pursued. They lie outside us, and we try to acquire them. This model might accurately describe a middle-class person deciding to seek a tax deduction on his second home, but does it work as well for someone more obviously embedded in the realm of necessity? If my children have inadequate health coverage and one of them is very sick, am I pursuing my "self-interest" if I support universal health care or, in desperation, rob a bank?

What if, following Du Bois, we were to replace "self-interest" with "an end to suffering" or "a diminishment of suffering"? The advantage of these terms is that they don't covertly enforce an untenable and misleading distinction between the self and its needs. As a number of feminist theorists have argued, those needs are *in* the self, so the self should not be imagined as a pure abstraction apart from them. Once we have named suffering, or undergoing, as what we "experience" that makes us turn to the democratic community for relief and redress, we can see that the opposition between what we were calling a "self-interest" model and a "deliberative" model of democracy is no longer quite so sharp or absolute. Suffering is the hinge that connects them, or reveals their unity. For suffering is what we are actually seeking to diminish when we pursue our so-called self-interest, and suffering is also the source of the distinctive knowledge we can contribute to democratic deliberation.

Readers familiar with the work of Iris Marion Young will know how close she is to the spirit of Du Bois as I have tried to render him here.[27] Her insistence on the importance of inclusion is very much in keeping with Du Bois's vision of enlargement, expansion, and the infinite. But perhaps even Young's approach can be enlarged somewhat by Du Bois's understanding of democracy. Young bases her argument for inclusiveness in democratic deliberations (which she would prefer to call, more inclusively, "communication") on the very reasonable assumption that citizens of a democracy have the right to be included. (Thus, if in a hypothetical polity all citizens just happened to be equally invested and competent in particular forms of democratic communication, Young would have no reason to advocate for the inclusion of other forms of communication.) The weak point of this line of argument is its practical circularity: more complete inclusion is justified by recourse to an already established right of inclusion. In the realm of logic, abstracted from the conflict-ridden nature of democracy, there's no problem here. But in the realm of actual democratic practice, where citizens vigorously contest the matter of who will be included, the universal right to inclusion has *not yet* been sufficiently established. Indeed, it is precisely the issue that's being contested.

Du Bois, by contrast, shifts the ground entirely. He presents the problem not as a denial of rights but as limitation of knowledge. Because some citizens have not been allowed to bring the knowledge their suffering has conferred on them into democratic deliberation, the democratic polity has deprived itself of the benefits of their distinctive and potentially important knowledge. Du Bois's argument for greater inclusiveness is based not on the assumption that everyone has a right to be included (although he did believe that everyone does have such a right) but on a democratic epistemology that understands differentiated suffering as the source of the community's knowledge.

If the citizens of a democracy could embrace this view, two things might follow. First, arguments like Young's on behalf of an elastic understanding of "giving reasons" would be more effectively based on what is good for all rather than on what would be fairer to some. Second, the problem of how to maintain civic unity in the face of the broadest possible recognition of difference would be frontally addressed (if not solved): we would understand that our unity is based on the fact that we *all* suffer. It is in the fact of our suffering, and in the added pain of its privacy, that we find our common humanity. In short, Du Bois invites us to see that democratic unity is *composed* of difference, not threatened by it.

Notes

Originally published in somewhat different form as "W. E. B. Du Bois and the Enlargement of Democratic Theory," *Raritan* 30, no. 4 (2011): 140–61. Reprinted with the permission of Rutgers University.

1. Charles W. Mills, *Blackness Visible: Essays on Philosophy and Race* (Ithaca, NY: Cornell University Press, 1998), 5–6.

2. Baldwin often uses the first-person-plural pronoun with startling effect, as when he writes: "What it comes to is that if we, who can scarcely be considered a white nation, persist in thinking of ourselves as one, we condemn ourselves, with the truly white nations, to sterility and decay . . ." (*The Fire Next Time* [New York: Vintage, 1993], 93–94). See Lawrie Balfour's fine discussion in "'A Most Disagreeable Mirror': Race Consciousness as Double Consciousness," *Political Theory* 26, no. 3 (1998): 346–69.

3. W. E. B. Du Bois, "Jefferson Davis as a Representative of Civilization" in *The Oxford W. E. B. Du Bois Reader*, ed. Eric J. Sundquist (New York: Oxford University Press, 1998), 243; hereafter cited parenthetically in the text.

4. W. E. B. Du Bois, *The Autobiography of W. E. B. Du Bois: A Soliloquy on Viewing My Life from the Last Decade of Its First Century* (New York: Oxford University Press, 2007), 92.

5. Ibid., 93.

6. W. E. B. Du Bois, "Booker T. Washington," in *Du Bois Reader*, ed. Sundquist, 247; hereafter cited parenthetically in the text.

7. W. E. B. Du Bois, "Abraham Lincoln," in *Du Bois Reader*, ed. Sundquist, 249; hereafter cited parenthetically in the text.

8. For a discussion of these key words in Douglass's political vocabulary, see Nick Bromell, "The Liberal Imagination of Frederick Douglass," *American Scholar* 77, no. 2 (Spring 2008): 34–45.

9. Anna Julia Cooper, in *The Voice of Anna Julia Cooper*, ed. Charles Lemert and Esme Bhan (Lanham, MD: Rowman and Littlefield, 1998), 122, 128.

10. W. E. B. Du Bois, *Souls of Black Folk,* in *Du Bois Reader*, ed. Sundquist, 124. As Robert Gooding-Williams has argued, Du Bois would soon abandon this conception of the relation between leaders and the led—but his abandonment was not as complete and unequivocal as Gooding-Williams suggests. To be sure, within the sphere of black politics, Du Bois did commit himself repeatedly to a conception of leaders as rulers. But this is not the only sphere in which Du Bois moved and thought. As we shall see, in the dimension of his political thought that addresses an imagined polity of blacks and whites and seeks to reimagine and reconstruct democracy, Du Bois returned repeatedly to what Gooding-Williams calls his "honest criticism model" (Robert Gooding-Williams, *In the Shadow of Du Bois: Afro-Modern Political Thought in America* [Cambridge: Harvard University Press, 2009], 55).

11. Du Bois, in *Du Bois Reader*, ed. Sundquist, 558.

12. Du Bois, *Autobiography*, 72; hereafter cited parenthetically in the text.

13. Du Bois, in *Du Bois Reader*, ed. Sundquist, 555, 556. Perhaps Du Bois's most eloquent expression of this vision of inclusion and democracy is spoken by one of the two main characters in his unfinished and unpublished novel "A World Search for Democracy." Democracy, she says, "is based on the widest recognition of human equality. It assumes that wisdom in government comes from the widest knowledge concerning the governed, a knowledge eventually so wide that it becomes in effect a pool of human experience to which all human beings contribute. Shut off one rill from this ocean of life and it becomes incomplete" (unpaginated).

14. Du Bois, in *Du Bois Reader*, ed. Sundquist, 544. Du Bois would thus qualify Richard Rorty's hope that human solidarity is achieved "by increasing our sensitivity to the particular details of the pain and humiliation of other, unfamiliar sorts of people." Like Rorty, Du Bois places human suffering at the center of his understanding of democratic citizenship, but he explicitly cautions that increased "sensitivity" to others' suffering should not be mistaken for knowledge or understanding of it (Richard Rorty, *Contingency, Irony, and Solidarity* [Cambridge: Cambridge University Press, 1989], xv).

15. It's crucial to distinguish between the reification and the preservation, or honoring, of difference. I agree with Ross Posnock that Du Bois is fundamentally misunderstood by those who have read him as an advocate of what Posnock calls "identity logic." Du Bois certainly did believe in the value of difference to a democratic polis, but he became increasingly careful to avoid suggesting that the content or meaning of any person's difference could be predicted on the basis of certain markers (age, race, gender, and the like); indeed, as I have just indicated, Du Bois believed that each individual was, in the last analysis, not knowable by others. Thus, the meaning of a person's difference was something that only each individual could explain herself to the community; it was not something that was given by the community to each individual.

16. Du Bois, in *Du Bois Reader*, ed. Sundquist, 596.

17. Du Bois, "The Vision of Phillis the Blessed," in *Du Bois Reader*, ed. Sundquist, 329.

18. W. E. B. Du Bois, *Color and Democracy: Colonies and Peace* (New York: Harcourt, Brace, 1945), 137.

19. Du Bois's most biting critique of religion and at the same time most fervent affirmation of "ultimate truth" appear in a piece he wrote for the *Crisis*, in 1933:

> He [the young Negro] should see in the church an expression of the desire for full and ultimate truth; that desire for goodness and beauty, which is ingrained in every human being; and on the other hand, and just as clearly, he should frankly denounce all attempts on the part of any organized body of human beings when they declare that they know it all and that God has personally told them about it. That is a plain lie and they know it and everybody else ought to know it. We must have religion in the sense of striving for the infinite, the ultimate, and the best. But just as truly we must straitly curb the effort of any exclusive guild to be the single and final arbiter of individual interpretation of desired and desirable truth. ("The Church and Religion." *Crisis* 40 [October 1933]; in *Selections from "The Crisis,"* ed. Herbert Aptheker [Millwood, NY: Kraus-Thomson, 1983], 2:720).

20. Du Bois, "The Possibility of Democracy in America." pt. 1, *Crisis* 35 (September 1928), in *Selections from "The Crisis,"* ed. Aptheker, 2:520.

21. Du Bois, "The Possibility of Democracy in America," pt. 2, *Crisis* 35 (October 1928), in *Selections from "The Crisis,"* ed. Aptheker, 2:526.

22. Du Bois, "Third Party," *Crisis* 36 (February 1929), in *Selections from "The Crisis,"* ed. Aptheker, 2:545.

23. Du Bois, "Strategy of the Negro Vote," *Crisis* 40 (June 1933), in *Selections from "The Crisis,"* ed. Aptheker, 2:706, 707.

24. Du Bois, *Autobiography*, 275.

25. George Kateb, "Democratic Individuality and the Claims of Politics," *Po-*

litical Theory 12, no. 3 (August 1984): 331–60; hereafter cited parenthetically in the text.

26. Although my argument pursues a different objective, I found very helpful and informative Jack Turner's "Awakening to Race: Ralph Ellison and Democratic Individuality," *Political Theory* 36, no. 5 (October 2008): 665–82.

27. In the discussion of Young that follows, I draw primarily from her essay "Communication and the Other: Beyond Deliberative Democracy," in *Democracy and Difference,* ed. Seyla Benhabib (Princeton: Princeton University Press, 1996), 120–36; and Iris Marion Young, *Inclusion and Democracy* (New York: Oxford University Press, 2000).

7

A Democracy of Differences

Knowledge and the Unknowable in Du Bois's Theory of Democratic Governance

Robert W. Williams

In numerous ways, works, and deeds, W. E. B. Du Bois championed democracy. He espoused political and civil rights for persons of color and supported women's suffrage. His long-standing Pan-Africanism called for the ending of colonial domination and the promotion of political rights for indigenous peoples. Moreover, as his turn toward socialism became more forceful, his ideals of democracy extended popular participation into democratic control over industry. Such facets of his thought increasingly have been studied by scholars and have contributed to his slow inclusion into a wider canon of US democratic theory.

In the pages that follow, I will argue that one of Du Bois's more important contributions to such theory was his fluid conception of difference, one that acknowledges what I will be calling the "unknowability" of others yet at the same time finds a role for scientific knowledge in democratic governance. To highlight the distinctiveness of Du Bois's conception of difference, I will juxtapose it with that of a more recent theorist of difference and democracy, Iris Marion Young. As will be discussed, what they share is notable. Both thinkers are concerned with the consequences of embodiment for a democracy that encompasses, even celebrates, difference among the humans within its territorial borders. Both believe that individuals are socially embodied, and both criticize the idea of the abstract, disembodied individual found in social contract theories and their modern variants. While Young argues that the fact of human embodiment undermines the possibility of impartiality in moral reasoning and in technocratic forms of policymaking, Du Bois similarly argues that neutrality becomes impossible both for those researching social issues and for those struggling for social justice. Both Du Bois and Young argue also that such differences must be respected, not homogenized, if true equality and justice are to be upheld. Finally, both strenuously assert that the different interests, viewpoints, and values must be given full play in political participation and policymaking.

Where Du Bois and Young disagree, however, is over two key points. One is the nature of difference, which Young takes to be unproblematically graspable, whereas Du Bois understands it to be ultimately unknowable. The second point of disagreement is over the nature and role of knowledge in governance, especially that of scientific knowledge. Du Bois would have accepted Young's critique of impartiality, but his work challenges her views that seem to equate all of science and scientific knowledge with the racist and sexist conclusions generated by numerous practitioners of recent centuries. Indeed, Du Bois affirms the possibility of scientific objectivity as well as the usefulness of scholarly explanations and interpretations of human actions. Du Bois's application of objectivity involves grasping the strengths and weaknesses of science in general, and thereby demarcating what science can and cannot discover—that is, what is scientifically knowable and what is unknowable (or "nescient") by those methodologies. Ultimately, and this is my central contention, from his critiques of science we can reconstruct Du Bois's use of both science and nescience in the support of good and just democratic governance, a governance that is necessarily coupled with participation by diverse citizens because science in crucial ways is fundamentally inadequate to the task of generating the range of knowledge(s) needed for governing.

Difference and Democracy in Du Bois and Young

Du Bois does not explicitly formulate a theory of democracy and difference, but he argues in numerous works that human differences are a central reason for disfranchisement and societal repression (e.g., "Democracy and the

Negro"; "The Negro Citizen"). Notable in this respect are "The Individual and Social Conscience" (IASC), published in 1905, and its draft counterpart, "How to Develop in the Individual a Social Conscience."[1] Both texts frame difference in a language of embodiment. In the draft version Du Bois writes: "But the differences emphasized [by others seeking to marginalize members of social groups] have been, if you remember, differences of body rather than soul—physical differences suited to an age of physics, material differences sprung from a world of bulk and mass and weight."[2]

That is, Du Bois believed that physical human differences are both literally and figuratively superficial, even though they have been used as the basis for exclusion. Accordingly, they are to be transcended and rendered moot insofar as a fundamental similarity between and among distinct humans is to be found in a religiously grounded realm denoted here by Du Bois's word "soul." This fundamental similarity among all human beings is the basis for according political equality as well as equality of opportunity to all.[3]

Du Bois's somewhat conventional idea of a common humanity clearly resembles the type of homogeneity that Iris Marion Young criticizes in *Justice and the Politics of Difference.*[4] For Young, such a definition of common humanity historically has assumed an elite white heterosexual male as the norm and has tended to socially and politically marginalize those persons not part of that particular social grouping. Likewise, Du Bois observes how physical and other forms of difference across racial, gender, and class lines have been used to justify oppression and segregation. Unlike Young, however, Du Bois and a number of his contemporary thinkers and activists retained their belief in fundamental similarities among all humans, such as the equal capacity to reason and to develop their skills. In addition, many in Du Bois's era and earlier (e.g., Anna Julia Cooper, Frederick Douglass, and Mary Church Terrell) grounded that basic equality both in a theological foundation and in the core US political principles enunciated in the Declaration of Independence and the Constitution.

However, Du Bois also conceptualizes difference in a second way, one that that accords more with Young's critique of homogeneity. In "Of the Ruling of Men" (and its related pamphlet, *Disfranchisement*), Du Bois suggests that differences between individuals and among individuals of various social groupings (such as race and gender) are fundamental because of their irreducibly unique, unbridgeable, perhaps even ineffable experiences.[5] In "Ruling," Du Bois sketches three regime types—aristocracy, monarchy, and democracy—and places the plurality of singular individuals at the heart of that schema, arguing that only an individual can know his or her condition and needs in life:

> [Wh]o shall elect [the rulers]. The earlier answer was: a select few, such as the wise, the best born, the able. Many people assume that it was corruption that made such aristocracies fail. By no means. The best and most effective aristocracy, like the best monarchy, suffered from lack of knowledge. The rulers did not know or understand the needs of the people and they could not find out, for in the last analysis only the man himself, however humble, knows his own condition. He may not know how to remedy it, he may not realize just what is the matter; but he knows when something hurts and he alone knows how that hurt feels. Or if sunk below feeling or comprehension or complaint, he does not even know that he is hurt, God help his country, for it not only lacks knowledge, but has destroyed the sources of knowledge.[6]

Like Young, then, Du Bois seem to believe that human differences and their embodied knowledges are indispensable to effective governance, regardless of the regime type.

The Difference That Embodiment Makes

As with his conception of difference, Du Bois does not explicitly formulate a theory of human embodiment. Yet throughout his works he employs examples and language that plainly recognize its importance. Although, for Du Bois, humans can soar figuratively in the heavens with their ideals and aspirations, in a world of racial indignities and violence they exist in corporeal form and live fully incarnated in the here-and-now, with all its discriminatory norms and practices. Likewise, while he believes that human knowledge accumulates over time and can transcend any given person, he is also aware that knowledge is embodied in individuals and develops within the social situations and relationships in which persons live. In a passage to which I will return, he writes:

> The vast and wonderful knowledge of this marvelous universe is locked in the bosoms of its individual souls. To tap this mighty reservoir of ex-

> perience, knowledge, beauty, love, and deed we must appeal not to the few, not to some souls, but to all. The narrower the appeal, the poorer the culture; the wider the appeal the more magnificent are the possibilities. Infinite is human nature. We make it finite by choking back the mass of men, by attempting to speak for others, to interpret and act for them, and we end by acting for ourselves and using the world as our private property. If this were all, it were crime enough—but it is not all: by our ignorance we make the creation of the greater world impossible; we beat back a world built of the playing of dogs and laughter of children, the song of Black Folk and worship of Yellow, the love of women and strength of men, and try to express by a group of doddering ancients the Will of the World.[7]

Accordingly, the justification for participation in government does not derive primarily from natural and political rights and the attendant conception of the supposedly rights-bearing individual. Rather, in "Ruling" Du Bois focuses on what makes an individual fundamentally distinct: namely, his or her embodied experiences of the world, which arise from being an irreducible and indivisible agentic self-in-the-world (as his thought could be stated). Ultimately, Du Bois considers embodiment to be inescapable for all races. It is therefore a necessary component of understanding others in the world. Indeed, the embodiment of blacks is something of worth for themselves, but it also offers value to humanity as a whole.[8]

Iris Marion Young specifically addresses embodiment in her theory of marginalization. Many well-known philosophies assume a reason/emotion dichotomy that privileges reason and subordinates emotion. Reason is associated with the mind and is supposedly universal. Emotions and feelings are particular to the body. The prevailing views of many centuries characterize women and persons of color as essentially, and typically immutably, embodied. Males purportedly can transcend, or at least moderate, their bodily passions because they are characterized as essentially reasoning beings. For Young, however, the supposedly universal standpoint of reason is problematic to its core. Such a view of reason is quite pointedly particular to and incarnated by elite white males. Consequently, all others are deemed inferior within a social hierarchy of inequality. Gender and racial differences are suppressed; they must be excluded from, or at least obstructed within, the public and its political processes. The supposedly universal standpoint of reason in the (atomistic) individual is belied in reality by how particular its application is to elite white males rather than to the range of humanity that actually exists.[9]

For both Young and Du Bois, then, the dominant value systems and social/political practices generate certain consequences. Individuals can be philosophically ignored and effectively marginalized in social and political practices. As a result, the pursuit of normative recognition and political participation historically has tended to require an acceptance of the goal to homogenize their differences—to be like white males and to embrace a narrower set of values and views than actually may be present among all. Writes Young:

> By assuming that reason stands opposed to desire, affectivity, and the body, this conception of the civic public excludes bodily and affective aspects of human existence. In practice, this assumption forces homogeneity upon the civic public, excluding from the public those individuals and groups that do not fit the model of the rational citizen capable of transcending body and sentiment. This exclusion has a twofold basis: the tendency to oppose reason and desire, and the association of these traits with kinds of persons. . . . Modern normative reason and its political expression in the idea of the civic public, then, attain unity and coherence through the expulsion and confinement of everything that would threaten to invade the polity with differentiation: the specificity of women's bodies and desire, differences of race and culture, the variability and heterogeneity of needs, the goals and desires of individuals, the ambiguity and changeability of feeling.[10]

About this implicit exclusion of rights effected by universalist theories of democracy, Du Bois seems to be in agreement with Iris Marion Young. She is noted for her critique of distributive theories of justice, such as those propounded by John Rawls and others. A distributive paradigm typically deals with measurable, material things for atomistic individuals—ahistorically conceptualized humans shorn of social situatedness—rather than individuals constituted by social relations and the norms undergirding them. Young's critique parallels the criticisms of the theories of the sexual contract and the racial contract of Carol Pateman and Charles Mills, respectively.[11]

As with Young, embodiment is integral to existence for Du Bois. He illustrates embodiment in various works. First, he argues against lynching and, in a graphic example of dismembering black bodies, he recounts his reflections on the racial violence of Sam Hose's lynching. Second, he criticizes the presumed standard of so-called Eurocentric beauty; he praises Afrocentric forms of beauty ("The Damnation of Women," in *Darkwater*). Third, as Nick Bromell has argued, his varied uses of "touch" as a metaphor underscored his belief that politics and governance always have a corporeal dimension. Du Bois writes, for example, that, "Politics have not touched the matters of daily life which are nearest the interests of the people—namely, work and wages; or if they have, they have touched it obscurely and indirectly."[12] Finally, his famous concept of double-consciousness in *The Souls of Black Folk* also has an embodied aspect: "It is a peculiar sensation, this double-consciousness, this sense of always looking at one's self through the eyes of others, of measuring one's soul by the tape of a world that looks on in amused contempt and pity. One ever feels his twoness,—an American, a Negro; two souls, two thoughts, two unreconciled strivings; two warring ideals in one dark body, whose dogged strength alone keeps it from being torn asunder."[13]

Du Bois emphasizes that whites for their part are also embodied. Most famously, in *Black Reconstruction* he writes of the embodiment of unearned white advantages, or as we may call it today, white privilege: to compensate for low wages and status relative to upper-class whites, poorer and working-class whites receive "a public and psychological wage" in the form of being white within a racist hierarchy. Less obviously, Du Bois often refers to whites' embodiment in his accounts of the interpersonal relations between blacks and whites. In passages of *The Souls of Black Folk* that articulate his idea of the "Talented Tenth," for example, he claims that white elites tend to interact mainly with the black working classes and very seldom with educated black professionals; consequently, he argues, whites usually form inaccurate conclusions regarding African Americans' skills and possibilities. Similarly, white researchers—including the "car window sociologists" who do not interpersonally relate with blacks—are also likely to draw the wrong conclusions about their black subjects.[14]

Indeed, Du Bois also emphasizes that all scholars practicing social-science research should be aware that they are embodied persons embedded in the society that they study:

> From the beginning, social scientists have envied the students of physical science and sought to imitate them in various ways. They have been especially intrigued by the detachment which is possible in the case of a physical scientist. No physical scientist has any particular personal interest in the rocks which he studies or even the fish, the snakes, or the animals. He views them and their action entirely from without and from above, and therefore presumably can come to utterly unprejudiced conclusions. The social scientists on other hand, including the historians, have to do with vital matters of which they are more or less a part.[15]

Although not using Young's terminology of public and private, Du Bois's idea of double-consciousness expresses a similar analysis. In the United States, African Americans face the prospect of denying themselves and their (ancestral) communities to the extent that they are expected to "bleach" their differences in white norms. In his often-quoted words:

> The history of the American Negro is the history of this strife,—this longing to attain self-conscious manhood, to merge his double self into a better and truer self. In this merging he wishes neither of the older selves to be lost. He would not Africanize America, for America has too much to teach the world and Africa. He would not bleach his Negro soul in a flood of white Americanism, for he knows that Negro blood has a message for the world. He simply wishes to make it possible for a man to be both a Negro and an American, without being cursed and spit upon by his fellows, without having the doors of Opportunity closed roughly in his face.[16]

Marginalization of differences should not be expected or justified simply because the individuals are unconventional or do not fit some norm or tradition. Based on the inescapable particularities arising from embodiment, Du Bois and Young each agree that such differences should not be homogenized if equality and justice are to be upheld. Accordingly, for Du Bois and Young, the different interests, viewpoints, and values deserve political participation and input into policymaking. Only thus will a democracy be one in practice and also in principle. Young incorporates a wide range of different groups into deliberative processes that extend beyond voting to include consideration of their views in legislatures and private interest groups. In her words: "To promote a politics of inclusion, then, participatory democrats must promote the ideal of a heterogeneous public, in which persons stand forth with their differences acknowledged and respected, though not perhaps completely understood, by others."[17]

For Du Bois, in sum, individuals are not abstract entities, such as one finds in various social contract and liberal theories (e.g., those of Hobbes, Locke, and Rousseau). Social contractarians may disagree with the argument that their conception of the individual formulates an abstract being. Nonetheless, they depict individuals who purportedly are universal in their acquisitiveness and in the formal qualities of their rationality and emotionality. As many critics have argued, such individuals often carry with them certain assumptions marking them as less (or more) than universal—for example, assumptions of their whiteness, their maleness, and the social, political, and economic privileges these attributes confer.[18]

The Importance of Unknowability

Despite their deep agreement on the importance of embodied difference to democracy, Du Bois and Young understand such difference in significantly different ways. Young tends to assume that the differences made by race, gender, age, sexuality, and the like are unproblematically knowable and categorizable. But as Nick Bromell has argued, Du Bois sees differences of experience as being in the last analysis mysterious, even unknowable.[19] In approaching the place of unknowability in his political thought, we might begin by noting that the two (somewhat contradictory) senses of difference we saw in "Social Conscience" and "Ruling" converge in the epistemological dimensions of each uniquely different human individual. In both texts, Du Bois holds that any particular person is directly unknowable to others. In "The Individual and Social Conscience," he writes: "Here in this my neighbor stand things I do not know, experiences I have never felt, depths whose darkness is beyond me, and heights hidden by the clouds; or, perhaps, rather, differences in ways of thinking, and dreaming, and feeling which I guess at rather than know; strange twistings of soul that curve between the grotesque and the awful."[20]

That passage bears a striking similarity to Du Bois's later view in "Ruling" that only the individual knows her/his own needs and life condition.

Such unknowability yields related consequences that connect the two sets of texts. In the "Social Conscience" works, one's incapacity to experience another's joys and pains prompts one, according to the dialectic set forth, to seek a more comprehensive understanding of what humans are by seeing past their particular bodily differences. In "Ruling" and "Disfranchisement," this incapacity to experience others' suffering justifies their inclusion in the voting processes, because governments require their heretofore "excluded wisdom." Paradoxically, then, in order to take full account of the specific differences of unique individuals, we will need to admit at the outset that some aspects of these cannot be known by us.[21]

Regarding democracy and difference, in "Disfranchisement" and "Ruling" Du Bois raises implicit challenges to the reduction of individual differences to statistical measures and means within masses of data. Certainly, Du Bois mentions the social groups of race, gender, and class in those texts. But he is explicit about the particularity of individuals within social groups and the importance of such individuals in governance. As I have already noted above, Du Bois writes that one's suffering is not known to, and indeed cannot be directly knowable by, others:

> Remember the foundation of the argument [for democracy] is that in the last analysis only the sufferer knows his sufferings, and that no state can be strong which excludes from its expressed wisdom, the knowledge possessed by mothers, wives, and daughters. Certainly we have but to view the unsatisfactory relations of the sexes the world over and the problem of children, to realize how desperately we need this excluded wisdom.
>
> The same argument applies to other excluded groups: If a race like the Negro race is excluded, then so far as that race is a part of the economic and social organization of the land, the feeling and the experience of that race is absolutely necessary to the realization of the broadest justice for all citizens. Or if the "submerged tenth" be excluded, then again there is lost from the world an experience of untold value, and the submerged must be raised rapidly to a place where they can speak for themselves.[22]

For Du Bois, the direct unknowability of an individual's experiences does not preclude and does not negate the shared experiences of that individual as a member of a racial group. Indeed, an African American possesses her/ his personal experiences, which, when considered in light of other African Americans, would share some commonalities together that would not be the experiences of the members of other races.

Iris Marion Young is certainly aware that persons within social groups can possess knowledge that others do not have and that such a variety of information and experiences may be helpful for policymaking. At the end of a list of advantages that emerge from including oppressed and marginalized groups within the policy processes of a democracy, Young writes:

> Finally, group representation promotes just outcomes because it maximizes the social knowledge expressed in discussion, and thus furthers practical wisdom. Group differences are manifest not only in different needs, interests, and goals, but also in different social locations and experiences. People in different groups often know about somewhat different institutions, events, practices, and social relations, and often have differing perceptions of the same institutions, relations, or events. For this reason members of some groups are sometimes in a better position than members of others to understand and anticipate the probable consequences of implementing particular social policies. A public that makes use of all such social knowledge in its differentiated plurality is most likely to make just and wise decisions.[23]

Thus, although in some ways similar to Du Bois, Young's understanding of difference does not connect the varying experiential bases of knowledge to a thematic of unknowability and in turn does frame the idea of unknowability as the foundation of democracy. Her emphasis falls consistently on the importance (and epistemological validity) of group experience.

The central place Du Bois accords to singular experiences may provoke charges that he is catering to personal whims and perspectives, and that as a consequence he is justifying governance based on an individual's (or individuals') irrationality, misperception, and delusions. As with much of Du Bois's underlying philosophy of social science, he does not address this issue in "Ruling." However, an unpublished document circa 1946 can help us to better understand how Du Bois may have sought to avoid solipsism with regard to unknowability. In "Steps toward a Science of How Men Act," he takes a philosophically skeptical line that we cannot have "direct knowledge" of anything except our own individual feelings. (Here he is following a point made by William James and others.)[24] For Du Bois, the world around us is present in our perceptions, but doubt remains about whether our perceptions correspond with that which is outside of us. In Du Bois's words: "Yet of this outer world; of everything except our own emotions there is and probably never can be any direct knowledge. Everything concerning that outer world must be assumption upon our part. But it is [a] natural assumption and for the most part makes our feelings and thoughts seem reasonable: the existence of other people is a perfectly natural assumption, but it cannot be directly perceived; it must be inferred from our emotions and thoughts."[25]

At times, the influence of James's pragmatism reverberates throughout this essay, as when Du Bois writes:

> Here the great scientific tool of the Hypothesis is discovered; we assume that certain things are true; we act as though this assumption is Truth. The ensuing facts of our experience arrange themselves in accord with our assumption. Therefore our assumption is True; or the facts agree except in certain particulars; we rearrange our assumptions to fit the new experience or more fully to explain the old. The new Hypothesis becomes accepted Truth. But all Truth, save our own feeling, we hold tentatively and watchfully, ready to change our conception, once a new explanation or phenomena fits the facts more perfectly.[26]

As part of their existence, individuals must act in the world. They encounter a continuous stream of experiences of the world that must be analyzed and reanalyzed constantly. Subsequent experiences can potentially modify previous experience, all in a never-ending process that helps humans to gain a better sense of the world, but a sense that is never fully complete or completed.

For Du Bois, then, the unknowability of others is not a nihilist concept of despair nor a justification of political apathy or inactivity. Rather, unknowability supports a democracy of differences by recognizing that what makes individuals irreducibly distinct, and thus not homogeneous, are their embodied experiences as agentic selves in the world.

Scientific Knowledge and Democratic Governance

Yet for all his commitment to the importance of unknowability, Du Bois is much more sanguine than Young about the role scientific knowledge can play in democratic governance.[27] Young herself does not address the role of scientific knowledge in governance. Severely critical of science, as we have seen, she is seemingly skeptical of the ability of the sciences to understand anything about humans at all. Young criticizes science and the forms of knowledge that are associated with technocratic styles of policymaking. Included in her criticisms is her critique of the idea of impartiality. Impartiality in politics assumes that particularity can be overcome via positing the precondition and/or the goal of a common (universal) good that all citizens are to embrace and promote. Such a common good, she argues, homogenizes difference. This homogenization has justified racial, gender, and class suppression in numerous historical cases.[28] Moreover, she also criticizes impartiality in terms of how natural science and medicine have studied women and persons of color: "In the developing sciences of natural history, phrenology, physiognomy, ethnography, and medicine, the gaze of the scientific observer was applied to bodies, weighing, measuring, and classifying them according to a normative hierarchy. Nineteenth-century theorists of race explicitly assumed white European body types and facial features as the norm, the perfection of the human form, in relation to which other body types were either degenerate or less developed. Bringing these norms into the discourse of science, however, naturalized them, gave the assertions of superiority and additional authority as truths of nature."[29]

Such sciences proclaim differences as natural and immutable based on a normative ideal of elite white males. Such scientists believe that they occupy a universal standpoint of reason, shorn of interest, power, and privilege. Perhaps this is why Young does not consider science to have a role in governing.[30]

Du Bois's position on this issue is more nuanced. On the one hand, he certainly agrees with the critiques of pseudo-science made by Young and others.[31] Du Bois is also keenly aware of the limitations of scientific knowledge. In an interview with William Ingersoll late in his life, Du Bois recounts a dialogue that he held when he was conducting the fieldwork for what became *The Philadelphia Negro:*

> Q: How did you find the attitude of the people you interviewed? Co-operative? helpful? [*sic*]
>
> DuBois: A good many of the better educated and well-to-do didn't like it at all. They didn't like to be investigated; they weren't wild animals or anything of that sort. And they didn't like to have a stranger come and investigate them.
>
> I remember one case in particular. There was a young man who graduated from the University of Pennsylvania in engineering, a young colored man belonging to a well-to-do and well known colored family. I went to his sister, and the story was, that I had heard—I think it was true—that he couldn't get a job and he had to work as a waiter in a place where many of his fellow-graduates were dining. I asked her about these facts, and she looked me over rather coldly and said, "Why do you want to know?"
>
> I said, "Well, I'd just like to get at the truth of the matter."
>
> "What are you going to do about it after you know?"
>
> "I'm not going to do anything about it."
>
> "Well, in that case, I'm not interested," and she wouldn't give me any information. Well, I could see her point of view. If this was an effort on the part of the people who had not given him a chance to open some chances for him, that was one thing; but if they were just 'coming to look us over like a herd of cattle'"—[32]

Du Bois also believed that the sciences can discover only part of what humans are and can become. In his essay "The Church and Religion," for example, he argues that science is "organized human knowledge," but it "does not pretend to give a complete answer to the riddle of the universe" and cannot provide "scientific proof" for "faith in the triumph of good deeds" and for "love of our relatives and our neighbors and of all humanity."[33] Means other than science are necessary. In the "Criteria of Negro Art," Du Bois suggests one appropriate way to address humans in the fullness of their possibilities and capacities:

> Thus it is the bounden duty of black America to begin this great work of the creation of Beauty, of the preservation of Beauty, of the realization of Beauty, and we must use in this work all the methods that men have used before. And what have been the tools of the artist in

> times gone by? First of all, he has used the Truth—not for the sake of truth, not as a scientist seeking truth, but as one upon whom Truth eternally thrusts itself as the highest handmaid of imagination, as the one great vehicle of universal understanding. Again artists have used Goodness—goodness in all its aspects of justice, honor and right—not for sake of an ethical sanction but as the one true method of gaining sympathy and human interest.[34]

Finally, Du Bois challenges the tenet of value-neutrality of the social science of his era. Value neutrality holds that intellectual concepts and frameworks must not judge the worth of the "what," including the "who," that is being studied. As Du Bois and others note, purportedly neutral scientific concepts on the races are laden with biases. Many scholars employing such conceptions also hold that the relative positioning is based on innate, often immutable, characteristics—characteristics they deem objective.[35] Du Bois certainly combats this approach. How, then, may we conceptualize the development of Africana peoples? For Du Bois, any racial group cannot be deemed a priori as homogeneous synchronically; this is a white-supremacist tenet that he disputes in "The Negroes of Farmville, Virginia." Moreover, for Du Bois no racial group can be deemed a priori as incapable of development diachronically; this is another supremacist tenet that he challenges, for example, in "The Evolution of the Race Problem." Indeed, in *Dusk of Dawn* he argues against conceptualizing blacks in static terms: "Thus, in my own sociology, because of firm belief in a changing racial group, I easily grasped the idea of a changing developing society rather than a fixed social structure." Accordingly, for Du Bois, researchers must use as a research postulate the fundamental humanity of Africana peoples not only in order to justify the importance of studying them but also (I suggest) to account for their volitional agency at the core of their capacity to advance as humans.[36]

Nonetheless, for all his doubts about the sciences (including the social sciences), Du Bois seeks to understand their strengths and weaknesses so as to better delineate the conditions under which they may be used productively. The sciences in general provide the data that allow us to formulate general observations about nature and society.[37]

To understand better how Du Bois builds on the strengths of social science in particular, we can turn to his unpublished text "Sociology Hesitant," a document considered vital for understanding his views on the scientific method and the social sciences.[38] Du Bois indicates that human actions can be studied sociologically in terms of "primary rhythms" and "secondary rhythms":

> As . . . we rise in the realm of conduct, we note a primary and a secondary rythm [*sic*]. A primary rythm depending, as we have indicated on physical forces and physical law; but within this appears again and again a secondary rythm which[,] while presenting nearly the same uniformity as the first, differs from it in its more or less sudden rise at a given tune, in accordance with prearranged plan and prediction and in being liable to stoppage and change according to similar plan. An example of primary uniformity is the death rate; of secondary uniformity, the operation of a woman's club; to confound the two sorts of human uniformity is fatal to clear thinking; to explain them we must assume Law and Chance working in conjunction—Chance being the scientific side of inexplicable Will. Sociology[,] then, is the Science that seeks the limits of Chance in human conduct.[39]

The categories of primary rhythm and secondary rhythm allow Du Bois to conceptualize, on the one hand, the causal determinism that is the hallmark of natural laws and social-scientific law-like behaviors. The categories also allow him to conceptualize the possibility of undetermined action (i.e., free will) which when he casts it in scientific terms can be called "chance."

What are the objective truths that Du Bois believed could be discovered, and conversely, what is not discoverable by scientific research because it would not be deterministic? Pursuing primary rhythm research, such as birth, death, and marriage rates, conventional social-scientific techniques will involve aggregating data of individual humans into a statistical mass. Such primary rhythm research would also entail simplifying, or reducing, different motivations and/or different life situations into a few categories or a few causal variables. Ultimately, for Du Bois and other (social) scientists such simplification and aggregation hopefully can be used to formulate general laws of human behavior.[40] Although Du Bois does not specify the laws of human behavior as such, he often sets down the historical conditions, including ending racial discrimination and fostering education and business entrepreneurship for persons of color, that have occasioned the opportunities for individuals and social groups to advance.[41]

Du Bois does not specifically ask in "Sociology Hesitant" about the limitations on the knowledge generated by studying primary rhythms. However, we can frame a tentative answer by examining his conception of secondary rhythms. In "Sociology Hesitant," he indicates that the unique aspects of humans—what is incalculable—are located in the secondary rhythms of human actions.[42] Discerning and demarcating chance is the sociological counterpoint to religious views on free will. As I may (para)phrase it in light of his other early 1900 texts (e.g., "The Individual and Social Conscience" and "Disfranchisement"), the data of primary rhythms can neither convey the utter uniqueness of an individual nor the knowledge and wisdom arising from that individual's experiences. Secondary rhythms conceptualize the subjectivity that separates humans from animals and plants. Accordingly, that which is "incalculable" (in Du Bois's wording) is that which we may also call conscious, volitional agency. And with this point we circle back to Du Bois's notion of individual unknowability.

Both W. E. B. Du Bois and Iris Marion Young address the importance of human differences in democratic politics and polities. Young's analysis of difference includes her critique of the historical role of the natural and social sciences in marginalizing humans within racial and gender hierarchies of repression and inequality. Her insightful criticisms, however, suggest no way by which the sciences may have a positive role in governance. Du Bois offers his own relevant criticisms of the sciences, especially the racist pseudo-science of his era. He also outlines the limitations of quantitatively based sciences when studying the irreducible and unique experiences of individuals.

Although he shares Young's criticisms of science, Du Bois also considers it to be a potentially positive tool for government policymaking: it can help us discern patterns in the interrelated natural and social realms, as well as understand better the development of human differences. All the while, the diverse knowledges of the people—including the unknowable "excluded wisdom" and experiences of marginalized persons—provide the information needed for governing that the sciences cannot effectively study. Accordingly, in Du Bois's theory of democracy, both the knowable and the unknowable, both science and nescience, are indispensable.

Du Bois's dynamic of science and nescience speaks to us in the twenty-first century. Scientific research in the United States today examines crucial environmental, social, and workplaces issues. Without such research neither citizens nor the politicians they elect could address those issues responsibly. Similarly, the social sciences increasingly have been wielded for the common good of equality, citizen participation, and government accountability.[43] Nonetheless, even in the midst of accumulating knowledge, Du Bois reminds us that the limits of knowledge and the knowable should prompt us to listen to, and perhaps to heed, the insights, the hopes, and the grief of our fellows. It is all of us—and certainly those with the least among us—that democracy in its fullest sense should serve.

Notes

During the revision process I have benefited from the thoughtful questions and useful comments posed by Nick Bromell. In addition, I wish to thank Philip Luke Sinitiere for directing my attention to Du Bois's "How to Develop in the Individual a Social Conscience," a typescript located in the W. E. B. Du Bois Collection at the Fisk University Archives.

1. W. E. B. Du Bois, "Democracy and the Negro," *City Club Bulletin,* 4, no. 14 (May 28, 1912): 229–36; W. E. B. Du Bois, "The Negro Citizen," in Charles S. Johnson, *The Negro in Civilization* (New York: Holt, 1930): 461–70. In mid-February 1905, Du Bois serves as a discussant at the Third Annual Convention of the Religious Education Association (REA), where he delivers "The Individual and Social Conscience" (IASC) (see Horace Bumstead, "Dr. Du Bois in Boston," *Bulletin of Atlanta University,* no. 153 [March 1905]: 2–3, Digital Collection of Robert W. Woodruff Library. Atlanta University Center, http://contentdm.auctr.edu/cdm/compoundobject/collection/rwwl/id/1331/rec/1). "Dangerous Classifying," *Friends' Intelligencer,* 62, no. 10 [Third Month 1905): 150–51. "How to Develop in the Individual a Social Conscience" (HTDT, ca. 1905) is an undated draft version held in the W. E. B. Du Bois Collection, 1867–1963, Box 55, Folder 2, Fisk University Archives, as a typescript (a handwritten version is also housed at the archives).

The IASC is the published version printed in the REA conference proceedings, but it is missing two paragraphs from the HTDT draft—paragraphs relevant to my analysis of Du Bois on difference. Does Du Bois actually deliver those paragraphs at the conference session? Based on a contemporaneous source I argue tentatively that he indeed does deliver the words of the draft HTDT. In an anonymous editorial in the *Friends' Intelligencer* published a few weeks after the conference ("Dangerous Classifying"), Du Bois is mentioned by name, and a portion of the draft HTDT version is printed, even quoted verbatim, including the missing two paragraphs not found in the IASC as published in the REA conference proceedings. If Du Bois did not deliver those "missing" two paragraphs when speaking, then he perhaps made the draft version available to the author of the anonymous essay. See W. E. B. Du Bois, "The Individual and Social Conscience" (originally untitled), in *Religious Education Association, The Aims of Religious Education. The Proceedings of the Third Annual Convention of the Religious Education Association,* Boston, February 12–16, 1905 (Chicago: Executive Office of the Religious Education Association, 1905): 53–55, www.archive.org/details/proceedingsofann03reliuoft (alternate source: www.webdubois.org/dbIASC.html).

2. Du Bois, "How to Develop in the Individual a Social Conscience," 5.

3. See Robert W. Williams and W. E. B. Du Bois [Primary source], "'The Sacred Unity in All the Diversity': The Text and a Thematic Analysis of W. E. B. Du Bois's 'The Individual and Social Conscience' (1905)," *Journal of African American Studies* 16, no. 3 (September 2012): 456–97.

4. Iris Marion Young, *Justice and the Politics of Difference* (Princeton: Princeton University Press, 1990).

5. W. E. B. Du Bois, "Of the Ruling of Men," in W. E. B. Du Bois, *Darkwater: Voices from within the Veil.* (New York: Harcourt, Brace and Howe, 1920), chap. 6; W. E. B. Du Bois, *Disfranchisement* (Pamphlet) (New York: National American Woman Suffrage Association, ca. 1912).

6. Du Bois, "Of the Ruling of Men," 142–43 (¶ 25).

7. Ibid., 140–41 (¶ 20).

8. W. E. B. Du Bois, "The Conservation of Races," *American Negro Academy Occasional Papers,* no. 2. (Washington, DC: American Negro Academy, 1897), www.webdubois.org/dbConsrvOfRaces.html.

9. Young, *Justice,* chaps. 4–5. See also Genevieve Lloyd, *The Man of Reason: 'Male' and 'Female' in Western Philosophy,* 2nd ed. (London: Routledge, 1993).

10. Young, *Justice,* 109, 111.

11. Ibid., 26–27; Carol Pateman, *The Sexual Contract* (Stanford, CA: Stanford University Press, 1988); Charles W. Mills, *The Racial Contract* (Ithaca, NY: Cornell University Press, 1997).

12. W. E. B. Du Bois, "My Evolving Program for Negro Freedom," in *What the Negro Wants,* ed. Rayford W. Logan, 31–70 (Chapel Hill: University of North Carolina Press, 1944), 53 (¶ 63), www.webdubois.org/dbMyEvolvingPrgm.html; W. E. B. Du Bois, "The Damnation of Women" in Du Bois, *Darkwater*; Du Bois, "Of the Ruling of Men," 150 (¶ 43). On this aspect of embodiment in Du Bois, see also Nick Bromell, "'Honest and Earnest Criticism" as the 'Soul of Democracy': Du Bois's Style of Democratic Reasoning," in this volume, 159–80.

13. W. E. B. Du Bois, *The Souls of Black Folk* (Chicago: McClurg, 1903), chap. 1.

14. W. E. B. Du Bois, *Black Reconstruction in America, 1860–1880* (1935; New York: Atheneum, 1992), 700; see also Du Bois, *Souls.*

15. W. E. B. Du Bois, "Phylon: Science or Propaganda," *Phylon*, 5, no. 1 (First Quarter 1944), 6.

16. Du Bois, *Souls*, chap. 1.

17. Young, *Justice*, 119.

18. For example, Lloyd, *The Man of Reason;* see also Pateman, *Sexual Contract;* and Mills, *Racial Contract.*

19. Bromell, "Enlargement of Democratic Theory"; Nick Bromell, *The Time Is Always Now: Black Thought and the Transformation of US Democracy* (New York: Oxford University Press, 2013).

20. Du Bois, "The Individual and Social Conscience," ¶ 3.

21. Although Du Bois never formulates a theory of unknowability, he does reference the idea of the unknowable in various places. For example, in his letter to Herbert Aptheker of 10 January 1956, Du Bois specifically mentions unknowability as part of his philosophy: "I assumed that Truth was only partially known but that it was ultimately largely knowable, although perhaps in part forever Unknowable" (in W. E. B. Du Bois, *The Correspondence of W. E. B. Du Bois, Vol. III: Selections, 1944–1963,* ed. Herbert Aptheker [Amherst: University of Massachusetts Press, 1978]: 394–96; capitalization in the original).

22. Du Bois, "Disfranchisement," 7. The words of the quotation are repeated, with small grammatical changes, a few years later in "Of the Ruling of Men," 143–44 (¶¶ 27–28).

23. Young, *Justice*, 186.

24. William James, in his *Principles of Psychology*, writes:

> Each of these minds keeps its own thoughts to itself. There is no giving or bartering between them. No thought even comes into direct *sight* of a thought in another personal consciousness than its own. Absolute insulation, irreducible pluralism, is the law. It seems as if the elementary psychic fact were not *thought* or *this thought* or *that thought,* but *my thought,* every thought being *owned.* Neither contemporaneity, nor proximity in space, nor similarity of quality and content are able to fuse thoughts together which are sundered by this barrier of belonging to different personal minds. The breaches between such thoughts are the most absolute breaches in nature. Everyone will recognize this to be true, so long as the existence of *something* corresponding to the term "personal mind" is all that is insisted on, without any particular view of its nature being implied. On these terms the personal self rather than the thought might be treated as the immediate datum in psychology. The universal conscious fact is not "feelings and thoughts exist," but "I think" and "I feel." No psychology, at any rate, can question the *existence* of personal selves. The worst a psychology can do is so to interpret the nature of these selves as to rob them of their worth. (William James, *Principles*

of Psychology, vol. 1 [New York: Henry Holt, 1890], 226; footnote omitted; emphasis in the original)

25. W. E. B. Du Bois, "Steps toward a Science of How Men Act, ca. 1946," 1, W. E. B. Du Bois Papers, Special Collections & University Archives, University of Massachusetts Amherst Library, http://credo.library.umass.edu/view/full/mums312-b213-i071.

26. Ibid., 3.

27. Du Bois's support for both knowledge and the unknowable should not be understood as contradictory but rather as an epistemological dynamic. That is, the domain of knowledge extends to the horizon framed by scientific methods and evidence. Beyond that horizon lies the domain of those unknowable aspects of human free will and personal experiences. In "Ruling," Du Bois employed the metaphor of the mountaintop and valley to convey the dynamic between science and the unknowable:

> Here in the heavens and on the mountaintops, the air of Freedom is wide, almost limitless, for here, in the highest stretches, individual freedom harms no man, and, therefore, no man has the right to limit it. ("Ruling," ¶ 56)
>
> On the other hand, in the valleys of the hard, unyielding laws of matter and the social necessities of time production, and human intercourse, the limits on our freedom are stern and unbending if we would exist and thrive. This does not say that everything here is governed by incontrovertible "natural" law which needs no human decision as to raw materials, machinery, prices, wages, news-dissemination, education of children, etc.; but it does mean that decisions here must be limited by brute facts and based on science and human wants. ("Ruling," ¶ 57)

Accordingly, for Du Bois, both knowledge and the unknowable exist simultaneously, and the categorical gap between the two will persist. Knowledge might be and probably will be increased because we can know increasingly more about others and about the world. However, what is unknowable now will remain so in the future because we will never know what others are directly experiencing and will never know the experiences they embody as knowledge.

28. Young, *Justice,* chap. 4.

29. Ibid., 128; emphasis in original.

30. Young does not include all of the sciences in her criticisms of impartiality; she specifically targets the medical and natural sciences for their studies of women and non-European peoples. Accordingly, we do not know her position on the use of science to study issues like climate change, animal extinction, or air pollution. Nevertheless, Young does not offer us the means by which to develop science for the public interest.

31. W. E. B. Du Bois, "Races," *Crisis* 2, no. 4 (August 1911): 157–58. See also

Carol M. Taylor, "W. E. B. DuBois's Challenge to Scientific Racism," *Journal of Black Studies* 11, no. 4 (June 1981): 449–60.

32. W. E. B. Du Bois, "Oral History Interview of W. E. B. Du Bois by William Ingersoll, ca. June 1960," 172–73, W. E. B. Du Bois Papers, Special Collections & University Archives, University of Massachusetts Amherst Library, http://credo.library.umass.edu/view/full/mums312-b237-i137; W. E. B. Du Bois, *The Philadelphia Negro: A Social Study* (Philadelphia: Ginn, 1899).

33. W. E. B. Du Bois, "The Church and Religion," *Crisis* 40, no. 10 (October 1933): 236–37 (¶¶ 2–3), www.webdubois.org/dbChurchAndReligion.html. See also Lewis R. Gordon, "Du Bois's Humanistic Philosophy of Human Sciences," *Annals of the American Academy of Political and Social Science* 568 (March 2000): 265–80; and Anthony Monteiro, "Being an African in the World: The Du Boisian Epistemology," *Annals of the American Academy of Political and Social Science* 568 (March 2000): 220–34.

34. W. E. B. Du Bois, "Criteria of Negro Art," *Crisis* 32 (October 1926): 290–97.

35. Stephen Jay Gould, "Human Equality Is a Contingent Fact of History," in *The Flamingo's Smile*, by Gould (New York: Norton, 1985), 185–98.

36. W. E. B. Du Bois, "The Negroes of Farmville, Virginia: A Social Study," *Bulletin of the U.S. Bureau of Labor* 14 (January 1898): 1–38; W. E. B. Du Bois, "Evolution of the Race Problem," in the *Proceedings of the National Negro Conference* (New York 1909), 142–52 (¶ 18), www.webdubois.org/dbEvolOfRaceProb.html; W. E. B. Du Bois, *Dusk of Dawn*, in W. E. B. Du Bois, *Writings*, ed. Nathan Huggins (1940; New York: Library of America, 1980), chap. 4; W. E. B. Du Bois, "The Study of the Negro Problems," *Annals of the American Academy of Political and Social Science*, 11 (January 1898): 17 (¶ 36), www.webdubois.org/dbStudyofnprob.html.

37. For Du Bois's programmatic statements, see "The Study of the Negro Problems" and "My Evolving Program for Negro Freedom."

38. W. E. B. Du Bois, "Sociology Hesitant" (ca. 1905), W. E. B. Du Bois Papers, Special Collections & University Archives. University of Massachusetts Amherst Library, http://credo.library.umass.edu/view/full/mums312-b212-i003. See also Nahum D. Chandler, introduction to W. E. B. Du Bois, *The Problem of the Color Line at the Turn of the Twentieth Century: The Essential Early Essays*, ed. Chandler (New York: Fordham University Press, 2015); and Ronald A. T. Judy, "Introduction: On W. E. B. Du Bois and Hyperbolic Thinking," *boundary 2*, 27, no. 3 (2000): 1–35.

39. Du Bois, "Sociology Hesitant," 9; capitalization in the original; included are all handwritten corrections made to the original.

40. Ibid.; Du Bois, "My Evolving Program," 57–58 (¶ 75).

41. Du Bois, "Oral History Interview of W. E. B. Du Bois by William Ingersoll,"

181. See also Du Bois's "The Development of a People," *International Journal of Ethics* 14, no. 3 (April 1904): 292–311.

42. Du Bois, "Sociology Hesitant," 4, 5, 6 (¶¶ 9, 10, 18).

43. For example, read Michael Burawoy, "From Max Weber to Public Sociology," in *Transnationale Vergesellschaftungen*, ed. Hans-Georg Soeffner (Wiesbaden: Springer, 2013), 741–55; Francie Diep, "The Research against Mississippi's Ban on Gay Adoption," *Pacific Standard*, August 14, 2015, www.psmag.com/politics-and-law/get-it-together-mississippi.

IV

Du Bois and the Challenges of Black Politics

8

The Cost of Liberty

Sacrifice and Survival in Du Bois's John Brown

Alexander Livingston

> I, John Brown, am now quite *certain* that the crimes of this *guilty land* will never be purged away but with *blood.* I had, as I now think vainly, flattered myself that without very much bloodshed it might be done.
>
> —John Brown, "Prison Letters" (1859)

> To-day we know at last: John Brown was right.
>
> —W. E. B. Du Bois, *John Brown* (1909)

Resurrecting John Brown

Madman, traitor, revolutionary, prophet. Few figures in American history have been more damned and more praised than John Brown. Even before he mounted the gallows in 1859 for leading an assault on the federal armory at Harpers Ferry, the spectrum of meanings that would become synonymous with Brown's life and death had begun to set. To Henry A. Wise, the governor of the Commonwealth of Virginia trying Brown on charges of treason, murder, and inciting insurrection, Brown was "a man of clear head, of courage, fortitude, and simple ingenuousness," but "a fanatic, vain and garrulous" nonetheless. What made Brown so dangerous to Wise was not his alleged madness, a charge made by many both then and since, but rather his conscientious commitment to see justice reign regardless of its costs. To white abolitionists, by contrast, Brown was celebrated as a Christian martyr whose death would atone for the nation's original sin of slavery. Ralph Waldo Emerson declared Brown a saint whose execution would make "the gallows glorious like the cross." And to the slaves, fugitives, and freedmen he sacrificed his life to lead into battle, Brown was an inspiring beacon of struggle. "To the outward eye of men, John Brown was a criminal, but to their inward eye he was a just man and true," declared Frederick Douglass. "His deeds might be disowned, but the spirit which made those deeds possible was worthy of highest honor."[1]

These diverse John Browns live on in contemporary American political discourse. To some, he figures as an example of the dangers absolute moral convictions pose to democratic politics. To others, he is a symbol of moral courage whose sacrifice prefigured those of the thousands of men who died in the war that followed his raid to rid the nation of slavery. And still to others, Brown is an inspiring beacon of militancy whose radicalism continues to indict liberalism's pursuit of compromise.[2]

W. E. B. Du Bois published his 1909 biography of John Brown at a moment of transition in national memory of abolitionism, slavery, and the Civil War. Lost Cause historiography was coming to displace the Unionist image of Brown as symbol of Christian atonement with a counternarrative of the Civil War as a tragically unnecessary conflict forced by religious fanatics in the North who made peaceful compromise impossible.[3] From within this nadir of Jim Crow revisionism, Du Bois's conclusion that "John Brown was right" rang out as an indictment of the nation's acquiescent acceptance of Reconstruction's defeat and called his readers to continue agitating for racial equality. The biography's historical intervention into national memory reflects Du Bois's personal relationship to Brown's symbolism. An unsettling tension was growing between Du Bois's academic career and his expanding civil rights activism, a tension that would culminate in 1910 with his resignation from Atlanta University to take a leadership role in the newly founded NAACP. "My career as a scientist," he observes of this period of his life in *Dusk of Dawn,* "was to be swallowed up in my role as master of propaganda."[4] Accordingly, scholars have seen in the biography's subversive recuperation of the abolitionist a testament of Du Bois's identification with his new role as race propagandist. As Arnold Rampersad observes, Brown served Du Bois as a "spiritual model" for the unity of prophetic leadership and political agitation.[5] Hence the biography's "adventurous presentism," which roots its resurrection of Brown's memory firmly within the personal and political questions Du Bois faced at the dawn of the twentieth century.[6]

John Brown is commonly considered to be one of Du Bois's weaker works.[7] Rushing to finish it in time for the fiftieth anniversary of Brown's raid, he conducted little original research. The result is a book containing entire pages excerpted from earlier biographies and secondary sources. Reviewers faulted the book for its numerous historical inaccuracies, and it was quickly surpassed the following year by Oswald Garrison Villard's celebrated *John Brown, 1800–1859: A Biography Fifty Years After.* Falling far short of the critical success of *The Souls of Black Folk*, *John Brown* sold fewer than seven hundred copies. It is therefore surprising that Du Bois later judged the biography "one of the best written of my books" and even published a revised version in 1962, shortly before his death.[8] Du Bois's retrospective praise invites a rereading of the biography today, one that looks beyond its historical inaccuracies and stylistic faults. What readers will find, as I hope to show, is a rich statement of Du Bois's thinking about the meaning and limits of sacrifice in politics—an issue with which he was wrestling in his role as a civil rights activist.

Readers have long overlooked the centrality of sacrifice within Du Bois's political thought.[9] The omission is a peculiar one given the persistence with which Du Bois returns to the theme of sacrifice across his corpus. In an 1898 commencement address at Fisk University, he cites "the law of sacrifice," along with those of work and service, as the key to the race's development. It is through sacrifice, work, and service that the black race will "develop our powers, gain the mastery of this human machine, and come to the broadest, deepest self-realization." Returning to the linkage of sacrifice with human flourishing in a subsequent commencement address, he revises this list of goods as work, love, and sacrifice. Work is good, he insists, but only when performed in the loving service of some higher ideal. And love of one's fellow man, in turn, is the stimulus for "the greatest thing in life—Sacrifice." Such espousal of sacrifice is similarly at the center of his famous dispute with Booker T. Washington in *Souls.* Du Bois there characterizes Washington's call for a politics of submission to white rule as a repudiation of self-respect and "the higher aims of life." Washington's "gospel of

Work and Money" is ethically hollow because it ignores the need for black self-respect. It is also politically self-defeating because it pursues economic prosperity without securing the rights and political representation needed to protect black citizens from the arbitrary rule of the white majority. Against the path of passive integration through adjustment to white rule, *Souls* proposes a politics of assimilation through agitation and self-assertion. Du Bois's name for this program of militant striving is "the Gospel of Sacrifice." Here and throughout his writings Du Bois presents selfless sacrifice as paradoxically synonymous with a politics of black self-assertion. Political advancement requires putting aside individual self-interests and the "deification of Bread" for the collective advancement of the race.[10]

The role of sacrifice in racial politics more broadly has been reexamined recently by Danielle S. Allen. For Allen, sacrifice is a "preeminent" ritual of democratic politics. Collective decision-making inevitably results in winners and losers, so some citizens are inevitably required to make sacrifices for the sake of others. Good citizenship means acknowledging loss as the very condition of collective political action. "The hard truth of democracy is that some citizens are always giving things up for others," she explains. In a robust democracy each citizen must accept her or his share of sacrifice. The flaw of democratic life in the United States lies in the unequal and unreciprocated burden of sacrifice that systematically falls on people of color. The deep inequality of sacrifice unravels the fabric of trust binding democratic life. Allen calls for new modes of citizenship to renew civic trust. Citizens of color in a racial democracy ought to prefiguratively trust that white citizens will recognize and reciprocate the burdens they bear in order to create the conditions for a more robust and equal democratic society.[11]

John Brown makes a similar claim for the ubiquity of sacrifice in democratic politics in its repeated call for black and white citizens to equally accept "the cost of liberty." Du Bois was not alone in such thinking. Democracy demands sacrifices of citizens because sacrifice "is a frank confession of interlocking lives," wrote George Herbert Palmer, one of Du Bois's mentors from his student days at Harvard University.[12] But this acknowledgment of interdependence pushes Du Bois's analysis in a direction different from Allen's call to affirm the inevitability of democratic loss. For Du Bois, loss is not something to be accepted but resisted through bold and assertive acts of political agitation. Du Bois reworks and resists Jim Crow's racialized economy of sacrifice through reinscribing black Americans within it as *sacrificial agents* rather than mere *sacrificial victims.*[13] This distinction raises a question different from Allen's concern with how to acknowledge the sacrifices citizens make for one another: namely, how vulnerable citizens can *survive* the demands of a sacrifice-making political struggle against a sacrifice-taking regime of white rule. As Juliet Hooker argues in a critique of Allen that illustrates the contemporary resonance of the paradox of sacrifice facing black citizens, "The question is how to square democracy's commitment to equally distributing the burdens of citizenship with the fact that racially subordinated groups are asked to bear primary responsibility for the work of racial justice."[14] Du Bois turns to the life and death of John Brown as a provocative symbol of the sacrificial burdens faced by people of color and a prophetic call for democratic redress.

Du Bois's identification with John Brown is at once a part of the Niagara movement's appropriation of abolitionist iconography and a means of stepping back from the urgencies of political organizing to reflect on the burdens of political action. In the pages that follow, I begin by situating *John Brown* within the historical and intellectual context of the Niagara movement in order to demonstrate that Du Bois identified political agitation with sacrifice in this period. I then show how Du Bois's questions and uncertainties about the viability of a sacrificial conception of political agency inform the biography's ambivalent portrayal of Brown's life and death. Brown's act of heroic sacrifice is depicted as both necessary *and* problematic through the biography's illustration of the disjuncture between Brown's selfless pursuit of justice and the less dramatic modes of black resilience that surround him. I argue that the biography's ambivalent portrait serves to illustrate a particular paradox of black politics I propose to call the paradox of sacrifice and survival. I articulate this paradox in order to show that acknowledging sacrifice demands something more than making a virtue of loss; it demands a radical reconstruction of the ways citizens distribute the burdens of citizenship in a democratic society. Against redemptive narratives of Brown's sacrifice, the biography recounts his life as a tragic warning concerning the "price of repression" that awaits a nation unwilling to make the equal and reciprocal sacrifices that constitute the cost of liberty. "The cost of liberty," Du Bois repeats throughout the biography, "is less than the price of repression." Working the intervals between prophecy and social theory, *John Brown* retells Brown's pursuit of divine violence in order to provoke contemporary readers to envision a more democratic economy of sacrificial reciprocity at the dawn of the twentieth century.[15]

The Niagara Movement and the Gospel of Sacrifice

George W. Jacobs & Co. Publishers approached Du Bois in the fall of 1903 to contribute a volume to their American Crisis Biographies series. The series proposed to "give an impartial view" of the causes, course, and consequences of the Civil War by inviting contemporary southern authors to pen biographies of historical southern figures and contemporary northern writers to contribute biographies on historical northern figures. Du Bois was invited to round out this supposed evenhandedness with a biography of Frederick Douglass that offered a black perspective on the war. The press withdrew the invitation the following year, however, when it informed Du Bois that his rival, Booker T. Washington, had accepted an earlier invitation to write the volume. In its place, Du Bois proposed to contribute a volume on Nat Turner as a lens through which to examine such topics as the transatlantic slave trade, transformations in the plantation economy, abolitionism, the Underground Railroad, and the black antislavery movement "from Toussaint down to John Brown." The history of Turner's bloody insurrection would serve as a vehicle for "the general reflections [*sic*] Negro point of view on the system of slavery." The series editor, Ellis Paxson Oberholtzer, was unenthusiastic about Du Bois's proposal. He suggested that Du Bois instead consider John Brown as a more appropriate figure for a study of slave insurrection and the cotton economy. Du Bois accepted the invitation and began working on the biography in early 1905.[16]

Du Bois's slow progress on the book over the next four years was in no small part due to his contemporaneous role in the Niagara movement. Named after the location of its founding meeting in Fort Erie, Canada, the movement was organized in opposition to Washington's self-proclaimed race leadership to push for a more aggressive civil rights agenda. The Niagarites may have considered themselves "the vanguard of the Talented Tenth," as David Levering Lewis puts it, but their politics of self-assertion and aggressive action was as intent on challenging Washington's autocratic leadership as on confronting national institutions of antiblack racism.[17]

Niagarites symbolized their break with Washington's pragmatic accomodationism by embracing antebellum abolitionism, a historical identification that affirmed the abolition of slavery as an unfinished task. Typical of this turn to abolitionist history was the "Garrison pledge" Du Bois prepared for the movement's founding meeting in 1905. Vowing to follow Garrison's model of service and sacrifice for human liberty, Niagarites intoned these words from the inaugural issue of the *Liberator* from 1831: "I am in earnest. I will not equivocate. I will not retreat an inch. *And I will be heard.*"[18] Similar was the choice of taking Augustus St. Gauden's sculpture of Robert Gould Shaw and the Massachusetts Fifty-Fourth Regiment as the movement's crest, the famed unit of African American soldiers who took up arms against slavery. The Niagarites deepened their identification as neo-abolitionists the following year by holding their second annual meeting at Harpers Ferry in 1906. The second day of the meeting began at dawn with a barefoot pilgrimage from Storer College to the firehouse where Brown and his men had valiantly fought their last stand. The pilgrimage was followed by a performance of the Union marching song "John Brown's Body" and addresses by Du Bois and others on Brown's living legacy.[19] "We do not believe in violence, neither in the despised violence of the raid nor the lauded violence of the soldier, nor the barbarous violence of the mob, but we do believe in John Brown," Du Bois proclaimed—"in that incarnate spirit of justice, that hatred of the lie, that willingness to sacrifice money, reputation, and life itself on the altar of right."[20] Association with Brown's name and his image remained a staple of the Niagara movement over the following years. Subsequent annual meetings included regular updates from the John Brown Memorial Committee on fund-raising efforts for a permanent monument to the abolitionist.[21] The *Horizon*, the movement's monthly periodical edited by Du Bois, commemorated the jubilee of Brown's death with his portrait on its cover.

Brown provided the Niagara movement with a resonant symbol of an antiracist politics focused on agitation, activism, and, of course, sacrifice. "Like the ghost of Hamlet's father, the spirit of John Brown beckons us to arise and seek the recovery of our rights, which our enemy, 'with the witchcraft of his wit, with traitorous gifts' has sought forever to destroy," observed Reverdy Ransom in a speech delivered at the Harpers Ferry meeting: "John Brown was thought by many, even amongst his friends, to be insane. But an exhibition of such insanity was required to arouse the nation against the crime of slavery and bring on the civil war."[22] The insanity Ransom celebrated was neither Brown's call to arms nor his supposed fanaticism. It was rather his courage to confront the seemingly insurmountable challenge of abolishing racial discrimination. The movement's declaration of principles announces, "We do not hesitate to complain, and to complain loudly and insistently" for "manly agitation is the way to liberty."[23] Agitation is indeed a key concept for Du Bois in these Niagara years. The role of the agitator is that of the herald who alerts the public to the evil they do not hear or refuse to see. His work is unpleasant to many as it demands telling the public what they do not want to know. Even more unpleasant are the costs for the agitator himself. His duty will jeopardize his friendships, his reputation, and possibly even his life. Agitation is a form of sacrifice.

Such attention to the costs of agitation leads Du Bois to characterize political agency itself as sacrificial. Sacrifice in his view is neither self-destruction nor absolute renunciation. It is a forgoing of some immediate personal good for a higher or more general good. By "sacrifice" Du Bois means "a plain practical facing of this fact that in order that there shall be the largest sum of joy in the world it is often necessary for *you* to give up some of *your* personal pleasures."[24] Du Bois links sacrifice, agitation, and emancipation in an early draft of his biography when he explains what made Brown's life a "tremendous triumph" despite the military failure of his raid: "First it produced a man; secondly it laid before the world the supreme technical [*sic*] of an unselfish sacrifice, and thirdly it brought freedom to four million of [*sic*] human beings."[25] The agitator's courage to suffer sacrifice for the advancement of the race is both an instrumental good and an intrinsic one; it is at once the driver of a collective struggle for emancipation and the virtuous means by which a people make themselves worthy to be free.

Du Bois discusses this sacrificial conception of political agency in greater detail in the famous third chapter of *Souls,* "Of Booker T. Washington and Others." Here he outlines a typology of three modes of political thought and action that African Americans have employed in response to white supremacy. They are: a politics of revolt, a politics of assimilation through self-assertion, and a politics of assimilation through submission. Each of these visions of African American politics presumes a different economy of sacrifice in the advancement of black freedom. The politics of revolt personified by Toussaint-Louverture and Nat Turner represents a willingness to sacrifice one's very survival for the sake of self-respect. By contrast, the politics of assimilation through submission (which Du Bois attributes to Washington) inverts the order of these goods to sacrifice self-respect and dignity for the sake of survival and wealth.

Between these two extremes, Du Bois proposes his militant vision of "the assertion of manhood rights of the Negro by himself." This third path folds in elements of both alternatives to propose a politics of self-assertion and self-respect that sacrifices Washington's promise of economic gain without taking this logic to the violent extreme of sacrificing survival itself. The doctrine preached in the history of great crises like that facing African Americans at the dawn of the twentieth century "has been that manly self-respect is worth more than lands and houses, and that a people who would voluntarily surrender such respect, or cease striving for it, are not worth civilizing." In short, Washington's politics of submission asks African Americans to make the wrong kind of sacrifice by putting aside their collective self-respect for the sake of individual economic gain. Du Bois, by contrast, looks to Frederick Douglass and John Brown as proponents of a more agonistic vision of "ultimate assimilation *through* self-assertion, and on no other terms," even if Brown admittedly represents this politics of sacrificial agitation taken to "the extreme of its logic."[26]

Du Bois returns to this linkage between agitation and self-respect elsewhere in *Souls* when he writes of black Americans' need to choose between sacrifice and what he calls "the lie." Recall his celebration of the spirit of John Brown at Harpers Ferry as his "hatred of the lie, that willingness to sacrifice money, reputation, and life itself on the altar of right." The lie is the bad faith with which African Americans disavow their need for self-realization and self-respect. White reprisals for Denmark Vesey and Turner's politics of revolt taught slaves to conclude that their only alternative was a pragmatic politics of bare survival through flattery and deception. "The price of culture," white violence had taught the slave and continues to teach many in the South, "is a Lie." The dawn of the twentieth century, *Souls* argues, is the time to be finally done with the lie and courageously embrace the path of advancement through self-assertion. African Americans must be "steeled by Sacrifice against Humiliation," as he describes Alexander Crummell, in order to abandon the comforts of the lie.[27]

In a 1904 commencement address delivered at Fisk University, Du Bois poses the question of the cost of the lie through a reflection on the life of Galileo Galilei. Galileo faced "the greatest moral problem that rises before men"; namely, whether to serve humanity and risk his life or lie and save himself. Galileo chose to lie when he denied that the earth revolved around the sun. The cost of his lie was stymying the development of the human race by bringing science's progress to a halt and entrenching the rule of prejudice. Du Bois argues that African American students face just such a "bribe of the Lie" in Washington's gospel of work. What will it continue to cost the nation to refuse truth and justice for fear of individual harm or loss? How much greater will be the costs the black race pays in the future if it continues to abide by the lie today? What is urgently needed is not simply work or leisure but freedom, Du Bois tells his audience, even if that freedom comes at a cost: "So then when a man offers a discovery for a lie or Education for a bribe then must the watchman on the outer wall cry Halt—In the King's name! And you graduates of Fisk University, are the Watchmen on the outer wall."[28]

Washington's lie offers individuals a path to security if they are willing to live a life of bad faith. The lie's promise of mere survival, however, is one it cannot keep. No individual African American can enjoy peace and the fruits of their labor without the collective political power, uplift, and fair value of rights won through a campaign of persistent agitation. As the sadism of the Atlanta race riot would viscerally illustrate, white southerners would not remain satisfied with the separate but equal terms of Washington's Atlanta compromise. Du Bois's gospel of sacrifice framed the choice facing black Americans as one between becoming sacrificial victims of the lynch mob or embracing their role as sacrificial agents of political agitation, leadership, and education. Describing the mission of the black college in "On the Wings of Atlanta," Du Bois writes that no other institution of higher learning better represents "an air of higher resolve or more unfettered striving; the determination to realize for men, both black and white, the broadest possibilities of life, to seek the better and the best, to spread within their own hands the Gospel of Sacrifice—all this is the burden of their talk and dream." Du Bois follows this passage with one of his favorite lines from Goethe's *Faust*, "*Entbehren sollst du, sollst entbehren*" [You shalt forgo, you shall do without].[29]

Du Bois's gospel of sacrifice has been criticized as an elitist vision of African American politics grounded in a Victorian ideology of hero worship.[30] Sacrifice, in this view, is a custodial act performed by black leaders who selflessly work to elevate and civilize the black masses. But Du Bois's gospel of sacrifice urges *all* African Americans to self-assertive sacrifice, not just the "Talented Tenth" among them. Additionally, reading Du Bois as a theorist of heroic leadership oversimplifies his conception of sacrifice by overlooking his own ambivalence toward it. This ambivalence is palpable in the very passage Du Bois takes from *Faust* as his gospel's motto. Here Faust does not celebrate a life of selfless striving but rather laments the burden of the scholar's life of service.[31] Du Bois shares Faust's complaint that a life of sacrifice in the service of humanity is not life enough: "What is Life? It is earth and air, health and appetite, books and knowledge, picture and song, and Friends." In his early "The Problem of Amusement," Du Bois faults black churches for teaching service and sacrifice to the exclusion of amusement and leisure. He is well aware, in other words, that a message of selfless devotion and deferred gratification fails to grasp the fact that amusement is a condition of fuller and richer sacrifice rather than its antithesis. "The Negro church is dimly grasping for that divine word of Faust: *Entbehren sollst du, sollst entbehren,*" he observes. "But in this truth—properly conceived, properly enunciated—there is nothing incompatible with wholesome amusement, with true recreation. For what is true amusement, true diversion, but the *re*-creation of energy which we may sacrifice to noble ends, to higher ideals—while without proper amusement, we waste or dissipate our mightiest powers."[32]

In sum, for Du Bois sacrifice is an indispensable *element* of human self-realization, not the whole of it. A life worth living also requires friendship, enjoyment, and leisure. The sacrifice of agitation can draw the energy to face the risks it takes only from the fullness of everyday life beyond politics and sacrifice alone.

Du Bois's ambivalence concerning sacrifice goes deeper than this, moreover. The very color line that makes agitation and sacrifice necessary also imposes unequal sacrificial burdens on black men and women. Du Bois characterizes the sectional reconciliation that followed the Civil War as a form of sacrificial cleansing at the cost of black freedom. Reconstruction saw the black race "sacrificed in its swaddling clothes on the altar of national integrity." National progress, Du Bois repeats throughout *Souls,* has historically been achieved through the sacrifice of black advancement and black life.[33]

He confronts the proximity of civic acts of sacrificial giving and a national history of sacrificial taking most dramatically in "Of the Passing of the First-Born." As Susan Mizruchi has observed, Du Bois draws on biblical imagery in this chapter to liken his grief over his son's death to Abraham's struggle with God's demand for sacrifice.[34] Du Bois wrestles to accept the loss of his son in terms of the promise of redemption in a world to come that does not know racial hatred and oppression. "Some morning this may be, long, long years to come," he prophesies of this coming world that would redeem his loss. "But now there wails, on the dark shore within the Veil, the same deep voice, *Thou shalt forego!* And all have I forgone at that command, and with small complaint,—all save that fair young form that lies so coldly wed with death in the nest I had builded."[35] Du Bois reiterates Faust's sacrificial motto to call himself back to the gospel of sacrifice, but that duty to serve now seems hollow and empty in the face of what is already a sacrifice too much. Unlike his earlier contempt for the bribe of the lie that afforded the conditions of everyday black survival, Du Bois here expresses a profound ambivalence toward sacrifice as a model of black politics. How can a politics of agitation call for an embrace of heroic acts of sacrifice without denigrating the practices of everyday life that energize and sustain political activism? How can a political program for confronting Jim Crow embrace a gospel of sacrificial offering without undermining the practices of care and security needed to survive the everyday terror of white rule?

The Paradox of Sacrifice and Survival

Bonnie Honig poses a similar question in *Emergency Politics,* where she argues that democratic theory's focus on political action in extraordinary conditions displaces the question of how a democracy survives ordinary politics once the emergency has subsided. "The propulsive generative powers of political action often seem at odds with its obligatory focus on the needs of mere life," Honig observes. "But if democratic politics is about risk and heroism, it is also just as surely about generating, fairly distributing, demanding, or taking the resources of life—food, medicine, shelter, community, intimacy, and so on."[36] Du Bois's opposition of sacrifice and the lie, or self-respect and survival, inserts just such a dichotomy between the ordinary and extraordinary into the heart of the political thought of *Souls.* The gospel of sacrifice repudiates Washington's compromise as an embrace of mere survival when nobler political ends are at stake. However, the traces of ambivalence in Du Bois's gospel suggest uneasiness with such a clear split between survival and sacrifice. At the boundaries of the text's call for agitation Du Bois acknowledges what Honig calls the "agonistic mutuality of mere and more life," the paradoxical need for both heroic action *and* caring sustenance as the grounds of any viable political program.[37] This paradox migrates from the margins to the center of Du Bois's political thought in *John Brown*. Unlike his earlier celebration of Brown's spirit as a model for civil rights agitation, the biography emplots Brown's sacrificial activism at Harpers Ferry as tragic rather than triumphant.[38] Brown's life and death represent the unavoidable "cost of liberty," a sacrificial cost that cannot be redeemed without remainders. If these remainders cannot be redeemed, however, they can serve as offerings for an expiatory ritual of sacrificial reciprocity from white Americans willing to honestly weigh the "price of repression."

Indeed, during his trial and imprisonment Brown promoted himself as precisely such a symbol of atoning sacrifice. In letters and interviews written from Charleston prison, he portrayed himself, alternatively, as Christ dying on the cross for humanity's sins and as Samson pulling down the pillars of the Philistines' temple.[39] Du Bois's biography resituates elements of Brown's biblical scripts into a transatlantic narrative of African striving and sacrifice in the New World. As he explains in the preface, *John Brown* appraises familiar historical material "from a different point of view"; namely, that of "the little known but vastly important inner development of the Negro Americans." John Brown came nearest of all Americans "to touching the real souls of black folk." This was more than mere sympathy, however. Brown was the very embodiment of the "mystic spell of Africa" that "is and ever was all over America." Along with the atonement of Christ and the militancy of Samson, Du Bois presents John Brown as a symbol for "the dark figure of Toussaint" and the rebellious spirits of Gabriel, Vesey, and Turner.[40] The biography doubles John Brown as both African and American to consecrate him as a provocative symbol of double-consciousness.[41]

This revisionary emplotment of Brown's life is characteristic of Du Bois's historical writings on slavery and the Civil War. As Lawrie Balfour explains, it "aspires both to right the historical record and to recast African Americans as central characters in the drama of their liberation and that of the nation."[42] John Brown serves Du Bois as the floating signifier he proposed to find in Turner in order to reconstruct a broader narrative of the black experience of the Civil War. Exemplary of this approach are the chapters "The Vision of the Damned" and "The Black Phalanx," in which the book's biographical narrative of Brown turns into a sociological examination of the role black agency played in bringing about the ultimate abolition of slavery in the United States: "A great unrest was on the land. It was not merely moral leadership from above—it was the push of physical and mental pain from beneath;—not simply the cry of the Abolitionist but the upstretching of the slave. The vision of the damned was stirring the western world and stirring black men as well as white." First among these stirrings from below were slave revolts. Revolts and the "old African warrior spirit" they awoke in the United States were seldom successful, but the heroism of these acts set the stage for the less suicidal forms of self-assertion that followed. "To be sure, the successful outbreaks were few and spasmodic; but the flare of Haiti lighted the night and made the world remember that these, too, were men," he writes.[43]

More significant than these acts of violent revolt, however, were those of slaves who dared to flee rather than fight or submit. The stream of fugitives fleeing north along "the Great Black Way" to safe harbor in cities like Boston, Cincinnati, and Philadelphia were the agents who showed the way to organize "a great black phalanx" that would march on the South in the Union army. Whereas in his later and better-known *Black Reconstruction in America* Du Bois centers his account of black agency in the "general strike" of fugitives who fled to the advancing Union lines, in *John Brown* he emphasizes a black politics of agitation and organizing in Canada and northern US cities in the decades prior to the war. No doubt finding parallels between these black abolitionists and the Niagara movement, Du Bois places great weight on the construction of a black civil society after 1830 through the establishment of schools, churches, newspapers, and the organizing of national conventions and reform societies. Thus, the stage for Brown's cataclysmic raid was set by the prior decades of black sacrifice and self-assertion in forcing the issue of slavery to the breaking point. Du Bois writes, "Without the long effective and self-sacrificing efforts of the Northern freed Negroes, the Abolition movement in the United States could not have been successful."[44]

The biography's emphasis on the historical role of a black politics of assimilation through self-assertion is in tension with its purported concern with Brown as the embodiment of a black politics of revolt. For example, Du Bois dates Brown's birth in terms of the year Gabriel planned his uprising in Virginia and while "the shudder of Haiti was running through all the Americas."[45] Brown studied Caribbean history, the Haitian revolution, and slaves' tactics of guerrilla warfare to succeed in striking a blow against slavery where others failed. Du Bois's depiction of Brown as "the figuration of black resistance in whiteface" has struck some readers as sitting awkwardly alongside the biography's broader arguments about the importance of the less heroic and more everyday forms of political organization and agitation in forcing the issue of slavery to the breaking point of civil war.[46] Yet such frictions in the text should alert us to the self-conscious limits of Du Bois's identification with Brown, limits Du Bois repeatedly brings to the foreground of his reading. The biography persistently frames Brown's heroism as both necessary *and* problematic for the way it fails to grapple with the agonistic mutuality of extraordinary sacrifice and everyday survival. The clear distinctions between the politics of revolt and assimilation put forward in *Souls,* with their respective economies of sacrifice, become less clear as Du Bois's polemical engagement with Washington gives way to an analysis that speaks in two registers at once in order to emphasize the paradoxical need for both politics despite their tensions. The question Du Bois poses is not whether black Americans ought to embrace the gospel of sacrifice but rather how to both *espouse* and *survive* the costs of liberty.

Brown is made to voice the gospel of sacrifice repeatedly throughout the biography. One example is "Sambo's Mistakes," a satirical narrative Brown published in a black weekly newspaper in 1847. The essay takes on the voice of a black persona, Sambo, to criticize free black northerners for their materialism and lack of discipline. While contemporary readers may find Brown's criticisms of African Americans paternalistic or even racist, Du Bois reads the act of impersonation in "this excellent paper" as a testament to Brown's radical sense of racial equality. Sambo confesses to "my colored brethren" that he has squandered his time and savings on petty amusements and tobacco when he ought to have been pursuing education, thrift, and uplift in the company of wise and good men. His appetite for the expensive clothes and luxuries enjoyed by whites meant that he "could never bring myself to practise any self-denial." The result was a life of poverty and idleness, but worse still was the bad faith and racial subservience this undisciplined pursuit of selfishness taught him: "I have always expected to secure the favor of the whites by tamely submitting to every species of indignity, contempt, and wrong, instead of nobly resisting their brutal aggressions from principle, and taking my place as a man, and assuming the responsibility of a man, a citizen, a husband, a father, a brother, a neighbor, a friend,—as God requires of every one (if his neighbor will allow him to do it)." Slavery taught Sambo the lie of survival; it is the work of freedom to learn the selfless discipline of noble resistance.[47]

Du Bois finds a connection between Brown's singular dedication to sacrifice and the moral idealism that defined his life, an idealism that often left him blind to life's complexities and paradoxes. As "more and more John Brown was becoming the man of one idea," less and less was he was able to cope with the nuances and contingencies of everyday life. The chapter "The Shepherd and the Sheep" presents Brown's failure in the wool industry as representative of this growing stress between his idealistic denigration of mere life and the interruptive need for more life. His attempts to organize his fellow wool producers into a cooperative economy may have succeeded had he been more attuned to the exclusion of morality by the logic of the marketplace. Brown's naïve presumption that business could be a moral enterprise shows "one weakness of his character: he did not know or recognize the subtler twistings of human nature." His simple moral point of view presumed clear distinctions between good and evil that failed to grasp the nuance and complexity that makes up the vast swath of gray between these two extremes. Of the "kinks and prejudices" of human life, "its little selfishnesses and jealousies and dishonesties, he knew nothing. They always came to him as a sort of surprise, uncalculated for and but partially comprehended. He could fight the devil and his angels, and he did, but he could not cope with the million misbirths that hover between heaven and hell."[48]

Brown's absolutist vision of a world clearly made up of devils and angels similarly contributed to his military failure at Harpers Ferry. Politics for Brown was applied morality. This moralism led him to conceive of American political development in strictly idealistic terms, as the redemption of the nation's moral ideals from the sin of the country's concrete history. Accordingly, Brown imagined his raid as a continuation of the American Revolution rather than a revolt against the United States. The slave's insurrection was to be a patriotic act of refounding that would redeem the Declaration of Independence's broken promise of freedom and equality. He makes this loyalty clear in the provisional constitution he drafted for the free black community in Chatham, Canada, in the spring of 1858. Containing some forty-eight articles concerning the membership, organization, and duties of the band of men he proposed to lead into war, the document denounces slavery as a violation of the nation's founding principles and an act of war against the American people. The aim of the constitution is "no dissolution of the Union, but simply to amend and repeal" the legal recognition of slavery in the United States. This prophetic vision of the divine purpose of the United States that so clearly distinguished pure and ideal principles from an impure and nonideal history left him deaf to the objections of the freedmen and fugitives training in Canada who refused to serve under the flag of the hated nation they had just escaped.[49]

These tensions and elisions are interpreted by Lawrie Balfour as signs of Brown's inability to transcend his own racial position so as to understand the complexity and burdens of the slave system from the perspective of those he sought to free from it. Du Bois indeed stages a conflict of perspectives here, but it is not one that can be reduced to racial experience alone. The elisions are symptomatic of how Brown's idealistic gospel of sacrifice blinds him to the paradox of mere life and more life facing a militant antiracist politics. For instance, it was Brown's persistent failure to grasp the vital particularities of the situations he found himself in that ultimately postponed the raid and cost him the support of the black phalanx waiting in Canada. Du Bois regards Brown's poor judgment concerning Hugh Forbes as especially damning in this regard. Forbes, a former lieutenant of Garibaldi's, was hired by Brown to drill the men waiting in Canada for their assault on the slave power. Forbes nearly bankrupted Brown, and when Brown was no longer able to pay his wages and flatter his vanity, he threatened Brown's New England financiers to reveal the planned raid unless he was placed in charge of a more ambitious war against slavery. The Secret Six, Brown's financiers, urged him to delay his raid, symbolically planned for the Fourth of July 1858, until the suspicions raised by Forbes's loose talk had abated. This delay, more than any other factor, foiled Brown's plan by costing him the support of freedmen in Canada, who lost their enthusiasm for the assault as time went on.[50]

Du Bois finds Brown's sacrificial idealism epitomized by his dramatic relationship to death. The "sense of overruling inexorable fate" and "the mystery and promise of death" that defined Brown's religious imaginary stoked the fire of his striving, a striving to sacrifice himself as a martyr in the historical drama ordained by his God. Du Bois presents this spiritual darkness as "the deeper, truer man, although it was not the whole man." In private moments Brown confessed a craving for more life, for friends and love and the will to survive. The year before the raid, he admitted to one correspondent that he longed to see his family and fears for the pain they will suffer once his terrible sacrifice is made. But, just as Du Bois invokes Faust when mourning the loss of his son in *Souls,* so he shows Brown rejecting mere survival and calling himself back to his duty of sacrifice. "But, courage, courage, courage!" he reminds himself, "— the great work of my life (the unseen hand that 'guided me, and who indeed holden my right hand, may hold it still,' though I have not known Him at all as I ought) I may yet see accomplished (God helping), and be permitted to return, and 'rest at evening.'"[51]

Yet, despite portraying this sacrificial denigration of mere life so critically, Du Bois does not hesitate to conclude that John Brown was right. The slave empire could be destroyed by nothing less than armed revolution. All men knew this, but only Brown refused to shrink or hesitate before the costs of liberty; he was "the sword on which struggling Kansas and its leaders could depend, the untarnished doer of its darker deeds, when they that knew them necessary cowered and held their hands." Du Bois does not repudiate Brown as a fanatic for the violent and sacrificial consequences of his religious idealism, as many liberal critics of idealism have been wont to do. Rather, he affirms the occasional need for the extraordinary heroism of a John Brown without losing sight of the paradoxical and tragic situation in which this puts an antiracist politics. "John Brown was a moral paradox," Du Bois writes in a speech from 1909, a paradox he identifies as "the world fight between the practical and the ideal." Although Brown embodied this paradox in an extraordinary fashion, all men and women struggle with it at some point in their lives. On the one hand, they pursue ease and safety as the goals of life; on the other, they sometimes recognize their obligation to sacrifice themselves to the moral ideal of the greater good. Du Bois poses this choice as a tragic choice, one that cannot be resolved without costs either way. "The truth is that both attitudes of mind are at times right," Du Bois explains. "But that does not mean that they are both right at the same time." *John Brown* does not ask whether Brown was justified to take up arms and sacrifice himself and others for the sake of justice. The biography instead poses the question of how a viable political movement can at once embrace and survive the clear conclusion that Brown was right.[52]

John Brown stages this need for a paradoxical politics that embraces both agonistic sacrifice and pragmatic survival in its portrayal of Frederick Douglass. Douglass was an ally who sheltered Brown in his Rochester home for a month in the winter of 1858, where Brown began his work on the provisional constitution. Brown had told Douglass that his plan was to liberate slaves from plantations in the South and guide them north along the Appalachian Mountains to liberty. It was only the following year that he revealed his true intention to attack the federal armory in Harpers Ferry. The plot to attack the federal government struck Douglass as suicidal. The two men argued their opposed positions on the raid for hours in a Pennsylvania stone quarry, with Brown inviting Douglass to join him on the assault and Douglass trying to warn Brown of the inevitable failure of his plan. Douglass "believed in John Brown but not his plan." He left the secret meeting anxious of the catastrophic consequences of Brown's plot.[53]

Was Douglass right to refuse Brown's call to fight? Du Bois's question brings home the paradox of sacrifice and survival. Brown and Douglass were both right. Brown saw the evil of slavery and the need to strike out. Douglass foresaw the deadly consequences that lay in store for slaves and freedmen. He and other African Americans understood the costs of Brown's raid in a way Brown could not: "They knew he was right, but they knew that for any failure of his project they, the black men, would probably pay the cost. And the horror of that cost none knew as they." Du Bois's Douglass provides another perspective on Brown's idealism, one rooted in the practical urgencies of survival and resilience under the terror of the slave system. The "moral evil" Brown would sacrifice his life to abolish was to Douglass an "evil of this world." This is not to say that Douglass disagreed with the validity of Brown's prophetic indictment of slavery. To describe slavery as an evil "of this world," rather than a metaphysical evil like sin, is still to know it as an evil—one that Douglass knew all too well; but it is an evil that must be confronted by a politics of this world, a politics that foregrounds the need to survive a long and protracted struggle rather than an apocalyptic act of purging violence. One element of such a politics is the tragic acknowledgment of how the unmasterable consequences of action can come to thwart human intentions, a tragic knowledge Du Bois invokes with the allusion to Oedipus in the title of the book's penultimate chapter, "The Riddle of the Sphinx."[54]

The encounter Du Bois stages between Brown and Douglass illustrates the paradox of sacrifice and survival in order to provoke the reader to reflect on what it could mean to negotiate it without bad faith. The paradoxical statement that both men are right affirms the insufficiency of a politics of sacrificial activism without a simultaneous counterpolitics of survival, care, and resilience.[55] Negotiating this paradoxical demand means reframing the project of African American politics beyond the narrow terms of Brown's heroic act. Sacrifice and survival can both be sustained only by resituating them within a broader economy of sacrifice, one that enlists not just black Americans but also the white Americans who cause and benefit from their sacrifices. Du Bois invokes such a sacrificial covenant among all Americans when he explains why Douglass and other African Americans were right *not* to follow Brown: "Was not their whole life already a sacrifice? Were they called by any right of God or man to give more than they already have given? What more did they owe the world? Did not the world owe them an unpayable amount?"[56] The world owes Douglass and millions of other black men and women something because sacrifice is not simply a moral gesture or a psychological precondition of action; it is a gift that creates a covenant between those who offer sacrifices and those who receive them. To say that black Americans have already sacrificed too much implies that they have consistently received too little; that white Americans have failed to acknowledge or reciprocate the black sacrifices from which they have profited. An egalitarian democracy, he suggests, would acknowledge the paradox of sacrifice and survival by honoring and reciprocating the burdens of sacrifice across the color line.

John Brown failed to grasp this truth, Du Bois emphasizes. By seeing himself as an American Christ whose wounds would cleanse the nation of its sins, he failed to see the need for a shared life beyond mere life to sustain the dangerous agon against white power. The tragedy of *John Brown*, however, lies not in its hero's downfall or his Oedipus-like failure of self-knowledge, but in the nation's failure to grasp the basic truth that "the price of repression is greater than the cost of liberty." If white Americans refuse to bear their share of the costs of liberty, they will pay a violent price *for* their repression.[57]

Prophecy, Democracy, and Divine Violence

John Brown illustrates a persistent paradox of black politics, what I have called the paradox of sacrifice and survival, whereby black citizens must strike assertively against white supremacy while at the same time protecting spaces and virtues that allow them to survive the hardships of political struggle and the terror of white rule. We turn now to the biography's prophetic and political response to this paradox. Surviving sacrifice, Du Bois insists, demands that the nation radically reconstruct the way it distributes the costs of liberty. Such reconstruction entails more than simply honoring the losses and sacrifices citizens make, as Danielle Allen has argued. It means militantly confronting white citizens with the continued price of repression. This price, as Brown's life illustrates, is divine violence.

Du Bois invokes this notion of a sacrificial economy binding white and black Americans together in the final chapter of *Souls*. Partly social science, partly prophetic criticism, "The Sorrow Songs" addresses the hyphenated nature of American identity. The sorrow songs name the music that sustained slaves' survival in the New World. These spiritual songs constitute "the greatest gift of the Negro people" among the many gifts black men and women have given to America. Du Bois recalls these national gifts—of song, of labor, and of spirit—to confront his white readers' claim to represent a truer or more authentic American identity:

> Your country? How came it yours? Before the Pilgrims landed we were here. Actively we have woven ourselves with the very warp and woof of this nation,—we have fought their battles, shared their sorrow, mingled our blood with theirs, and generation after generation have pleaded with a headstrong, careless people to despise not Justice, Mercy, and Truth, lest the nation be smitten with a curse. Our song, our toil, our cheer, and warning have been given to this nation in blood-brotherhood. Are not these gifts worth the giving? Is not this work and striving? Would America have been America without her Negro people?

Du Bois recovers this history of gifts in order to disclose American nationhood as always already interracial in itself, if not yet for itself. The sorrow songs are at once the greatest gift of the Negro people and "the sole American music."[58] In an insightful discussion of Du Bois's sacrificial rhetoric, Jonathon Kahn remarks how this passage deploys the notion of sacrifice both to authorize and to criticize a conception of shared nationhood that traverses the color line. On the one hand, black sacrifices of work, sorrow, and blood are offerings that authorize black claims to membership and recognition in the nation. On the other hand, to recall this list of gifts is to confront white citizens' failure to acknowledge their intertwined identity with people of color. The discourse of sacrifice upholds the language of nation "in the name of black America against America itself."[59] Achieving a truly democratic society of equals demands reciprocal and compensatory acts of white expiation to reset the balance of black sacrifices. Honoring the nation's covenant demands democratizing sacrifice.

The same mix of politics and prophecy in passages like this one informs Du Bois's discussion of the most controversial aspect of Brown's legacy: violence. Read in a political register, Du Bois's invocation of the nation bound together by a sacrificial covenant normatively prescribes the duties that putatively equal citizens owe one another. White Americans' refusal to acknowledge black gifts and sacrifices is a democratic failure, a failure to honor the responsibilities of equal sharing of sacrifices that democratic citizens owe to one another. Read in a prophetic register, Du Bois is issuing a warning to recall a wayward nation to their covenant "lest the nation be smitten with a curse." A nation that fails to honor its sacrificial covenant is one that will be struck low.

These two critical registers of Du Bois's rhetoric of sacrifice converge in *John Brown.* The "cost of liberty" for both white and black Americans must be a willingness to put self-interest and advancement aside for the collective pursuit of the nation's founding ideals of liberty and equality. What will liberty cost? "It would cost something," a something that white Americans persistently refuse to pay when they consider the eventuality of intermarriage or that "many a white man would be blackening black men's boots." The nation's unwillingness to pay liberty's cost—whether in wealth, or advancement, or privilege—lies at the root of its race problems. "The trouble with us," Du Bois writes in the voice of a national subject, "is not that the problems fronting us are insoluble, but that we are unwilling to pay the cost." The alternative to paying the cost of liberty, however, is risking the much more costly price of repression. John Brown's divine violence is that price. Du Bois repeats this ultimatum throughout the biography like the watchman on the city walls he would ask Fisk graduates to become. The memory of John Brown "stands today as a mighty *warning* to this country."[60]

Unlike his earlier speech at Harpers Ferry, in which he sought to distance Brown's inspiring spirit from the violence of his deeds, Du Bois's biography squarely confronts the bloody legacy of Brown's war against slavery. He does not flinch from reconstructing the night Brown and his sons captured five proslavery men in Potawatomi, Kansas, and hacked them to death with broadswords, an act of terror often forgotten in depictions of Brown as a symbol of sacrificial atonement or moral protest. The "cost of liberty" that night in Kansas was "five twisted, red and mangled corpses."[61] It is the same price of repressions paid when the Haitian revolution showed "the fearful cost that the western world was paying for slavery."[62] Du Bois bears witness to this tragic violence like a herald who warns rather than a philosopher who justifies. He does not ask under what conditions such acts of violence would be legitimate; he presents these tableaux of mangled corpses and bloody hands to warn the nation of a violence it tragically imposes upon itself. America's sacrificial taking of black life is the *covenant-breaking* violence that summons the *sacrifice-taking* violence of retribution. "Violence," as René Girard writes in his classical study of sacrifice, "is like a raging fire that feeds on the very objects intended to smother its flames."[63] The tragedy of this violence lies in its circularity, in the actor's own will turning back upon him like fate. John Brown is that fate.

Vengeance represents the price inevitably exacted by repression taken to its logical extreme; but the price is paid in less spectacular ways as well: "The degradation of men costs something both to the degrader and those who degrade." The price of repression for both races of men is ignorance, vice, and the stunting of human development. Under the slave regime, a system of racial inequality thwarted the nation's moral progress, "twisting them backwards towards darker ages of force and caste and cruelty, while forward swirled currents of liberty and uplift." This price continues to be paid under Jim Crow. Along with the nation's "moral retrogression," race prejudice wastes the nation's economic potential. The racial segregation of labor power makes both white and black workers vulnerable to exploitation and elite domination. Moreover, American race hatred of colored people destroys the good faith and cooperation the nation requires to export its capital overseas.[64]

The biography's final chapter, "The Legacy of John Brown," extends this reflection on the price of repression into Du Bois's contemporary moment. American race prejudice at the dawn of the twentieth century is not only struggling to hold down the uplift of people of color domestically. United States imperialism exports race hatred across the globe to repress the striving of the colored peoples of the world. The more expansive the United States' repression of the world's peoples of color, the more costly will be the price the nation will pay. Du Bois invokes the horizon of anti-imperialist retribution, however, only to shift focus away from violence per se. The year of Brown's death on the gallows was also "the year that first published the *Origin of Species*," the work that set the terms of contemporary race prejudice. Social Darwinism epitomizes the "moral retrogression in social philosophy" in the decades since Brown's death, a regression that makes Brown's warning both all the more needful and more difficult to hear.[65] As Thomas McCarthy explains in a genealogy of race ideology in the American social sciences, social Darwinism proved particularly adept at naturalizing relations of power by closing the "is/ought" gap.[66] The fact that white Americans and Europeans *in fact do* exercise colonial rule over peoples of color across the globe is taken as proof that white Americans and Europeans *ought* to exercise colonial rule over peoples of color across the globe. The existing system of racial hierarchy and domination is the result of a natural process of selection that demonstrates the natural inferiority of nonwhite racial groups. African Americans are not merely "the unlifted"; they are "the unliftable."[67] Agitating against racial discrimination, naturalized in stark Spencerian terms, is struggling against nature itself. The implication of this reductive naturalization of human development is that political interference with nature's hierarchy of races can only produce an unanticipated racial degeneration of the species as a whole.

The biography's concluding turn to evolutionary biology comes as a surprise. But even more surprising is Du Bois's appropriation of these evolutionary arguments to restate in naturalistic terms the book's prophetic warnings about the price of repression. The final chapter seeks to recuperate Darwin from the social Darwinists as the basis for a new vision of egalitarian democracy. If, as Darwin argues, nature is an open and unfinished system without a final or fixed teleology, then social scientists must acknowledge "the boundlessness and endlessness of human achievement." Du Bois, like his Harvard mentor William James, stresses the creative power of evolutionary variation as a rejoinder to social Darwinism's one-sided emphasis on the deterministic aspects of environmental selection. To borrow McCarthy's formulation again, the is/ought gap cannot be closed so seamlessly because of the inexhaustible contingency of Darwin's nature. The evolutionary potentiality of species is no longer defined by a final *telos* or constrained by a fixed natural hierarchy. Rather, the contingency of variation means that species remain forever open to future development, mutation, and transformation. Du Bois extends this same argument to destabilize the idea of a fixed ceiling for racial development and criticize the naturalization of white rule. The construction of racial barriers hinders the possibilities of mutual exchange between groups that alone can promote the richer realization of the species' development. Du Bois mobilizes this argument to portray Western imperialism, *pace* the imperialists, as an "outrageous program of wholesale human degeneration." Imperialism places "some of the worst stocks of mankind" in absolute authority over the rest. Such an anomaly represses the potential development of colonized peoples, but it also harms the development of the white race as well. White racial degeneration is evident in falling birth rates, waning stamina, and increasing difficulty maintaining the race's rule over the colored peoples of the world. Darwin's lesson is the same as John Brown's: the cost of liberty is less than the price of repression.[68]

Why does Du Bois give such prized attention to evolutionary biology in the concluding chapter of a biography dealing with slavery and abolition in antebellum America? William Cain argues that Du Bois "went astray" in this final chapter "because he recognized on some level and, furthermore, wished to avoid the powerful logic of his book—a logic that propelled him toward an acknowledgment and, indeed, an acceptance of violence as the inevitable final stage of social and political protest."[69] Du Bois's repeated claim that "the cost of liberty is less than the price of repression, even though that cost be blood," presents violent resistance as a legitimate possibility in the struggle against white supremacy. At the same time, the book's ambivalent depiction of Brown continually warns black readers that they would be mistaken to emulate Brown's martial tactics. Cain reads this "contradiction at the heart of his book" as an artifact of Du Bois's reluctance to follow the historical logic of his argument to its revolutionary conclusion. We do better to read the "logic" of Du Bois's account of revolution as prophetic rather than dialectical, however. Prophecy foretells a coming *future* in order to call a community to a moment of decision in the *present* as to whether they will honor *past* covenants and agreements.[70] Violence is a price the nation will pay tomorrow unless it decides today to embrace the equal burdens of its past covenant. Du Bois invokes the specter of violence to call the nation to embrace a different future, one grounded in the nonviolence of a democratizing economy of sacrifice. In framing Brown as an agent of retributive violence, a violence the nation can choose to forgo by honoring its covenant, Du Bois invokes a well-worn piece of abolitionist rhetoric: "Oppression and insurrection go hand in hand, as cause and effect are allied together. In what age of the world have tyrants reigned with impunity, or the victims of tyranny not resisted unto blood?" asked William Lloyd Garrison.[71] Garrison refused all complicity with violent means in his war against slavery, but this did not stop him and other nonresistors from characterizing slave rebellions as righteous punishment for the nation's sins. Garrison's and Du Bois's theodicies of avenging violence are not meant as predictions; they are calls to their audience to act now to avert the coming catastrophe: "The cost of liberty is thus a decreasing cost, while the cost of repression ever tends to increase to the danger point of war and revolution."[72] Abolitionist prophecies of divine violence to come are calls for the *urgency* of action in the present. Thus, whereas Cain sees Du Bois's reflections on violence as marking the *limit* of his democratic imagination, this chapter's emphasis on Du Bois's prophetic mode shows divine violence to be a spur to deepen democratic commitments.

And it is this urgency of sacrifice—the need to act courageously and selflessly in the present moment—that brings Du Bois to Darwin and race science in the book's concluding chapter. The scientific consensus that races are fixed and immutable natural kinds with unequal intellectual and moral capabilities saps the strength from the gospel of sacrifice. Sacrifice for the sake of uplifting a people unable to change is not selflessness; it is masochism. Reading this chapter in light of Du Bois's broader understanding of the gospel of sacrifice reveals how scientific racism is only another face of "the lie." Theories of black inferiority are an apology for political inaction, no less disabling than Washington's lie that equal freedom is possible without equal development and respect. And just as inspiring black agitation means overcoming the bad faith that locks African Americans into accepting their unequal status, so urging white reciprocity means provoking whites to confront the bad faith with which they disavow their democratic failures and dishonesties. The spirit of John Brown was his hatred of the lie. He sacrificed his wealth, his well-being, and even his life in the pursuit of equality because he refused to abide by the bad faith with which the nation forgets its founding covenant. Furthermore, Brown's agitation inspired others to hate the lie as well. Du Bois recalls how free state men in Kansas at first recoiled from Brown's violence and denounced his bloody deed. But his example ultimately broke through their bad faith.

John Brown is therefore something other than a revolutionary cry for Americans to seize their rifles and lay siege to the nation's racial caste system. It is a call to acknowledge and reject the lie within which both black and white Americans refuse to accept the burdens required to democratically reconstruct the nation's economy of sacrifice and loss. James Baldwin grasped this deeper truth of Brown's legacy when he described his raid on Harpers Ferry as a profound act of love: "He attacked the bastions of the federal government—not to liberate black slaves, but to liberate a whole country from a disastrous way of life. And as horrible as it may sound, it was an act of love."[73]

Du Bois thus deploys Brown as an icon of agonistic love in order to unsettle the nation's democratic complacencies at the dawn of the twentieth century. Agitation is necessary to awake the nation from the bad faith that keeps both white and black Americans locked in the stultifying lie. Without it, he writes in the inaugural issue of the *Crisis,* "many a nation has been lulled to false security and preened itself with virtues it did not possess." Agitation for racial equality is the cost of liberty African Americans must be willing to pay if they are going to enjoy security and freedom in the United States. But this is not a cost to be paid by people of color alone. In order to survive the burdens of agitation, African Americans need to cultivate a counterpolitics of more life, of care and joy at a safe distance from the risks and persecutions of activism. Cultivating this counterpolitics of care depends in part on whites becoming willing to shoulder equally the costs of democratic liberty—sacrificing their wealth, social standing and privilege, and perhaps even their lives. Such white sacrifices will not be forthcoming, however, without persistent agitation and striving on the part of black activists willing to agonistically take the rights they are denied. This more democratic economy of sacrifice was a cost the nation refused to pay at the time of the Revolution, and the Civil War was the price of repression. Will the nation pay this cost today? And if not, what greater price of repression awaits us reading *John Brown* in the twenty-first century?[74]

Notes

I would like to thank Saladin Ambar, Lawrie Balfour, Michael Gorup, Bronwyn Leebaw, Neil Roberts, and Joel Schlosser for insightful comments on earlier drafts of this chapter. Special thanks to Nick Bromell for his challenging criticisms and thoughtful editorial guidance.

1. Henry Wise, "Comments in Richmond Virginia (October 21, 1859)," in *The*

Tribunal: Responses to John Brown and the Harpers Ferry Raid, ed. John Stauffer and Zoe Trodd (Cambridge: Belknap Press at Harvard University Press, 2012), 233; Ralph Waldo Emerson, "Courage," ibid., 114; Frederick Douglass, "John Brown, speech delivered at Storer College Harper's Ferry, West Virginia, May 30 1881," in *Frederick Douglass: Selected Speeches and Writings*, ed. Philip S. Foner (Chicago: Lawrence Hill, 1999), 640.

2. For liberal criticisms of Brown as an antidemocratic absolutist, see Louis Menand, "John Brown's Body," *Raritan* 22, no. 2 (2002): 53–61; and Andrew Delbanco's lead essay in *The Abolitionist Imagination* (Cambridge: Harvard University Press, 2012), 3–55. David S. Reynolds's call for a pardon to be issued on the hundredth anniversary of Brown's death draws on elements of the second interpretation (see Reynolds, "Freedom's Martyr," *New York Times*, December 1, 2009, A35). Brown's militancy has been a guiding beacon for radicals from Malcolm X to Timothy McVeigh. For a democratic reconstruction of Brown's fanaticism, see "Radically Democratic Extremism: An Interview with Joel Olson," *Revolution by the Book*, May 26, 2010, www.revolutionbythebook.akpress.org/radically-democratic-extremism-an-interview-with-joel-olson/; and Olson, 'Rethinking the Unreasonable Act' *Theory & Event* 17, no. 2 (2014), https://muse.jhu.edu/article/546468. The capacious history of Brown's symbolism in the century and a half since his death is discussed in Benjamin Quarles, *"Allies for Freedom" and "Blacks on John Brown,"* rev. ed. (Boston: De Capo, 2001); and R. Blakeslee Gilpin, *John Brown Still Lives! America's Long Reckoning with Violence, Equality, and Change* (Chapel Hill: University of North Carolina Press, 2011).

3. David W. Blight, *Race and Reunion: The Civil War in American Memory*, new ed. (Cambridge: Belknap Harvard University Press, 2002); Eyal J. Naveh, *Crown of Thorns: Political Martyrdom in America from Abraham Lincoln to Martin Luther King, Jr.* (New York: New York University Press, 1990), 42–43.

4. W. E. B. Du Bois, *Dusk of Dawn: An Essay Toward an Autobiography of a Race Concept*, in *Writings*, ed. Henry Louis Gates Jr. (New York: Library of America, 1986), 622. Cf. *The Autobiography of W. E. B. Du Bois: A Soliloquy on Viewing My Life from the Last Decade of Its First Century* (New York: International, 1968), 252.

5. Arnold Rampersad, *The Art and Imagination of W. E. B. Du Bois* (Cambridge: Harvard University Press, 1976), 109, cf. 112. Du Bois's identification with Brown as a model leader of civil rights agitation is discussed in Keith E. Byerman, *Seizing the Word: History, Art, and Self in the Works of W. E. B. Du Bois* (Athens: University of Georgia Press, 1994); William E. Cain, "Violence, Revolution, and the Cost of Freedom," *boundary 2* 17, no. 2 (1990): 305–30; Dominic J. Capeci and Jack C. Knight, "Reckoning with Violence: W. E. B. Du Bois and the 1906 Atlanta Race Riot," *Journal of Southern History* 62, no. 4 (1996): 727–66; and

Lawrie Balfour, *Democracy's Reconstruction: Thinking Politically with W. E. B. Du Bois* (Oxford: Oxford University Press, 2011), 54. An exception to this view is Edward J. Blum, who views Du Bois's John Brown as a proposed model for white Americans (Blum, *W. E. B. Du Bois, American Prophet* [Philadelphia: University of Pennsylvania Press, 2007], 112).

6. Gilpin, *John Brown Still Lives!*, 84.

7. Levering Lewis calls it "an uneven product"; Rampersad writes, "*John Brown* is the strangest book in the Du Bois canon" (Lewis, *W. E. B. Du Bois: Biography of a Race, 1868–1919* [New York: Henry Holt, 1993], 357; Rampersad, *Art and Imagination*, 109).

8. *Autobiography*, 259. Du Bois's revised edition was published as *John Brown*, centennial edition (New York: International, 1962). On sales figures, see Rampersad, *Art and Imagination*, 109. Du Bois laid much of the blame for the book's failure on Villard's machinations as the editor of the *Nation* (*Dusk of Dawn*, 750–51). The professional and intellectual relationship between the two biographers is examined in Gilpin, *John Brown Still Lives!*, 79–105.

9. The few scholars who have commented on the persistence of sacrifice in Du Bois's writings have seldom connected it to his political thought. For example, Byerman reads Du Bois's concern with sacrifice in psychoanalytic and autobiographical terms. Susan Mizruchi places Du Bois's writings within the context of sociological discourses of sacrifice, but her interest is primarily textual and rhetorical rather than political. An important exception to this omission is Jonathon Kahn's thoughtful and provocative reading of Du Bois's religious naturalism as the key to his political thought. My reading of *John Brown* is indebted to Kahn's insightful reconstruction of the sacrificial logic of Du Bois's lynching parables (Byerman, *Seizing the Word*, 6; Mizruchi, *The Science of Sacrifice: American Literature and Modern Social Theory* [Princeton: Princeton University Press, 1998], 269–366; Jonathon Kahn, *Divine Discontent: The Religious Imagination of W. E. B. Du Bois* [Oxford: Oxford University Press, 2009], 107–28).

10. W. E. B. Du Bois, "Careers Open to College-Bred Negroes," in *Writings*, ed. Gates, 829, 832; "The Joy of Living," in *Writings of W. E. B. Du Bois Published in Periodicals Edited by Others*, ed. Herbert Aptheker (Millwood: Kraus-Thomason, 1982), 1:220; *Souls of Black Folk*, ed. Henry Louis Gates Jr. and Terri Hume Oliver (New York: Norton, 1999), 40, 40, 59, 57. George Herbert Palmer uses a strikingly similar expression in his essay on self-sacrifice published a year before *Souls*: "Our men, and still more our women, need as urgently the gospel of self-development as that of self-sacrifice; though the two are naturally supplemental" (*The Nature of Goodness* [Boston: Houghton Mifflin, 1903], 177; originally published as "A Study of Self-Sacrifice. Delivered June 26, 1902," *Harvard Graduates' Magazine* 9 [1902]: 12–27). Kwame Anthony Appiah discusses the relationship of Palmer's

essay to Du Bois's early thought briefly in *Lines of Descent: W. E. B. Du Bois and the Emergence of Identity* (Cambridge: Harvard University Press, 2014), 70–71.

11. Danielle S. Allen, *Talking to Strangers: Anxieties of Citizenship since "Brown v. Board of Education"* (Chicago: University of Chicago Press, 2004), 28, 29.

12. Palmer, *The Nature of Goodness,* 171.

13. Kahn, *Divine Discontent,* 111. Cf. Mizruchi, *The Science of Sacrifice,* 354, 365.

14. Juliet Hooker, "Black Lives Matter and the Paradoxes of U.S. Black Politics: From Racial Sacrifice to Democratic Repair," *Political Theory* 44, no. 4 (2016): 9.

15. W. E. B. Du Bois, *John Brown,* ed. David Roediger (New York: Modern Library, 2001), 230.

16. George W. Jacobs & Co. to W. E. B. Du Bois, November 11, 1903; George W. Jacobs to W. E. B. Du Bois, January 25, 1904, 1 (Du Bois's response on reverse); both in W. E. B. Du Bois Papers (MS 312), Special Collections and University Archives, University of Massachusetts Amherst Libraries (hereafter "Du Bois Papers"). See further in Du Bois Papers: Ellis P. Oberholtzer to W. E. B. Du Bois, February 3, 1904; Ellis P. Oberholtzer to W. E. B. Du Bois, February 16, 1904; George W. Jacobs & Co. to W. E. B. Du Bois, March 29, 1904.

17. Levering Lewis, *W. E. B. Du Bois: Biography of a Race,* 318. "I was greatly disturbed at this time, not because I was in absolute opposition to these things that Mr. Washington was advocating, but because I was strongly in favor of more open agitation against wrongs and above all I resented the practical buying up of the Negro press and choking off of even mild and reasonable opposition to Mr. Washington in both the Negro press and the white" (Du Bois, *Dusk of Dawn,* 609).

18. W. E. B. Du Bois, "Garrison and the Negro," in *Against Racism: Unpublished Essays, Papers, Addresses, 1887–1961,* ed. Herbert Aptheker (Amherst: University of Massachusetts Press, 1985), 83.

19. "The Niagara Movement: Second Annual Meeting, August 15, 1906," Du Bois Papers; Du Bois, *Dusk of Dawn,* 618–21; Quarles, *Allies for Freedom,* 3–14, 174–79. On the crest, see "Niagara Movement Logo, ca. 1905," Du Bois Papers. I discuss the significance of this monument to William James, Du Bois's teacher at Harvard, as a model of tragic political conviction and its relationship to Du Bois's *John Brown* in Alexander Livingston, *Damn Great Empires! William James and the Politics of Pragmatism* (Oxford: Oxford University Press, 2016), 103–25.

20. W. E. B. Du Bois, "The Niagara Movement: An Address to the Country," in *Pamphlets and Leaflets by W. E. B. Du Bois,* ed. Herbert Aptheker (White Plains: Kraus-Thomson, 1986), 64.

21. W. E. B. Du Bois, "Third Annual Meeting of the Niagara Movement," in *Pamphlets and Leaflets,* ed. Aptheker, 74; "Report of the Fifth Annual Niagara

Movement Conference, Sea Isle, New Jersey, ca. August 15, 1909," Du Bois Papers.

22. Reverdy C. Ransom, "The Spirit of John Brown," *Voice of the Negro* 3, no. 10 (1906): 417.

23. W. E. B. Du Bois, "The Niagara Movement: Declaration of Principles, 1905," in *Pamphlets and Leaflets,* ed. Aptheker, 58.

24. W. E. B. Du Bois, "The Joy of Living," in *Writings by W. E. B. Du Bois in Periodicals Edited by Others,* ed. Aptheker, 1:220. Compare Palmer, "I mean by self-sacrifice any diminution of my own possessions, pleasures, or powers, in order to increase those of others" (*The Nature of Goodness,* 165).

25. Du Bois, "John Brown, ca. 1909 [ID #mums312-b196-i047]," 19–20, Du Bois Papers. The dating of this document is unclear. While catalogued as 1909 in the Du Bois Papers, the paper follows the outline of a draft chapter dated as 1905 ("John Brown: The Hour and the Man, ca. 1905"). Moreover, Du Bois's narrative of Brown's life in this draft and the 1905 outline focus on details such as Brown's poor eyesight and education not included in the 1909 biography or Du Bois's other writings on Brown from 1909 to 1910. For these reasons, this paper most likely represents Du Bois's earliest remaining draft of the biography. Cf. "John Brown, ca. 1909 [ID #mums312-b196-i048]," Du Bois Papers.

26. Du Bois, *Souls,* 39, 40, 39, 39.

27. Du Bois, "Address to the Country," 64; *Souls,* 128, 141

28. W. E. B. Du Bois, "Galileo Galilei, June 1908 [ID# mums312-b196-i042]," 6, 11, 11, Du Bois Papers.

29. Du Bois, *Souls,* 59, 59.

30. Cornel West, "Black Striving in a Twilight Civilization," in *The Cornel West Reader* (New York: Basic Civitas, 1999), 93. Compare the competing readings of Du Bois as an elitist in Adolph Reed Jr., *W. E. B. Du Bois and American Political Thought: Fabianism on the Color Line* (Oxford: Oxford University Press, 1997), and Robert Gooding-Williams, *In the Shadow of Du Bois: Afro-Modern Political Thought in America* (Cambridge: Harvard University Press, 2009) with the democratic readings of Du Bois in Manning Marable, *W. E. B. Du Bois: Black Radical Democrat,* updated ed. (New York: Routledge, 2005), and Melvin L. Rogers, "The People, Rhetoric, and Affect: On the Political Force of Du Bois's *The Souls of Black Folk,*" in this volume (pages 123–58).

31. The passage continues:

Renounce all that you long for, all-renounce!
That's the truth that all pronounce
So sagely, so interminably,
The non-stop croak, the universal chant:
You can't have what you want, you can't!
I awake each morning, how? Horrified,

On the verge of tears, to confront a day
Which at its close will not have satisfied
One smallest wish of mine.

Goethe, *Faust: A Tragedy. Part One and Two,* trans. Martin Greenberg (New Haven: Yale University Press, 2014), lines 1571–79. Felipe Smith discusses this ambiguity and Du Bois's citations of this passage in *American Body Politics: Race, Gender, and Black Literary Renaissance* (Athens: University of Georgia Press, 1998), 222–30.

32. Du Bois, "The Joy of Living," 218; "The Problem of Amusement," in *Writings in Periodical Literature Edited by Others,* 1:36–37; emphasis in original.

33. Du Bois, *Souls,* 32.

34. Mizruchi, *The Science of Sacrifice,* 354.

35. Du Bois, *Souls,* 134.

36. Bonnie Honig, *Emergency Politics: Paradox, Law, Democracy* (Princeton: Princeton University Press, 2009), 10–11.

37. Ibid., 11.

38. Lawrie Balfour discusses the viability of triumphant and tragic readings of *John Brown* in *Democracy's Reconstruction,* 66–70.

39. John Brown, "Prison Letters," in *The Tribunal,* ed. Stauffer and Trodd, 62–63, 67, 69–70. David S. Reynolds discusses Brown's active promotion of the narrative of his Christian martyrdom in *John Brown, Abolitionist: The Man Who Killed Slavery, Sparked the Civil War, and Seeded Civil Rights* (New York: Vintage, 2005), 334–401.

40. Du Bois, *John Brown,* xxv, xxv, 6, 40. Cf. 45, 46.

41. Nahum Dimitri Chandler, *X—The Problem of the Negro as a Problem for Thought* (New York: Fordham University Press, 2014), 112–28. One consequence of this way of doubling Brown in a narrative that is both transnational and transracial is to interrupt his easy incorporation into the national narrative of atonement for slavery that Emerson and other white admirers place him in. In doing so Du Bois recovers Brown from the redemptive narrative of American exceptionalism to mobilize him as a symbol of the colored world's global struggle against colonialism and imperialism. Du Bois's racial doubling of John Brown is discussed further in Gilpin, *John Brown Still Lives!,* 79–86; Balfour, *Democracy's Reconstruction;* and Ted A. Smith, *Weird John Brown: Divine Violence and the Limits of Ethics* (Stanford: Stanford University Press, 2015), 157–77.

42. Balfour, *Democracy's Reconstruction,* 55.

43. Du Bois, *John Brown,* 67–68, 44, 43.

44. Du Bois, *John Brown,* 44, 142. Compare W. E. B. Du Bois, *Black Reconstruction in America, 1860–1880* (New York: Free Press, 1992), 55–83.

45. Du Bois, *John Brown,* 40.

46. Balfour, *Democracy's Reconstruction*, 66; Levering Lewis, *W. E. B. Du Bois: Biography of a Race*, 358.

47. Du Bois, *John Brown*, 55, John Brown, "Sambo's Mistakes," in *The Tribunal*, ed. Stauffer and Trodd, 3, 5, 5–6, cited in Du Bois, *John Brown*, 55.

48. Du Bois, *John Brown*, 63, 33, 35, 35.

49. Ibid., 154, 152. See John Brown, "Provisional Constitution and Ordinances for the People of the United States," in *The Tribunal*, ed. Stauffer and Trodd.

50. Balfour, *Democracy's Reconstruction*, 57.

51. Du Bois, *John Brown*, 19, 22, 137. Chandler provides an alternative reading of the significance of death in *X—The Problem of the Negro as a Problem for Thought*, 112–15.

52. Du Bois, *John Brown*, 204; "John Brown, ca. 1909," 24, 27.

53. Du Bois, *John Brown*, 206.

54. Ibid., 61, 60.

55. On the paradoxical character of a counterpolitics of "more life," see discussion in Honig, *Emergency Politics*, 141. Nick Bromell helpfully discusses the ways Du Bois's democratic theory provides a framework for sustaining such active tensions in *The Time Is Always Now: Black Thought and the Transformation of US Democracy* (Oxford: Oxford University Press, 2013), 112–21.

56. Du Bois, *John Brown*, 206.

57. Ibid., 4.

58. Du Bois, *Souls*, 162–63, 166; cf. 6.

59. Kahn, *Divine Discontent*, 117. Rogers similarly reads Du Bois's ambiguous placement of the black "we" both inside and outside the nation as invoking a future to be claimed and constructed in the present (see "The People, Rhetoric, and Affect," 192).

60. Du Bois, *John Brown*, 230; "William Lloyd Garrison, Oct 16, 1909," 11, Du Bois Papers; Du Bois, *John Brown*, 231, emphasis added. In saying this, I agree with Rampersad's description of *John Brown* as "a study in the sociology of modern prophecy," while disagreeing with his claim that Brown provided Du Bois with a clear model of prophetic leadership worthy of emulation (Rampersad, *Art and Imagination*, 112).

61. Du Bois, *John Brown*, 82.

62. Ibid., 40.

63. René Girard, *Violence and the Sacred*, trans. Patrick Gregory (Baltimore: Johns Hopkins University Press, 1977), 27.

64. Du Bois, *John Brown*, 4, 4, 230.

65. Ibid., 225, 225.

66. Thomas McCarthy, *Race, Empire, and the Idea of Human Development* (Cambridge: Cambridge University Press, 2009), 81.

67. Du Bois, *John Brown,* 226.

68. Ibid., 227, 237, 228. Compare William James's pragmatic interpretation of Darwin against the Spencerians in "Great Men and Their Environment," in *The Will to Believe and Other Essays in Popular Philosophy,* ed. Frederick Burkhardt, Fredson Bowers, and Ignas K. Skrupskelis (Cambridge: Harvard University Press, 1979), 163–89. I discuss Du Bois's complicated relationship with James's pragmatism further in Livingston, *Damn Great Empires!,* 126–52.

69. Cain, "Violence, Revolution, and the Cost of Freedom," 328. Byerman similarly reads *John Brown* as legitimating revolutionary violence (Byerman, *Seizing the Word,* 172).

70. George Shulman, *American Prophecy: Race and Redemption in American Political Culture* (Minneapolis: University of Minnesota Press, 2008), 30–31. Cf. Du Bois's revised statements on revolution in the 1962 edition of *John Brown,* 395–96.

71. William Lloyd Garrison, *Selections from the Writings and Speeches of William Lloyd Garrison, With an Appendix* (Boston: R. F. Wallcut, 1852), 190.

72. Du Bois, *John Brown,* 237.

73. Russell Banks, "John Brown's Body: James Baldwin and Frank Shatz in Conversation," *Transition* 9, no. 1 (2000), https://muse.jhu.edu/article/35041.

74. Du Bois, "Agitation," 1132.

9

On Democratic Leadership and Social Change

Positioning Du Bois in the Shadow of a Gray To-come

Arash Davari

Recent movements to address racialized police violence have been celebrated by many as being "leaderless." This development reflects a broader global trend. Since the late 1960s, social movements across the world have made a discursive shift away from centralized, vanguard models of self-governance toward ones that are more diffuse and collective—characterized by fragmentation, spontaneity, and individual autonomy—and hence more in tune with current democratic ideals.[1]

In black political culture, a similar discursive shift has appeared as a rejection of individual (and male) charismatic leadership. As Erica Edwards writes, an older style of leadership rested on the assumption "that political advancement is best achieved under the direction of a single male leader believed to be gifted with a privileged connection to the divine." Emerging in the wake of Reconstruction as a response to "the containments and terrors of Western modernity," black charismatic leadership usually drew on a narrative, or a "charismatic scenario," in which a heroic individual rises from "self-doubt and convention" to assume "the promise of his calling." Critics like Edwards have argued that this model tends to silence nonelite perspectives, reinforce oppressive gender norms, and contribute to the cultivation of antidemocratic social and political relations.[2]

This critique of charismatic leadership in black political thought aligns with the broader global trend away from leadership in contemporary social movements. The question remains, however, as to whether the most effective strategy for achieving a democratic future—one that, by necessity, involves the realization of racial justice—requires the dissolution of leadership altogether. In other words, is the answer to the problem of charismatic black leadership a leaderless movement? Should movements regard themselves (and be presented in terms of) horizontal strategies of resistance? Or are there alternatives between these extremes—alternatives that address the limits of each approach while retaining an orientation toward racial justice and radical democracy?

Recent work in the field of political theory has paralleled—even anticipated—the rise in leaderless social movements. Emphasis has been placed on the constitutive significance of the means adopted for the ends pursued, a point that stands in contrast to the "by any means necessary" mantras of a previous historical moment. Inspired by Marxist models, theorization in that earlier moment subordinated the political to the social, justifying inequality and a lack of freedom within the act of social change as required to attain a more just world in the future. More recent political theory has instead operated in the realm of the present and the political, directly engaging and resignifying democracy in the act of social change itself. An extension of the spirit found in the classical democratic revolutions of the late eighteenth century, scholarship in this register has articulated conditions for increased equality and freedom by challenging normative and centralized power wherever and whenever it might appear.[3]

Against the broader global trend, I would argue, the neoliberal context of contemporary social movements compels a reassessment of this theoretical disposition. Today's leaderless formations are at least partly a result of neoliberal policy and its accompanying political rationality. These policies and preferences have encouraged the dissolution of "the people" (which had previously appeared as an alliance of various collective formations such as trade unions and political parties) into a gathered mass of individuals. In undermining existing collectivities, neoliberalism simultaneously undermines the basis of charismatic leadership: actors in mass-based movements no longer appear as members of smaller collectives represented by individual leaders but as autonomous individuals representing themselves. At the same time, celebrations of today's social movements as being leaderless comport all too easily with the ethos of "communicative capitalism" marking neoliberal reforms. From this perspective, the collective formation of "a mass of individuals" is essentially a matter of participation—of having one's voice heard in a consumer world organized to discover and cater to our individual desires. It follows that movements not oriented toward challenging the material conditions structuring democratic exchange risk co-optation and fragmentation before they realize their goals.[4]

This erosion of traditional group solidarities seems to require a choice among three unappealing representational alternatives. We must either nostalgically grasp at what critical reflection and historical change are setting aside (liberal democracy, group formation, and/or charismatic leadership), celebrate the void (leaderless movements), or defer the political to the realization of social revolution before all else. Taking the occasion of contemporary black social movements as a point of departure, this essay suggests that W. E. B. Du Bois's early writings help us imagine a fourth alternative.

In his reflections on the prospect of social change on behalf of greater racial justice, I argue, Du Bois affirms one of the central precepts of radical and plural democracy—the idea that power cannot be eliminated but instead must be reconstituted in ways that are "compatible with democratic values." Yet by infusing "the political" with a revised and democratically inclined vision of "politics"—a gesture that goes against the grain of radical democratic theory—Du Bois's early writings provide tools to better represent and articulate processes of social change as they occur today. That is, where theorists of radical democracy tend to understand "politics" as the management and administration of human life for the purposes of ensuring peace and security, and "the political" as the fleeting yet genuinely democratic disruption of those managerial patterns, Du Bois presents "the political" as a process requiring practices our contemporaries would associate with "politics." Drawing on his early writings, we may fill the void left by our rejection of charismatic and socially determinist models while redefining radical democracy within it concretely. Herein, radical democracy appears as the constant movement of individuals and perspectives in and out of positions of authority on the basis of differences in lived experience—a process of exchange only produced by the preservation of positional distinctions in the first place.[5]

In the pages that follow, I present this fourth alternative through a close reading of 1899's *The Philadelphia Negro* (hereafter *PN*) and 1903's *The Souls of Black Folk* (hereafter *Souls*). The first section of this essay affirms the need to appreciate form (genre, in particular) when reading Du Bois's early writings as political theory. I apply this approach in the immediately ensuing sections. In the second section of this essay, I turn to *PN*'s narrative composition, where I locate an understanding of the elite as subject to open-ended and unscripted transformation through engagements with everyday peoples' lived experience. In the third, I present *PN* and *Souls* as parallel variations of a bildungsroman. It is my contention that an understanding of democratic leadership may be found in the formal continuity between the two texts. For instance, the democratic effects of producing *PN* on Du Bois—effects reflected in *PN*'s narrative structure—reappear in the manifest content of *Souls* through Du Bois's autobiographical self-representation.

I take these readings as an invitation for a broader theorization of democratic leadership in the context of social change. The fourth section of this essay considers the content of *Souls* in detail, focusing in particular on the shadowing relationship between Du Bois's authorial persona and the fictional figure of John Jones. Their differences reveal the limits of the bildungsroman and, moreover, reject the charismatic scenario of black political leadership as the most effective strategy for social change. Instead, Du Bois articulates a projected scenario where positional distinctions between a leader and the led are maintained. Herein, individuals from among the led may come to speak with the authority of leadership when and where necessary. As I argue in conclusion, this understanding of democratic leadership is consistent with core precepts informing radical democratic theory and popular representations of contemporary social movements alike.

Reading Du Bois for Form and Genre

For all his insight, the early Du Bois is not the most obvious choice for theorizing more radically democratic forms of social change. Critics have cast him as the intellectual architect of an elitist and antidemocratic model of leadership dominating black political life for over a century. In these accounts, Du Bois's influence is partly to blame for the excesses of charismatic political leadership in movements for racial justice. Writing at the turn of the twentieth century—a context where an elite-centered collectivist outlook had captured the imaginations of American Progressive scholars—Du Bois could not but proffer a vanguard model of black political leadership. His mostly widely read and influential text, *Souls,* is said to present a roadmap for implementing that model. The politics of what Robert Gooding-Williams calls "expressive self-realization" contained therein aspired to solve the problem of assimilation within, while simultaneously expressing the spiritual identity of, the African American community. In this sense, *Souls* offers a paradigmatic expression of charismatic leadership, arguing for legitimate and self-determined forms of governing black people in an authoritarian and decidedly undemocratic manner—a model that wields a democratic spirit for the sake of its undoing.[6]

To be sure, the early Du Bois has had his defenders, and radical democratic critiques of his leadership model have not gone unquestioned. Some have argued that the kind of leadership presented in *Souls* is not predicated on charisma or force but rather on persuasion and critical appraisal. An elite undoubtedly exists in Du Bois's political thought—indeed, all leadership calls for elitism—but Du Bois insists that leaders should be "subject to public scrutiny" and "responsive to the criticism of their followers." In a less celebratory fashion, others have argued that leadership and elitism comprise an unavoidable aspect of governance. Despite the continued presence of distinctions between leaders/followers and elite/mass, political contestation from below must continue to hold leaders and elites accountable. From this perspective, critiques of Du Bois's model of elite leadership are unrealistically utopian and impractical.[7]

And yet, in assuming that leadership necessarily implies elitism, both critics and these defenders of Du Bois alike overlook key features of the rhetoric, formal composition, and, I would suggest, genre conventions found in *Souls.* Attention to these aspects of the text more convincingly challenges characterizations of Du Bois as simply elitist and antidemocratic. For instance, when read with close attention to its rhetoric, *Souls* appears as an act of democratic persuasion—one that appeals to the judgment of its audience. In so doing, the text presumes that audience's continued self-possession, a presumption that differs markedly from the self-abandonment and submission required by charismatic leadership.[8]

This point can and should be extended to readings of Du Bois broadly construed. In this respect, in reading for form and genre across Du Bois's early writings, we discover a projected ideal of political leadership predicated on the movement between mass and elite lived experience. This is not necessarily elitism. Rather, it indicates that different people are able to speak with authority at different moments and in different contexts based on differences in what they have been through—not who they are. Although the problem of vanguard politics certainly persists, Du Bois's early writings also allow for a reassessment of leadership in the process of radical democratic change. Instead of situating leadership and democracy in opposition to one another, *Souls* advocates conserving positional distinctions between leader and led as a basis for the very democratic virtues and open-ended ethos critics seek to defend through the rejection of leadership *tout court*.

Reading *The Philadelphia Negro* as Ethnographic Narrative

PN was researched and written over the course of fifteen months between the summer of 1896 and the winter of 1897. The study was commissioned to address the prevalence of crime in the Seventh Ward, a predominantly African American neighborhood that also housed "many of the city's most distinguished white families." Despite an expectation that he present the "nature and duration of the quarantine that the city's notables intended to impose" on the neighborhood's black inhabitants, Du Bois took the occasion to examine the relationship between poverty and racism in an effort to scientifically correct the fact that "the world was thinking wrong about race."[9]

There are, as a result, two apparently contradictory premises underwriting the text. On the one hand, Du Bois affirms his sponsor's preconceived notions when he refers to the moral depravity of the black inhabitants in the Seventh Ward. Along these lines, he argues for the "training" of the masses according to a civilizational ideal—a task he bestows on "the better classes" of the city's African American population. This aspect of the text affirms the suspicions harbored by Du Bois's critics regarding his designs for assimilation. On the other, every central point in the study refers to "color prejudice" as an explanatory principle, deflecting primary responsibility from "the masses" for any "lack" in their progress along the "scale of civilization." The presence of both strands of thought seems to reinforce Du Bois's own retrospective assertion that he wrote *PN* with a "hidden agenda."[10]

In his introduction to *PN*, Du Bois more straightforwardly presents the text as comprising four parts. The first part presents a history of African Americans in the city (two chapters). The second part presents "their present condition considered as individuals" (six chapters), and the third, "their condition as an organized social group" (two chapters). A chapter on crime and pauperism is also included in the third part under the category of "group life." Du Bois's fourth section concerns the topic of environment, both physical and social.[11]

This outline signals a seemingly straightforward narrative, moving from individual life to organized (read: "civilized") collectivity. What it actually contains is a carefully plotted account of individual realization through group life—an almost dialectical relationship between the individual and the collective that inverts in emphasis as the text progresses. At first, although Du Bois investigates "their present condition considered as individuals," he offers no individual portraits. Instead, the text presents a portrait of the community as a whole, one in which each individual's information provides a single tile in a larger mosaic of general trends. Conversely, the chapters that consider "their condition as an organized social group" offer an abundance of individualized portraits. This second portion of the text abounds with narrative vignettes meant to capture what it feels like to be a member of the African American community in Philadelphia.[12]

The text's structural progression—from iterations of individual life in general terms to iterations of group life through specific examples—is accompanied by a series of methodological choices. As *PN* shifts to a focus on individual portraits in its medium of communication, Du Bois shifts from the exclusive use of statistics to the increased use of qualitative and mixed methodologies. By necessity, these methodological choices call our attention to Du Bois's presence as author and interpreter; that is, they signal his involvement in the production of the text. In the first part of *PN*, Du Bois is an impersonal medium through which the life of the black community is communicated as a whole. By contrast, in the second portion of the text where he turns to present the lived experience of its primary subject (i.e., the black "masses" of the Seventh Ward), Du Bois directly expresses his own thoughts and sensibilities. He no longer presents information to the reader in a passive fashion; instead, he reveals his own argumentative agenda, an agenda that statistical methods alone inadequately capture.[13]

The pattern points to an important yet overlooked biographical detail regarding the effects of producing *PN. The Philadelphia Negro* is the founding example of empirical methods in modern American sociology—in particular, ethnography. The process of ethnographic research requires an investigator to see the imprints of his own production—and by extension himself—as an object apart from who he is. The ethnographer asks a question, which in turn produces a response taken to be data. Similarly, when writing vignettes, the ethnographer paints a portrait of human life rather than taking a snapshot. Ideally, the ethnographer is not only implicated but also changed by the process.[14]

True to the exigencies of the form, Du Bois reflects on writing *PN* in a retrospective essay published more than forty years after his initial study: "I became painfully aware that merely being born in a group does not necessarily make one possessed of complete knowledge concerning it. I had learned far more from the Philadelphia Negroes than I had taught them concerning the Negro Problem."[15] Like the "truth" produced by portraiture, the "truth" produced by ethnographic investigation is inherently imprecise, suggestive and, above all, self-reflective. The ethnographic portrayal of that which has otherwise been rendered invisible or perceived incorrectly—in this case, the experiences of members of the African American community in the Seventh Ward—goes hand in hand with a process of self-exposure and eventually autobiographical self-depiction.

The transformation that occurs for Du Bois in the production of *PN*—the transformation of the ethnographer, alongside the unfolding presentation of the ethnographic subject in one and the same text—reappears in the content of *Souls.* There, Du Bois expressly weaves his authorial persona into the narrative. As I argue in the sections that follow, this reflects a formal continuity between the two texts. What is more, it occasions a theory of democratic leadership in processes of social change.

Reading *The Philadelphia Negro* and *The Souls of Black Folk* as Bildungsroman(s)

Du Bois's critics have presented arguments positing the elitism in 1899's *PN* as the basis for the antidemocratic model of leadership in *Souls.* This section presents a different relationship between *PN* and *Souls.* When we consider the composition as well as points of formal continuity between the two texts (as opposed to focusing solely on their manifest content), reading

Souls in light of *PN*, we may find the basis for a nonelitist articulation of democratic leadership.[16]

To be precise, *The Philadelphia Negro* and *The Souls of Black Folk* contain both a parallel and a shared narrative arc. On the one hand, just as *PN* turns from quantitative to qualitative analysis (from statistical analysis to ethnographic description), *Souls* turns from a sociology of black folk to an autobiography of Du Bois (from accounts of contemporary black life in general to a directly personal account of Du Bois's life experience). Each of these turns is phenomenological: broad descriptions of black folk as a mass become affective portraits through which Du Bois attempts to capture what it feels like to be the object of white racism in Jim Crow America.[17]

At the same time, the relationship between *PN* and *Souls* is linearly developmental: where *PN* ends, *Souls* begins, occupying the previous work's shell while exploring an affective dimension toward which *PN* only begins to gesture. Because he increasingly incorporates his autobiography into the fabric of both, Du Bois's personal development is central to the shared narrative arc between the two texts. When read together, that narrative arc constitutes a variation on the genre of the nineteenth-century bildungsroman—a genre in which grand historical transformations are figured as the developmental process of a single "protagonist." In this case, the grand transformation is that of the black "masses," and the single protagonist is Du Bois's authorial persona. Or rather, the emergence of Du Bois's authorial persona runs hand in hand with the development of the masses, who in turn achieve their self-development only when and where the "environment" of race prejudice changes.[18]

The first hints of a bildungsroman appear in *PN*. There, Du Bois presents the black inhabitants of the Seventh Ward as a version of the black "masses," incrementally taking steps to assimilate into an evolving and yet-to-be realized model of civilization. According to his own straightforward outline of the text, we begin the story seeing facets of their individual lives before slowly moving toward organized social life—or what Du Bois understands to be the incomplete realization of human civilization.[19] Yet, as I have suggested, Du Bois too is a "hidden" protagonist, changing his authorial presence in step with his subject of study as the narrative unfolds; in this interaction, he "learns far more" than he teaches. This kind of development—in which the masses, Du Bois, and the sociopolitical environment must all genuinely change—anticipates the model of democratic leadership implied by *Souls*.[20]

Reading *Souls* as a similarly cohesive and linear narrative challenges prevalent scholarly interpretations. *Souls* has often been misunderstood to be a fragmented collection of disparate essays—a conclusion abetted by the publication of its various chapters in article form prior to the book's release. Against these interpretations, Victor Wolfenstein suggests a cohesive and unified underlying structure. The narrative in *Souls* develops in a "palindromic" fashion, moving from the collective to the individual dimension of African American life in a nonlinear manner. This move is accompanied by a change in Du Bois's role as author such that, in the first part of *Souls,* he appears as a "vehicle for displaying the facts of the racial matter," whereas in the second part of the book the "racial matter" becomes the "medium through which we experience the sensibility of the author."[21]

And yet, within this nonlinear life-world, *Souls* also contains a two-pronged linear narrative. In line with its "palindromic" quality, the text tells the coming-of-age story of the black "masses" and Du Bois's authorial persona, both of whom are presented in an interrelated process of self-realization. *Souls'* linear narrative begins in Tennessee before moving to Atlanta and then farther south into the Black Belt. With each move, Du Bois unveils increasingly advanced stages in the life trajectory of the masses as "protagonist." This time around, however, the narrator's autobiography is directly woven into the fabric of the text. Du Bois comes of age right alongside the development of the masses. When and where he appears in the chapters that rest along what Wolfenstein calls the "horizontal plane" of sociological analysis, we find Du Bois progressively growing older. What is more, all of the chapters in the subsequent section are cast under the shadow of death. Like all living things, the narrative progresses from childhood to youth and then finally from (the "current" Du Bois's) adulthood to death.[22]

Behind the veil—where the text shifts to consider individual experience in an affective register, and the experience of living death defines the lives of African Americans under Jim Crow—Du Bois enacts a parallel coming-of-age story. These chapters present the experience of death at a progressively later stage in human life. In chapter 11 ("Of the Passing of the First Born"), death strikes in infancy. In the ensuing chapter 12 ("Of Alexander Crummell")—despite the fact that the protagonist's physical death occurs in old age—Du Bois presents Crummell's "deeper death" occurring in his formative youth. Chapter 13 ("Of the Coming of John") recounts the fictitious tale of a man from a small town in the South who, unlike Crummell, not only completes his formative training in the North but also, again unlike Crummell, begins to realize his soul's duty when he returns down South to become a schoolteacher. John Jones too has his path obstructed by prejudice and, like the others, suffers a premature death—only now as a mature adult.[23]

Importantly, just as Du Bois's ethnographic work teaches him more than he himself could teach, the notion of an unrealized promise of leadership appears in *Souls* in the form of persons other than the text's author. Put differently, in a continuation of the autobiographical dimensions woven into *Souls*' "palindromic" narrative, the portions of the text that arrive behind the veil depict people who both are and are not Du Bois. Each is a shadow of Du Bois's personality—including, especially, John Jones.[24]

While partially affirming criticisms of the politics found therein (a novel of formation ultimately recounts a process of assimilation), reading the narrative arc shared by *PN* and *Souls* as a variation on the bildungsroman also opens avenues for a reevaluation of Du Bois's account of political leadership. Precisely because the coming-of-age narrative told in *Souls* is "palindromic," it is not simply an account of progressive development for the black masses in accordance with white norms; it is also an account of interrelated and mutual development between African Americans and Du Bois. Du Bois—as the representative bearer of white norms in the black community—is not a passive observer in this scenario, instrumentally guiding his people along a predetermined path. Rather, insofar as the narrative contains dual protagonists in a bildungsroman, it tells the story of their coming together (and mutual transformation) as the medium for their coming together with (and mutual transformation of) American society. We may discern a democratic conception of political leadership in the duality of their developmental process—the fact that it includes prescriptions for the text's author, or the elite, alongside a program for the masses.

Democratic Leadership in *The Souls of Black Folk*

While *Souls* follows the general structure of a bildungsroman, it ultimately does not end as a bildungsroman would. Instead, the text is characterized by what Daphne Lamothe calls generic hybridity.[25] *Souls* replays the scenario of the bildungsroman alongside the scenario of charismatic black political leadership in order to break from both. These breaks disrupt the possibility of rigidly mapping elite/mass relations onto a democratic/undemocratic axis. In what follows, I present the limits of the bildungsroman and the charismatic scenario in *Souls*—that is, the fact that the text does not end with the realization of self-development and the related fact that its projected ideal of political leadership does not appeal to everyday folk culture. These breaks, or limits, invite us to imagine self-development and democracy anew.

To this end, this section retraces the parallels between *PN* and *Souls*. Taking the aforementioned analysis of form and genre as a point of departure, I directly consider the discussion of leadership in *Souls'* manifest content, paying particular attention to the shadowing relationship between Du Bois's authorial persona and John Jones. Where *Souls* recounts Du Bois's personal process of formation alongside that of the masses, Jones encapsulates both stories in one (fictional) figure. Like Du Bois, he possesses elite training and the will to "develop" the masses. Like Du Bois, he experiences misrecognition as double-consciousness by virtue of his elite training. Unlike Du Bois, however, he chooses the path of revolt and rebellion. This signals a further and more fundamental difference. Where Du Bois's bid to leadership is tainted by his lack of legitimacy, the question of legitimacy has already been answered for Jones. He is of the masses and therefore legitimate in a way Du Bois can never be. In other words, Jones represents the figure of self-development Du Bois wished to be.[26]

The text's limitations as bildungsroman and the possibilities for theorizing democratic leadership through it occur by way of this shadowing relationship. On the one hand, Du Bois appears as the incomplete shadow of Jones, who for his part exemplifies political leadership. It is fitting, then, that *Souls* attempts to end twice: first with the presentation of Jones as the telos of an unrealized bildungsroman and only afterward, provisionally, with the sorrow songs. The two endings correspond with a distinction made by Manning Marable between political and cultural leadership. Du Bois turns to the sorrow songs (a source of charisma) only in light of Jones's inability to realize his promise as political leader. By contrast, the turn to the written text—a return to Du Bois as authorial persona—presents a form of cultural leadership. In this respect, charisma appears as a second-best option and the only viable one under Jim Crow in the aftermath of failed political leadership. At the same time, by virtue of Jones's association with Du Bois's authorial persona as shadow—a persona we see changing across the texts—

ideal political leadership itself appears as a necessarily open and malleable position. The John Jones we encounter by the end of chapter 13 is an empty signifier for the movement of the masses into positions of leadership.[27]

Much akin to the imaginative democratic possibilities expressed by the figure of Abraham Lincoln Jones in 1937's incomplete novel *A World Search for Democracy*, "Of the Coming of John" speaks in future time and in a fictional register. The deaths in the second section of *Souls* signal obstructions to the realization of racial justice and hence the momentary yet inherent failures of the narrative as bildungsroman. All of the formal components of a bildungsroman may exist, yet the script of harmonized social change falls short because of realities beyond the text. *Souls* instead retains a sense of uncertainty where the bildungsroman might lead us to expect completion—a sense felt all the more by its evocative parallels to the genre. This is not to suggest that Du Bois adapts the bildungsroman to present the tragedy of American life in a pessimistic register. Rather, what *Souls* offers in place of an actual bildungsroman is the incomplete projection of one as a site of possibility—a text whose closure rests in the "gray To-come."[28]

Jones's temporal location in *Souls'* narrative structure incorporates the open-ended quality of reception into the text; in other words, the end of the narrative is itself indeterminate. In chapter 11, the death of Du Bois's infant son happens "before" the experience of "living death." His passing represents one possible response to an environment marked by white supremacy—to die before the pain of the present may occur. In the following chapter, Crummell's story offers a full portrait of the present: "Some seer he seemed, that came not from the crimson Past or the gray To-come, but from the *Pulsing Now*—that mocking world which seemed to me at once so light and dark, so splendid and sordid. Four-score years had he wandered in this same world of mine, within the Veil."[29] Crummell's is a "living death" (the kind Du Bois's son had avoided); his experience encapsulates what it feels like to be a "problem" in the historical present ("the Pulsing Now"). Indeed, while the other personages in this section of *Souls* die prematurely, Crummell stays alive and completes the course of his physical (present) existence. In John Jones's story, however, everything is a matter of anticipation, of the uncertainty of the future, or the "gray To-come." Throughout the story, the entire town, black and white, waits for a promised time when each of their respective Johns will return home. And yet, despite the story's overwhelming sense of anticipation, in the end we receive no ending. In what we might expect to be the culminating act of a bildungsroman, John Jones's return is cut short by his death. His story represents the failed promise of the future—the unrealized telos of self-development.[30]

Parallel to his approach in *PN,* Du Bois changes formal registers to accommodate and express the content in question. The use of fiction in chapter 13 signals the culmination of a general movement from quantitative to qualitative forms of analysis across the narrative arc shared between the two texts. At the same time, it communicates the uncertainty of the future. At the conclusion of the first (horizontal) portion of *Souls,* Du Bois uses words that could as easily facilitate the parallel transition from quantitative to qualitative methods in *PN.* In an echo of the pedagogical process marking the researcher's experience with ethnography, he describes the difficulty of recounting to strangers "the atmosphere of the land, the thought and feeling, the thousand and one little actions which go to make up life." For the "casual observer" to come to an "awakening" he must "linger long enough" until he "gradually" reaches a sense of things "he had not at first noticed." The second section of the text takes a further step. Where ethnographic research offers the truth of portraiture in its effort to capture the "atmosphere" of an intangible experience, fiction presents a medium through which to understand a related intangible promise, one that only exists as a potentiality in "the Pulsing Now."[31]

A similar pattern underlies Du Bois's reenactment of the charismatic scenario. As his critics claim, *Souls* culminates in a model of self-development that replays that scenario: Jones overcomes a sense of "self-doubt and convention" in order to ultimately "rise to the promise of his calling" back home. The quality of the iteration as elitist and antidemocratic, however, should be assessed in terms of the specificity of the account. Unlike Du Bois, who appeals to folk culture through the sorrow songs, Jones's legitimacy derives from what he has lived as a child of the South once removed—not what he must now say as a product of elite training in the North. The lived experiential differences between Du Bois and Jones determine the latter's more legitimate claim to leadership.

Instead, the rendering of Jones as the projected yet unrealized and (at the time) unrealizable telos of black self-development suggests that true self-development, or ideal political leadership, results from the movement of the masses into elite positions. That is, where elitism assumes an exclusive class determining an agenda of self-development for others—framing democracy (at best) in terms of collectives who simply select leaders that make decisions on their behalf—Du Bois's depiction of Jones suggests regular movement from the collective into positions among the leadership class.[32]

Indeed, "Of the Coming of John" is a tale of "immigration" from South to North and back South again. On the one hand, Jones's story parallels the story of the "submerged tenth" in Philadelphia—the masses who migrate to the city and return what appear to be strides in development by the already established inhabitants of the city to a low level on the "scale of civilization."[33] On the other, his story is like Du Bois's journey as an observer in *Souls,* moving from North to South. In making that same move, Jones is able to occupy a position of leadership by virtue of his lived experiences when and where Du Bois cannot. He speaks to the "masses" not of folk appeal but rather of the experience of having once come from them. Yet Du Bois makes a point of showing that Jones's appeal as a leader does not lie in his ability to act charismatically: upon returning home, Jones fails as an orator. In *Souls,* only Du Bois's authorial persona appeals to folk culture—a point made explicit in chapter 14 in the immediate wake of Jones's political failure. This rendering of political leadership—that is, the rendering of John Jones—imagines different people (mass and elite alike) speaking with authority across differences in time, context, and lived experience. To dismiss the possibility of these authoritative speech acts in a wholesale critique of leadership is to work against the radical promise of democracy, not for it.[34]

The ethnographic sensibility that carries over from *PN* to *Souls* informs this rendering; the rendering, in turn, coincides with nonunitary modes of subjectivity central to radical democratic theory. For Chantal Mouffe, radical democracy is defined by practical reason: "This 'ethical knowledge,' distinct from knowledge specific to the sciences (episteme), is dependent on the ethos, the cultural and historical conditions current in the community, and implies a renunciation of all pretense to universality. This is a kind of rationality proper to the study of human praxis, which excludes all possibility of a 'science' of practice but which demands the existence of a 'practical reason,' a region not characterized by apodictic statements, where the reasonable prevails over the demonstrable."[35] An example of the practical reason that emerges from "human praxis," *PN* captures the heterogeneity of black life not only in its depiction of the inhabitants in the Seventh Ward but also in the self-reflective relationship between its subject of study and its author. The culmination of the narrative thread originally planted in that text reappears with the fictional figure of John Jones. Jones epitomizes "two-ness" in his situation between mass and elite culture. He represents ideal leadership not because of an assimilated white education or folk charisma but rather because of the particularity of his lived experience—because he embodies "situated knowledge."[36]

Along these lines, a pedagogical ethos underwrites Du Bois's conclusions across *PN* and *Souls*—an ethos that preserves authority without relinquishing freedom. Jones's projected leadership is predicated on his ability to establish a school. With reference to Du Bois's own process of development in the production of *PN*—a process he explicitly characterizes in pedagogical terms—this part of the fictional narrative should be taken to mean more than the inculcation of already known truths. The most transformative models of pedagogy lie somewhere between dictating information to students and hands-off approaches to student-centered learning. This opposition echoes an analogous dichotomy between charismatic or elitist political leadership and leaderless movements. In contrast to both, democracy in a classroom involves a dialogical and mutually responsive relationship between teacher and student without absolving the teacher's authority and expertise altogether. The parallels between *PN* and *Souls*, and the "shadowing" relationship between Du Bois's authorial persona and John Jones, suggest that the kind of teaching (i.e., leadership) Du Bois had in mind in chapter 13 similarly involved Jones learning "more from the [black masses] than he taught them."[37]

Reconstructing Radical Democratic Theory

How might we "think politically with [this] W. E. B. Du Bois" in the effort to reimagine radical democracy in our contemporary moment?[38] How does Du Bois's work suggest we accept the critique of charismatic black leadership without swinging to the opposite extreme of advocating a leaderless movement? What are the prospects for articulating an open-ended and nonteleological social movement, driven by the disorderly energies of the "masses" from below, without the pretense of abandoning leadership altogether? How can the spirit of theory and practice oriented against authoritarian models of leadership be retained without relinquishing the strategic and organizational benefits of leadership for the prospects of affecting tangible social change? In fact, how might the institution of leadership within processes of social change help realize the radical democratic potential of contemporary social movements?

In line with the ethos prevalent at the time, the process of social transformation Du Bois envisioned in the 1930s required governance. Beneath these later formulations, we find yet again the pattern Du Bois attributed to the experience of producing *PN*. In a 1939 essay, Du Bois called for a new black vision of democracy, one that stresses self-governance rather than inclusion—"the building-up of democracy and democratic power among themselves."[39] "The Position of the Negro in the American Social Order" made explicit the approach guiding 1935's *Black Reconstruction in America* (hereafter *BR*)—an intervention in historiography recast as an agenda for radical democratic social change. In *BR*, Du Bois situates African American history in a dialectic: that which had been most forcibly denied in the American political order was in fact the essential agent in the realization of American democracy. Drawing inspiration from moments of self-governance in the Freedmen's Bureaus of Reconstruction, these writings argued for open-ended experiments required by the specific condition of black political life as the basis for the reconstruction of global democracy. Instead of Du Bois learning "far more from the Philadelphia Negroes than [he] had taught them concerning the Negro Problem," now world civilization would learn from black Americans far more than it could teach.[40]

Despite their historical specificity, the resonance between these formulations and John Jones's story is striking. In chapter 13 of *Souls*, an experiment in self-governance is cut short. Where such an experiment succeeds, according to "The Position of the Negro," leaders are to be discerned and selected by the community itself—not through the imposition of principles from without. In other words, while specific skills may be developed from without the community, the determination of when, where, and how to apply those skills appears through collective self-governance: "When real and open democratic control is intelligent enough *to select of its own accord* on the whole the best, most courageous, most expert and scholarly leadership, then the problem of democracy within the Negro group is solved and by that same token the possibility of American Negroes entering into world democracy and taking their rightful place according to their knowledge and power is also sure."[41] Du Bois goes on to argue that the role of the "mass" is not merely to select and then relinquish control. Rather, the "triumph" of "exceptional men" proves that "down among the mass, ten times their number with equal ability could be discovered and developed," moving the masses into positions of leadership. While the qualification in the passage ("intelligent enough") suggests a process of assimilation and even vanguard politics, the emphasis on selection "of its own accord" suggests terms of movement from mass to elite not to be determined by abstract (i.e., white normative) intelligence. Rather, those terms are to be autonomously determined within the process of governance itself. Du Bois accordingly posits "group leadership" as the projected ideal of democracy within as well as beyond the group.[42]

This formulation occasions a revision to contemporary iterations of radical democratic theory. Radical democratic theory imagines democracy as episodic and on the move—what Sheldon Wolin, relying on a distinction between "politics" and "the political," calls "fugitive." Again, "politics" refers to the management and administration of human life for the purposes of ensuring peace and security; management operates through the institution of leadership, producing the simulacra of democracy as it contains its actual enactment. By contrast, true democracy is tied to revolutionary social change and hence the disruption of "politics." It is a fleeting "moment," an "experience," that emerges through the act of those who are excluded from participating in conventional political experience, thereby re-creating and remembering "the political."[43]

Despite the sense of interiority suggested by this account (Wolin's argument presumes the embedded nature of democracy within systems of order inimical to what it is), it nevertheless conveys a sharp distinction between "the political" and "politics." That distinction is not as sharp as Wolin claims. As Melvin Rogers argues, the operation of "politics"—in ordinary and mundane moments, through the mechanism of contestation—may involve experiences of "the political" without the revolutionary dissolution of institutions. In other words, freedom and authority need not be fundamentally opposed. Rather, the management identified with the institution of the executive—the "expertise" of leadership—may be situated in response to the demands and authority of a citizenry. The practice of democracy as "politics" must be assessed by whether it ensures freedom through the prevention of arbitrary power. By way of a relationship of mutual responsiveness between state and citizen, the pursuit of democracy may retain a suspicion of institutions without requiring their dissolution.[44]

In moving beyond the rigidity of these distinctions, we also move beyond renderings of "the political" strictly in terms of the spontaneous, the disordered, the anarchic. In a sense, Rogers's argument realizes part of Du Bois's suggestion: that is, how practices of African American experiments in democratic self-governance may act as a model for reorganizing democracy in the broader political order. This argument may be generalized. In other words, where the move from particular group experience to universal order arrives after significant social change, a similar argument may be applied to the process of social change itself. Reframing Du Bois in Wolin's terms, the exercise of "politics" *within* the black counterpublic simultaneously acts as "the political" *for* a broader order. This is not all. The kind of "politics" practiced within "the political"—what Du Bois in 1939 called "the problem of democracy within the Negro group"—also contains a more fluid and less oppositional conceptual relationship between "politics" and "the political." In this regard, the process of social change may be theorized in a concrete fashion—or rather, "politics" may be discerned within "the political" without compromising what "the political" is.

To illustrate the point, we might imagine an analogy between the concept of "a position," which Du Bois articulates between African Americans and the rest of the world, and the relationship between mass and elite within the group itself. Wolin's argument follows from the identification of nation-state boundaries, which (through constitutions) are said to "contain" democracy.[45] But boundaries are not merely repressive; in fact, the democracy Wolin imagines would not make sense as "fugitive" without them. In a related fashion, the imagined dissolution of positional distinctions within expressions of "the political" conveys a disavowal. Instead, understanding social change with, instead of simply against, institutions of authority—specifically, those pertaining to positional distinctions between leader and led—allows for movement within the movement that defines radical democracy. A member of "the masses" may come to speak from the authority of lived experience at a moment in time only if a platform of authority exists in the first place. As a projected ideal of political leadership, John Jones's story exemplifies this dynamic. His claim to leadership requires the movement of "mass" to "elite" positions in response to the contextual relevance of particular lived experiences—a movement produced and preserved by adopting a specific kind of pedagogical disposition in the articulation of leadership.

The conceit of leaderless social change overlooks, even aggressively challenges, these positional distinctions. Yet this conceit need not be a definitive feature of radical democratic theory. Reading Du Bois alongside that tradition adds concrete theorization to "the political": in addition to the effort to expand our understanding of political life beyond what assumed forms foreclose (be they institutional, normative, or otherwise), an understanding of leadership that coheres with the ethos of radical democratic theory allows us to articulate tangible steps within processes of social change. That understanding helps us move beyond the perceived need to represent today's movements as leaderless in order to stand against yesterday's excesses made in the name of a charismatic vanguard.

Notes

I would like to thank Yousef Baker, Libby Barringer, Anuja Bose, Nick Bromell, Sohail Daulatzai, Andrew Dilts, Megan Gallagher, Kirstie McClure, Amir Moosavi, Raul Moreno, Ella Myers, Raymond Rocco, Melvin Rogers, Mark Sawyer, Althea Sircar, and Victor Wolfenstein for their helpful questions, suggestions, and comments.

1. Leaderless movements can offer an effective strategy of mobilization in a context of police violence where, after the passage of civil rights legislation, the leaders of black radical movements have been systematically criminalized and assassinated. But recognizing the merits of a diffuse model of leadership as an organizing strategy should not preclude our ability to question the model's merit as a purported democratic ideal. To this end, this essay addresses the representation of contemporary social movements in popular culture and media, not the actual organization of contemporary social movements. The portrayals considered here employ a celebratory register to describe movements as leaderless, when and where such a dynamic may not exist in practice. In so doing, these portraits foster a false choice between an acceptable ideal of leaderless social change and undesirable forms of charismatic leadership from the past. This essay theorizes alternatives to that false choice—alternatives that very well may already be worked out in practice. For one example of the popular representations in question, see Jay Caspian Kang, "Our Demand Is Simple: Stop Killing Us," *New York Times Magazine,* May 4, 2015.

2. Erica R. Edwards, "Moses, Monster of the Mountain: Gendered Violence in Black Leadership's Gothic Tale," *Callaloo* 31, no. 4 (Fall 2008): 1085; Erica R. Edwards, *Charisma and the Fictions of Black Leadership* (Minneapolis: University of Minnesota Press, 2012), 4, 17, 21–22.

3. Chantal Mouffe, "Radical Democracy: Modern or Postmodern?," trans.

Paul Holdengräber, *Social Text* 21 (1989): 31–45. These theorizations also repeat select features of the black freedom struggle. Martin Luther King Jr famously argued for nonviolent tactics of resistance by insisting that "the means we use must be as pure as the ends we seek" (see "Letter from Birmingham Jail [1963]," in *Call and Response: Key Debates in African American* Studies, ed. Henry Louis Gates Jr. and Jennifer Burton [New York: Norton, 2011], 610).

4. Neoliberalism is alternatively defined as an ideology or a condition of precarity brought about not just by political economic reforms but also by forging a peculiar type of reason where all aspects of existence, including most notably the political, are understood in terms of economics. For (conflicting) accounts of neoliberalism as a policy transformation, see David Harvey, *A Brief History of Neoliberalism* (Oxford: Oxford University Press, 2007); and Terry Flew, "Six Theories of Neoliberalism," *Thesis Eleven* 122, no. 1 (2014): 49–71. For a discussion of neoliberalism as political rationality, see Wendy Brown, *Undoing the Demos: Neoliberalism's Stealth Revolution* (Brooklyn: Zone, 2015). For the effects of neoliberal policy on the dissolution of "the people" in contemporary social movements, see Robin Celikates and Yolande Jansen, "Reclaiming Democracy: An Interview with Wendy Brown on Occupy, Sovereignty, and Secularism," *Critical Legal Thinking: Law and the Political,* January 30, 2013, http://criticallegalthinking.com/2013/01/30/reclaiming-democracy-an-interview-with-wendy-brown-on-occupy-sovereignty-and-secularism/. I draw the phrase "communicative capitalism," which refers to "democracy that talks without responding," from Jodi Dean, *Democracy and Other Neoliberal Fantasies: Communicative Capitalism and Left Politics* (Durham: Duke University Press, 2009), 22. For a discussion of neoliberalism as ideology (and not political rationality)—wherein liberal democracy acts as a barrier (and not a platform) for the realization of new political possibilities (such as a "collective emancipatory egalitarian ideal")—see Jodi Dean, "Neoliberalism's Defeat of Democracy," *Critical Inquiry*, October 27, 2015, http://criticalinquiry.uchicago.edu/neoliberalisms_defeat_of_democracy/.

5. Chantal Mouffe, "Deliberative Democracy or Agonistic Pluralism?," *Social Research* 66, no. 3 (1999): 753–55; Sheldon Wolin, "Fugitive Democracy," *Constellations* 1, no. 1 (1994): 11–25. Like Wolin, Mouffe presents "the political" as inevitable social antagonism and "politics" as social practices that establish order.

6. Adolph Reed, *W. E. B. Du Bois and American Political Thought: Fabianism and the Color Line* (Oxford: Oxford University Press, 1997); Robert Gooding-Williams, *In the Shadow of Du Bois: Afro-Modern Political Thought* (Cambridge: Harvard University Press, 2009). According to Gooding-Williams, Du Bois's model of political leadership advocated the assimilation of the black "masses" in accordance with "the constitutive norms of modernity" through the ability to evoke "the ethos of the black folk." The claim requires a distinction between the masses and

the folk. On the one hand, Du Bois is said to describe African Americans as "an aggregate of uncultured, premodern slaves or former slaves"—the "masses." As "folk," the same community possesses "a collectively shared ethos or spirit" (4). *Souls* exhibits a democratic strain of thought when discussing Booker T. Washington's model of leadership—that is, a leader is legitimate when and where the ruled have selected him through search and criticism. Du Bois's failure to elaborate this process in depth, however, leads Gooding-Williams to identify an "expressivist" model of leadership (54–55). Instead, with reference to the writings of Hannah Arendt and Wolin, *In the Shadow* identifies a tension between interpretations of politics as a "practice of ruling" and democracy; the latter contains an unpredictable quality that contravenes any effort to impose rule (24).

7. Tommie Shelby locates persuasion within the text, i.e., between the Talented Tenth and its audience (see Shelby, "Reparations, Leadership, and Democracy," *Du Bois Review* 8, no. 2 [2011]: 395–99). Shelby's interpretation draws on Du Bois's critique of Booker T. Washington (see note 6 above). Rogers Smith claims that Gooding-Williams draws too sharp a distinction between politics-as-rule and politics as action-in-concert—and hence between elitism (associated with the former) and mass-based politics (meant to comprise the latter). According to Gooding-Williams, Smith's point is already contained in the notion of politics as action-in-concert (see Smith, "Toward a Progressive Democratic Politics of Race: Reflections on Du Bois' Legacy"; and Gooding-Williams, "Anti-Foundationalism, Leadership, Black Politics: Rejoinders to Smith, Shelby, and Beltrán," *Du Bois Review* 8, no. 2 [2011]: 389–93, 401–7).

8. For the democratic quality of Du Bois's style of argumentation, see Nick Bromell, "'Honest and Earnest Criticism' as the 'Soul of Democracy': Du Bois's Style of Democratic Reasoning," in this volume, 159–80; and Melvin Rogers, "The People, Rhetoric, and Affect: On the Political Force of Du Bois's *The Souls of Black Folk*," *American Political Science Review* 106, no. 1 (2012): 188–203. Unlike Shelby (see note 7 above), Rogers locates persuasion in the rhetoric of the text, attending to what the writing is doing in the world. Rogers makes a similar argument in *The Undiscovered Dewey: Religion, Morality, and the Ethos of Democracy* (New York: Columbia University Press, 2009), 210. In both cases, "elites" (Du Bois as author or experts in the abstract) perform a function that is circumscribed by a self-possessed audience. That audience frames and ultimately determines the trajectory of expert action.

9. David Levering Lewis, *W. E. B. Du Bois, 1868–1919: Biography of a Race* (New York: Owl, 1993), 186–87; W. E. B. Du Bois, *Dusk of Dawn* (New Brunswick: Transaction, 2009), 58.

10. For references to "training," see W. E. B. DuBois, *The Philadelphia Negro: A Social Study* (Philadelphia: University of Pennsylvania Press, 1996), 11, 32, 66,

257, 385–93. Conversely, Du Bois identifies "poverty and crime" as the central problems facing black inhabitants of the Seventh Ward. They constitute "the darker side of the picture," or the "disease," which *PN* attempts to investigate. He not only links the two together, arguing that poverty leads to crime; he directly argues that "race prejudice" causes poverty by determining the employment opportunities available for black citizens. The same revisionist logic is applied in his evaluation of health statistics and his discussion of property ownership (see ibid., 145–47, 160–61, 184–85). These divergent objectives led Lewis to claim that *PN* comprises "two books in one" (see Lewis, *Biography of a Race,* 189–90, 210).

11. DuBois, *The Philadelphia Negro,* 8–9. There are some discrepancies between Du Bois's stated organization of the book and the organization found in the most recent edition. In the latter, the chapters on "organized social life" are in fact four in number, whereas Du Bois refers to three. He seems to suggest that the three chapters are divided between "a study of the family, of property, and of organizations" with a discussion of crime and pauperism somewhere included. In the current edition, the discussion of property is subsumed in the chapter on family life with crime and pauperism constituting their own separate chapters. In addition to these four parts, we would be warranted to consider two additional sections that book-end Du Bois's organizational schema: a set of introductory remarks (including one chapter on methodology and another on the definition of "the problem") and three concluding chapters, each of which offers a programmatic commentary on contemporary race relations.

12. While graphs and charts are interspersed throughout *PN,* they are particularly prominent in chapters 5–10. For representative examples, see ibid., 54–57, 66–71, 78, 85–88, 99–109. For the pattern identified in the second part of the text, see ibid., 189–90, 259–68, 275–77, 332–36, 341–47.

13. The transition begins to occur in a chapter just before he concludes the section on "their present condition as individuals," or rather before he moves out of a general representation of individual life and into an individualized depiction of collective life. The chapter notably argues for a new reading of available statistics, one that considers the differing "conditions of life" between (racial) "classes" of people. It is divided in two subsections, both of which (in a move unique to the book) directly engage methodology and epistemology: subsection 25 is titled "The Interpretation of Statistics," and subsection 26 is titled "The Statistics of the City" (see ibid., 147–49). Within the logic of the text, Du Bois justifies the methodological move by referring to the need to consider "environmental" factors—meaning, social attitudes—in any effort to adequately assess the prospects for self-development among the black population. Because environmental factors are marked by "human choice, wish, whim and prejudice," it follows that a less systematic method of analysis must be employed (see ibid., 98). The ensuing chapters attempt to

capture these conditions through anecdotes and vignettes as statistical analysis falls away.

14. For *PN*'s place in the history of sociological methods, see Aldon D. Morris, *The Scholar Denied: W. E. B. Du Bois and the Birth of Modern Sociology* (Oakland: University of California Press, 2015), 45–54. The rendering of ethnography presented here echoes contemporary critiques of scientism. For instance, against modern depictions of a subject unmoved by truth, Michel Foucault cites premodern traditions where the transformation of a subject acts as the basis for accessing truth (see *The Hermeneutics of the Subject: Lectures at the Collège de France, 1981–82*, ed. Frédéric Gros, trans. Graham Burchell [New York: Picador, 2005], 16–17). For a discussion of "New Negro" intellectuals (like Du Bois) anticipating the later emergence of these critiques with respect to anthropology and ethnography, see Daphne Lamothe, *Inventing the New Negro: Narrative, Culture, and Ethnography* (Philadelphia: University of Pennsylvania Press, 2008), 5, 9, 15–16, 20.

15. W. E. B. DuBois, "My Evolving Program for Negro Freedom," in *What the Negro Wants*, ed. Rayford V. Logan (Chapel Hill: University of North Carolina Press, 1944), 45. This passage contrasts with even sympathetic accounts of Du Bois as elitist. For example, in "Reparations, Leadership, and Democracy," Shelby writes: "There is no question that Du Bois's vision is unjustifiably *elitist:* Du Bois assumes that the masses have much to learn from the Black elite but that the Black elite have little or nothing to learn from the masses" (399).

16. The most prominent critics of Du Bois on these terms are Reed and Gooding-Williams. Where Reed offers a direct and detailed consideration of *PN*, Gooding-Williams focuses on a shorter essay titled "The Study of the Negro Problems." For Gooding-Williams, "Study" expresses the essential components of the reform agenda and model for leadership found in *PN*. The substitution is said to allow for more focused conceptual analysis (see Gooding-Williams, *In the Shadow*, 58–65, 277n140). It also, however, leads us to overlook parallels in the formal composition of *PN* and *Souls* as monographs.

17. For a discussion of the phenomenological turns in *Souls*, see Eugene Victor Wolfenstein, *A Gift of Spirit: Reading "The Souls of Black Folk"* (Ithaca, NY: Cornell University Press, 2007).

18. For a discussion of the biographical events that prompted stylistic and substantive changes in *Souls*, see ibid., 44–47. For Du Bois's references to "environmental" factors in *PN*, see note 13 above. On the distinction between Du Bois as an "empirical individual" and an "authorial persona" in *Souls*, see Gooding-Williams, *In the Shadow*, 131. For a discussion of the bildungsroman as genre, see Tobias Boes, "Modernist Studies and the *Bildungsroman:* A Historical Survey of Critical Trends," *Literature Compass* 3, no. 2 (2006). Generally speaking, the bil-

dungsroman (or "novel of formation") involves a process of "teleological and organic growth, in the manner of a seed that develops into a mature plant according to inherent genetic principles" (232). The genre depicts this process through a story that "intimately links personal to historical development" (236). Boes, however, presents the bildungsroman as a novel of development (as opposed to formation) in an effort to "highlight the intimate connection between personal and historical change" (241–42). Mikhail Bakhtin similarly presents a number of types when discussing the "novel of emergence." The "most significant one" presents "man's individual emergence" as "inseparably linked to historical emergence" (see M. M. Bakhtin, *Speech Genres and Other Late Essays,* trans. Vern W. McGee, ed. Caryl Emerson and Michael Holquist [Austin: University of Texas Press, 1986], 23–24). I adhere to this formulation of the bildungsroman, shared between Boes and Bakhtin, here. It should be noted that Shamoon Zamir similarly interprets *Souls* as a "*bildungsbiographie*" (see Zamir, *Dark Voices: W. E. B. Du Bois and American Thought, 1888–1903* [Chicago: University of Chicago Press, 1995], 113–17, 158–60). In so doing, however, he too closely associates *Souls* with Hegel's *Phenomenology of Spirit.* Moreover, Zamir's reading of the early Du Bois as three distinct and "contradictory" thinkers at once (1–6) overlooks the formal continuities across *PN* and *Souls.* For a critique of Zamir's interpretation, see Robert Gooding-Williams, Review of *Dark Voices: W. E. B. Du Bois and American Thought, 1888–1903,* by Shamoon Zamir, *American Literature* 69, no. 4 (December 1997): 855–56.

19. On civilizational assimilation, see DuBois, *The Philadelphia Negro,* 19; and Reed, *W. E. B. Du Bois and American Political Thought,* 34–41. It may be objected that my depiction of "the masses" counteracts one of Du Bois's central aims and perhaps his most important contribution with *PN:* his effort to respond to and correct sensibilities that understand different classes of African Americans as homogenous (see DuBois, *The Philadelphia Negro,* 73–74, 309–18). For a detailed demonstration of the lasting significance of Du Bois's insight and methodological approach, see Marcus Anthony Hunter, "W. E. B. Du Bois and Black Heterogeneity: How *The Philadelphia Negro* Shaped American Sociology," *American Sociologist* 46, no. 2 (2015): 219–33. For the difference between *PN* and *Souls* on this count, see Lamothe, *Inventing the New Negro,* 52, 56–57. And yet, as Gooding-Williams suggests, Du Bois's study does not offer a portrait of differentiation within these classes. My characterization of "the masses" as one protagonist in *PN*'s "plot" ironically follows Gooding-Williams's argument, that is, that Du Bois characterizes all of the individuals within a class on a shared path of development.

20. In *PN,* crime is the pivot around which the text's various plots and protagonists come together. For Du Bois's sponsors, the prevalence of crime in the Seventh Ward constitutes an immediate concern. For Du Bois, who seeks to articulate the *real* "Negro problem," crime represents a lack of assimilation and thus a failure

on the part of the black masses to live up to their historical epoch's civilized ideal (see DuBois, *The Philadelphia Negro,* 235, 241). In Du Bois's redefinition, the formal relationship between the black masses and their broader social context echoes the structure of the bildungsroman (see Bakhtin, *Speech Genres,* 30). The resolution to this "real" problem would simultaneously allow the "protagonist" (i.e., the masses) to achieve self-realization while pushing the American political order to live up to its civilized ideals; all aspects of the plot occur in a simultaneous and interrelated process of change and emergence. The same dynamic plays out with regards to Du Bois's role and presence as author. For instance, the chapter on crime contains the first significant instance where qualitative evidence is incorporated in the body of the text (see Du Bois, *The Philadelphia Negro,* 259–68). The inclusion of individual stories corresponds with the suggestion that "environmental" factors—or rather, attitudinal factors such as "color prejudice"—prevent the plot (i.e., self-development) from progressing as it should. In the effort to redescribe the alleged developmental "failure" of the black masses, the investigator must accordingly change his methodological approach and interpretive perspective. Because they operate on more "whimsical" terms, those same "environmental" factors (i.e., "color prejudice") permit a less objective and more obviously rhetorical voice on Du Bois's part. In the end, the storyteller presents himself as intimately invested in the story he tells—his work, his voice, his perspective (in short, his methodology) change in step with the protagonist's development.

21. Wolfenstein, *A Gift of Spirit,* 1–2, 102. For a related articulation of this point, see Robert Gooding-Williams, "Du Bois, Politics, Aesthetics: An Introduction," *Public Culture* 17, no. 2 (2005): 206.

22. The narrative begins with the initial, Reconstruction-era effort to establish schooling (in "Of the Meaning of Progress") before presenting chapters that discuss the purpose of university education (in "Of the Wings of Atlanta" and "Of the Training of Black Men"). As if those masses have graduated from a period of formative education, the following chapters ("Of the Black Belt" and "Of the Quest of the Golden Fleece") offer portraits of economic life. Meanwhile, Du Bois's authorial persona first appears as a New England schoolboy whose visiting card is rejected. He then appears at the beginning of chapter 4 as a young (eighteen- or nineteen-year-old) Fisk student turned schoolteacher in Tennessee. He makes his final appearance in chapters 7 and 8 in what we might take to be his most present guise as an investigative sociologist riding through the Deep South (see Du Bois, *The Souls of Black Folk,* ed. Henry Louis Gates Jr. and Terri Hume Oliver [New York: Norton, 1999], 10, 46, 74–88, 96, 100).

23. When Bishop Onderdonk refuses to allow him to sit in his diocese because of race, Du Bois describes Crummell as experiencing "a death that is more than death,—the passing of a soul that has missed its duty" (see Du Bois, *Souls,*

139–40). My interpretation follows Gooding-Williams's argument that the younger Crummell represents a sublime figure in Du Bois's eyes, whereas the older Crummell fails to do so (see "Du Bois's Counter-Sublime," *Massachusetts Review* 35, no. 2 [1994]: 202–24). For Jones's progressive realization of his calling and "life-work," see Du Bois, *Souls,* 146–48.

24. Each of these figures arrives at a death Du Bois had escaped or could not "achieve." Du Bois's son, an extension of himself and his legacy, "achieves" death before the injustice of life in Jim Crow America; Du Bois laments that he himself did not die in his place, while tragically envying his preemptive escape. When Crummell experiences "living death" in his formative years, his age parallels Du Bois's while at Fisk University. Finally, there is Jones. Focusing on the affective dimensions of Du Bois's response to misrecognition, Wolfenstein characterizes Jones's story as expressing a "temptation" or impulse toward "revolt and revenge." Du Bois identifies with the temptation but does not wish to act on it. In other words, Jones is Du Bois's shadow self—a shadow that acts on this impulse where Du Bois does not, leading Wolfenstein to characterize him as the man Du Bois "was determined not to become" (see Wolfenstein, *A Gift of Spirit,* 128). My reading departs from Wolfenstein on this count. Jones is, I argue, the man Du Bois was determined to become but, by virtue of differences in life experience, could not.

25. Lamothe, *Inventing the New Negro,* 62. Where Lamothe, like Zamir, draws too sharp of a distinction between "generic hybridity" and *PN*'s scientific empiricism, my reading of the text imagines a more fluid relationship between fiction and ethnography.

26. Double-consciousness, or doubling, is represented in the story through the presence of two Johns—a black John and a white John. For a discussion of the story's Hegelian resonances, see Wolfenstein, *A Gift of Spirit,* 118.

27. For a discussion of shadow imagery in Du Bois's work, see Lawrie Balfour, *Democracy's Reconstruction: Thinking Politically with W. E. B. Du Bois* (Oxford: Oxford University Press, 2011), 9–13. According to Balfour's reading, the failure to address the "shadow" of historical injury (the "present-past") has the capacity to "foreclose democratic futures." A different feature of the imagery Balfour considers, that is, Du Bois's shadowing relationship to John Jones, complements this reading. Here, the "present-past" obstructs the realization of ideal political leadership ("forecloses democratic futures"), leading Du Bois (as shadow) to adopt the only means available—cultural leadership, or charisma. For the distinction between political and cultural leadership, see Marable, *Black Leadership* (New York: Columbia University Press, 1998), xi–xvii. As in *PN,* the "problem" of "crime" plays a pivotal role in the narrative, in this case marking the difference between political and cultural leadership. In *PN,* "crime" signaled the limits of scientific empiricism. Du Bois defines it as "the open rebellion of an individual against his social envi-

ronment" (see note 20 above; and DuBois, *The Philadelphia Negro,* 235). In *Souls,* crime signals the limits of the bildungsroman. If not for it, Jones's bid for leadership and the corresponding self-realization of the black masses would be realized. He ends chapter 13 of *Souls* with a rebellious "criminal" act: the tragedy of Jones's story lies in the fact that his social environment gives him no choice but acquiescent subordination or revolt and revenge. The story presented in chapters 11–13 of *Souls* may accordingly be interpreted as the (mal)formation of an ideal black leader turned "criminal." For an interpretation of Du Bois's context-based sympathy for people who, like John Brown, are narrowly cast as "terrorists" and "criminals," see Balfour, *Democracy's Reconstruction,* 63–64.

28. Abraham Lincoln Jones, who also acts as a shadow of Du Bois, personifies an understanding of democracy as incomplete—as the recognition of partial truth, an infinite and thus necessarily imaginative relationship to others and the unknown (see Bromell, "W. E. B. Du Bois and the Enlargement of Democratic Theory," 140–51). I am grateful to Nick Bromell for pointing out this parallel.

29. Du Bois, *Souls,* 135, emphasis mine.

30. Gooding-Williams rightly points out that Jones, upon returning from the North, is alienated from the people in his hometown in a manner that signals his illegitimacy (see Gooding-Williams, *In the Shadow,* 118–20). But Gooding-Williams does not adequately consider the role of time in these three chapters. To judge the entirety of a character cast in future time, one who changes as much as Jones does, with reference to a single instantiation of his persona (the church scene where Jones's speech falls flat) precludes a consideration of the chapter's overall rhetorical framing and the text's related parallels with the mutability found in a bildungsroman.

31. Du Bois, *Souls,* 115. Du Bois projects this experience of "awakening" not only onto his readers but also, in a sense, onto the black masses as they await the coming of John. Just as the first portion of *Souls* ends with the promised "coming" of understanding to casual observers who have witnessed the life-world of African Americans from afar, so too does the second, inverted portion of the text end with the promised "coming" of the ideal leader from within the life-world of African Americans.

32. For an expressly elitist account of democracy, see Joseph Schumpeter, *Capitalism, Socialism, and Democracy* (New York: Harper and Row, 1950), 269–73.

33. DuBois, *The Philadelphia Negro,* 11, 45, 76–82.

34. Gooding-Williams takes the sorrow songs as representations of Du Bois's "authorial persona" and, moreover, as projections of charismatic and authoritative leadership where Crummell and Jones fail. His reading is ambivalent. On the one hand, he presents Jones in a state of double-consciousness—one that mirrors the condition of the older Crummell. Both are unable to connect with a slave

past that Du Bois, via the sorrow songs, identifies with folk identity. The primary textual evidence used to support this claim comes from the scene in the church after Jones's return to Altamaha; his secular and lofty speech contrasts sharply with what Du Bois takes to be the "religion of the slave" (see Gooding-Williams, *In the Shadow,* 118–19; cf. Du Bois, *Souls,* 149–50). On the other hand, the sorrow songs themselves do not offer a definitively hopeful resolution for Du Bois (see Gooding-Williams, *In the Shadow,* 125). If chapter 13 were to end with the church scene, Gooding-Williams's broader framing of the text in terms of "expressive self-realization" would be entirely correct. Ideal political leadership would have to involve charismatic appeals to folk culture in an instrumental fashion and John Jones fails on that front. However, Jones does not return North after his failure in the church or suffer a "deeper death" like Crummell. Where Crummell is a picture of "living death" objectified, Jones is the living dead as subject. He walks the earth having suffered double-consciousness and yet he continues to strive until actual death prevents him from striving further. In fact, he establishes his school after this incident and begins to "see at last some glimmering of dawn" when the injustice of Jim Crow physically prevents him from going further (see Du Bois, *Souls,* 152).

35. Mouffe, "Radical Democracy," 36.

36. Hunter, "W. E. B. Du Bois and Black Heterogeneity." With reference to Donna Haraway's formulation, Balfour uses the phrase "situated knowledge" to argue that Du Bois's double vision "lives on" in his "capacity to convey the universality of his particular perspective and, simultaneously, the partiality of all perspectives" (see Balfour, *Democracy's Reconstruction,* 7, 146n27).

37. For the critique of "banking" education, see Paolo Freire, *Pedagogy of the Oppressed,* trans. Myra Bergman Ramos (New York: Bloomsbury, 2000). For an articulation of a third way between teacher- and student-centered learning, see Kris Gutierrez, Betsy Rymes, and Joanne Larson, "Script, Counterscript and Underlife in the Classroom: James Brown versus *Brown v. Board of Education,*" in *Harvard Educational Review* 65, no. 3 (1995): 445–72.

38. I follow Balfour's example here in examining "why and how revisiting Du Bois's work makes a particular kind of political critique possible in the present" (see *Democracy's Reconstruction,* 22).

39. W. E. B. Du Bois, "The Position of the Negro in the American Social Order: Where Do We Go From Here?," *Journal of Negro Education* 8, no. 3 (1939): 564, 568. Du Bois explicitly distinguishes this argument from the concept of a Talented Tenth.

40. Nikhil Pal Singh, *Black Is a Country: Race and the Unfinished Struggle for Democracy* (Cambridge: Harvard University Press, 2004), 58–100, 66; Balfour, *Democracy's Reconstruction,* 24–25, 27–35. Balfour links this aspect of *BR* directly to arguments in *Souls.* We might similarly substantiate a comparative read-

ing of *PN* and *BR* with reference to the parallel recognition of black heterogeneity in both texts (see notes 19 and 36 above; and Du Bois, *Black Reconstruction,* 125). In this regard, *BR* and the related argument in "The Position of the Negro" illuminate an unresolved tension in *PN.* Despite "cultural differentiation," a common experience of racial discrimination leads Du Bois to argue for strategic essentialism in the 1930s. The rendering of the masses as one protagonist in *PN*'s coming-of-age narrative may accordingly be read as foreshadowing Du Bois's more explicitly articulated vision for radical democratic change later in life.

41. Du Bois, "The Position of the Negro," 570, emphasis mine.

42. Ibid., 569. For a contrary reading of this essay as advocating assimilation via vanguard politics, see Reed, *W. E. B. Du Bois and American Political Thought,* 72–79.

43. Wolin, "Fugitive Democracy," 11, 13–14, 18–19, 23–24. Wolin argues that "politics" presents "an illusion of perpetual political motion." In contrast to "the political," which represents genuine movement, "politics" (the civic order) is actually a matter of *stasis:* "Democracy is not about where the political is located but how it is experienced . . . Thus revolutionary transgression is the means by which the demos makes itself political. It is by *stasis* not *physis* that the demos acquires a civic nature" (18). For a discussion of Du Bois's political thought as "fugitive" in light of Wolin's formulation, see Balfour, *Democracy's Reconstruction,* 19.

44. Rogers, *The Undiscovered Dewey,* 191–236. On the related "overlap" between radical democracy and liberal constitutionalism, see Jack Turner, "The Constitution of Radical Democracy," *Polity* 47, no. 4 (2015): 558–65.

45. Wolin, "Fugitive Democracy," 13.

10

A Splendid Failure?

Black Reconstruction *and Du Bois's Tragic Vision of Politics*

Vijay Phulwani

Near the end of his 1940 autobiography, *Dusk of Dawn,* Du Bois paused to mock the genre of historical writing that Kenneth Stampp would later call "the tragic legend of Reconstruction." As Du Bois described it, the legend held that "Reconstruction was 'tragic,' 'terrible,' a 'great mistake,' and a 'humiliation,' not because of what actually happened. . . . No, the 'tragedy' of Reconstruction was because here an attempt was initiated to make American democracy and the tenets of the Declaration of Independence apply not only to white men, but to black men."[1] In this particular passage, the target of his rancor was undoubtedly Claude Bowers's *The Tragic Era,* an immensely popular history of Reconstruction published in 1929. Bowers "sought to recreate the black and bloody drama of those years, to show the leaders of the fighting factions at close range, to picture the moving masses, both whites and blacks, in North and South, surging crazily under the influence of the poisonous propaganda on which they were fed."[2] His aim in thus depicting Reconstruction was to shore up the fracturing coalition of the Democratic Party following its disastrous defeat in the election of 1928, in which five southern states voted for Republican Herbert Hoover over Al Smith, the Democratic candidate and Catholic governor of New York. By reminding southerners of the purported indignities of "black Republican" rule after the Civil War, Bowers thought he could alert them to the dangers of siding with the Republicans in his own day. Reconstruction's "prevailing note was one of tragedy," he wrote, because "the Southern people literally were put to the torture" for the political and economic gains of "daring and unscrupulous men" (preface).

Given Du Bois's scorn for this "tragic legend" in *Dusk of Dawn*, it is surprising to find that he leaned heavily on the language of tragedy in his 1935 magnum opus, *Black Reconstruction in America*. There, he called Reconstruction "a tragedy that beggared the Greeks; it was an upheaval of humanity like the Reformation and the French Revolution. Yet we are blind and led by the blind. We discern in it no part of our labor movement; no part of our industrial triumph; no part of our religious experience."[3] At the end of the book's penultimate chapter, he wrote, "The unending tragedy of Reconstruction is the utter inability of the American mind to grasp its real significance, its national and worldwide implications" (*BR* 708). For all his anger about the way white historians like Bowers used the language of tragedy to discredit Reconstruction and the role African Americans played in it, Du Bois did not disavow the view that Reconstruction was a political tragedy. Instead, he used *Black Reconstruction* to invert the tragic legend, showing how the real harm done to American democracy was not the rule of "black Republicanism" but the reimposition of white supremacy, which both stymied the practical possibility of political progress and closed white Americans off to the historical self-understanding they needed to make sense of their own condition. This inversion allowed Du Bois to rethink the political implications of the tragic and to derive from them a radical political and economic program for black politics in his own day.

Today, in our day, *Black Reconstruction* is probably more popular than it has been at any time since it was first published. Even outside of the historical profession, many of Du Bois's key ideas have recently been resurrected, from Angela Davis's appropriation of the concept of "abolition-democracy" as a name for her program of resistance to the carceral state, to Gayatri Spivak's interest in his account of "the general strike" as a way of rethinking the Eurocentric biases of classical Marxism. In the *Atlantic*, where Du Bois published his first article on the Freedmen's Bureau in 1901, prominent public intellectuals like Annette Gordon-Reed and Ta-Nehisi Coates have recently written about *Black Reconstruction* and what it can still teach us about race in America.[4] And in the field of political theory, a renewed interest in Du Bois's political thought and advocacy has produced a number of works that treat *Black Reconstruction* as an important theoretical text. Thanks to Adolph Reed, Lawrie Balfour, Nikhil Pal Singh, and others, Du Bois's work from the 1930s no longer suffers from scholarly neglect as compared to *The Souls of Black Folk* and his other writings from the first decade of the twentieth century.[5] Although these scholars emphasize the linkage between Du Bois's political thought and his historical work, the specifics of this connection have yet to be worked out in detail. Building on this body of scholarship, I show that *Black Reconstruction* and Du Bois's 1930s activism for African American consumers' cooperatives are united by a tragic vision of American democracy that emphasizes the constraints and limitations created by white supremacy so as to better envision alternative strategies for building black political and economic power.

Du Bois wrote about Reconstruction a number of times throughout his long career. In this essay, I describe the ways he used Reconstruction—from the publication of *Souls* in 1903 to that of *Dusk of Dawn* in 1940—to rethink his ideas about the organizational form and programmatic content of black politics. In his reflections on Reconstruction, Du Bois returned again and again to the problem of how to build durable political institutions for African Americans out of the fragmented and loosely organized forms of collective agency available to them after centuries of slavery and white supremacy. Over the course of his career, Du Bois moved from an emphasis on internal racial uplift and external political agitation (in the early twentieth century) to a theory of economic separatism and a strategic embrace of segregation in the 1930s. As I will argue, this shift in his thinking was driven by his growing appreciation of possibilities for political agency exercised outside the official realm of state institutions and electoral politics, particularly in decentralized forms of black economic power that could use segregation as a weapon against white capitalism. This shift both informed and was informed by his changing understanding of the role of slaves and freedmen in the Civil War and Reconstruction.

The arc from *Souls* to *Black Reconstruction* and *Dusk of Dawn* also reveals Du Bois's increasingly tragic vision of American democracy and the form that black politics must take in it.[6] Advocating segregation even on limited, strategic terms was seen by many of his contemporaries as an abandonment of a long-standing commitment to integration as the sine qua non of racial equality. Although his position was never as simple as this characterization would suggest, it is nevertheless true that Du Bois's turn away from integration as a political strategy mirrored a change in how he viewed the history of African American political struggles from Reconstruction to his own day. To make sense of this change, I focus on the relationship between his claim that slavery was ended by a general strike on the part of the slaves themselves and his advocacy in the 1930s for a separate "group economy" made up of African American consumers' cooperatives. The group economy was Du Bois's plan for reconstructing American democracy without falling into the conventional opposition between the reformism of the NAACP and the revolutionary exhortations of communist activists. Seen against the background of black history from Reconstruction to the Great Migration, co-ops served a dual role as both a kind of economic marronage that weakened capitalism and white supremacy in America, as well as a positive, institution-building method for developing new forms of power and collective identity among African Americans. Du Bois presented the group economy as a strategy for organizing and institutionalizing the kinds of spontaneous agency exercised by slaves in the general strike while also recognizing the tragic limitations of black politics that were dramatically revealed in the failure of Reconstruction.

Reconstruction and the Problem of Black Politics in Early Du Bois

Du Bois's 1901 *Atlantic Monthly* article is better known today as "Of the Dawn of Freedom," the second chapter of *The Souls of Black Folk*. *Souls* spends little time on the lives of blacks during slavery. Instead, by beginning his story of the meaning of life behind the veil with the Civil War, Du Bois figured Reconstruction as a founding moment for black politics and the source of the educational program for which he argued throughout the book. However, "Of the Dawn of Freedom" is not a general survey of Reconstruction or even a specific history of the role slaves and freedmen played in the period. Instead, "This tale of the dawn of Freedom is an account of that government of men called the Freedmen's Bureau,—one of the most singular and interesting of the attempts made by a great nation to grapple with the vast problems of race and social condition."[7] Du Bois concentrated on the years from 1861 to 1872, which was the life span of the Freedmen's Bureau, and dealt only briefly with the last six years of Reconstruction, the period when a few states actually had black-majority legislatures. By focusing on the Freedmen's Bureau, he seems to have implicitly agreed with other Reconstruction historians that the freedmen themselves were not the main political protagonists of the period. Thus, the overall historical trajectory that Du Bois traced from Emancipation to his present day was largely set by the actions of a white-led political institution, not the strivings of blacks themselves.

Moreover, when "Of the Dawn of Freedom" does discuss the actions of slaves and freedmen, it does so in naturalistic terms, rendering them more as a force of nature than as deliberate or conscious political agents. Thirty years later, Du Bois would see the movement of slaves to the Union army as a something much more agentic and purposive, but here he emphasizes the pathetic condition of the "steady stream" of human misery as "fugitive slaves appeared within their lines," particularly after the Emancipation Proclamation, when "the stream of fugitives swelled to a flood" (*Souls* 373–74) Similarly, Du Bois describes the slaves who accompanied Sherman on his march to the sea as a "dark cloud that clung like remorse on the rear of those swift columns, swelling at times to half their size, almost engulfing and choking them. In vain were they ordered back, in vain were bridges hewn from beneath their feet; on the trudged and writhed and surged, until they rolled into Savannah, a starved and naked horde of tens of thousands" (*Souls* 377). Nonetheless, in Du Bois's account the actions of the slaves did have important political consequences. For example, Sherman was forced to issue his famous Field Order Fifteen granting land to fugitive slaves who defected to his army. The agency of slaves and freedmen thus consisted primarily of their ability to make themselves a problem to which the government had to organize a response. And the most importance response they engendered was the creation of the Freedmen's Bureau.

Du Bois argued that the Freedmen's Bureau was far more than an administrative agency. Instead, "The Freedmen's Bureau became a full-fledged government of men. It made laws, executed them and interpreted them; it laid and collected taxes, defined and punished crime, maintained and used military force, and dictated such measures as it thought necessary and proper for the accomplishment of its ends" (*Souls* 382). In other words, the Bureau exercised sovereignty in the postwar South and was the chief agent in carrying out the work of Reconstruction. It had to take care of the freedmen and organize their relief, starting from "a heterogeneous and confused but already existing system of relief and control" that Du Bois describes as a "curious mess" of "little despotisms, communistic experiments, slavery, peonage, business speculations, organized charity, almsgiving—all reeling on under the guise of helping the freedmen (*Souls* 379–80). At the same time, it had to create new political and social institutions now that the Emancipation Proclamation and the Fourteenth Amendment had abolished slavery, which had previously been the Confederacy's foundational institution. Du Bois argued that both of these goals could have been accomplished had there been "a permanent Freedmen's Bureau, with a national system of Negro schools; a carefully supervised employment and labor office; a system of impartial protection before the regular courts; and such institutions for social betterment as savings-banks, land and building associations, and social settlements" (*Souls* 390). Note that Du Bois describes these as institutions created by the state for the social betterment of the freedmen, not for their political or economic power. In any case, the actual Freedmen's Bureau was conceived as a temporary expedient and never had the financial or political support it needed to carry out either of its main tasks, let alone both.

Du Bois identified the legacies of the Freedmen's Bureau as the guiding threads in the subsequent history of black politics. Most importantly, he held that "the greatest success of the Freedmen's Bureau lay in the planting of the free school among Negroes, and the idea of free elementary education among all classes in the South" (*Souls* 385). The chapter immediately after "Of the Dawn of Freedom" in *Souls* is "Of Mr. Booker T. Washington and Others," his famous attack on Washington's educational program, and the sequence of the chapters makes it clear that he viewed his own educational program as the rightful heir to the work of the Freedmen's Bureau. The second of the Bureau's legacies also pertains to his critique of Washington's program, namely the suffrage guarantees of the Fifteenth Amendment. Du Bois argued that universal manhood suffrage was an inferior replacement for his preferred program of a permanent Freedmen's Bureau backed up by a limited suffrage. "The alternative thus offered the nation," he argued, "was not between full and restricted negro suffrage; else every sensible man, black and white, would easily have the chosen the latter" (*Souls* 389). In the absence of a reforming quasi-state, like the Freedmen's Bureau, the freedmen needed the ballot to compel the state's protection through electoral means. This, of course, was not how events actually worked out, but Du Bois did not examine or try to defend the record of African American voters and legislators in *Souls*. Instead, he worked to rehabilitate the reputation of the Freedmen's Bureau as a statist and white-led agent for black emancipation. This led him to describe the project of black politics is his own day—"the heavy heritage of this generation"—as that of finding a way to convince the US government to complete "the large legacy of the Freedmen's Bureau, the work it did not do because it could not" (*Souls* 391).

Du Bois took a wider view of Reconstruction in a 1910 article for the *American Historical Review*, "Reconstruction and its Benefits." In the years since *Souls*, he had been increasingly active politically, founding first the Niagara movement in 1905 and then the NAACP in 1909. His views in 1910 reflected a growing interest in the possibilities of political agency being exercised directly by blacks, though his overall model of political agency was largely the same as it was in 1903. Although the Freemen's Bureau still played the leading role in trying to reconstruct the Confederacy, it was no longer the sole creative force behind other Reconstruction-era institutions. He wrote: "Three agencies undertook the solution of this problem at first and their influence is apt to be forgotten. Without them the problems of Reconstruction would have been far graver than they were. These agencies were: (a) the negro church, (b) the negro school, and (c) the Freedmen's Bureau."[8] Just as he later would in *Black Reconstruction*, Du Bois had neglected the role of black churches in "Of the Dawn of Freedom," choosing instead to treat them (fairly critically) in chapter 10 of *Souls*, "Of the Faith of Our Fathers." Here he acknowledged their importance as "the most powerful negro institutions in the world" and "the first institution fully controlled by black men in America." Similarly, Du Bois now interpreted the demand for education as something that came from the freedmen themselves. "The movement started with the negroes themselves," he wrote, "and they continued to form the dynamic force behind it" (*RIB* 782).

Du Bois claimed that "negro churches and schools stood as conservative educative forces" in the unstable world of Reconstruction (*RIB* 782). Unlike the Freedmen's Bureau, they were not sources of wider social transformation and political action so much as centers for internal uplift that sought to prepare the freedmen for the role they would have to play in the political life of the nation. Du Bois still wished that the Bureau had been made permanent, but now he mounted a defense of the conduct of black voters and officeholders as acting mostly honorably on the basis of the preparation they had been given by the churches and schools. "The theory of democratic government," he argued, "is not that the will of the people is always right, but rather that normal human beings of average intelligence will, if given a chance, learn the right and best course by bitter experience" (*RIB* 792–93). When judged by this standard, "the negro governments in the South accomplished much positive good." Specifically, "We may recognize three things which negro rule gave to the South: 1. Democratic Government. 2. Free public schools. 3. New social legislation" (*RIB* 795). Thus, Du Bois defended the contribution of black-led institutions, like schools and churches, by way of the legislative accomplishments of black politicians. This strategy reveals both the importance Du Bois attached to leadership in thinking about political agency and his continued emphasis on the state as the central agent in modern politics.

Another notable consequence of Du Bois's focus on the state was his careful examination of the state constitutions created during Reconstruction. He was "surprised at the comparatively small amount of change in law and government which the overthrown of negro rule brought about," noting that the Reconstruction constitution of South Carolina, the state where freedmen had the most legislative power, remained in force for twenty-seven years and was revised primarily to prevent blacks from voting (*RIB* 795). By focusing on the durability of state constitutions and lesser forms of legislation passed during Reconstruction, Du Bois demonstrated that even the governments that overthrew them found the constitutional framework created by the freedmen and their allies to be acceptable on matters other than white supremacy. As Du Bois put it at the end of his paper: "Practically the whole new growth of the South has been accomplished under laws which black men helped to frame thirty years ago. I know of no greater compliment to negro suffrage" (*RIB* 799).

Du Bois's use of state constitutions to make this argument had a surprising source in the work of William Archibald Dunning, professor of political science and history at Columbia University and mentor to the generation of Reconstruction historians often referred to as the Dunning School. Dunning was there in person when Du Bois read "Reconstruction and Its Benefits" at the 1909 meeting of the American Historical Association, and it is quite possible that this argument was directed specifically to him. Unlike Bowers, who used the history of Reconstruction to intensify partisan divisions, Dunning studied Reconstruction in order to heal the still-sharp divisions between North and South, writing consensus-building histories that tried to acknowledge the legitimate points raised by northern and southern partisan alike.[9] The underlying problem of Reconstruction, Dunning insightfully argued, was that of creating in the southern states "a new political people" after the Civil War, and the question of whether the freedmen would be included in that people. He admired the political skill shown by the North in carrying out that task, and he defended the conduct of military governors during the early years of Reconstruction against southern critics of martial law. In all this, Du Bois would have found much to agree with. However, Dunning deplored the ends of Reconstruction as much as he commended the means, and the price of his fair-mindedness on sectionalism was an utter disregard for the freedmen and a blank dismissal of their ability to be part of the political people. In "The Undoing of Reconstruction," an article than ran in the *Atlantic Monthly* seven months after Du Bois's article on the Freedmen's Bureau, Dunning lamented, "The negroes exercised an influence in political affairs out of all relation to their intelligence or property," and concluded that, "the ultimate root of the trouble in the South had been, not the institution of slavery, but the coexistence in one society of two races so distinct in characters as to render coalescence impossible."[10] Here, Du Bois would naturally have disagreed, but this disagreement did not prevent Du Bois from reinterpreting arguments and data taken from Dunning and his students, something he would continue to do even in *Black Reconstruction*—its celebrated critique of the Dunning School in "The Propaganda of History" notwithstanding.

It would be a mistake, however, to think that Du Bois was simply tailoring his argument to a Dunning-ite audience when he depicted the state as the primary political actor in Reconstruction. Abstracting a bit from both "Of the Dawn of Freedom" and "Reconstruction and Its Benefits," we can say that these were some of the central assumptions of Du Bois's early model of black politics. Put schematically, the strategy for overcoming white supremacy was for blacks to force the state, primarily the federal government, to resume the work of the Freedmen's Bureau. The ballot was essential to making the condition of black people in the United States a problem to which the state must respond, but because most blacks were disenfranchised, they would also have to rely on other means. Rather than reproducing the formless and undirected mass activity of fugitive slaves during the

Civil War, leaders from the dominant black institutions (primarily schools and churches, but eventually including the NAACP) had to channel popular activity into campaigns of information, agitation, and, when necessary, protest. In the inaugural issue of the *Crisis*, Du Bois said: "Agitation is a necessary evil to tell of the ills of the Suffering. Without it many a nation has been lulled to false security and preened itself with virtues it did not possess."[11] While the leadership worked externally to spur the state to action, it also worked internally upon the black masses by using their educative institutions to make the masses ready for citizenship. The problem of black politics was therefore one of finding a way for African Americans to influence and, eventually, be incorporated into a state that refused to acknowledge them. This diagnosis was presented as an extension of the problem of Reconstruction, which Du Bois depicted as an admittedly imperfect moment of foundation, but one to which black politics, and black political leaders, needed to stay faithful if they wanted to establish racial equality.

World War I and the Changing Idea of Reconstruction

Following the widespread destruction and social dislocation of the First World War, governments and intellectuals embraced the term "reconstruction" as a way of talking about how to respond to the war's shattering changes. According to historian Daniel T. Rodgers, "From its origins in France in discussions of the physical reconstruction of the war devastated northeast, it soon swelled into a general term for postwar planning," particularly for Progressives who wanted "to secure for the peace the collectivist spirit and institutions of the war."[12] Du Bois was actively involved in conversations about the meaning and scope of reconstruction in the postwar years, and it is hardly surprising that these conversations, and the events that spurred them, reshaped the way he thought about the Civil War and Reconstruction. In his 1924 book, *The Gift of Black Folk*, we can see Du Bois attempting to assimilate these changes into his existing ideas. What emerges from this period is less a fully articulated model of black politics and more a mind in transition, being pulled in new directions toward ideas that would not be fully worked out until *Black Reconstruction* was finished a decade later.

Far and away the most important influence on Du Bois's ideas in this period was the experience of the war itself. Du Bois supported US involvement in war, which he saw largely as a product of European imperial competition in Africa, and he devoted himself to chronicling the role African Americans played in the war effort. Of particular importance was the question of whether the US military would exclude blacks from the higher levels of military service entirely or create segregated military institutions, like a segregated training camp for black officers in Des Moines and a segregated military hospital in Tuskegee. Though it was highly controversial to do so, Du Bois and the NAACP supported these segregated institutions as the best way to provide fair treatment to African American soldiers. In the 1930s, Du Bois referred back to this decision constantly when he was accused of betraying his previous ideals in his advocacy for economic separatism. At the time, however, he was less than sure this was the right course. In a 1919 article for the *Crisis,* he argued, "You cannot build up a logical scheme of a self-sufficing, separate Negro American inside America or a Negro world with no close relations to the white world" while also admitting that "Unless we had welcomed the segregation of Fort Des Moines, we would have had no officers in the National Army." Du Bois offered no solution to this dilemma. Instead he called for "thought and forbearance" because "not every builder of racial co-operation and solidarity is a 'Jim Crow' advocate," and "not every Negro who fights prejudice and segregation is ashamed of his race."[13]

This was also the period in which Du Bois began to examine cooperative economic institutions more carefully. Du Bois had earlier looked at cooperatives in his 1907 Atlanta University study, *Economic Cooperation among Negro Americans,* but this study did not distinguish between black capitalism and cooperatively owned economic enterprises, a distinction that would be fundamental to his later thought. Starting in 1918, he began writing about co-ops in the *Crisis* and corresponding with experts on the Rochdale Principles, a framework for running cooperative organizations created in the nineteenth century by the Rochdale Society of Equitable Pioneers in England.[14] In "Reconstruction," a *Crisis* article from 1919, Du Bois placed co-ops in a larger program for black politics. Though he continued to insist on the importance of fighting segregation in educational institutions, he argued that the most autonomous black institutions, the churches, should engage in "character building through economic co-operation."[15] Churches, he added, "can easily begin co-operative buying of coal, bread, and meat" as a way to "extend its economic functions" and "organize the Negro laborer so that his entire wage will not go in rent and supporting [white] storekeepers who despise and cheat him." A year later, he wrote another article arguing that cooperatives were the only way blacks could compete against white businesses, though he also criticized businessmen who embraced the label of cooperative without its substance. "Don't be afraid," he implored his readers, "Try the whole co operative program. Write us."[16]

Du Bois's interest in cooperative economics for blacks was driven by his disillusionment with the racism of the white working class. In "The Class Struggle," he admitted: "Theoretically we are a part of the world proletariat in the sense that we are mainly an exploited class of cheap laborers; but practically we are not part of the white proletariat and are not recognized by that proletariat to any great extent. We are the victims of their physical oppression, social ostracism, economic exclusion and personal hatred."[17] Demobilization at the end of World War I produced a new bout of racial violence in American cities, which Du Bois later called "the worst experience of mob law and race hate the United States had seen since Reconstruction" (*DoD* 734). He attributed this violence to "the competition of emigrating Negro workings, pouring into Northern industry out of the South and leaving Southern plantations with a shortage of their customary cheap labor," and "the resentment of American soldiers, especially those from the South, at the recognition and kudos which Negros received in the World War" (*DoD* 747). Though Du Bois identified himself as a socialist, the violence of the white working class and the segregation of American labor unions made him doubt that an interracial proletarian politics would be possible in the foreseeable future.[18]

One of the driving forces behind postwar racial conflict was the Great Migration, which began during World War I when wartime industries in the North were experiencing severe labor shortages. Immigration quotas meant that there were not enough new migrants from Europe to provide an adequate labor supply. Southern blacks took the opportunity to flee Jim Crow in search of higher wages and greater freedom in northern and western cities, often in spite of restrictions on migration and violent efforts by southern whites to keep blacks in their place. Isabel Wilkerson describes the migrants of World War I as "the first volley of a leaderless revolution" that "crept along so many thousands of currents over so long a stretch of time as to be difficult for the press truly to capture while it was under way."[19] In fact, many local and national black leaders, including Booker T. Washington, actively opposed the mass migration of African Americans from the rural South to the urban North, but their warnings were easily ignored by people hoping for a better life. Du Bois, on the other hand, became an enthusiastic supporter of the Great Migration early on, providing detailed documentation of how many people were leaving and what the general migratory patterns were in a 1917 issue of the *Crisis*. In 1920, he wrote, "The migration of Negroes from South to North continues and ought to continue."[20] Although he sometimes expressed anxiety at the disorderly character of mass migration and the immorality of urban life, he saw that moving out of the South increased the economic and political power of blacks by giving them higher wages and the right to vote, and he knew that migration also put pressure on the South to end Jim Crow. Of all the ideas and events that shaped Du Bois's thought in this period, the influence of the Great Migration has been least appreciated, but it was crucial in showing him a form of mass political action where previously he had seen only disorder.

We can see the effects the Great Migration and the other forces of postwar Reconstruction were having on Du Bois's political thought in 1924's *The Gift of Black Folks.* Though the book's title came from the "Afore-thought" of *Souls, Gift* narrated black politics in a very different way, beginning not with Reconstruction but with the role of black people in the exploration of the Americas. From there, Du Bois turned to consider life under slavery as he examined the contribution of black labor to the building of America in chapter 2. He also jumped ahead to highlight the power of black labor in his own day by way of the Great Migration, pointing out how "in a few short months 500,000 black laborers came North to fill the void made by the stoppage of immigration at the rush of white workingmen into the munitions industry. This is simply a foretaste of what will continue to happen."[21] In the next chapter, Du Bois chronicled the participation of black soldiers in US wars, paying particular attention to the Civil War and ending with World War I.

Chapter 4 of *Gift* addressed the "more indefinite" question of "how the black slave by his incessant struggle to be free has broadened the basis of democracy in America and in the world." To answer this question, Du Bois pointed out that "the democracy established in American in the eighteenth century was not, and was not designed to be, a democracy of the masses of men" (*Gift* 65). He argued that the labor movement was not the major agent of democratization in America because it "sought to raise the white servant and laborer on the backs of the black servant and slave." Instead, "it was the rise and growth among the slaves of a determination to be free and an active part of American democracy that forced American democracy continually to look into the depths" of its original sin (*Gift* 66–67). Most of the chapter is a catalogue of the different forms of resistance slaves used to force white Americans to institute mass democracy, most notably insurrection, appeals to reason, marronage, and bargaining over the conditions of slave labor.[22] Perhaps as a result of his study of the Great Migration, Du Bois treated fugitive slaves as agents of democratization, thereby moving beyond his purely naturalistic depiction in *Souls* and toward the idea of the general strike in *Black Reconstruction.* But the general strike is not invoked in *Gift,* and Du Bois had no other overarching concept for relating different kinds of slave resistance, giving the chapter an unorganized feel. Still, his insistence that "the motive force of democracy has nearly always been a push from below rather than the aristocratic pull from above" marked an increasing appreciation for assertive forms of mass politics (*Gift* 93).

In chapter 5, Du Bois returns to Reconstruction itself. Given the novelty of Du Bois's arguments in chapter 4, it is somewhat surprising that his history of Reconstruction is largely the same as it was in "Reconstruction and Its Benefits." However, this consistency makes it easier to see just how Du Bois's thoughts were shifting in this period, particularly on questions of political agency. In contrast to what he had written in the previous chapter, Du Bois maintained here that "the Negro was not freed by edict or sentiment but by the Abolitionists backed by the persistent action of the slave himself as fugitive, soldier and voter," thereby continuing to cast slaves in a supporting role in their own emancipation (*Gift* 95). He did, however, emphasize the extent to which Reconstruction government was a form of economic self-emancipation. "The North being unable to free the slave," he wrote, "let him try to free himself. And he did, and this was his greatest gift to the nation" (*Gift* 112).[23] By this, Du Bois meant that Reconstruction government accomplished enough to ensure that even after it was overthrown, the full reenslavement of blacks was no longer possible—an accomplishment achieved despite half-hearted and inconsistent federal support. He also saluted his old rival when he reminded his readers that it was a freedman, "the late Booker T. Washington[,] who planned the beginning of industrial democracy in the South" (*Gift* 140). The language of industrial democracy was a staple of post–World War I reconstruction discourse, and through Washington, Du Bois linked the achievements of Reconstruction to the guiding political problems of his own day. The way forward, however, remained elusive.

Black Reconstruction and the Politics of Tragedy

Du Bois's readers have often noted the way he used historical inquiry to make political arguments. According to Lawrie Balfour, "he dedicated himself to the presentation of a past that was not just known but creatively reworked to sustain a critique of the present . . . to craft a usable past from unspeakable loss."[24] Similarly, Nikhil Pal Singh draws on Jacques Rancière to argue that *Black Reconstruction* "rejected the separation of literature and truth" in order to "dramatize a social movement of black people into the new symbolic space of democratic history-making."[25] For Du Bois, however, a past was usable only if it was also factual. At the end of *Black Reconstruction,* he excoriated historians and political leaders "who would compromise with truth in the past in order to make peace in the present and guide policy in the future," which is what, in their differing ways, white-supremacist historians like Dunning and Bowers tried to do. For Du Bois, learning from Reconstruction required learning the truth about Reconstruction, however painful that truth turned out to be.

Du Bois saw clearly that most white Americans resisted interpretations of Reconstruction that presented its tragic character truthfully and not through the manipulative racism of Bowers or the Dunning School. When placed against decades of racist scholarship and propaganda, "one reads the truer deeper facts of Reconstruction with a great despair. It is at once so simple and so human, and yet so futile. There is no villain, no idiot, no saint. There are just men" (*BR* 728). *Black Reconstruction* does not offer anything that might be called a theory of the tragic, and despite the influence of Hegel on his intellectual development, Du Bois does not present the tragedy of Reconstruction in a progressive, dialectical fashion. However, the way he uses the term "tragedy" in *Black Reconstruction* makes it clear that he agreed with many theorists of the tragic that the redeeming feature of tragedy is that one can learn from it. Only when its possible lessons are ignored does tragedy give way to despair. As Hayden White argues in *Metahistory,* "the fall of the protagonist and the shaking of the world he inhabits" give rise to "a gain in consciousness for the spectators of the contest. And this gain is thought to consist in the epiphany of the law governing human existence which the protagonist's exertions against the world have brought to pass."[26] It was precisely the fact that white Americans were so resistant to this gain in consciousness that provoked Du Bois's previously mentioned insistence that "the unending tragedy of Reconstruction is the utter inability of the American mind to grasp its real significance." Thus, *Black Reconstruction* must be read as complex, multilayered tragedy. First, it documents the tragic events of Reconstruction itself, namely the failure of Emancipation to turn into real racial equality and the eventual rise of Jim Crow as a successor to slavery. Second, it works to expose the unending tragedy of thwarted historical memory, and it is in this second tragedy that the real political force of *Black Reconstruction* is to be found. Put simply, Du Bois held that as long as white Americans were unable to recognize the truth of Reconstruction, they would be unreliable allies in the struggle for democracy and racial equality.

Du Bois begins to build this argument at the start of *Black Reconstruction,* which opens with a history of "the black worker" in the United States that moves from the origins of the slave trade through the institutionalization of slavery and the resulting practices of slave resistance, especially marronage. "The White Worker" is the subject of the next chapter, which contains a stinging critique of the American labor movement's refusal to embrace abolitionism. Du Bois argued there were "two labor movements: the movement to give the black worker a minimum legal status which would enable him to sell his own labor, and another movement which proposed to increase the wage and better the condition of the working class in America" (*BR* 20). Anticipating later arguments about whiteness, Du Bois presented a litany of immigrant labor agitators coming to America and gradually embracing white supremacy, even when it conflicted with their earlier views and was still denounced by activists abroad. "Thus the majority of the world's laborers," he wrote, "by the insistence of white labor, became the basis of a system of industry which ruined democracy and showed its perfect fruit in World War and Depression. And this book seeks to tell that story" (*BR* 30).

Following a summary of the political dominance of the planter class in the antebellum United States, Du Bois turned to examine "how the Civil War meant emancipation and how the black worker won the war by a general strike which transferred his labor from the Confederate planter to the Northern invader" (*BR* 55). He positioned his argument against two opposed stories about the conduct of slaves during the Civil War, "one that the Negro did nothing but faithfully serve his master until emancipation was thrust upon him; the other that the Negro immediately, just as quickly as the presence of Northern soldiers made possible, left serfdom and took his stand with the army of freedom" (*BR* 57). What both these stories miss, he argues, is the importance of careful waiting and calculated hesitation on the part of the slaves, who acted not automatically but deliberately in choosing sides: "What the Negro did was to wait, look and listen and try to see where his interest lay."[27] However, "as soon as it became clear that the Union armies would not or could not return fugitive slaves, and that the masters with all their fume and fury were uncertain of victory, the slave entered upon a general strike against slavery by the same methods he had used in the period of the fugitive slave. He ran away to the first place of safety and offered his services to the federal army" (*BR* 57). Though Du Bois continued to use some the same naturalistic metaphors he deployed in *Souls*, he now placed them alongside clear statements of strategic intentionality. Now, "the swarming of the slaves" showed their "quiet but unswerving determination," and "this whole move was not dramatic or hysterical, rather it was like the great unbroken swell of the ocean before it dashed on the reefs" (*BR* 65). The appearance of slave defection as a sudden, spontaneous, uncontrollable force was an illusion created by the necessary invisibility of the forms of deliberation and communication that existed among slaves before Emancipation.[28]

The idea of the general strike united the various sorts of slave resistance that Du Bois had described earlier in *Gift* but was unable to put together. The general strike was a loosely coordinated intensification of the ways slaves had always resisted slavery, one that became something vastly more powerful in the context of the Civil War. Slaves who ran away withdrew their labor power and weakened the southern economy, while those who stayed were able to use the resulting labor shortage to challenge the conditions of their work in ways that all but destroyed slavery in many parts of the South well before the Emancipation Proclamation.[29] "Simply by stopping work," Du Bois wrote, "they could threaten the Confederacy with starvation. By walking into the Federal camps, they showed to doubting Northerners the easy possibility of using them as workers and as servants, as farmers, and as spies, and finally, as fighting soldiers" (*BR* 121). In this limited sense, the general strike was able to transition from the negative act of slaves removing their labor power to the positive projects of joining the army or creating new communities and institutions of their own. Thus, Du Bois reverses his earlier judgment about priority of different groups in bringing about Emancipation. Though he continued to esteem the abolitionists and emphasized their important role, he now wrote, "It was the fugitive slave who made the slaveholders face the alternative of surrendering to the North, or the Negros" (*BR* 121).

When it was published, the general strike argument was one of the most frequently criticized parts of *Black Reconstruction*. Communists aligned with the Third International were unhappy with Du Bois's heterodox use of a concept strongly associated with Sorelian syndicalism, while other leftists were content to point out that Du Bois did not seem to understand what a general strike was. Even his most sympathetic readers, like Alrutheus Ambush Taylor, who was one of the only black scholars to have published extensively on Reconstruction during the 1920s, remained unconvinced. "The work is hardly persuasive when it interprets the wholesale abandonment of plantations by Negroes as a general strike against the slave-regime," he wrote in the *Journal of Negro History:* "It does not show that this movement constituted an organized breaking away from work on the plantations with a view to forcing immediate economic or political concessions either from the planters or from the government of the Confederacy."[30] Du Bois might have agreed with some of these points, for he had not argued that the general strike was the result of an agreed-upon plan, an authorized decision, a general will, or any of the other concepts we ordinarily use to guide our thinking about the prerequisites for collective action. Instead, Du Bois's inspiration for the general strike was the leaderless revolution of the Great Migration. Like the Great Migration, it was a variation on the old slave practice of marronage, a form of agency born of the limitations placed on opportunities for black political organizing by the structures of white supremacy as they existed at the time. It used hesitation, exit, and other practices rarely seen as political, and turned them into a source of power that that was accessible to slaves across the South, whether they understood themselves to be coordinating or not.

As effective as the general strike was in ending the Civil War, however, it was unable to provide for real freedom after the Civil War. Insofar as slaves and freedmen were forced to join with the federal government, especially the Union army, in building their positive program, they were dependent on the continued support of northern whites. Most of all, the freedmen needed to have the land of the slave owners confiscated and redistributed to them because "beneath all theoretical freedom and political right must lie the economic foundation" (197). The North was unwilling to do this, and the freedmen had no preexisting organizations, institutions, or resources that would enable them to press their case or act autonomously on a sufficiently large scale. Furthermore, both the freedmen and their sympathizers had to contend with a rebellion against Emancipation that was carried on by southern whites through both legal and extralegal means well after the war had officially ended. As Du Bois argued, the power of the freedmen "could only be shown by refusal to work under the old conditions, and it had neither permanent organization nor savings to sustain it in such a fight" (*BR* 586). Reconstruction required the end of the general strike because it required that blacks reenter the capitalist economy as a condition of white alliance, foreclosing the possibility of independent subsistence farming outside the national economy, which had the objective of so many of the freedmen. But without either the economic basis for autonomy or the sustained support of the federal government and northern public, the freedmen were powerless to prevent the eventual demise of Reconstruction government and the redemption of white supremacy in the South.

None of this is to say that seeing Reconstruction as a tragedy necessitates seeing its failure as inevitable. In tragedy, Raymond Williams writes, "limits on human action are discovered in real actions, rather than known in advance or in general."[31] What is important about these limits is that they are not defined by abstract necessity but instead created by human interactions in specific historical situations. In other words, the tragic flaw that doomed Reconstruction was not that the freedmen were inferior but that whites refused to recognize them as human. Du Bois brought this out in *Black Reconstruction*'s longest chapter, "The Transubstantiation of a Poor White." Ostensibly an account of Andrew Johnson's presidency, Du Bois used Johnson as a representative figure for the white working class as whole. The chapter is bookended by invocations of tragedy, beginning with the claim, "Like Nemesis of Greek tragedy, the central problem of America after the Civil War, as before, was the black man," and ending with an account of how Johnson personified the contradiction between white supremacy and economic democracy (*BR* 237). "Because he could not conceive of Negroes as men," Du Bois wrote, "he refused to advocate universal democracy, of which, in his young manhood, he had been the fiercest advocate." This change "did not come by deliberate thought or conscious desire to hurt—it was rather the tragedy of American prejudice made flesh; so that the man born to narrow circumstances, a rebel against economic privilege, died with the conventional ambition of a poor white to be the associate and benefactor of monopolists, planters and slave drivers" (*BR* 322). Although Du Bois has often been criticized for being unsympathetic to poor whites in South, his account of how Johnson was led to choose race over democracy emphasized not only the blandishments of the planters but also the self-interested designs of northern politicians like Seward and the class snobbery of northern elites. Although poor whites might have chosen a different path for Reconstruction, they, like the freedmen, were confronted by tragic limitations on the exercise of their political power and agency.

In sum, *Black Reconstruction* maps both the successes and the unsolved problems of black politics. On the one hand, slaves were able to destroy slavery by way of general strike that redeployed long-established forms of slave resistance in the context of the Civil War. On the other hand, without an economic and institutional basis that blacks themselves could control, the general strike could not avoid its eventual reincorporation into the American capitalist order, nor could the freedmen prevent the return of white supremacy once the North lost interest in Reconstruction. The problem that Reconstruction could not solve was that of developing an organizational form of black politics that could further the cause of economic democracy while providing security and safe harbor against changing white sentiments. It was a tragedy because it showed, as Bernard Williams puts it, "that social reality can act to crush a worthwhile, significant, character or project without displaying either the lively individual purpose of a pagan god or the world-historical significance of a Judaic, a Christian, or a Marxist teleology."[32] Reconstruction was a failure, but it was splendid failure. "It did not fail where it was expected to fail," Du Bois wrote, not with the incompetence of the freedmen, but in a valiant, doomed struggle "against the massed hirelings of Religion, Science, Education, Law, and brute force" (*BR* 708). Du Bois used this tragic history to frame a program for black politics in the New Deal that began by acknowledging the existential vulnerability of racial minorities and the compulsory character of segregation as a precondition for developing a positive form of collective agency that would institutionalize black economic power in consumers' co-operatives and provide the material basis for freedom that was impossible during Reconstruction.

The Group Economy and the Lessons of Reconstruction

Du Bois never detailed the connections he saw between Reconstruction and the politics of the 1930s, but his political writings from the period implicitly draw the connection through their narration of the tragic history of black politics. In *Dusk of Dawn,* which begins with a chapter entitled "A New England Boy and Reconstruction," he wrote that after finishing *Black Reconstruction,* "I naturally turned my thought toward putting into permanent form that economic program of the Negro which I believed should succeed, and implement the long fight for political and civil rights and social equality" (*DoD* 787). That more permanent form was meant to be a short book entitled "The Negro and Social Reconstruction," in which Du Bois would chart the history of black politics from enslavement, Emancipation, and Reconstruction through to the New Deal, ending with one his most developed accounts of his plan for a black cooperative economy.[33] The book was to be published in a series edited by Alain Locke, but Locke ultimately rejected the manuscript for fear that it would antagonize the white foundations that were supporting the series, principally the Carnegie Corporation. Between this unpublished book and *Dusk of Dawn,* and alongside his journalism from the 1930s, we can see why Du Bois hoped that building a segregated black economy out of consumers' cooperatives could avoid the failure of Reconstruction, however splendid that failure was.

The importance Du Bois placed on the idea of the group economy can be best be appreciated by looking at what it cost him to promote it. Du Bois's advocacy for this plan in the years following the onset of the Great Depression brought him into a series of conflicts with other leaders in the NAACP, culminating in June 1934 with his resigning the editorship of the *Crisis,* which he had run for a quarter century, and his complete withdrawal from the organization. In his resignation letter he wrote, "I have since the beginning of the Great Depression, tried to work inside the organization for its realignment and readjustment," but "my program for economic readjustment has been totally ignored." Du Bois charged that the NAACP, "which has been great and effective for nearly a quarter of a century, finds itself in a time of crisis and change, without a program, without effective organization, without executive officers, who have either the ability or the disposition to guide the National Association for the Advancement of Colored People in the right direction."[34] As emphatic as he was in cutting his ties with the organization he had helped create, he found few allies in the NAACP's radical young critics because the economic program he was calling for—a cooperatively owned black economy operating independently of American capitalism—struck them as outdated and dangerously naïve. Ironically, his vision of black political organization forced him to renounce his existing organizational ties, leaving him more politically isolated than he had been at any time since the founding of the Niagara movement in 1905.

Though Du Bois disagreed with both the NAACP and many of its most strident critics, he did not position his alternative program as a middle ground between the two. Instead, he faulted both sides for being too dependent on forms of political agency beyond the control of African Americans and, therefore, unable to articulate plausible visions of black politics on their own. The NAACP, Du Bois felt, was stuck on the protest and uplift model of black politics he had articulated in the first decade of the twentieth century. In his resignation letter, he said the NAACP was "founded in a day when a negative program of protest was imperative and effective[;] it succeeded so well that the program seemed perfect and unlimited." However, "by World War and chaos, we are called to formulate a positive program of construction and inspiration. We have this far been unable to comply."[35] In one of his last articles in the *Crisis*, Du Bois rejected the claim that strategic segregation was a "counsel of despair" and scorned those who thought that "the fight against segregation consists merely of one damned protest after another. That the technique is to protest and wait and protest again, to keep this thing up until the gates of public opinion and the walls of segregation fall down." Not that he believed protest was unnecessary and should be given up, but it was insufficient. There were many ways in which segregation had increased during the years in which the NAACP had been active, and the severe economic effects of the Great Depression on African Americans meant black politics had new priorities and required new methods. "This program," he argued, "must be modified by adding to it a positive side. Make the protest, and keep making it, systematically and thoughtfully. Perhaps now and then even hysterically and theatrically; but at the same time, go to work to prepare methods and institutions which will supply those things and those opportunities which we lack because of segregation."[36]

The nature of this positive program preoccupied Du Bois and divided him from other critics of the NAACP. He saw the choice of positive strategy in tragic terms defined by the limits placed on black agency by the various manifestations of white supremacy in American society and government as they emerged out of the failure of Reconstruction. Though Du Bois praised the New Deal for having "entered for good into the social and economic organization of life," he also knew that southern Democrats were able to ensure segregation in nearly all its activities. "We could wish, we could pray, that this entrance could absolutely ignore lines of race and color," he wrote in the *Crisis,* "but we know perfectly well it does not and will not, and with the present American opinion, it cannot."[37] With the New Deal under the thumb of the Jim Crow South, younger radicals like Ralph Bunche and E. Franklin Frazier at Howard University, and George Streator, Du Bois's former assistant at the *Crisis,* advocated an alliance with the left wing of the American labor movement, particularly the Socialist and Communist Parties.[38] But Du Bois did not believe that white workers were willing to work with blacks in any large number and distrusted the American Communist Party for parroting the Soviet Union's call for national self-determination in the Black Belt.[39] "We cannot use the power of the state because we do not form a state," he wrote; "We cannot dictate as a proletariat, because we are in a minority, and not as Marxism and Socialism usually assume an overwhelming majority with power in the reach of its outstretched arms."[40] With the power of the state out of reach and interracial alliance not forthcoming, Du Bois looked to creation of a group economy out of networks of cooperatives that would trade directly with each other, sell to black consumers, and hire black workers as the most promising strategy for working within these limitations in order to organize the power that blacks in the United States already had (*NSR* 145).

Before he left the *Crisis,* Du Bois had described the kind of struggle he was envisioning in terms strikingly similar to those Antonio Gramsci was then using in his Italian prison cell, half a world away. "When an army moves to attack," Du Bois told his readers, "there are two methods which it may pursue." What he called "the older method" was what Gramsci called the war of maneuver, while his "modern method of fighting" was the war of position. It emphasized "careful planning" and "slow, calculated forward mass movements." The modern method of fighting recognized that mass political action requires long and careful organizing if it is to bear fruit. As Du Bois argued in *Black Reconstruction,* "The rise of a group of a people is not a simultaneous shift of the whole mass; it is a continuous differentiation of individuals with inner strife and differences of opinion, so that individuals, groups and classes begin to appear seeking higher levels, groping for better ways, uniting with other like-minded bodies and movements" (411).

Like the slaves of the general strike, practitioners of the modern method of fighting knew the value of waiting, hesitating, and recognizing the limits of what was possible in a world where being on the right side of history is no protection against the crushing indifference of social reality. Whereas the NAACP looked to the New Deal state, and communists looked to the white-dominated labor movement, Du Bois saw in the seemingly bourgeois cooperative movement something far more radical: a way for African Americans to develop their political and economic agency through autonomous institutions that could also provide them with material security. "This is the kind of method," Du Bois insisted, "which we must use to solve the Negro problem and to win our fight against segregation."[41]

In arguing for consumers' cooperatives as the driving institutions for organizing a separate black economy, Du Bois did not simply reapply the analytical framework of *Black Reconstruction* so much as he drew on the underlying method of moving from shared identities to institutions to the forms of collective agency they enabled. In *Black Reconstruction,* he had emphasized the importance of the slave's identity as a worker to understanding the nature of the general strike. In his own day, however, Du Bois argued that the most important economic identity African Americans had was as consumers, and it was specifically as consumers that their power could be organized. "As a consumer the Negro approaches economic equality much more nearly than he ever has as a producer," he wrote. "Organizing then and conserving and using intelligently the power which twelve million people have through what they buy, it is possible for the American Negro to help in the rebuilding of the economic state" (*DoD* 707) . This turn toward consumer citizenship may have angered Du Bois's Marxist critics, who were primarily interested in organizing at the site of production, but it was widespread in Depression-era politics and served as a particularly useful identity around which to organize African Americans. Federal legislation like the Social Security Act and the National Labor Relations Act defined labor in narrow terms that were designed to exclude southern blacks by leaving out categories like agricultural and domestic workers, thereby making it harder for them to claim the legal rights to which white workers had access. Also, focusing on consumption provided a greater role for women, whose contributions as workers were often devalued by both the state and the labor movement. Ella Baker, for example, began her political career as an organizer for the Young Negroes' Co-operative League (YNCL), and many of the groups she organized were led by women. Consumption, therefore, offered a more encompassing identity around which to organize the country's black population.

The increased consumer power African Americans possessed in the 1930s was a result of the social and economic changes brought about by the Great Migration. Though it was in many ways an extension of slave marronage, the Great Migration, unlike the general strike, was in no way anticapitalist. By leaving the South, with its system of sharecropping and debt peonage, for industrial jobs in urban areas, African Americans entered further into the cash economy, creating a larger and more varied workforce than existed in the past. While migration increased purchasing power and broadened the scope of the black economy, urbanization led to the development of a thicker institutional life among migrants. As Du Bois wrote, "Groups of Negroes in their own clubs and organizations, in their own neighborhoods and schools, were formed, and were not so much the result of deliberate planning as the rationalization of the segregation into which they were forced by racial prejudice" (*DoD* 697). Alongside black churches and schools, the two major institutional legacies of Reconstruction, these new organizations provided an economic and social foundation for the development of consumers' cooperatives, precisely what the freedmen lacked during Reconstruction.

Du Bois knew his plan for a black cooperative economy was seen by many as plainly incredible, but just as consumer identity was becoming increasingly important during the Depression, so too was the idea of organizing consumption around cooperative rather than capitalistic lines. New Deal administrators traveled the globe to study how cooperatives worked in other countries, and Marquis Childs's 1936 book on the role of cooperatives in the Swedish economy became a surprise best seller.[42] The growth of cooperatives in African American communities started somewhat earlier, when George Schuyler founded the YNCL in 1930. As economic historian

Jessica Gordon Nembhard argues, "The Great Depression probably saw the rise of more African American–owned cooperatives than any other period in U.S. history."[43] It is clear that Du Bois was aware of this wider situation because, at the end of *The Negro and Social Reconstruction,* he both cited Childs and obliquely referenced some of the campaigns of the YNCL (*NSR* 157, 147). In calling for a more coordinated approach to developing cooperatives, Du Bois was trying to organize something that blacks in many parts of the country were already trying to do. These cooperatives made it possible to transform the Great Migration into a new form of economic marronage in which blacks could leave the white, capitalist economy without having to go anywhere, thereby uniting the negative power of the general strike with the positive, institution-building program with which Du Bois was so concerned.

Seeing the group economy as an extension of marronage allows us to better appreciate the ways in which it responds to the tragic situation of black politics. The group economy begins with the reality of compulsory segregation and, in the near term, abandons some cherished ideals of integration. At the end of *The Negro and Social Reconstruction,* Du Bois admitted, "Momentarily the greater plans of the Niagara Movement and the N.A.A.C.P. for the emancipation of the American Negro cannot be realized because of the depression, and especially because white America is not ready to have them realized" (*NSR* 157). He did not reject integration as a good; he rejected it as a good political program for the moment in which he was living. "What I propose," he wrote, "is that into the interstices of this collapse of the industrial machine, the Negro shall search intelligently and carefully and farsightedly plan for his entrance into the new economic world" (*DoD* 706). In pulling back from the capitalist world, the group economy was also a prefigurative effort to make a place for African Americans in the world that would be. Not that Du Bois claimed to know what that world would look like in detail. "We are not called upon to be dogmatic as to just what the end of this change will be and what form the new organization will take," he insisted (*DoD* 699). As a form of marronage, the group economy was less a vision of a just society than what Neil Roberts calls a "liminal and transitional social space *between* slavery and freedom."[44] Du Bois's tragic vision of political agency allowed him to see, against the protestations of both the liberal NAACP and leftist radicals, that creating such a space sometimes requires acting and organizing in ways that cut against values in which you deeply believe but do not have the power to realize.

Du Bois never lost sight of the difficulty of his plan for the group economy. "It has to be admitted this will be a real battle," he granted at the end of *Dusk of Dawn*. Echoing his assessment of Reconstruction as a "splendid failure," he then added, "There are chances of failure, but there are also splendid chances of success" (714). However, the bombing of Pearl Harbor and the entrance of the United States into the Second World War dramatically changed the political and economic situation in the United States. Wartime industry created demand for African American workers that surpassed even the levels reached during World War I. Patriotic sentiment made Du Bois's strategic embrace of segregation and separatism seem disloyal to many progressives, even bordering on treasonous. Meanwhile, the Roosevelt administration's efforts to position itself against the racism of Nazi Germany created new opportunities for civil rights groups like the NAACP to challenge racism in the United States. If there was a window of opportunity in the 1930s for the creation of a group economy, that window was effectively closed by World War II.

Why, then, should we concern ourselves with a political program whose window of opportunity closed before it could be seriously attempted? The answer is not to be found in the specifics of Du Bois's proposals for the group economy, though many of these have had an enduring influence on black political thought. More broadly, Du Bois's thought from this period matters because it helps us see how an awareness of the tragic nature of politics can contribute to and even strengthen our commitment to radical forms of democratic agency. As was the case with the tragic legend of Reconstruction, tragedy has often been seen as a conservative discourse, one that either opposes efforts at radical political change or calls on us to chasten our ideals and aspirations for the world in which we want to live. For Du Bois, this interpretation of tragedy missed the point. By presenting Reconstruction as a tragedy, he tried to show his readers how they could learn from past efforts at social transformation. The point of tragedy is not to alter our ideals but to remind us of the importance of the how. In this sense, an awareness of the tragic is indispensable for thinking strategically about politics.

As Cornel West writes: "A sense of the tragic is an attempt to keep alive some sense of possibility. Some sense of hope, some sense of agency. Some sense of resistance in a moment of defeat and disillusionment and a moment of discouragement."[45] The failure of Reconstruction was such a moment of defeat, and over the course of his long life, Du Bois saw many more. But his ability to keep fighting, and to keep thinking about how the fight should be carried on, was premised on the kind of hope that can only come from an unflinching sense of the tragic, what he elsewhere called "a hope not hopeless but unhopeful" (*Souls* 507). The core of this tragic hope is not to be found in the belief that our ideals will eventually be realized but in the conviction that, if we think and act carefully, we have it in ourselves to go on fighting for those ideals indefinitely. In other words, Du Bois used tragedy to teach his readers to hope wisely by using history to hold the balance between political vision and political strategy. Today, as the struggle to reconstruct American democracy seems to be entering a new and troubling phase, we continue to have need of this kind of vison. And what Du Bois told his readers in 1934 is still worth hearing today: "The real battle is a matter of study and thought; of the building up of loyalties; of the long training of men; of the growth of institutions; of the inculcation of racial and national ideals. It is not a publicity stunt. It is a life."[46]

Notes

1. W. E. B. Du Bois, *Dusk of Dawn: An Essay toward an Autobiography of a Race Concept*, in *W. E. B. Du Bois: Writings*, ed. Nathan Huggins (New York: Library of America, 1986), 787; hereafter cited parenthetically as *DoD.* On the "Tragic Legend," see Kenneth M. Stampp, *The Era of Reconstruction 1865–1877* (New York: Vintage, 1967), chap. 1. I would like to thank Libby Anker, David Bateman, Richard Bensel, Nick Bromell, Kevin Duong, Jason Frank, Jill Frank, Murad Idris, Jordan Jochim, Alex Livingston, Ed Quish. Aziz Rana, Anna Marie Smith, and Erin Pineda.

2. Claude Bowers, *The Tragic Era: The Revolution after Lincoln* (Cambridge: Houghton Mifflin, 1929), preface. On the motivation behind Bowers's book and the political stakes of Reconstruction historiography in the period, see Bruce E. Baker, *What Reconstruction Meant: Historical Memory in the American South* (Charlottesville: University of Virginia Press, 2007).

3. W. E. B. Du Bois, *Black Reconstruction in America 1860–1880* (New York: Free Press, 1998), 727; hereafter cited parenthetically as *BR.*

4. See Angela Y. Davis, *Abolition Democracy: Beyond Empire, Prisons, and*

Torture (New York: Seven Stories, 2005); Gayatri Chakravorty Spivak, "General Strike," *Rethinking Marxism* 26, no. 1 (2014): 9–14; Ta-Nehisi Coates, "But This Latter Person, I Am Not Trying to Convince," *Atlantic*, www.theatlantic.com/notes/2016/06/but-this-latter-person-i-am-not-trying-to-convince/488408/; Annette Gordon-Reed, "What If Reconstruction Hadn't Failed?" *Atlantic*, www.theatlantic.com/politics/archive/2015/10/what-if-reconstruction-hadnt-failed/412219/. The most famous history of Reconstruction to have been inspired by Du Bois is, of course, Eric Foner, *Reconstruction: America's Unfinished Revolution, 1863–1877* (New York: Harper and Row, 1988), but historians like Steven Hahn, Heather Cox Richardson, David Roediger, and David Williams have all written about their debts to *Black Reconstruction*.

5. See Lawrie Balfour, *Democracy's Reconstruction: Thinking Politically with W. E. B. Du Bois* (New York: Oxford University Press, 2011), chap. 2; Adolph L. Reed, *W. E. B. Du Bois and American Political Thought: Fabianism and the Color Line* (New York: Oxford University Press, 1997); and Nikhil Pal Singh, *Black Is a Country: Race and the Unfinished Struggle for Democracy* (Cambridge: Harvard University Press, 2004), chap. 2. Whereas these authors treat Du Bois's work from the 1930s quite sympathetically, the most important recent book that has been critical of Du Bois's politics, Robert Gooding-Williams's *In the Shadow of Du Bois: Afro-Modern Political Thought in America* (Cambridge: Harvard University Press, 2009), focuses on Du Bois's early work, particularly *Souls*.

6. The literature on tragedy in political theory is too vast for me to summarize here, but I would like to thank Libby Anker for helping me think about *Black Reconstruction* in relation to it. On her idea of "tragedies of emancipation," see Elizabeth R. Anker, "Three Emancipations: *Manderlay*, Slavery, and Racialized Freedom," *Theory & Event* 18, no. 2 (2015).

7. W. E. B. Du Bois. *The Souls of Black Folk*. Collected in *Writings*, ed. Huggins, 373; hereafter cited parenthetically as *Souls*.

8. W. E. B. Du Bois, "Reconstruction and Its Benefits," *American Historical Review* 15, no. 4 (July1910): 781; hereafter cited parenthetically as *RIB*. I follow the original text in not capitalizing "negro," though Du Bois strenuously objected to this.

9. On the Dunning School, see A. A. Taylor. "Historians of the Reconstruction," *Journal of Negro History* 23, no. 1 (January 1938): 16–34; and John David Smith and J. Vincent Lowery, eds., *The Dunning School: Historians, Race, and the Meaning of Reconstruction* (Lexington: University Press of Kentucky, 2013). The wider impulse toward reconciliation to which Dunning's work belonged is the subject of David W. Blight, *Race and Reunion: The Civil War in American Memory* (Cambridge: Belknap Press of Harvard University Press, 2001).

10. William A. Dunning, "The Undoing of Reconstruction," in *Essays on the Civil War and Reconstruction* (New York: Harper and Row, 1965), 354, 384.

11. W. E. B. Du Bois, "Agitation," *Crisis,* November 1910, in *Writings,* ed. Huggins, 1132.

12. Daniel T. Rodgers, *Atlantic Crossings: Social Politics in a Progressive Age* (Cambridge: Belknap Press of Harvard University Press, 1998), 290. One possible transatlantic connection between Reconstruction after the Civil War and post–World War I Reconstruction that Rodgers does not explore is the career of French prime minister Georges Clemenceau, who covered Reconstruction as a journalist while exiled from France in the late 1860s. Clemenceau wrote favorably on the efforts of Radical Republican leaders like Stevens and Sumner to bring the South to heel, and his articles were republished in the United States in book form shortly before his death in 1929. Du Bois draws on Clemenceau's observations throughout *Black Reconstruction.*

13. W. E. B. Du Bois, "Jim Crow," *Crisis,* January 1919, in *Writings,* ed. Huggins, 1177–78.

14. W. E. B. Du Bois, *Economic Co-Operation among Negro Americans* (Atlanta: Atlanta University Press, 1907). On the history of African American cooperatives, and the difference between Du Bois's early and later uses of the term, see Jessica Gordon Nembhard, *Collective Courage: A History of African American Cooperative Economic Thought and Practice* (University Park: Pennsylvania State University Press, 2014).

15. W. E. B. Du Bois, "Reconstruction," *Crisis,* July 1919, 130–31.

16. W. E. B. Du Bois, "Cooperation," *Crisis,* February 1920, 171–72.

17. W. E. B. Du Bois, "The Class Struggle," *Crisis,* June 1921, in *W. E. B. Du Bois: A Reader,* ed. David Levering Lewis (New York: Holt, 1995), 555.

18. This argument is made most forcefully in W. E. B. Du Bois, "The Negro and Radical Thought," *Crisis* July 1921, in *Reader,* ed. Lewis, 531–37.

19. Isabel Wilkerson, *The Warmth of Other Suns: The Epic Story of America's Great Migration.* (New York: Random House, 2010), 42, 9. The most comprehensive scholarly treatment of the Great Migration is James N. Gregory, *The Southern Diaspora: How the Great Migrations of Black and White Southerners Transformed America* (Chapel Hill: University of North Carolina Press, 2005).

20. W. E. B. Du Bois, "The Migration of the Negros," *Crisis,* June 1917, 63–66; W. E. B. Du Bois, "Brothers, Come North," *Crisis,* January 1920, in *Reader,* ed. Lewis, 529.

21. W. E. B. Du Bois, *The Gift of Black Folk: The Negros in the Making of America* (New York: Washington Square, 1970), 20; hereafter cited parenthetically as *Gift.*

22. The importance of marronage is explored in Neil Roberts, *Freedom as Marronage* (Chicago: University of Chicago Press, 2015); and Steven Hahn, *The Political Worlds of Slavery and Freedom* (Cambridge: Harvard University Press, 2009).

Thanks to Jordan Jochim for pushing me on the significance of marronage to my argument.

23. On self-emancipation, see David Williams, *I Freed Myself: African American Struggle for Freedom in the Civil War Era* (New York: Cambridge University Press, 2014).

24. Balfour, *Democracy's Reconstruction*, 6.

25. Singh, *Black Is a Country*, 93.

26. Hayden V. White, *Metahistory: The Historical Imagination in Nineteenth-Century Europe* (Baltimore: Johns Hopkins University Press, 1973), 9.

27. Du Bois's emphasis on the strategic importance of waiting in his 1930s writings may be connected to the debates on "revolutionary waiting" that took place in Germany's Social Democratic Party (SPD) around the time Du Bois was living in Germany. Like Du Bois, the SPD leadership emphasized a program of building parallel institutions, but their efforts to withdraw from bourgeois political and social life were very different from Du Bois's economic separatism, which was intended to be a weapon within American politics. On revolutionary waiting, see James T. Kloppenberg, *Uncertain Victory: Social Democracy and Progressivism in European and American Thought, 1870–1920* (New York: Oxford University Press, 1986), 207–37.

28. On patterns of slave communication and resistance, see Steven Hahn, *A Nation under Our Feet: Black Political Struggles in the Rural South, from Slavery to the Great Migration* (Cambridge: Belknap Press of Harvard University Press, 2003).

29. The use of exit as a political strategy is most famously discussed in Albert O. Hirschman, *Exit, Voice, and Loyalty: Responses to Decline in Firms, Organizations and States* (Cambridge: Harvard University Press, 1970). Hirschman's account of the interplay between exit and voice provides a useful way to think about strategies southern blacks used to resist white supremacy from Reconstruction through the civil rights movement.

30. Taylor "Historians of the Reconstruction," 33. Some of difficulties surrounding the general strike seem to be connected with the influential formulation given by Georges Sorel in *Reflections of Violence.* But Du Bois never mentions Sorel, whose work he probably would have known, and Du Bois's emphasis on the historical reality of the general strike contrasts with Sorel's interest in its status a myth for energizing class conflict. Du Bois's silence on Sorel should almost certainly be read as an effort to quietly distance himself from a thinker whose work had already acquired unsavory connections with fascism.

31. Raymond Williams, *Modern Tragedy* (London: Chatto and Windus, 1966), 18. David Roediger connects William's idea of "social tragedy" with Du Bois in *Seizing Freedom: Slave Emancipation and Liberty for All* (New York: Verso, 2014). However, Roediger's insistence on reading Du Bois through the Benjaminian lens of "revolutionary time" unhelpfully obscures Du Bois's focus on the con-

tinuous operation of political constraints and has, at best, a slender basis in the text of *Black Reconstruction.*

32. Bernard Williams, *Shame and Necessity* (Berkeley: University of California Press, 1993), 165.

33. W. E. B. Du Bois, *The Negro and Social Reconstruction*, in *Against Racism: Unpublished Essays, Papers, Addresses, 1887–1961* ed. Herbert Aptheker (Amherst: University of Massachusetts Press, 1985), 102–57; hereafter cited parenthetically as *NSR*.

34. "Dr. Du Bois Resigns," *Crisis*, August 1934, in *Writings*, ed. Huggins, 1260–61. On the early history of the NAACP, see Patricia Sullivan, *Lift Every Voice: The NAACP and the Making of the Civil Rights Movement* (New York: New Press, 2009).

35. "Dr. Du Bois Resigns," 1260.

36. W. E. B. Du Bois, "Counsels of Despair," *Crisis*, June 1934, in *Writings*, ed. Huggins, 1257.

37. W. E. B. Du Bois, "Segregation in the North" *Crisis*, April 1934, in *Writings*, ed. Huggins, 1243. The impact of southern congressional power on the New Deal is treated extensively in Ira Katznelson, *Fear Itself: The New Deal and the Origins of Our Time* (New York: Liveright, 2013). On black politics in the period, see Nancy J. Weiss, *Farewell to the Party of Lincoln: Black Politics in the Age of FDR* (Princeton, NJ: Princeton University Press, 1983); and Eric Schickler, *Racial Realignment: The Transformation of American Liberalism, 1932–1965* (Princeton, NJ: Princeton University Press, 2016).

38. Singh provides the best guide to this debate in chapter 2 of *Black Is a Country*. The larger context is explored by Michael C. Dawson, *Blacks in and out of the Left* (Cambridge: Harvard University Press, 2013).

39. The most powerful defense of the role communist activists played in the struggle against white supremacy is Glenda Elizabeth Gilmore, *Defying Dixie: The Radical Roots of Civil Rights, 1919–1950* (New York: Norton, 2008).

40. W. E. B. Du Bois, "The Right to Work," *Crisis*, April 1933, in *Writings*, ed. Huggins, 1236–37.

41. Du Bois, "Counsels of Despair," 1258–59.

42. On the international spread of interest in consumers' cooperatives, and Childs's book in particular, see Kiran Claus Patel, *The New Deal: A Global History* (Princeton, NJ: Princeton University Press, 2016), 222–33.

43. Nembhard, *Collective Courage*, 146.

44. Neil Roberts, *Freedom as Marronage*, 4.

45. Cornel West, "Pragmatism and the Tragic," in *Prophetic Thought in Postmodern Times*, vol. 1: *Beyond Eurocentrism and Multiculturalism* (Monroe, ME: Common Courage, 1993), 32.

46. Du Bois, "Counsels of Despair," 1259.

11

"Love Is God, and Work Is His Prophet"

Decolonial Extension and Gandhian Exploration in Du Bois's Interwar Years

David Haekwon Kim

The work of W. E. B. Du Bois spanned roughly seventy productive years. More than fifty years after his death, we are still trying to realize the full extent of its importance. The scholarship on his political theory in particular has focused primarily on the period of his masterpiece *The Souls of Black Folk* (1903) and the themes generated out of that text and milieu. As with any truly great work, there is yet more to learn from *Souls*. But it is also true that Du Bois had, remarkably, some sixty years beyond *Souls* in which to modify and extend his outlook. This is a point that he *politically* thematized in *Dusk of Dawn* (1940), where he characterized the *Souls* stage of his career in terms of ignorance of political economy and the expression of forces in an age of "Empire."[1]

This chapter considers Du Bois's transition during the interwar years from an early "political expressivism" to a post-*Souls* "black Marxism." On Robert Gooding-Williams's account, Du Bois was committed in his early years to a political expressivist agenda that encouraged black elites to lead their people in modernizing uplift and ethos cultivation.[2] Cedric Robinson's work highlights how Du Bois's political theory gained a critical edge through the infusion of Marxist ideas, which accords with Du Bois's self-understanding and places him within a radical tradition of black politics sometimes referred to as "black Marxism."[3] These and other works clarify that there is genuine complexity and sometimes tension in Du Bois's progressive, and sometimes regressive, politics. In trying to sum up his complex life and shifting perspectives, Manning Marable, following Herbert Aptheker, describes Du Bois as a "radical democrat."[4] In this chapter, I try to articulate a Du Bois during the interwar years whose outlook was wider and more complex than that of a black Marxist but more specific than what is conveyed by "radical democrat." Drawing from a largely Latin American–derived political theory—decolonial thought—I will show how and why Du Bois should be regarded as a decolonial democrat, paying special attention to how he was a rather unusual variant of it by virtue of espousing a black Marxism-Gandhism.[5]

In the first section of this chapter, I situate Du Bois's political theory generally and describe some of the key features of decolonial thought. In the second, I explain how Du Bois was a forerunner of decolonial thought because he produced concepts that anticipated many of its major ideas, especially the constituent features of what decolonial thinkers call "coloniality," a world-like condition generated by global Western imperialism. In the third and longest section, I argue that Du Bois was a distinctive type of decolonial thinker by virtue of developing an Afro-Asian conception of South-South decoloniality and, within this framework, experimenting with a fusion of black radicalism and Gandhian notions of moksha (liberation) and satyagraha (nonviolent resistance).

Situating Du Bois's Political Theory

Broadly speaking, a theory can be understood and evaluated in terms of its application to various salient objects of inquiry. We might ask, for example, whether Du Bois's political theory adequately treats the topic of black subjectivity by means of the notion of double-consciousness. But theory can also be understood in terms of its orienting or framing perspectives rather than its objects of inquiry. Here, organizing rubrics of thought and evaluative criteria play a major role, delivering or configuring elements of the world as intelligible for inquiry. This is also where the issue of intellectual traditions emerges explicitly, since traditions are enduring, broadly collaborative social networks committed to developing theoretic frameworks as well as improving and expanding their application to relevant objects of inquiry. For example, was it a pragmatist orientation, perhaps learned from William James, that led Du Bois to a flexible sociohistorical conception of race? Did Marxism eventually replace pragmatism as the central framing viewpoint on race, such that class analysis emerged as the dominant optic on race relations? Was it the Afro-modern tradition that led Du Bois to think about race in terms of conservation rather than elimination? Importantly, orienting perspective and object of analysis are linked in dynamic ways as when a shift in perspective generates new objects or a reanalyzed (or anomalous) object leads to a modified or abandoned perspective.[6] This distinction between orienting perspective and object of analysis is important, and I will return to it later when I discuss the strong anti-Eurocentrism of decolonial theory and, in the final section, the creative theoretical hybridity of Du Bois's type of decolonial theory.

In the work of Du Bois, complexity characterizes both aspects of his political theory, but arguably the orienting perspective is the more ambiguous of the two. As a political theorist, Du Bois was a rare synthesist. His coordination of disparate conceptual elements was often experimental in a way that makes his synthesizing efforts hard to track. This hybridization or harmonization process also evolved across many decades in a manner that requires careful longitudinal study. Unsurprisingly, scholars have situated the orienting perspective of his work in many traditions: Herderianism, Hegelianism, Marxism, pragmatism, romanticism, the black radical tradition, black existentialism, black radical liberalism, black feminism or protofeminism, Afro-modernism, Afrocentrism, and even Afro-Orientalism.[7] For the purposes of this essay, I will more or less assume that at various stages of his life Du Bois drew from, mixed, or stood within most and perhaps all of these traditions and possibly more. Throughout his life, Du Bois was positioned and also positioned himself at the margins of the academy and the polity. So, unlike many conventional academicians, he was not disposed to hagiographical allegiance to a single tradition. Moreover, his commitment to social transformation encouraged, even sometimes required, a strategy of hybridization of theoretic resources, like the traditions already mentioned, and of academic disciplines, like sociology and philosophy.[8] For our purposes, it will be the quality of hybridization that concerns us, not the mere instantiation of multiple traditions.

In his important book on the early Du Bois, Robert Gooding-Williams delineates an Afro-modern tradition by which to situate early black political theorists and explain the centrality of Du Bois. The Afro-modern tradition began roughly in the late eighteenth century and was configured by "genre-defining thematic preoccupations" like "the political and social organization of white supremacy, the nature and effects of racial ideology, and the possibilities of black emancipation."[9] This body of thought, concerned with intranational and transnational white supremacy, can be distinguished from roughly historically parallel traditions of modern political theory that focused on the nation-state proper, like the classic social contract tradition of Hobbes and Locke and the French liberal tradition of Tocqueville. Working with this characterization of the Afro-modern tradition, which seems maximally inclusive of black political thinkers, I will regard Du Bois as (1) a political thinker whose primary concerns and objects of analysis included white supremacy and black liberation; (2) a central figure in the Afro-modern tradition, and thus one whose theoretic orientation was informed by a complex dialogue between Western frameworks and black critiques and transformations of them; and (3) a potential participant in *other critical traditions* that are also concerned with a dominative modernity and unrealized democracy. In characterizing Du Bois during the interwar years as a decolonial democrat, we will see that in regard to (1), Du Bois contextualized his initial focal points in a wider anticolonial critique that both centered political economy and an Afro-Asian model for empire's underside. Regarding (2), he enriched his theoretic orientation in a way that aligns him more closely with what has come to be called comparative political theory (and comparative philosophy) through the introduction of not so much Marxist but Gandhian ideas. As to point (3), Du Bois could very well show up as a figure in not only, say, European critical traditions but also Indian critical or democratic traditions that involve such figures as Gandhi, Tagore, Ambedkar, Nehru, Ashis Nandy, and current subaltern studies scholars. As well, he can be juxtaposed with "Third World intellectuals" more broadly, perhaps within a "colored-modern" or "dark modern" tradition, like José Mariátegui, M. N. Roy, Lu Xun, Aimé Césaire, and others. I turn now to a brief characterization of decolonial theory so that we can better conceptualize Du Bois's perspective as wider and more complex than "black Marxism" and narrower than "radical democrat."

Although Du Bois famously prophesied that the problem of the twentieth century would be that of the color line and understood this to be a global phenomenon, it took some decades for him to develop a critical and theoretically integrated conception of domestic racial subordination, on the one hand, and global colonial domination, on the other. Currently, the most famous body of thought that addresses colonialism and its aftermath is the field of postcolonialism, especially the branch that comes under the heading of "subaltern studies." The emergent field of decolonial thought is a peer and a rival to postcolonialism, especially subaltern studies.[10] Both postcolonial and decolonial thought share a vision of the world as systemically transformed by global Western imperialism, from the domination of the politics and economies of the non-Western world to the centering of the West in the global epistemic landscape. Moreover, it is typically understood that the material force of global imperialism enabled the conceptual hierarchy of Eurocentrism and that both can persist even after formal decolonization of nation-states. In terms of history, these theories have a corresponding critique of modernity as harboring these profoundly suppressive structures while obscuring them through a Eurocentric grand narrative of Western progress and non-Western emulation.

Where they differ seems to be priorities and overall synthesis.[11] Although there are differences within postcolonial theory, arguably a composite sketch of the field would indicate that postcolonial thought supports a fairly general collation, as opposed to a tightly patterned one, of the political, economic, cultural, and epistemic critiques mentioned. In terms of disciplines, there seems to be a strong showing of literary and cultural studies. And for critical sources, there is, with the exception of Frantz Fanon, a heavy reliance on Derrida, Foucault, Deleuze, and other Western critical theorists. In decolonial theory, however, the overall pattern in the literature is a commitment to a *strongly unified radical political economy and anti-Eurocentric political epistemology,* where each of these two elements involves an important, though not absolute, difference from what we find in roughly similar elements in postcolonial theory.[12] Decolonial theory tends (1) to support an empirically grounded, unified critique of modern global racism, sexism, and capitalism, typically through the filter of world-system's theory and the geographical heuristic of the Americas, and (2) issues a mandate to decolonize thought, which includes a rejection of the uncritical or overuse of critical Western sources of the kind commonly cited by postcolonial theorists, like Derrida and Foucault.

Regarding the first point, the political economy, decolonial theory borrows from and emends world-systems theory to argue that modernity would not have transpired were it not for the founding of global capitalism in the post-1492 genocidal domination of the Americas and the subsequent African slave trade and New World slavery. For example, many or most decolonial thinkers rely on the work of Aníbal Quijano, who, with the world-systems theorist Immanuel Wallerstein, argues that "the Americas were not incorporated into an already existing capitalist world-economy. There could not have been a capitalist world-economy without the Americas."[13] This founding structure in turn became the basis for what was by the early twentieth century, a truly global white Western imperium. Elsewhere, Quijano contends that what has been called "modernity" was fundamentally framed by the rise of this global capitalism, which was constituted by (1) a dominative control of labor and (2) a racially hierarchical configuration of that dominative control. This entire phenomenon, or world-condition, decolonial thinkers call the "coloniality of power," or simply "coloniality."[14] The upshot is that modernity unmasked turns out to be coloniality, and instances of colonialism were not deviations from the promise of modernity but the normatively consistent expressions of a planet-wide racially hegemonic capitalist system or simply coloniality. Importantly, as Nelson Maldonado-Torres points out, coloniality's origin in the conquest of the Americas deeply affected gender relations because the sexualization of the wars of conquest persisted in the racial-gendered dehumanizing structures of the subsequent colonial enterprise: "Once vanquished, they [the indigenous of Latin America] are said to be inherently servants and their bodies come to form part of an economy of sexual abuse, exploitation, and control."[15] María Lugones maintains that conquest and colonial control also significantly disfigured by means of an oppressive binaristic logic the many relations that composed precolonial gender as gender, both transforming gender fundamentally in the Americas and rendering coloniality also an oppressive racial-gendered condition.[16] Turning to class, decolonial theorists tend not to be orthodox Marxists, as is typically the case with world-systems theorists as well, but there seems to be a range of views of how to conceptualize the force of material relations. In clarifying one position on the relation between culture and economy in the world-systems model, Ramón Grosfoguel claims: "I take global ideological/symbolic strategies and colonial/racist culture as constitutive, together with capitalist accumulation processes and the inter-state system, of the core-periphery relationships at a world-scale. These different structures and processes form a heterarchy . . . of heterogeneous, complex and entangled hierarchies that cannot be accounted for in the infrastructure/superstructure paradigm."[17] Finally, it is important to note that the *overall* theoretic structure and directionality of the political economy described above derives from experience and perspective generated from what Enrique Dussel has called "the underside of modernity."[18]

Regarding the second point, the political epistemology, decolonial theory urges a divestment of colonially configured thought. This involves a serious commitment to theorize *out of the vantage point* of, and not merely about, the "underside of modernity" or the suppressed of coloniality. Thus, there is a strong opposition to Eurocentrism. In fact, many or most decolonial thinkers regard standard Marxism as Eurocentric, and some decolonial thinkers criticize postcolonialists, like subaltern studies scholars, of also being Eurocentric since they tend to draw primarily from Western thinkers, even if they are critical theorists. Whether or not this last is warranted, the concern with Eurocentrism is crucial. To put the matter in terms of the distinction raised earlier, many Euro-based theories, like Marxism or Foucauldian poststructuralism, can make people of color or "Third World" peoples important objects of inquiry, perhaps through an effort to defend them from hegemonic ideologies that justify their subordination. Certainly, these theories can illuminate much. But, insofar as we are concerned with ending Eurocentrism, the epistemic dimension of coloniality, we will need at some point to shape our orienting perspectives with concepts drawn from the "underside of modernity" or "the wretched of the Earth." We will need to liberate our theories. Or, as Walter Mignolo puts it, we need to "delink" our theoretical orientation from traditions emerging out of the dominant zones of coloniality and center the viewpoints or orientations of the underside of coloniality, like those of Ottobah Cugoano, José Mariátegui, Du Bois, Fanon, and the like. This is not to deny the value of critical traditions of the West; after all, decolonial theory shows indebtedness to Marx, the Frankfurt school, and the like. Rather, delinking is about what consolidates the core of the theoretical orientation. Here, the viewpoints of the underside must have a strong presence. Indeed, in characterizing the foundational influence of Quijano's political economy and concept of coloniality, Mignolo is keen to emphasize that Quijano's own theoretic orientation is not beholden to purely Western, even if critical, voices. As he notes, Quijano was influenced heavily by the Peruvian radical thinker José Mariátegui, who wrote in the 1920s, and then later by dependency theory in the 1970s, which was itself influenced by deep consideration of Africa and by the impact of Fanon.[19] Given how saturated the radical and the liberal academy is in the works of Western thinkers, even anti-establishment critical thinkers, the call to theoretical decolonization is an enormously challenging demand of decolonial theory.

Du Bois as Decolonial Democrat

In short, I take decolonial theory to be a naming of and intervention against coloniality, one that is distinguished by its strongly unified radical political economy and delinking political epistemology. In the literature of this theory, Du Bois is often hailed as a precursor and sometimes even a progenitor. For example, an important contributor to decolonial theory, Nelson Maldonado-Torres, notes that though there were decolonial voices at the inception of coloniality, a "more substantial decolonial turn was announced by W. E. B. Du Bois in the early twentieth century and made explicit in a line of figures that goes from Aimé Césaire and Frantz Fanon in the mid-twentieth century, to Sylvia Wynter, Enrique Dussel, Gloria Anzaldúa, Lewis Gordon, Chela Sandoval, and Linda Tuhiwai Smith, among others."[20] In the decolonial literature, there is recurring mention of Du Bois's claim that the twentieth century is the problem of the color line, as we have just seen, but his remarks on double-consciousness are also highlighted.[21] The idea of the color line is taken to be an emblematic way of characterizing some central features of the political economy of coloniality, especially the racial structure of domestic disenfranchisement and of colonial subjection. The idea of double-consciousness is regarded as a crucial motif for both existential experience of and the epistemic vantage point from within coloniality's underside, which underscores the political epistemology crucial to confronting coloniality.[22] I think a good deal more can be said to consolidate this widespread notion that Du Bois was an early decolonial thinker, but I will only quickly summarize some relevant material to firm up this notion and then move on to Du Bois's distinctive brand of decolonial thought.[23]

It is well known, perhaps to the chagrin of many sympathetic liberals, that across the interwar years Du Bois became increasingly confident that Marxism offered significant theoretic tools for the fight against white supremacy and that in his final years he insisted upon his allegiance to the Communist Party. I leave aside his final decades, but in the decade of World War I, he clearly began to use the vocabulary of Marxist diagnosis and critique: labor exploitation, the fundamental positions of proletariat and capital, class struggle, state control of the means of production, imperialism as capitalist expansion, etc. Famously, he offered in his 1915 essay "The African Roots of War" an analysis of World War I that fundamentally appealed not to European civilizational hubris or mere political predation as the causal engine but to capitalist processes of interimperial competition for material access to and labor exploitation in African nations. Du Bois also hoped, even against repeated frustration, that socialist organizations would accept blacks so that more empowered and inclusive social movements would develop. As his own writings during that period show and as the work of Cedric Robinson clarifies, Du Bois united elements of his growing black radicalism (specially energized during the Niagara movement just after the 1903 publication of *Souls*) with attractive critical tools from Marxism.[24] Across the interwar years, Du Bois became set upon the notion that political economy must be united with his long-standing race analytic and this integrated outlook brought to bear on the analysis of white supremacy and the means for its abolition. Though not an orthodox Marxist, Du Bois had become a kind of black Marxist or perhaps a semi-Marxist black radical. This development played a significant role in Du Bois generating an early concept of coloniality. Even prior to his two most obviously relevant texts, *Black Reconstruction* (1935) and *Color and Democracy* (1946), traces of a sense of coloniality can be found as early on in his corpus as *The Negro* (1915), *Darkwater* (1920), and *The Gift of Black Folk* (1924). In what follows, I focus on *The Negro* because it is such an early text in Du Bois's corpus, and in the next section I will argue that Du Bois's understanding of decoloniality receives creative elaboration some years before *Black Reconstruction*, namely in the often-overlooked or underappreciated *Dark Princess* (1928).

In *The Negro* (1915), Du Bois already reveals a fairly consistent use of a political economy, the implementation of which connects elements of race and class, culture and economy, and the domestic and the global in a relatively comprehensive way. On his account, the plight of blacks in the modern world involves two major world-historical developments, international slavery and colonialism, and these are explicitly depicted as stages of a globalizing economy: "The Negro slave trade was the first step in modern world commerce, followed by the modern theory of colonial expansion."[25] Du Bois also suggests that the moral discourse that helped end the first stage of the globalizing economy, namely abolitionism, gained some efficacy due to slaves becoming less crucial to the evolving economy, implying that ideological legitimation weakens as the relevant economic necessity lessens: "When the Americas had enough black laborers for their immediate demand, the moral action of the eighteenth century had a chance to make its faint voice heard" (233).

Du Bois goes on to contend that from roughly the middle of the nineteenth century and in response to the exploitation that characterized the Industrial Revolution, "the modern working class," a predominantly white coalition, emerged to collectively empower white workers to limit suppression and gain greater access to industry's profits (234–35). Roughly concurrently, blacks were striving to gain a foothold after having recently been liberated from enslavement in the Caribbean, the Americas, and regions of Africa. In principle, newly emancipated black laborers could join their white counterparts in the modern working class, but as we know deep and pervasive racist attitudes prevented inclusion and ultimately divided the working class. But interestingly Du Bois does not dwell on this obvious point. Instead, revealing political economic thinking, he asserts a structural tendency relation, specifically that the new type of colonialism of the nineteenth and twentieth centuries created conditions that systematically encouraged white laborers to mitigate their disenfranchisement and disempowerment by joining the white industrial elite in exploiting their black counterparts. As he puts it: "The new colonial theory transferred the reign of commercial privilege and extraordinary profit from the exploitation of the European working class to the exploitation of backward races under the political domination of Europe. For the purpose of carrying out this idea the European and white American working class was practically invited to share in this new exploitation" (245). Du Bois then rounds out his discussion by drawing attention, in the midst of World War I itself, to the European colonial focus on Africa and how the ensuing interimperial rivalry over the exploitation of Africans became a trigger for World War I.

Importantly, the foregoing claims—racial slavery and racial colonialism as two stages of a globalizing capitalist economy, the formation of the modern working class through deep racial division in labor and a system of racial colonialism, and the significant role played by racial global capitalism in European interimperial rivalry and warfare—together form a collative template and critical lens that would endure in Du Bois's thinking through the coming decades. Many regard his *Black Reconstruction*, published twenty years later, to be one of his most conceptually mature expressions of a political economy united with a race analytic and specifically a kind of a "black Marxism." I do not doubt this. But consider that one of the basic framing conceptions of this book is an elaboration upon what he had already expounded in *The Negro*. We see this in his own introduction of the guiding perspective of *Black Reconstruction:*

> The plight of the white working class throughout the world today is directly traceable to Negro slavery in America, on which modern commerce and industry was founded, and which persisted to threaten free labor until it was partially overthrown in 1863. The resulting color caste founded and retained by capitalism was adopted, forwarded and approved by white labor, and resulted in subordination of colored labor to white profits the world over. Thus the majority of the world's laborers, by the insistence of white labor, became the basis of a system of industry which ruined democracy and showed its perfect fruit in World War and Depression. And this book seeks to tell that story.[26]

Clearly, Du Bois's account lacks many details that political economists would want to see, and it is not exactly world-systems theory, which reaps the benefits of late twentieth-century theoretical development and hindsight. For example, there is an implicit sense but not a committed thematization of the world as a whole as the primary unit of analysis, and relatedly the same can be said of Du Bois on the transnational system by which "core" nations exploit "peripheral" nations (to which worlds-systems analysts would add semi-peripheral nations). At best, Du Bois is an early kind of dependency theorist, something that world-systems theory, by its own lights, grew out of and beyond. In addition, Du Bois's story of colonial globalization and the economic unification of the world starts with transatlantic slavery rather than conquest of the Americas, which for Quijano begins the narrative one stage too late. Indeed, there is a general absence of consideration of the Americas as a whole: the United States, the Caribbean, the Atlantic, Europe, and Africa are highly visible in Du Bois's geopolitical consciousness, with the rest of the Americas (including the indigenous of North America) largely a kind of afterthought or mere background.

Nonetheless, Du Bois exhibits here a clear and powerful use of a political economy, which is globally integrative and globally historicized, that adds depth and a critical edge to Du Bois's long-standing race analytic. In addition, there does not appear to be anything in his account that would stand against empirical correction so that his political economy could be modified to begin with colonial subjection of the Americas. Moreover, since his concern with these worldly developments is as much ethical as it is political and economic, it seems fairly easy to imagine him developing a sense of ethical solidarity with Latin Americans and Latino/as in the way that later generations of African American thinkers and activists have. So, as it happens, decolonial theory's central notion of coloniality relies heavily on Quijano's modification of world-systems theory, but there is in principle no reason why there could not currently be alternative bases for the concept or why sufficiently related frameworks could not count as legitimate predecessors to Quijano's proposed basis. Indeed, Du Bois's account seems like an early version of dependency theory, and it is dependency theory that helped to generate world-systems theory in the first place.

Thus, in light of such an early work as *The Negro* (1915), Du Bois's prophecy about the centrality of the color line in the twentieth century was by World War I no longer a mere collation of many types of anticipated racism. Du Bois produced a compelling template of an intersectional analysis of race and class that is also part of the story of global modernity and global colonialism, the basic constituents of the concept of coloniality.[27] It also makes blacks as causal actor central to modern history because slavery and colonialism were central to the political economy of the modern globalizing world. Relatedly, as he considered black agency and resistance in this context, he posited the need for a matching and thus globalizing racial- and class-consciousness. He claimed in *The Negro*: "The Pan-African movement when it comes will not, however, be merely a narrow racial propaganda. Already the more far-seeing Negroes sense the coming unities: a unity of the working classes everywhere, a unity of the colored races, a new unity of men. . . . Most men in this world are colored. A belief in humanity means a belief in colored men" (241–42).

Earlier I mentioned that decolonial theory tends to strongly integrate radical political economy with a delinking political epistemology. *The*

Negro, then, can also be understood as serving the relevant epistemic aim, specifically by providing a refutation of Hegel's claim that Africa has no history. Du Bois lays out, with what he took to be the best history of his day, a multifaceted portrayal of the origin and precolonial cultures of Africans as well as the modern collective life, struggles, achievements, and centrality of Africans and their diaspora. The book attempts in some sense to normalize black collective life in the global story of civilizations in order to pave the way for taking blacks as human beings seriously. He strives to let an accurate historical record of black life, at many points posed with a kind of documentarian neutrality and matter-of-factness, to clarify there is no inferiority in Africans and their diaspora, only the distortions of colonially imposed practices of dehumanization. Later, in *The Gift of Black Folk* (1924), Du Bois ups the ante, as it were, and argues in a sustained fashion that given America's self-professed identity as a democracy, the historical facts of slavery and Jim Crow radically weakens the nation's identity claim and that black democratic resistance to such dehumanization makes black agency central to the nation's ethical aspiration to be a genuine democracy. Thus by virtue of blacks being both a central economic and ethical actor in modernity, their epistemic vantage point is crucial for engaging with the problems of the day.

A good deal more might be said of Du Bois's pioneering efforts as a decolonial democrat, especially with a sustained treatment of *Darkwater* and *Black Reconstruction*, but the foregoing clarifies how some of his early work, like *The Negro* (1915), offered some of the earliest contributions to the concept of coloniality and other commitments of decolonial theory. As it happens, he did not only advance what would turn out to be familiar central features of decolonial thought; he experimented with his political theory in other ways that are difficult to characterize but important for political epistemology and activism.

Du Bois's South-South Decoloniality: Afro-Asian Allegory and Gandhian Experiments

I turn now to Du Bois's Afro-Asian decolonial perspective and within it his working out of ideas that mingled elements of the Afro-Modern, Marxist, and Gandhian traditions. I focus in particular on his romance novel *Dark Princess* (1928) and on his *Crisis* articles about black and Indian freedom struggles. I begin with some preliminary remarks on the very idea of black Marxism-Gandhism. I then lay out what I take to be a plausible interpretation of the narrative of *Dark Princess,* one that centralizes the symbolic potency of romantic union and characterizes the romantic bond as a unity developed dialectically between a prophet and a seer, as it were. These considerations help to clarify Du Bois's evolving hybridity in ways that his nonfiction does not. I conclude with a fuller discussion of Du Bois's black Marxism-Gandhism.

Du Bois's anti-Eurocentrism, again a key component of decolonial theory, is far more complex and interesting than many have noted. He synthesizes frameworks that not only take up the epistemic vantage point of the black "underside of modernity," helping to constitute a decolonial tradition, but also the epistemic perspective of modern Asian traditions, taking the decolonial tradition in an unusual direction, that of South-South, even East-South, dialogue.

Black Marxism-Gandhism: The Very Idea

As we shall see, *Dark Princess* is a particularly dense site of Afro-Asian and specifically black Marxist–Gandhian thinking. Such thinking proceeds as an exploratory and experimental synthesis. Importantly, it does not seem that Du Bois had in the novel or in related essays a very detailed or definitive position on Gandhism as political theory. Beyond the novel itself, at most, there are short essays scattered across the years about the rightness and efficacy of satyagraha, ethical nonviolent resistance. Although such essays are not trivial, Gandhism is much wider than satyagraha-as-strategy. Gandhi carefully embedded satyagraha in an ethico-spiritual worldview.[28] Thus, what we find in the novel is a window onto a midcareer stage of experimentation with Gandhian (and Marxist) concepts, ideas that are provocatively raised but left largely undeveloped in subsequent writings. Current scholars have the benefit of a rich commentarial tradition on Gandhi and a host of scholarly translations and commentaries on ideas and texts of the Vedic tradition in which Gandhi was steeped and which he hybridized in complex ways. Very little of this was available to Du Bois.

In the foregoing sections, I have described how elements of the political economic thinking of Marxism enhanced Du Bois's race analytic. As we have seen, Du Bois endorsed an early kind of dependency theory as a part of his decolonial theory. So Marxism offered Du Bois a *diagnostic framework* for analyzing local and global race. But it seemed to offer far less in the areas of ethics, spirituality, and praxis, which is to say, the normative and constructive elements for the enhancement of his race analytic. Here the tentative Gandhian explorations are more relevant. Although much can be said about how to understand Du Bois's preliminary efforts at synthesizing elements of Marxist diagnostics and Gandhian ethico-spiritual praxis with the black radical tradition, I focus very briefly on three elements before I turn to the novel's narrative. I wish here simply to say enough to make the very notion of Du Boisian exploration of Gandhi's ideas even minimally plausible.

First, from the interwar years onward, Du Bois seemed to espouse a Vedic-resonant immanentist worldview. Famously, in the *Upanishads*, the Vedic tradition asserts both that Brahman, the ground of being, metaphysically encompasses all reality and that Atman, the deep soul, which underlies the self, is one and the same as Brahman. This offers a broadly pantheistic account of the world that differs conspicuously from the conventional Christian worldview according to which God is distinctly not one with creation and not one with a pervasive soul that manifests in the human self.[29] As far as I can tell, Du Bois was not a black Vedic thinker in this precise sense. Nevertheless, he seemed to lean in this general direction and away from the standard metaphysics of the black church. His was at least a Vedic-resonant view. For example, at the conclusion of his book *Darkwater,* Du Bois offers a poem, "A Hymn to the Peoples," in which he beseeches a "World-Spirit," a "Human God," to make "Humanity divine."[30] Clearly, his invocation of such a permeating divinity places Du Bois in the general camp of pantheism or panentheism. And in the novel *Dark Princess,* Du Bois, using the mouthpiece of the character Kautilya, speaks of a spark of divinity in human beings that is continually reincarnated and claims, "We are eternal because we are God."[31] As we will see later, Du Bois often uses the character Kautilya to present his more considered views.

Second, extending his work in *Souls,* Du Bois conceptualized a Douglas-Gandhian ethico-political middle way between accommodationism (of the kind attributed to Booker T. Washington) and insurrectionism (of the kind ascribed to Nat Turner and John Brown). In *Souls,* Du Bois argued that Frederick Douglass's project of moral suasion and legal public protest for equality was the right normative path for black Americans by virtue of its moral rightness and causal efficacy. A central feature of its moral rightness was its combination of nonviolence and its maintenance of self-respect. With his Gandhian explorations, Du Bois adds the concept of a deeper kind of freedom than mere political liberty as the ultimate goal of freedom struggles. Gandhi extended the classic Vedic concept of moksha, or ethico-spiritual liberation, as the defining feature of the pursuit of Indian independence from England. Specifically, he contended that self-rule, or swaraj, has both an inner and outer face, both an inner ethical endeavor and an outer civic project, that have to be seamlessly interwoven as the pursuit of moksha.[32] Du Bois did not formally espouse the classic Vedic idea of moksha. But, as *Dark Princess* makes clear, he insisted upon the achievement of a deeper utopic freedom that is reminiscent of moksha, namely what he called "Divine Anarchy" or "anarchy of the spirit." This will be explained later, when the novel's narrative is discussed.

Third, by considering satyagraha as political praxis, Du Bois enriched his thinking in a couple ways. He began to play with the idea of systematic, ethically configured lawbreaking as a mode of moral suasion, a mode that radicalized what he took to be the Douglassian project. In addition, this would offer a praxis extension of his earlier notion in *The Gift of Black Folk* that blacks were both the focal point of the great ethical contradiction of America-as-democracy and the great ethical actor in the making of America into a true democracy. Specifically, if thousands of black satyagrahi crossed legal lines in the right way, the moral contradiction of antiblack racism in America would be driven into the hearts of white Americans and eventually move them affectively and ethically into humane and egalitarian ways of thinking and feeling. As he tells the story in *Dark Princess,* a utopic level of success in such black swaraj, as it were, would result in Divine Anarchy.

The Narrative: The Dialectics of Revelation

Numerous topics addressed in Du Bois's primary organ of propaganda, the *Crisis,* find stylized expression in the novel—workaday subordination, lynching, mulattos, women's status, white unions, black nationalism, the Bolshevik revolution, Indian anticolonialism, and so on. What makes the narrative distinctive is how it is fundamentally configured by a romance. This might be an unusual literary form for someone often regarded as a "race man." And the partners in the romance, a black man and an Asian woman, make an unusual couple in the United States, then as now. Yet in spite of the many aspects of the novel that have received commentary and critique, there seems to be relatively little elaboration on the romance itself as central to Du Bois's political message. Most of the commentarial work focuses on the identities—gender, race, nation—of the lovers, which is clearly important. But to grasp fully the political message of the novel, we need to concentrate attention also on Du Bois's depiction of the romance itself, and the child born of it, as a particularly potent exemplification of liberation, what he calls Divine Anarchy, and to regard Du Bois as proffering this special union as a symbol for transformative race, gender, and class solidarity. And the key to understanding the romance is to regard it as an unfolding revelatory dialectic between the black male protagonist as a kind of prophet of black cultural traditions and the female protagonist as a kind of seer of Indian cultural traditions. I think Du Bois's own considered view is the overall union or resolution of this dialectic. Most commentators have not made much of this revelatory dialectic and its import for the romance and the romance as fecund symbol, and some have misunderstood Du Bois as presenting only the black male protagonist's viewpoints as his own, viewpoints that tend to favor violence and are often caught up in a kind of spiritual malaise. But I think better sense of the novel and Du Bois's many surrounding essays can be made by supposing Du Bois to be presenting the resolution or synthesis of the lovers' dialectic as his own position. As it turns out, the dialectic has many features that reveal Du Bois's experimentation with a kind of black Marxism–Gandhism.

Many objections have been raised against this novel: tiresome prose, aesthetic discordance, problematic gendered figurations, and outmoded Orientalist tropes.[33] I largely agree with these criticisms. There is nevertheless much political theory that can be done with this text. Here I join the pioneering efforts of Bill Mullen. *Dark Princess,* with all its shortcomings, is nevertheless one of the most significant literary moments in a rich but largely undertheorized history of Afro-Asian internationalism, including what Mullen calls Afro-Orientalism.[34] Moreover, its expression of an emerging Marxism would seem to make the novel an unusual instance of proletarian literature. And if for no other reason, the novel deserves some attention because Du Bois explicitly claimed twelve years after its publication, specifically in his important autobiography *Dusk of Dawn,* that it was his "favorite book."[35]

The story opens with the main character, Matthew Towns, quietly raging aboard a ship bound for Europe.[36] He has exiled himself from America after racism has ended his ability to graduate from medical school. Later, at a Berlin café, his lonely seething dissipates before the dark loveliness of a South Asian woman, the Princess Kautilya of Bwodpur: "Many, many times in after years he tried to catch and rebuild that first wildly beautiful phantasy which the girl's face stirred in him. He knew well that no human being could be quite as beautiful as she looked to him then. . . . Never after that first glance was he or the world quite the same" (8).

They begin a conversation that leads to his disclosure of the conditions under which he has exiled himself. And he finds a sympathetic ear, for she has recently returned from Moscow and acquired an interest in the revolutionary events of her day, including the Bolshevik revolution and the internationalization of the "Negro question." In the course of their exchange, he wins enough of her trust to be invited to a clandestine meeting of an anti-imperialist conspiracy, the "Great Council of the Darker Races of the World." The members include, in addition to Kautilya, one Japanese, two Indians, two Chinese, two Egyptians, and one Arab (262). Recognizing that her largely pan-Asian group represents "the darker world except the darkest," she invites Matthew's participation on behalf of Africa and black Americans. But except Kautilya and, interestingly, the Chinese, the members doubt the ability of blacks to contribute to their cause, or to their own civilizational advancement for that matter. But Kautilya invokes the "black and curly-haired Lord Buddha" to insist upon some sort of shared ancestry and ethical connection with Matthew and the African diaspora.

Merging a classic figure of Asian spirituality with a conventional mark of African descent, this is one of several Afro-Asian unities that emerges in the story, and it anticipates the idea of Divine Anarchy that appears later in the novel. After asserting this distant blood connection with Matthew, Kautilya appeals to the political logic of an alliance between Pan-Asia and Pan-Africa for resisting white imperialism. In doing so, she produces another Afro-Asian unity. But in spite of her efforts, most of the Dark Council remains doubtful of black contribution to global emancipation. Unlike the racism to which Matthew is accustomed, theirs is a partial inversion of classic white supremacy, namely a brown-yellow supremacy that holds whites in contempt and apparently blacks too.[37] Moreover, they exhibit a general disdain of working classes everywhere. So their version of racial supremacy is a brown-yellow bourgeois elitism. And with insult after insult, Matthew's mounting frustration finally reaches the breaking point, and he uncontrollably erupts in a Song of Emancipation:

> *Go down Moses!*
> *Way down into the Egyptland.*
> *Tell old Pharaoh*
> *To let my people go!* (26)

After such an outburst, the council might think Matthew peculiar, but in fact the Song of Emancipation meets with approval. And it manages to reorient the discussion more favorably, even if for a brief moment, toward the ignored laboring masses, including black Americans (25–27). More importantly, the Song of Emancipation has a quickening effect on the princess, and it establishes one of the most significant events in the early half of the novel. It marks the moment at which Kautilya begins to fall in love with Matthew, though he will not learn of her love until some years and many tribulations later. Moreover, and no less important, it simultaneously marks the onset of revelation for the princess. The "doors of a world" are sprung open before her, and a liberatory "madness" begins to alter her being and to define the nature of their love. This vision and this madness will mature as their relationship develops. The chaos, delirium, and creative surge of their boundary-crossing union forms a microcosm, and offers a foretaste, of utopic liberation, what they call "Divine Anarchy." Appropriately, Kautilya later calls Matthew's words "prophecy" and describes her experience with spiritual grandeur (225): "It came to me like a great flash of new light, and *you, the son of slaves, were its wonderful revelation.* I determined to go to America, to study and see. I began to feel that my dream of the world based on the domination of an ancient royal race and blood might not be all right, but that as Lord Buddha said and *as we do not yet understand,* humanity itself was royal" (248, italics mine).

In fact, earlier, she had a premonition of this life-changing event when her prophet defended her from a racist white American at the Berlin cafe.[38] Without fully understanding its significance at the time, she mused: "It had never happened before that a stranger of my own color should offer me protection in Europe. I had a curious sense of some *great inner meaning to your act—some world movement.* It seemed almost that *the Powers of*

Heaven had bent to give me the knowledge which I was groping for; and so I invited you, that I might know more" (17, italics mine).

Informing the backdrop is Kautilya's travels to Russia. She visited presumably during one of the several Congresses of the Third Communist International, which began in 1919 and extended through and beyond the decade of the Harlem Renaissance. So she would be familiar with Lenin's historic 1920 "Theses on the National and Colonial Questions."[39] In fact, she may have witnessed Lenin's exchange with her countryman M. N. Roy over the draft of the Theses, which led to revisions more accommodating to revolutionary national liberation struggles.[40] But real exposure to the Negro Question probably first came from Claude McKay's 1922 "Report on the Negro Question" before the audience of the Comintern, and later from the Comintern's issuance of the Black Nation Thesis, which accorded black America the status of a nation and, hence, the right to self-determination.[41] So, by the time Kautilya meets Matthew, she has been specially attuned to revolutionary possibilities, and of course her leading of the Dark Council is an attempt to realize some of them. But, significantly, none of the debates or documents of the Comintern were revelation; none produced the impact of the Song of Emancipation. So, in spite of the misgivings of her comrades, the princess, now partially transformed, entrusts Matthew with a mission. He is asked to investigate and report on the revolutionary potential of black Americans.

Later that evening, some disgruntled members of the Dark Council, led by the Japanese baron, visit Matthew at his hotel room and attempt to dissuade him from joining their efforts. When his refusal makes a group assault on him imminent, Kautilya suddenly appears and with regal authority stays the hand of the Dark Council. Matthew is the more resolved to complete his mission. But, as we shall see, the faith of Kautilya's prophet will degenerate in her absence; the tribulations of racial caste will prove too much.

This near altercation and the earlier incident in the café reveal the beginnings of a pattern. Throughout the novel, Matthew is beset by the temptation to respond violently to oppression and by what seems to be a related spiritual fatigue. Correspondingly, Kautilya is a rejuvenating force and repeatedly leads Matthew away from such temptations and toward nonviolent alternatives. This pair of patterns comprises a large part of what might be described as a dialectical romance, and its significance will be discussed shortly.

After returning to America, Matthew investigates a Garvey-like Miguel Perigua only to discover that he is too undisciplined and his men too disorganized for the group to be an effective force. Although he maintains infrequent contact with Perigua, Matthew turns his attention to broadening his knowledge of antiblack oppression and therein the possible sources of subversion of the system. To encounter a wide array of people and places, he enlists as a Pullman porter and thereby intensifies his subjection to Jim Crow life. He is also deeply lonely since he has been separated from his love, and his frustration mounts as the months go by without any reply from Kautilya.

Events accelerate when he is caught up in a conspiracy to blow up KKK members on a train, which leads to his being sentenced to prison. Eventually, he is released from prison through the machinations of aspiring local politicians Sammy Scott and Sara Andrews.[42] As the story unfolds, Matthew loses his moral bearings and eventually joins "the political machine" and even marries Sara out of political aspirations. But on the night that he is to be nominated to Congress, a night on which all of the city's political players are present at his and Sara's home, salvation comes to the battered soul of the prophet. The president of the box-cutter union wishes to meet Matthew during the high-society dinner, and that leader turns out to be none other than the Princess of Bwodpur. Upon realizing her identity, past epiphanies suddenly flood his consciousness. They are discovered locked in embrace. And in a whirl, the party is ruined, the nomination is lost, and Sara has a nervous breakdown.

The final chapter of the novel begins with Matthew and Kautilya's love affair. In what could have been a whole chapter devoted to the showing of her life, Du Bois instead has Kautilya merely tell her life story. Given the importance of the romance as the configuring literary vehicle, this failure in character development is one of the serious aesthetic flaws in the text. At Matthew's behest, she unveils her past under the exotic pretext of a Scheherazade telling 1001 Arabian tales. She traces her story from court life in her northeast Indian kingdom to her involvement with the Dark Council, where she was transformed by Matthew's Song of Emancipation, and finally to her "proletarianization" as a box-cutter union organizer. Throughout these 1001 tales, the lovers are entirely engrossed in each other, their immediate world falling away into a dreamy haze, and their shared vision resonating emotionally and erotically. Eventually, Kautilya feels the call of duty pulling her back to her kingdom of Bwodpur. We learn from their exchange that there is no royal male to assume the throne in accord with the conventions of the kingdom and that British colonizers may exploit the situation to take control of Bwodpur. So she must return to India to seek a mate and thwart a British takeover. So after finally finding truest love, circumstances force them to make the profound sacrifice of separation.

Matthew begins grueling labor as a construction worker, excavating the earth to build a subway system. And Kautilya stops over in Virginia, at Matthew's mother's home, en route to India. Between long days of digging, he writes Kautilya and waxes philosophical. In their exchanges, we learn that Matthew has become obsessed with the drudgery of his work, insisting that "Work is God." Kautilya, however, repeatedly reminds him that as the Buddha says, "Love is God, and Work is his Prophet" (279).[43] In connection with this theme, their liberatory vision, nurtured during their "1001 nights" together, continues to develop, though now in fits and starts as Matthew struggles with his spiritual fatigue and labor alienation. In yet another Afro-Asian unity, one involving religious hybridity, Kautilya reads Christian scriptures with Matthew's mother, whom Kautilya deifies as the Hindu goddess Kali, the Black One, Wife of Siva. In the course of sharing devotionals, Kautilya exalts in a vision of the future, a partially formed conception of what Matthew will later call "Divine Anarchy" (283).

After receiving word of this, Matthew replies, "But always, everywhere, massed and concentrated power is necessary to accomplish anything worth while doing in this muddled world, hoping for divine Anarchy in some faraway heaven" (283). And suffering from the burden of his work and a spiritual malaise, he fixates on power and oligarchy and begins once again to valorize violence. He declares that "only great strokes of force—clubs, guns, dynamite in the hands of fanatics—that only such Revolution can bring the Day" and calls for "world-tyranny which will impose by brute force a new heaven on this old and rotten earth" (284–85). In her rejoinder, Kautilya affirms Matthew's idea of Divine Anarchy but dwells upon another means to it. She introduces the idea of a global "Talented Tenth," marking a significant advance in the visionary madness initiated by the Song of Emancipation: "And, oh, my Matthew, your oligarchy as you conceive it is not the antithesis of democracy—it is democracy, if only the selection of the oligarchs is just and true. Birth is the method of blind fools. Wealth is the gambler's method. Only Talent served from the great Reservoir of All Men of All Races, of All Classes, of All Ages, of Both Sexes—this is real Aristocracy, real Democracy—the only path to that great and final Freedom which you so well call Divine Anarchy" (285).

And she adds that even though Asia and Africa comprise the "real world," global justice can only be achieved if a united Afro-Asia works within and out of America, the primary site of power in the world. In particular, the effects rendered by such an alliance will be magnified if they radiate out from an enlarged "Black Belt," a geopolitical arc that stretches out from the American South down to the Caribbean and across to Africa and India.[44]

Finally, the protracted dialectic is brought back to the relationship itself. When Matthew and Sara finally divorce, Kautilya summons Matthew to Virginia, to his mother's home. Completely unknown to him is the gift and wonder that awaits him, their child, "a palpitating bubble of gold." And in a suddenly transfigured setting, Matthew and Kautilya are finally wedded. But the pageantry quickly takes on much larger proportions as the newlywed parents oversee the consecration of their child. In a final Afro-Asian unity, representatives of both of the child's lineages partake in the ceremony. Matthew's mother, deified as Kali, sanctifies the child as a black preacher presides. After the family finishes singing spirituals, an Asian procession of Hindu, Muslim, and Buddhist holy men emerges to complement the consecration. Receiving the royal child from his grandmother, the Brahmin places a jeweled turban on the child's head and passes the child to his mother to finalize the coronation of the infant messiah.

> She raised her son toward heaven and cried:
>
> "Brahma, Vishnu, and Siva! Lords of Sky and Light and Love! Receive from me, daughter of my fathers back to the hundredth name, his Majesty, Madhu Chandragupta Singh, by the will of God, Maharajah of Bwodpur and Maharajahdhirajah of Sindrabad."
>
> Then from the forest, with faint and silver applause of trumpets:
>
> "King of the Snows of Gaurinsankar!"
>
> "Protector of Ganga the Holy!"
>
> "Incarnate Son of the Buddha!"
>
> "Grand Mughal of Utter India!"
>
> "Messenger and Messiah to all the Darker Worlds!" (311)

From his mother's line, the child acquires the royal appellations of "King," "Protector," "Incarnate Son," and "Grand Mughal." Indeed, part of his full name, "Chandragupta," is derived from the legendary empire-builder of ancient India, Chandragupta Maurya. Subsequent Indian rulers were sometimes given that same name, so Matthew and Kautilya's child is to be the most recent installment in the grand succession, spiritually speaking. But his first name, Madhu, which means Matthew, is his father's. This is the man who gave new meaning to royalty and emancipation, who helped a princess make a home of the real world, the world of the global proletariat. A child of slavery and royalty, and Africa and Asia; a child of equal partners and transformed laborers—Madhu is raised before all as the Dark Messiah, the future of race and the great unifier of humankind. Needless to say, this depiction differs dramatically from that of the golden child "above the Veil" memorialized in *The Souls of Black Folk.*[45] There, the child, having passed into death, would not know the pain of the color line; here, the child having passed into life will someday tear the veil asunder. Matthew and Kautilya, their romance defined by their great and evolving revelation, now have before them its embodiment. Symbolically, the child is a manifestation of Divine Anarchy, but he is so precisely by virtue of being an Afro-Asian unity.

The Union

> Only Talent served from the great Reservoir of All Men of All Races, of All Classes, of All Ages, of Both Sexes—this is real Aristocracy, real Democracy—the only path to that great and final Freedom which you so well call Divine Anarchy.

As noted, Kautilya's utterance of these words marks a special advance in her vision of the future.[46] To understand the nature of this Divine Anarchy, we might derive insight by considering the proposed means for this end. Du Bois maintains here that at least with respect to concrete strategy, we must amass capable leaders and workers from an expansively inclusive cross-section of humanity, something like a global Talented Tenth. But why precisely should such a massive mixed array of talent inaugurate utopia? Presumably, such an army of talent will have both the ability to transform the exiting order and the social diversity to effect such transformation in every region of which the members are representatives. And the social diversity—and, hence, range of perspectives and experiences—is likely to be a part of their collective ability. This suggests that Du Bois could have adequately conveyed his conception of Divine Anarchy without the literary vehicle of a romance. All that would have been needed is the conspiratorial theme. The romance might have been merely a sidelight to a centered focus on the actions of the Dark Council to raise up a global Talented Tenth army.[47] But this, of course, is not *Dark Princess*. The novel, as its subtitle explicitly states, is a romance. It is not conspiratorial work, but love, that is divine—or so the dark Buddha might be invoked to say. Although a document is produced toward the end of the story, bearing to the white world an ultimatum demanding racial equality by 1952, it is overshadowed by the wedding of Matthew and Kautilya, and the glorious celebration of the golden "Messenger and Messiah to all the Darker Worlds." Its open-ended conclusion, then, is not preparation for mass or military action but the consecration of a messianic child. And so it must be emphasized that what a romance delivers is an evocative intimacy, a specially constructed unity. I submit then that for the purposes of the novel, the global array of talent that forms the path to Divine Anarchy is significant not so much for its purported efficacy, a matter that Du Bois takes up in his nonfictional writings, but for the special character of the unity it *exemplifies*. We need then to consider the sorts of unities salient in the novel. The central one is obviously that of Matthew and Kautilya.

In the literature on romantic love, a common theme is the nature of the romantic union, both as an intersubjective fact and as it is perceived or felt by the individual lovers. It seems uncontroversial to claim that romantic love crucially involves a kind of we-formation or shared identity. This is why people with a strongly individualist sense of autonomy experience some aspects of this union as a form of bondage. In any case, the formation of a shared identity seems always to be the basis of individual transformation in real and literary romances. This is sometimes cast in terms of love having a creative will. As we have seen, Matthew and Kautilya's love transforms their lives permanently, creating a liberatory yearning and vision, and ultimately a Child of Emancipation. But what makes the we-formation and ensuing potential for transformation distinctly romantic, as opposed to familial or friendship-configured, is a special sort of perception run through desire: a sense of beauty that is erotically modulated. There is, for example, the common tendency to exaggerate the other's qualities aesthetically and to not only delight in such exaggeration but feel sensually charged and sometimes desirous in profoundly somatic ways.[48] The delirium and ecstasy enable the lovers to *feel* what is not yet. Their earlier hope, a mere anticipation of the future, is now laced with urgent longing. And no small part of this urgency is the foretaste of lawlessness or release in Divine Anarchy. Specifically, their interracial union, felt precisely as such, is boundary-crossing or law-suspending both erotically and politically. It is not simply that their union is affectively unruly or chaotic. It is also normatively or ideologically tumultuous and expansive. So when, finally, the call of duty separates them, Matthew deifies their interembodiment: "The magnificent fact of our love remains, whatever its basis or accident. It rises from the ecstasy of our bodies to the communion of saints, the resurrection of the spirit, and the exquisite crucifixion of God. It is the greatest thing in our world" (259–60). Du Bois exploits, therefore, the phenomenological structure of erotic love as a conduit through which to convey the imagined experience of utopic liberation.

In sum, these reflections lend support to my characterization of the narrative in which I have suggested that the romance exemplifies the vision of Divine Anarchy, that the messianic child, precisely as a product of the romantic union, exemplifies more intensively that same vision, and finally that the global Talented Tenth is the enlargement of the couple and of the child.

Black Marxism–Gandhism Expanded

Written in the 1920s, *Dark Princess* reveals the impact of three important developments during the Harlem Renaissance that in different ways brought together the Negro Question and the Oriental Question: the notoriety of Lothrop Stoddard's global white supremacism, the black populist acclaim of Gandhi, and the expansion of black Marxism inspired by the Comintern. As Matthew Guterl has noted: "Stoddard, Nordicism, and white world supremacy had become, by the 1920s, thoroughly intertwined with the New Negro Movement, changing the nature of race in the process. Local libraries, newspapers, and political organizations began scrutinizing Stoddard's writings, clipping articles from the daily papers, and cheering whenever a member of 'the race' struck down in print the man many African Americans equated with the white leviathan himself."[49] It is in this context that Du Bois's own reputation, then beginning to wane, received some new vitality. He publicly debated Stoddard on a number of occasions and was widely regarded to have "defended the race" well.[50] Moreover, in his racist *locus classicus,* Stoddard singles out Du Bois to his white-supremacist brethren, which of course only consolidated Du Bois's status as a worthy race man. After a fearful discussion of the Japanese defeat of Russia, the rise of Pan-Asianism, and Europe's self-immolation during World War I, Stoddard cites a passage from Du Bois's acclaimed article "The African Roots of War" to alert readers of an impending colored revolt: "The Afro-American author, W. E. Burghardt Du Bois, wrote of the colored world: 'These nations and races, composing as they do a vast majority of humanity, are going to endure this treatment just as long as they must and not a moment longer. Then they are going to fight, and the War of the Color Line will outdo in savage inhumanity any war this world has yet seen. For the colored folk have much to remember and they will not forget.'"[51]

This Stoddard–Du Bois pairing, especially around the issue of colored revolt and white horror of it, was surely part of Du Bois's mental backdrop as he created *Dark Princess.* For example, the Japanese baron of the Dark Council seems to be modeled after Count Okuma, prime minister of Japan from 1914 to 1916, whom Stoddard described as having founded the "Pan-Asiatic Association." And the leadership of the Dark Council seems to be a literary rendition of an actual incipient Indo-Japanese alliance that intrigued and concerned Stoddard enough to remark upon it, and this in conjunction with Count Okuma.[52] But consider as well that one of the recurring and existentially significant themes of the novel is the dilemma of whether violence should be used to end white supremacy—the very possibility to which Stoddard returns repeatedly in his book. During every episode of his spiritual malaise, Matthew hovers over the line of violence. At the seething start of the novel, he actually beats down a racist white American in what he takes to be an act of chivalry on Kautilya's behalf. After being separated from his love, he nearly joins Perigua's attempt to destroy a train filled with KKK members. And throughout the novel, he is constantly faced with the temptation to pursue violence or a ruthless utilitarianism, as in the near assault by members of the Dark Council, and the seductive amoralism of Sammy and Sara. Finally, he flirts again with a violent militancy at the end of the novel when he is separated from Kautilya in what he thinks may be the conclusion of their relationship:

> But always, everywhere, massed and concentrated power is necessary to accomplish anything worth while doing in this muddled world, hop-

> ing for divine Anarchy in some faraway heaven. . . . I am afraid that only great strokes of force—clubs, guns, dynamite in the hands of fanatics—that only such Revolution can bring the Day.
>
> I wish I could see the solution of world misery in a little Virginia cottage with vines and flowers. I wish I could share the surging happiness which you find there; but I cannot, I am too far from there. I am far in miles, and somehow I seem insensibly to grow farther in spirit. (283–84)

This passage foreshadows Du Bois's actual response to the dilemma of violence. For in that "little Virginia cottage with vines and flowers" lies the embodiment of the "one far-off divine event," the "Messiah and Messenger to all the Darker Worlds." As his prophetess declares, "Love is God," and the dilemma of violence, which forms a part of the dialectics of revelation, finds its resolution in peaceful dark unities. But this resolution has a racio-national specificity, and it reveals the second important development in the black 1920s alluded to earlier. The wife and seer, Kautilya, seems to represent the Gandhian response to the white-supremacist nightmare. In the passage cited earlier, Stoddard wrongly depicts Du Bois as advocating Pan-Colored violence against white oppressors. Rather, Du Bois merely claims on a descriptive front that colored revolt is likely to occur if racism and colonialism persist, not that it is something to encourage or celebrate. As noted earlier, Du Bois struggled for a middle way between violence against white supremacy and acquiescence before it. He encouraged intrablack and, in *Dark Princess* and thereafter, intracolored coalitions, a global Talented Tenth. And this conception, though generated by independent considerations, was especially fueled by his animated sense of what was developing halfway around the world: the rise of an anticolonial India through the nonviolent philosophy of Mahatma Gandhi.

Sudarshan Kapur has surveyed publications of twelve prominent black American journals from 1919 to 1955 to establish the significance of the recurring theme of Gandhian politics and the Indian struggle for independence (swaraj) in the black liberatory imagination.[53] Black Americans, including Hubert Harrison, Marcus Garvey, W. E. B. Du Bois, and other "New Negro" leaders, felt a strong kinship of color and oppression with their Indian counterparts. But though black activists had written pro-Indian propaganda, and white transcendentalists, like Ralph Waldo Emerson, had referenced Indian spirituality, it was Du Bois who was the first to incorporate broadly Vedic and specifically Gandhian perspectives into the kind of emancipatory vision displayed in *Dark Princess.* And as Arnold Rampersad has pointed out, he was surely helped in his understanding of Indian philosophy and politics by the Indian anticolonialist Lala Lajpat Rai, a colleague of Gandhi's who castigated alike the subjection of blacks in America and Indians in their own land.[54] In fact, Du Bois may have learned through Lajpat Rai of the fourth-century BCE male Indian politician Kautilya and hence come upon a name and a concept for his female protagonist. He may have also learned from Rai the history of the Mauryan Empire with Chandragupta Maurya as its unifier and Kautilya as his advisor.

The politician Kautilya was the author of *Arthashastra,* the classic Indian text on politics and material acquisition (artha). Artha is one of the fundamental human aims postulated by classic Indian philosophy, the others being duty (dharma), sensual pleasure or enjoyment (kama), and liberation or self-realization (moksha). Although much of the *Arthashastra* seems perfectly compatible with what we might call ordinary conceptions of duty, ethics, or dharma, many passages have a distinctly Machiavellian character. The text includes, for example, advice on gaining diplomatic advantage through trickery, assassination, and the secret use of poison, and it praises the "skill for intrigue."[55]

It is conceivable that Du Bois developed the character Sara Andrews, with all her cunning and "skill for intrigue," on the model of the ideal politician delineated by Kautilya. And note too that some of Matthew's tendencies toward a valorization of violence seem to assume a shape that also may have been developed from the Kautilyan model. If this is the case, the *character* Kautilya may have been so named in order to stand as the antithesis of the historical Kautilya by virtue of her embrace of the idea that "Love is God, and Work is his Prophet" and that "Humanity itself is royal." And it must be recalled that early in her life, she did espouse the framework of the historical Kautilya. She was committed to political violence and the aristocracy of royalty until she heard the Song of Emancipation. After the ensuing epiphany, she holds fast to her contradiction of the historical Kautilya, even as her prophet struggles in doing the same. And after telling Matthew that the Dark Council has issued an ultimatum to the white world demanding equality by 1952, she reveals clearly her Gandhian and not Kautilyan stance on the matter by siding with "the path of Peace and Reason, of cooperation among the best and poorest, of gradual emancipation, self-rule, and world-wide abolition of the color line, and of poverty and war" (297). She goes on to say that although most of her comrades prefer force and aspire to make Stoddard's nightmare a reality, she herself is committed to the way of satyagraha: "They may be right—that's the horror, the nightmare of it: they may be right. But surely, surely we may seek other and less costly ways. Force is not the first word. It is the last—perhaps not even that" (297). And this is the point in the novel where the narrative moves into fanfare and pageantry, leaving the reader to muse upon the peculiar import of the wedding and the coronation of the infant messiah.

Thus Stoddard was correct in thinking that the white tide was ebbing, but he was wrong to think that Du Bois championed the way of the gun.[56] Quite the contrary, through the character Kautilya, Du Bois rejected militarism and ruthless utilitarianism and revealed instead his commitment to love, alliance, and nonviolent transformative action. And his repudiation cross-cut the white/colored divide: Choosing Gandhian swaraj and satyagraha, he rejects Sammy and Sara's Arthashastran diplomacy and barely tolerates the militant Japanese baron, who is cast in an unflattering light throughout the novel. However, Du Bois has often been misunderstood on this point.[57] Several years after the publication of *Dark Princess,* he wrote an article on the similarly oppressive conditions faced by Indians and blacks. It generated a reply from an Indian educator, N. S. Subba Rao, who condemned what he took to be Du Bois's warmongering.[58] In response, Du Bois defended his position and thereby, I would contend, clarified the final outcome of the romantic and revelatory dialectic of *Dark Princess.*

> It is too true that only two awful paths seem to face the suppressed peoples of today: The path of humiliation, and the path of war. . . . [W] hat I propose is a hearty and even a desperate attempt to find *a third path*—a path that will not necessarily range the forces of the world into "two camps, sullen, suspicious and menacing," but which will aim at inner cohesion and understanding among the colored peoples, and especially organizations designed to meet and solve their pressing economic problems. I believe that by consumers' cooperation and production, a thoughtful and scientific blending of the preachments of Gandhi and Kagawa, we can stop the dependence of colored consumers upon

white exploitation; that we can establish new ideals of mutual respect which shall not be exclusively and continually white ideals.[59]

Let me note here that we have already gone a long way toward illuminating the relevance of the third development of the black 1920s mentioned earlier, namely the rise of black Marxism in America. From *Darkwater* (1920) to *Dusk of Dawn* (1940), Du Bois wrote a good deal about both the special importance and the limitations of Marxist thought for black antiracism and anti-imperialism. After World War II, he had less to say about the limitations. His primary reservations were threefold, and they amount to significant emendations of Marxism. First, he believed that Marxists often underestimate how deeply race divides the world, including the global and the American proletariat. Thus, in *Black Reconstruction* (1935) and elsewhere, Du Bois argued that racial division was *constitutive* of the construction of the American working class after the Civil War and a *configuring principle* of the formation of global industrial imperialism. So even if the emancipation of humanity flows from the emancipation of the proletariat, racist ideology is no mere strategy of division. And this is why Du Bois also asserted that the emancipation of the proletariat follows from the emancipation of the colored world.[60] Correspondingly, the effort to develop global class-consciousness and solidarity ought not to proceed by a transcendent proletarianism. Rather, recalling the earlier remarks about decolonial theory, Du Bois advises that solidarity be rooted in the immanent categories of coloniality.

Second, Du Bois repeatedly contends that many Marxists fail to consider the special features of black subordination, which complicate any automatic application of praxis-oriented Marxist doctrines. Specifically, because blacks are both a visibly distinct numerical minority and seriously disempowered by the racism of both white capitalist and proletariat classes, violent revolutionary action on the part of black Americans would amount to group suicide.[61] Indeed, in a 1943 article, "Doubts Gandhi Plan," Du Bois contended that even the sort of mass nonviolent civil disobedience propounded by Gandhi ought not to be pursued by blacks in the American context.[62] The reasons given are the same as those invoked against violent black revolution. By 1957, however, Du Bois had changed his position and looked hopefully across black protest movements for a black American Gandhi.[63]

Third and finally, Du Bois retained for many decades his pre-Marxist moral opposition to any form of violence.[64] In "The Negro and Social Reconstruction," for example, he writes: "In any real social revolution, every step that saves violence is to the glory of the great end. We should not forget that revolution is not the objective of socialism or communism rightly conceived; the real objective is social justice."[65]

One way of drawing these three emendations of Marxism together, especially the first two, is to see Du Bois as reversing the charge of abstractionism that the Comintern issued against what it called "bourgeois democracy." Consider, for example, the first of Lenin's 1920 agenda-setting "Theses on the National and Colonial Questions:" "An abstract or formal conception of equality in general, and of national equality in particular, is characteristic of the very nature of bourgeois democracy. Under a show of the equality of the human personality in general, bourgeois democracy proclaims the formal equality in law of property owners and proletarians, of exploiters and exploited, thereby deeply deceiving the oppressed classes. . . . [The Communist Party] should not advance abstract and formal principles on the national question, but should undertake first of all a precise analysis of the given environment, historical and above all economic."[66]

Two primary concerns were raised by the Indian communist M. N. Roy and others at the Comintern in the effort to avoid such abstractionism. First, in anticolonial struggles for national liberation, revolutionary nationalists must be distinguished from bourgeois democratic nationalists, even if for strategic ends the former would sometimes have to share political space with the latter. Second, given the semi-feudal economies of large portions of Third World colonies, special attention must be paid to the revolutionary potential of the peasant class, not just their industrial counterparts. Be these as they may, note that typically these colonized nations consist of a populace that numerically overwhelms the class of foreign imperial liaisons. Moreover, the revolutionary nationalists can borrow some of the force or gains of their bourgeois democratic counterparts in the name of national liberation. But all this is simply to say that the standard colonial case over which abstractionism was condemned reveals the black American situation to be anomalous. The specific reasons for this have already been clarified by Du Bois. Again, blacks, a mere tenth or so of the population, were almost completely shut out of avenues of empowerment by not only white capitalists but nearly the whole of the white proletariat, including many white socialists and communists. So just as it would be abstractionist to model colonial insurgency after European proletariat revolution, black American transformation cannot be modeled after colonial insurgency. This is why, as I've discussed above, Du Bois sought a third way, a Douglassian-Gandhian route between acquiescence and violent revolution. That third way was the development of racially segregated economic cooperatives, in addition, of course, to the continuation of political agitation and legal reforms. And, as noted, Du Bois struggled with the question of whether political agitation should include Gandhian collective law-breaking.

The cooperatives project, pushed by Du Bois throughout the 1930s, ultimately failed. But significant for our purposes is the formation of a revised Marxism in the crucible of the black 1920s that contrasted, sometimes pointedly, with the views of important black Marxists of the period. Specifically, we have what seems to be a kind of black Marxism–Gandhism. Here, it is interesting to observe the links and separations between Du Bois, Rai, and Roy. As noted earlier, Du Bois befriended Rai during Rai's exile from India, which he spent mostly in the United States before returning to India and to his death. From their interactions, Du Bois was able to learn a good deal about Indian anticolonialism, and clearly this aided his formulation of *Dark Princess.* As it turned out, Roy also met Rai in the United States. They met during Roy's pre-Marxist days, specifically after Roy failed to acquire arms for the national liberation movement in India. As described in Roy's memoirs, Rai was stridently opposed to Marxism. Rai was a bourgeois democratic nationalist and had no qualms about declaring this fact before socialist and communist audiences. In fact, it was precisely the limitations of his viewpoint that ultimately compelled Roy to seek books by Marx in the New York Public Library.[67] Du Bois, then, was indebted to Rai for an understanding of Indian anticolonialism, and indirectly Roy owed Rai his eventual conversion to Marxism.

Given these relations, consider that Rai and Du Bois were separated by a significant ideological gulf, specifically regarding Marxism, but they converged on their pro-Gandhism. As for Roy, he and Du Bois, though both Marxists of a kind, diverged significantly on the matter of Gandhism. In his historical materialist analysis of the rise of Gandhi's popularity, Roy condemned Gandhi's spiritualized nonviolent philosophy as a distraction to real revolution, which requires, according to Roy, violent mass struggle.[68] And so had he an interest in and an opportunity to assess Du Bois's convictions, Roy may have viewed Du Bois as a black counterpart to Rai and accordingly criticized Du Bois's apparent bourgeois democratic nationalism. As I have argued, however, Du Bois's political philosophy was not nearly so simple. Ironically, Du Bois would have had available to him as a response to Roy the charge of abstractionism. Let me note that I am not defending the legitimacy of Du Bois's view, only suggesting that it attains the more modest epistemic status of plausibility. And I am principally concerned with showing that these ideas have their provenance in Du Bois's decolonial "experimentalism." At any rate, these three figures offer an illuminating triangle of positions, occupying an important place in a "dark modern" or more global critical theory tradition. So, whether or not Du Bois's Marxism-Gandhism is correct, this triangle throws into sharp relief the emergent creolized Marxism that Du Bois propounded in the format of a romance. As Kautilya reminds Matthew, "Love is God, and Work is his Prophet."

Understood this way, *Dark Princess* turns *The Rising Tide of Color* on its head: white supremacy will indeed be abolished—not by guns and dynamite but rather by an infant messiah, an ancient intimacy restored, an Afro-Asian unity, a moral federation of race, gender, and class equality and solidarity. And just as the revelatory dialectic is produced by a black American man and an Asian woman, the political conception of the novel is developed through the integration of black American and Asian revolutionary ideas and offers an important experimental effort that differs from black and Asian revolutionary ideas of the time.

Dark Princess is the most curious aesthetic experiment Du Bois ever produced. Part of its unusual nature has to do with its having a complexity that many critics regard as nearly incoherent. The novel gives play to virtually every major idea with which Du Bois struggled in his mature political thought. So there is a sense in which the novel has something for everyone. But part of the peculiarity has also to do with its aesthetic oddity. Its merging of global politics and romantic epiphany could be more seamless. Nevertheless, his efforts to unify romantic passion and global liberation have produced a set of ideas, perhaps more a dream matrix, that can serve as a prism through which we can understand Du Bois's lifelong writings on the nature of race and liberation. The ideas are also important in their own right and offer us considerations relevant in our own day about the qualitative nature of the "coming unities" anticipated in *The Negro* and the "great humanity" longed for in *Darkwater.* Finally, the novel affords us an appreciation of what liberating a theory might look like. Both white people and white theories are strongly decentered. And it is interesting to consider what this might look like in a real context of white domination. Here we can consider the United States in the late 1960s. Just prior to his assassination, there was a distinctive power to the moral vision of Martin Luther King Jr. as he tied together his increasing radicalism on the domestic front, his outrage on behalf of the Vietnamese people, and the inspiration he drew from Gandhian politics.

Notes

For his vision and generous editorial assistance, I am grateful to the editor of this volume, Nick Bromell; this essay was improved greatly by his help.

1. W. E. B. Du Bois, *Dusk of Dawn: An Essay Toward an Autobiography of a Race Concept* (New Brunswick, NJ: Transaction, 1997), 40–41, 96.

2. Robert Gooding-Williams, *In the Shadow of Du Bois: Afro-Modern Political Thought in America* (Cambridge: Harvard University Press, 2009). Importantly, Gooding-Williams aims to critique and replace Du Bois's political expressivism with the politics of Frederick Douglass. Implied in this essay is that Du Bois lost much of this earlier outlook across the interwar years.

3. Cedric Robinson, *Black Marxism: The Making of the Black Radical Tradition* (Chapel Hill: University of North Carolina Press, 1983).

4. Manning Marable, *W. E. B. Du Bois: Black Radical Democrat* (Boston: Twayne, 1986), ix.

5. For a sampling of decolonial thought, see Mabel Moraña, Enrique Dussel, and Carlos A. Jáuregui, eds., *Coloniality at Large: Latin America and the Postcolonial Debate* (Durham, NC: Duke University Press, 2008). See also Walter Mignolo, *The Darker Side of Western Modernity: Global Futures, Decolonial Options* (Durham, NC: Duke University Press, 2011).

6. Famously, Thomas Kuhn expounded one account of this link in *The Structure of Scientific Revolutions* (Chicago: University of Chicago Press, 1962).

7. Wilson Jeremiah Moses, *The Golden Age of Black Nationalism, 1850–1925* (New York: Oxford University Press, 1978); Robinson, *Black Marxism;* Cornel West, *The American Evasion of Philosophy: A Genealogy of Pragmatism* (Madison: University of Wisconsin Press, 1989); Shamoon Zamir, *Dark Voices: W. E. B. Du Bois and American Thought, 1888–1903* (Chicago: University of Chicago Press, 1995); Adolph L. Reed Jr., *W. E. B. Du Bois and American Political Thought: Fabianism and the Color Line* (New York: Oxford University Press, 1997); Charles Mills, *The Racial Contract* (Ithaca, NY: Cornell University Press, 1997); Joy James, *Transcending the Talented Tenth: Black Leaders and American Intellectuals* (New

York: Routledge, 1997); Lewis Gordon, *Existentia Africana: Understanding Africana Existential Thought* (New York: Routledge, 2000); Ronald T. Judy, ed., *boundary 2,* 27, no. 3 (2000); Bill Mullen, *Afro-Orientalism* (Minneapolis: University of Minnesota Press, 2004); Nikhil Singh, *Black Is a Country: Race and the Unfinished Struggle for Democracy* (Cambridge: Harvard University Press, 2004); Tommie Shelby, *We Who Are Dark: The Philosophical Foundations of Black Solidarity* (Cambridge: Harvard University Press, 2005); Gooding-Williams, *In the Shadow of Du Bois;* Lawrie Balfour, *Democracy's Reconstruction: Thinking Politically with W. E. B. Du Bois* (New York: Oxford University Press, 2011); and Nick Bromell, *The Time Is Always Now: Black Thought and the Reconstruction of US Democracy* (New York: Oxford University Press, 2013).

8. For more on theoretical hybridization, see Jane Gordon, *Creolizing Political Theory: Reading Rousseau through Fanon* (New York: Fordham University Press, 2014).

9. Gooding-Williams, *In the Shadow of Du Bois,* 3.

10. I think, technically, postcolonialism is broad enough to accommodate decolonial thought as a branch alongside subaltern studies, but many decolonial theorists link postcolonial studies with subaltern studies and reject them together. To avoid confusion, I will follow the lead of decolonial thinkers and contrast decolonial thought with both postcolonialism and subaltern studies. For a broad postcolonialism that would be sympathetic to decolonial thought, see Robert Young, *Postcolonialism: An Historical Introduction* (Malden, MA: Blackwell, 2001).

11. See Walter Mignolo's position in *The Darker Side of Western Modernity,* xxvi–xxviii, 54–58; and Ramón Grosfoguel, "Decolonizing Post-Colonial Studies and Paradigms of Political-Economy: Transmodernity, Decolonial Thinking, and Global Coloniality," *Transmodernity: Journal of Peripheral Cultural Production of the Luso-Hispanic World* 1, no. 1 (2011): 1–37, esp. 15–20. Another helpful comparison is Gurminder K. Bhambra, "Postcolonial and Decolonial Dialogues," *Postcolonialism,* 17, no. 2 (2014): 115–21.

12. This characterization of strong unification of political economy and political epistemology is very clear in the work of one of the leading spokespersons of decolonial theory, namely Walter Mignolo (see his *The Darker Side of Western Modernity*). But another decolonial theorist offering different inflections on the strong unification idea can be found in the important work of Linda Martín Alcoff (see her "An Epistemology for the Next Revolution," *Transmodernity: A Journal of Peripheral Cultural Production of the Luso-Hispanic World,* 1, no. 2: [2011]: 67–78), which draws from her larger treatment of knowledge and subordination, *Visible Identities: Race, Gender, and the Self* (New York: Oxford University Press, 2005).

13. See Aníbal Quijano and Immanuel Wallerstein, "Americanity as a Concept, or the Americas in the Modern World-System," *International Journal of Social*

Sciences 134 (1992): 549. Interestingly, Wallerstein cites Fanon as one of three of the most influential figures in his intellectual career (see Wallerstein, "The Development of an Intellectual Position," http://iwallerstein.com/intellectual-itinerary/).

14. Aníbal Quijano, "Coloniality of Power, Eurocentrism, and Latin America," *Nepantla: Views from the South* 1 (2000): 533–80.

15. Nelson Maldonado-Torres, "On the Coloniality of Being," *Cultural Studies*, 12, no. 2 (2007): 248.

16. Maria Lugones, "Decolonial Feminism," *Hypatia*, 25, no. 4 (Fall 2010): 742–59.

17. Grosfoguel, "Decolonizing Post-Colonial Studies and Paradigms of Political-Economy," 16.

18. Enrique Dussel, *The Underside of Modernity: Apel, Ricoeur, Rorty, Taylor, and the Philosophy of Liberation*, ed. and trans. Eduardo Mendieta (Atlantic Highlands, NJ: Humanity Press, 1996). For a richer sense of the Latin American tradition of philosophy, see Jorge J. E. Gracia and Elizabeth Millan-Zaibert, eds., *Latin American Philosophy for the 21st Century: The Human Condition, Values, and the Search for Identity* (Amherst, NY: Prometheus, 2004).

19. See Mignolo, *The Darker Side of Western Modernity*, xxv. I think the issue of Eurocentrism and whether decolonial thinkers themselves have escaped it is actually more complex than what Mignolo indicates; see Manuel Vargas, "Eurocentrism and the Philosophy of Liberation," *APA Newsletter on Hispanic/Latino Issues in Philosophy* 4 (2005): 8–17; Katherine Gordy, "No Better Way to Be Latin American: European Science and Thought, Latin American Theory?" *Postcolonial Studies* 16 (2013): 358–73; and David Haekwon Kim, "José Mariátegui's East-South Decolonial Experiment" *Comparative and Continental Philosophy*, 7, no. 2 (November 2015): 157–79.

20. Nelson Maldonado-Torres, "Thinking through the Decolonial Turn: Post-Continental Interventions in Theory, Philosophy, and Critique—An Introduction," *Transmodernity: Journal of Peripheral Cultural Production in the Luso-Hispanic World* 1, no. 2 (2011): 2.

21. Ibid.; Mignolo, *The Darker Side of Western Modernity*, 109.

22. For contrasting views on double-consciousness, see Lewis Gordon, *Existentia Africana: Understanding Africana Existential Thought* (New York: Routledge, 2000), chap. 4; and Gooding-Williams, *In the Shadow of Du Bois*, chap. 2. A great overview of accounts on this topic can be found in John Pittman, "Double Consciousness," http://plato.stanford.edu/entries/double-consciousness/.

23. See Maldonado-Torres on Du Boisian double-consciousness in "On the Coloniality of Being," 262.

24. Robinson, *Black Marxism*, esp. chap. 9.

25. W. E. B. Du Bois, *The Negro* (Philadelphia: University of Pennsylvania Press, 2001), 233; hereafter cited parenthetically in the chapter text.

26. W. E. B. Du Bois, *Black Reconstruction in America 1860–1880* (New York: Free Press, 1997), 30.

27. His treatment of gender does not seem to emerge in distinctive ways (beyond a generic gender egalitarianism) until after *The Negro* (1915). See, for example, *Darkwater*, esp. chap. 7 ("The Damnation of Women"). For some important commentary and critique, see Farah Jasmine Griffin, "Black Feminists and Du Bois: Respectability, Protection, and Beyond," *Annals of the American Academy of Political and Social Science* 568 (March 2000): 28–40; Lawrie Balfour's *Democracy's Reconstruction*, chap. 5; Alys Eve Weinbaum, "Gendering the General Strike: W. E. B. Du Bois's *Black Reconstruction* and Black Feminism's 'Propaganda of History,'" *South Atlantic Quarterly* 112, no. 3 (2013): 437–63; and Ange-Marie Hancock, *Intersectionality: An Intellectual History* (New York: Oxford University Press, 2016).

28. See Mohandas K. Gandhi, *Hind Swaraj and Other Writings*, ed. Anthony Parel (New York: Cambridge University Press, 2009); Mahatma Gandhi, *Selected Political Writings*, ed. Dennis Dalton (Indianapolis: Hackett, 1996); Veena Howard, *Gandhi's Ascetic Activism: Renunciation and Social Action* (Albany: State University of New York Press, 2014); and Farah Godrej, *Cosmopolitan Political Theory: Method, Practice, Discipline* (New York: Oxford University Press, 2011).

29. For an introduction to early Indian philosophy, see Bina Gupta, *An Introduction to Indian Philosophy: Perspectives on Reality, Knowledge, and Freedom* (New York: Routledge, 2012).

30. W. E. B. Du Bois, *Darkwater: Voices from within the Veil* (Mineola, NY: Dover, 1999), 161–62.

31. W. E. B. Du Bois, *Dark Princess: A Romance* (Jackson, MS: Banner, 1995), 295; hereafter cited parenthetically in the chapter text.

32. See Anthony Parel, *Gandhi's Philosophy and the Quest for Harmony* (New York: Cambridge University Press, 2006); and Farah Godrej, *Cosmopolitan Political Theory*.

33. Arnold Rampersad, *The Art and Imagination of W. E. B. Du Bois* (New York: Schocken, 1976); and Arnold Rampersad, "Du Bois' Passage to India: *Dark Princess*," in *W. E. B. Du Bois on Race and Culture: Philosophy, Politics, and Poetics*, ed. Bernard Bell, Emily Grosholz, and James Stewart (New York: Routledge, 1996), chap. 7; Wilson Jeremiah Moses, *Black Messiahs and Uncle Toms: Social and Literary Manipulations of a Religious Myth* (University Park: Pennsylvania State University Press, 1982); Claudia Tate, "*Race and Desire: Dark Princess, A Romance*, by William Edward Burghardt Du Bois," in *Psychoanalysis and Black Novels: Desire and the Protocols of Race* (New York: Oxford University Press, 1998), chap. 2; Alys Eve Weinbaum, "Reproducing Racial Globality: W. E. B. Du Bois and the Sexual Politics of Black Internationalism," *Social Text* 19, no. 2 (Sum-

mer 2001): 15–41; Ross Posnock, "Divine Anarchy: Du Bois and the Craving for Modernity," in *Color and Culture: Black Writers and the Making of the Modern Intellectual*, by Posnock (Cambridge: Harvard University Press, 1998); Mullen, *Afro-Orientalism.*

34. But I understand Du Bois to be a far more creolized Marxist than Mullen does. Indeed, it is Afro-Asian *theoretical*, not just literary, resources that help constitute the hybridization.

35. Du Bois, *Dusk of Dawn*, 270.

36. For an interesting perspective on black expatriates in Europe and on *Dark Princess* generally, see Moses, *Black Messiahs and Uncle Toms*, chap. 9.

37. If their yellow-brown supremacy were a total inversion of white supremacy, they would hold Matthew and many black Americans in contempt because their ancestry has been "contaminated" by "drops of white blood"!

38. A still earlier and less complete conception of Divine Anarchy seized her as she gloried in the cessation of World War I: "There was no real line of birth or race or color. I loved them all. The nightmare was ended. The world was sane. The world was good. The world was Peace" (236).

39. For various documents produced during the Third Comintern, see Jane Degras, ed., *The Communist International, 1919–1943 Documents*, 3 vols. (London: Cass, 1971).

40. See M. N. Roy, *M. N. Roy's Memoirs* (Bombay: Allied, 1964); M. N. *Selected Works of M. N. Roy, 1917–1922*, ed. Roy Sibnarayan Ray (Oxford: Oxford University Press, 1987); M. N. Roy, *Selected Works of M. N. Roy, 1923–1927* (Oxford: Oxford University Press, 1988); Sankar Ghose, *Socialism and Communism in India* (Bombay: Allied, 1971); and John Patrick Haithcox, *Communism and Nationalism in India: M. N. Roy and Comintern Policy 1920–1939* (Princeton: Princeton University Press, 1971).

41. We know that Du Bois was familiar with McKay's visit to Russia because he encouraged McKay to write about it in the *Crisis*. And of course Du Bois himself traveled to Russia in 1926 and repeatedly thereafter. He wrote frequently about Russia, including in his autobiographies, and even produced a large unpublished manuscript in 1950 entitled "America and Russia: An Attempt at an Interpretation."

For more on black America's Russia during this period, see Harry Haywood, *Black Bolshevik: Autobiography of an Afro-American Communist* (Chicago: Liberator, 1978); Mark Naison, *Communists in Harlem during the Depression* (Urbana: University of Illinois Press, 1983); Robin D. G. Kelley, *Race Rebels: Culture, Politics, and the Black Working Class* (New York: Free Press, 1994); William J. Maxwell, *New Negro, Old Left: African-American Writing and Communism between the Wars* (New York: Columbia University Press, 1999), chap. 2; and Kate A. Baldwin, *Beyond the Color Line and the Iron Curtain: Reading Encounters be-*

tween Black and Red, 1922–1963 (Durham: Duke University Press, 2002), chap. 3.

42. The latter is depicted as a "mulatto" and is cast in a suspiciously unflattering light.

43. An earlier expression of this general idea appears in *Darkwater*, 96.

44. This passage anticipates the Third Comintern's 1928 endorsement of the "Black Belt" Thesis, according to which southern black Americans constitute an oppressed nation and hence can lay claim to the discourse and practice of national liberation.

45. Du Bois, *The Souls of Black Folk*, chap. 11

46. Du Bois, *Darkwater*, 285.

47. This narrower view of the novel seems implied in Marable, *W. E. B. Du Bois*, 133.

48. Here, I follow philosophers who contend that loving perception can often be an epistemic asset. One becomes specially attentive in a way that makes one "finely aware and richly responsible." So evaluations of the loved one can enter substantive, albeit nonclassical, epistemic categories, like personal "awakenings" or deep knowledge. And we overlook these positive features of romantic perception because we mistake the species of warped evaluations for the larger genus of "love's truths." It seems clear that Du Bois has a generally positive estimation of romantic perception. He sometimes writes artfully and often struggles in portraying lovers as deep evaluators.

I have learned from Martha Nussbaum, *Love's Knowledge: Essays on Philosophy and Literature* (New York: Oxford University Press, 1990); Roger Lamb, ed., *Love Analyzed* (Boulder, CO: Westview, 1997); Michael Stocker, *Valuing Emotions*, with Elizabeth Hegeman (New York: Cambridge University Press, 1996); and Audre Lorde, "Uses of the Erotic: The Erotic as Power," in *Sister Outsider*, by Lorde (Trumansburg, NY: Crossing, 1984).

49. Matthew Pratt Guterl, *The Color of Race in America, 1900–1940* (Cambridge: Harvard University Press, 2002), 142.

50. One debate between Stoddard and Du Bois is recorded in "Report of the Debate Conducted by the Chicago Forum" in *Pamphlets and Leaflets by W. E. B. Du Bois*, ed. Herbert Aptheker (White Plains, NY: Kraus-Thomson, 1986), 222–29.

51. Lothrop Stoddard, *The Rising Tide of Color against White Supremacy* (New York: Scribner's Sons, 1921), 14; W. E. B. Du Bois, "The African Roots of War," *Atlantic Monthly* 115 (May 1915): 707–14, in *W. E. B. Du Bois: A Reader*, ed. David Levering Lewis (New York: Holt, 1995), 642–51.

52. Stoddard, *The Rising Tide of Color*, 31–33. Interestingly, Count Okuma Shigenobu, a hypernationalist, imperialist Pan-Asianist, actually met at length with Rabindranath Tagore during Tagore's Pan-Asian travels. At some point dur-

ing his stay, Tagore was apparently hoodwinked by Okuma into publicly endorsing Japanese imperial leadership of Asia. Soon after, though, Tagore repudiated his earlier remarks. For more on their meeting, see Stephen N. Hay, *Asian Ideas of East and West: Tagore and his Critics in Japan, China, and India* (Cambridge: Harvard University Press, 1970), chap. 2.

53. Sudarshan Kapur, *Raising up a Prophet: The African-American Encounter with Gandhi* (Boston: Beacon, 1992).

54. Arnold Rampersad, "Du Bois' Passage to India: *Dark Princess*," in *W. E. B. Du Bois on Race and Culture*, ed. Bernard W. Bell, Emily R. Grosholz, and James B. Stewart (New York: Routledge, 1996), chap. 7.

55. Sarvepalli Radhakrishnan and Charles A. Moore, eds., *A Sourcebook in Indian Philosophy* (Princeton: Princeton University Press, 1957), 211–12, 222. For more on Kautilyan diplomacy, see Bharati Mukherjee, *Kautilya's Concept of Diplomacy: A New Interpretation* (Columbia, MO: South Asia Books, 1976).

56. Wyndham Lewis, in *Paleface,* also significantly misinterprets Du Bois's novel. Whereas Stoddard focuses on violent colored revolution, Lewis reveals great angst about the colored world resentfully inverting the valuation structures of the existing racial hierarchy and replacing it with a black- or colored-supremacist worldview. Lewis takes *Dark Princess* to be a paradigm example of this (see Lewis, *Paleface: The Philosophy of the "Melting Pot"* [New York: Gordon, 1972], chap. 11).

57. Arnold Rampersad, in his fine essay "Du Bois' Passage to India," also misconstrues Du Bois on this score when he asserts on page 173: "In his weakness for royalty and wealth, in his unwillingness to repudiate even justifiable violence or to rise above racial antagonism, Du Bois (as the guiding spirit of *Dark Princess*) begs comparison and contrast with Gandhi. The Mahatma's life and career offer a practical critique of Du Bois' romance." I think the reason why Rampersad starkly contrasts Du Bois and Gandhi is that he takes Matthew alone to be Du Bois's mouthpiece, when in fact Du Bois divided his consciousness between Matthew and Kautilya to generate a revelatory dialectic, as I have argued earlier in this essay.

58. W. E. B. Du Bois, "The Clash of Color: Indians and Negroes," *Aryan Path* 7 (March 1936): 111–15 (Bombay, India), reprinted in *Writings by W. E. B. Du Bois in Periodicals Edited by Others*, ed. Herbert Aptheker, vol. 3 (Millwood, NY: Kraus-Thomson, 1982). N. S. Subba Rao's rejoinder is in *Aryan Path* 7 (May 1936): 213–16.

59. Du Bois, "The Union of Color," *Aryan Path* 7 (October 1936): 438–84 (Bombay, India), reprinted in *Writings by W. E. B. Du Bois in Periodicals Edited by Others*, ed. Aptheker, vol. 3; the passage cited is ibid., 44.

60. For an important articulation of this idea, see Charles Mills, *From Class to Race: Essays in White Marxism and Black Radicalism* (Lanham, MD: Rowman and Littlefield, 2003).

61. For more on these two criticisms, see chap. 9 of *Dusk of Dawn,* in addition to *Black Reconstruction.*

62. See *W. E. B. Du Bois: A Reader,* ed. Lewis, 409–10.

63. See "Gandhi and the American Negro," republished in *W. E. B. Du Bois: A Reader,* ed. Lewis.

64. On the contemporary relevance of Gandhi for modern civic politics, see Farah Godrej's excellent "Gandhi's Civic Ahimsa: A Standard for Public Justification in Multicultural Democracies," *International Journal of Gandhi Studies* 1 (2011): 75–106.

65. Du Bois, "The Negro and Social Reconstruction," in *Against Racism: Unpublished Essays, Papers, Addresses, 1887–1961,* ed. Herbert Aptheker (Amherst: University of Massachusetts, 1985), 142.

66. Jane Degras, ed., *The Communist International 1919–194, Documents,* vol. 1 (London: Cass, 1956), 139–40.

67. M. N. Roy, *M. N. Roy's Memoirs* (Bombay: Allied, 1964), 27–29.

68. "The Cult of Non-Violence: Its Socio-Economical Background," in *Selected Works of M. N. Roy, 1923–1927,* 152–57.

Acknowledgments

Editing this volume has been a truly collaborative effort, and my deepest thanks go to all the contributors: your dedication to excellence and your patient perseverance through multiple revisions have made my own work both pleasurable and rewarding.

I extend a warm thanks to those colleagues who first welcomed me into the field of political theory. These include especially Lawrie Balfour, Chip Turner, Melvin Rogers, George Shulman, and Brandon Terry, as well as the ever-changing cast of participants in "Democratic Vistas: An Interdisciplinary Seminar."

My thanks go also to the Charles Warren Center for Studies in American History, where a fellowship in 2016–2017 enabled me to bring this volume to completion.

Versions of two chapters have already appeared in print. I would like to thank the *American Political Science Review* for permission to republish Melvin L. Rogers's "The People, Rhetoric, and Affect: On the Political Force of Du Bois's *The Souls of Black Folk*," and *Raritan* for permission to republish my own "W. E. B. Du Bois and the Enlargement of Democratic Theory."

At the University of Massachusetts, I have received generous support from Dean Julie Hayes and the College of Humanities and Fine Arts and from my colleagues in the English Department, especially its Chair, Jennie Spencer.

As always, I send my deepest thanks to my partner and soulmate Laura A. Doyle, whose love, wit, and wisdom have enriched my life and work for more than thirty years.

I dedicate this book to Kathleen ("Kay") Dodd and her late husband, William ("Bill") Dodd. Their love has meant everything to me, and their energetic founding of a chapter of Healing Racism in the southern suburbs of Chicago has been a constant inspiration.

Contributors

Nick Bromell is professor of English at the University of Massachusetts, Amherst. His most recent book is *The Time Is Always Now: Black Thought and the Transformation of U.S. Democracy.*

Arash Davari is assistant professor of politics at Whitman College.

James Edward Ford III teaches in the English Department at Occidental College. His first book, on Depression-era black literature, theory, and politics, is forthcoming. His published and forthcoming articles in *Cultural Critique, Novel, Black Camera* and other journals address political theory's intersections with literature, film, and contemporary popular culture.

Lewis R. Gordon is professor of philosophy at UConn–Storrs; European Union Visiting Chair in Philosophy at Université Toulouse Jean Jaurès, France; core professor at the Global Center for Advanced Studies; and honorary professor at the Unit of the Humanities at Rhodes University (UHURU), South Africa. His most recent books are *What Fanon Said: A Philosophical Introduction to His Life and Thought* (2015; in Swedish, 2016) and *La sud prin nord-vest: Reflec ii existen iale afrodiasporice,* trans. Ovidiu Tichindeleanu (2016).

David Haekwon Kim is associate professor of philosophy at the University of San Francisco. He has published widely in the philosophy of race, decolonial thought, and comparative philosophy. His current research is on East-South decolonial dialogue, focusing on shared political struggle and resources for theoretical hybridity in the wider South or non-West.

Alexander Livingston is assistant professor of government at Cornell University. His book *Damn Great Empires! William James and the Politics* *of Pragmatism* (2016) examines the political thought of William James's pluralistic pragmatism through the lens of his writings on American imperialism in the Philippines. His writings have appeared in *American Political Science Review*, *Political Theory*, *Contemporary Political Theory*, *Theory & Event*, *Humanity*, *Philosophy and Rhetoric*, and *Contemporary Pragmatism*. His current research explores the politics of nonviolence in the American radical tradition.

Charles W. Mills is Distinguished Professor of Philosophy at the CUNY Graduate Center. He works in the general area of oppositional political theory, with a particular focus on race. He is the author of six books: *The Racial Contract* (1997); *Blackness Visible: Essays on Philosophy and Race* (1998); *From Class to Race: Essays in White Marxism and Black Radicalism* (2003); *Contract and Domination* (with Carole Pateman) (2007); *Radical Theory, Caribbean Reality* (2010); and *Black Rights/White Wrongs: The Critique of Racial Liberalism* (2017).

Vijay Phulwani is a doctoral candidate in the Department of Government at Cornell University whose work has been published in the *American Political Science Review*. He is currently completing his dissertation on theories of popular organizing in the work of Thomas Hobbes, Karl Marx, W. E. B. Du Bois, and Saul Alinsky.

Anthony Reed is associate professor of English and African American studies at Yale University. In 2014, he published *Freedom Time: The Poetics and Politics of Black Experimental Writing*, which received the William Sanders Scarborough Prize from the Modern Language Association. His essays have appeared in such journals as *African American Review* and *Souls: A Critical Journal of Black Politics, Culture, and Society*. He is currently finishing a book on the recorded collaborations between poets and musicians in a shifting political and technological context.

Melvin L. Rogers is associate professor of political science at Brown University. He is the author of *The Undiscovered Dewey: Religion, Morality, and the Ethos of Democracy* and editor of John Dewey, *The Public and Its Problems*. He is currently at work on a book that explores the rhetorical and aesthetic features of democratic theorizing by African Americans in their struggle to reimagine the boundaries of the polity and achieve freedom.

Robert W. Williams is associate professor in the political science program at Bennett College in Greensboro, North Carolina. His research has typically focused on metatheoretical analyses, addressing the assumptions and implications that underpin the social and political theories themselves. Over the years he has studied environmental justice and the spatiality of politics. His recent research efforts emphasize the philosophical dimensions of W. E. B. Du Bois's thinking, including the intellectual context of Du Bois's era. In particular, Williams has examined Du Bois's underlying philosophy of social research and its implications for governance, democracy, and conventional scholarship.

Index

Political Companions to Great American Authors

Series Editor
Patrick J. Deneen, University of Notre Dame

Books in the Series

A Political Companion to W. E. B. Du Bois
Edited by Nick Bromell

A Political Companion to Philip Roth
Edited by Claudia Franziska Brühwiler and Lee Trepanier

A Political Companion to Saul Bellow
Edited by Gloria L. Cronin and Lee Trepanier

A Political Companion to Flannery O'Connor
Edited by Henry T. Edmondson III

A Political Companion to Herman Melville
Edited by Jason Frank

A Political Companion to Walker Percy
Edited by Peter Augustine Lawler and Brian A. Smith

A Political Companion to Ralph Waldo Emerson
Edited by Alan M. Levine and Daniel S. Malachuk

A Political Companion to Marilynne Robinson
Edited by Shannon L. Mariotti and Joseph H. Lane Jr.

A Political Companion to James Baldwin
Edited by Susan J. McWilliams

A Political Companion to Frederick Douglass
Edited by Neil Roberts

A Political Companion to Walt Whitman
Edited by John E. Seery

A Political Companion to Henry Adams
Edited by Natalie Fuehrer Taylor

A Political Companion to Henry David Thoreau
Edited by Jack Turner

A Political Companion to John Steinbeck
Edited by Cyrus Ernesto Zirakzadeh and Simon Stow

www.ingramcontent.com/pod-product-compliance
Lightning Source LLC
LaVergne TN
LVHW050147080826
844660LV00002B/102